Recruitment and Selection

Theories and Practices

Dipak Kumar Bhattacharyya

Xavier Institute of Management

Xavier University, Bhubaneswar

Odisha, India

Cengage

Australia • Brazil • Canada • India • Mexico • Singapore • United Kingdom • United States

Cengage

Recruitment and Selection: Theory and Practices

Dipak Kumar Bhattacharyya

For product information and technology assistance, contact us at **asia.infoindia@cengage.com**

For permission to use material from this text or product, submit all requests online at **www.cengage.com/permissions**

ISBN-13: 978-81-315-3160-0
ISBN-10: 81-315-3160-0

Cengage Learning India Pvt. Ltd.
T-303, 3rd Floor
DAV Complex, Plot 3
Mayur Vihar Phase 1
Delhi-110091

Cengage is a leading provider of customized learning solutions with employees residing in nearly 40 different countries and sales in more than 125 countries around the world. Find your local representative at **www.cengage.com**

Cengage is committed to creating inclusive and diverse products, including perspectives that represent the diversity of people across all backgrounds, identities, opinions, and experiences. If you have any feedback related to this, please contact us at **support.cengage.com**

To learn more about Cengage products, platforms and services, visit at **www.cengage.co.in**

Printed by:
Saurabh Printers Pvt Ltd
67A-68 Ecotech Ext-I Greater Noida, Tel-0120-2341180

Printed in India
Print Number: 25 **Print Year:** 2025

To my wife Sutapa and children Sudip and Tapodeep,
whose relentless support could make this project successful

Contents

Preface xi

1. ESSENTIALS OF RECRUITMENT AND SELECTION **1**

Introduction 2
Definitions and Concepts of Recruitment and Selection 4
Recruitment 5
Selection 7
Difference Between Recruitment and Selection 8
Recruitment and Selection Functions 10
Internal Recruitment 10
Recruitment Policy 11
Recruitment Policy of XYZ Company 12
E-recruitment 22
Outsourcing 23
Induction 23
Objectives 24
Steps in Induction Program 25
Employees Socialization 25
Placement 26
Importance of Induction and Placement 27
Onboarding 27
Recruitment Matrices 28
Recruiting Generation Y 30
Expectations of Generation Y from Their Organizations 32
Recruiting Generation Z 33
Recruitment and Selection in India 34
Summary 35
References 43
Appendix-1 45
Personal Data 45
Education 45
Extra Curricular Activities 46

2. HUMAN RESOURCE PLANNING FOR RECRUITMENT AND SELECTION **49**

Introduction 50
Importance of HRP for Recruitment and Selection 51
Challenging Role of HR Planners 53

HRP Activities 53
Steps for HRP 54
Objectives of HRP 57
Manpower Demand Forecasting 57
Macro and Micro Level HRP 59
HRP at Macro-Level 59
Macro-Level HRP Models 61
Rate of Return Approach (RRA) 62
Labor Economics 63
Labor Markets 64
HRP Micro Level 64
Example of Markov Chain Model 71
Monte Carlo Simulation 75
Illustration 75
Determination of Demand and Stock Levels 79
Advantages and Disadvantages of Simulation 79
Staff Replacement 80
Predictive Statistics for Organization Level Human Resource Planning 83
Regression Analyses 83
Linear Regression 83
Least-Squares Model 84
Line of Best Fit 84
How to Find the Least Squares Line 86
Managerial Judgment 87
Difficulties in Manpower Forecasts Using Quantitative Tools 87
Use of Qualitative Models for Better Managerial Judgment 89
Summary 90
References 98

3. JOB ANALYSIS AND PROFILE MATCHING **99**
Introduction 100
Profile Matching 101
Position Analysis Questionnaire (PAQ) and Other Job Analysis Methods 102
Job Questionnaire 104
Job Sculpting 104
Culture Job-Fit 107
Personality-Based Job Analysis 108
Personality and Recruitment 108
Measurement of Personality Traits 109
Personality and Employment Testing 111
Validity and Reliability of the Selection Tests 111
Test of Intelligence as Employability Test 112
Performance Intelligence Test 112
Emotional Intelligence (EI) 113

The Five Domains of EQ 114
Ethical Guidelines for Psychological Testing 115
Personality and Career Choice 115
Johari Window and Personality and Training on Personality 116
Personality Assessment 118
Transactional Analysis (TA) and Personality 119
Summary 120
References 127

4. POLICIES AND PROCEDURES FOR RECRUITMENT AND SELECTION 131
Introduction 132
Recruitment and Selection Policy 133
Importance and Significance of Recruitment and Selection Policy 135
Developing Recruitment and Selection Policies 136
Aligning Recruitment and Selection Policies with HR Strategies and Business Goals 139
Summary 141
References 149

5. STRATEGIC RECRUITMENT AND SELECTION 151
Introduction 152
Definitions and Concepts 153
Issues Driving the Need for Strategic Recruitment and Selection 156
Important Components of Strategic Recruitment and Selection 156
Purpose of Strategic Recruitment and Selection 157
Benefits of Strategic Recruitment and Selection Strategy 157
Dimensions of Recruitment and Selection Strategy 158
Features of Strategic Recruitment and Selection 159
Importance of Strategic Recruitment and Selection 161
Steps for Developing Effective Recruitment and Selection Strategies 162
Connecting Recruitment and Selection with Business Plans 164
Connecting Recruitment and Selection with Strategies 165
Summary 167
References 171

6. TOOLS AND TECHNIQUES FOR RECRUITMENT AND SELECTION 173
Introduction 174
Traditional Recruitment Tools 175
Modern Recruitment Tools 176
E-Recruitment 176
Benefits and Risks of E-Recruitment 178
SNS-Based or E-Recruitment Tools 179
Recruitment Models 181

Interviewing 182
Effective Interviewing 183
Types of Interview 184
Structured Standardized Interview 184
Depth Interviews 185
Telephone Interviews 185
Psychological Test for Recruitment 185
Test of Personality for Recruitment 186
Measurement of Personality Traits 188
The Big Five Model 190
Personality and Employment Testing 190
Validity of the Psychological Tests 191
Validity and Reliability 192
Test of Intelligence as Employability Test 192
Emotional Intelligence 194
Emotional Intelligence—Two Aspects 195
Emotional Intelligence—the Five Domains 195
Neuro-Linguistic Programming (NLP) 195
Ethical Guidelines for Psychological Testing 195
Recruitment Metrics as Recruitment Tools 196
Recruitment Analytics 197
Ability Tests for Recruitment 197
Summary 198
References 204

7. LEGAL ISSUES IN RECRUITMENT AND SELECTION 205

Introduction 206
Benefits of Legal-Compliant Recruitment and Selection Process 207
Snapshots on Labor Laws Governing Recruitment and Selection 208
Diversity Inclusivity in Recruitment and Selection 208
Different Approaches to Diversity 209
Gender Diversity 211
Gender Diversity in India 212
Equality in Recruitment and Selection 213
Equality in Compensation Design 217
Legal Briefing on Recruitment and Selection in India 219
Summary 221
References 225

8. ETHICAL ISSUES IN RECRUITMENT AND SELECTION 229

Introduction 230
Definitions and Concepts 231
Dimensions of Ethics in Recruitment and Selection 233

Importance of Ethics in Recruitment and Selection 235
Ethical Due Diligence 236
Gender Mainstreaming and Recruitment Ethics 238
Ethics Strategy 239
The Ethics of Lateral Recruitment 240
Developing Ethics-Compliant Recruitment Policy 241
Ethical Recruitment and Selection Framework 241
Social Media and Recruitment Ethics 243
Recruitment and Selection Ethics in PSEs 243
Ethical Breaches for Senior-Level Recruitment and Selection 244
Unethical Recruitment and Selection Process 246
Summary 246
References 252

9. INTERNATIONAL RECRUITMENT AND SELECTION 257

Introduction 258
International Recruitment and Selection Concepts 259
Approaches to International Recruitment and Selection 261
Types of International Recruitment and Selection 263
Selection of Employees in MNCs and TNCs 263
Diversity and Cross-Cultural Issues in International Recruitment and Selection 264
Guidelines for Recruitment and Selection Across Cultures 265
International Selection Process 266
Training and Development for International Recruitees 267
Compensation and Benefits Programme for International Recruitees 268
Assignment-Specific International Recruitment 270
Performance Management For International Employees 270
Summary 272
References 278

10. EMPLOYEE ONBOARDING 279

Introduction 280
Definitions and Concepts 281
Difference Between Onboarding and Orientation 282
Strategic Onboarding Program 282
Designing Onboarding Program 285
Onboarding and Employer Branding 287
Succession Planning and Onboarding 288
Co-Creating Individual-Level Onboarding Program 289
Gamification in Onboarding 289
Summary 290
References 295

11. CAREER PLANNING, CAREER DEVELOPMENT, AND EMPLOYEES' SUCCESSION **297**
Introduction 298
Definitions and Concepts 299
Essential Elements of Career 301
Importance of Career Development 301
Types of Career Development Programs 303
Importance of Career Planning 304
Difference Between Career Development and Career Planning 305
Difference Between Career Planning and Human Resource Planning 305
Difference with Succession Planning 306
Career Development Cycle 307
Career Anchors 309
Succession Planning 311
Steps of Succession Planning 312
Management Development 313
Summary 314
References 318

12. RESEARCH ON RECRUITMENT AND SELECTION **319**
Introduction 320
Types of Recruitment Research 321
Concept Mapping for Recruitment and Selection Research 323
Literature Review for Recruitment Research 323
Model Building in Recruitment Research 324
Significance of Recruitment and Selection Research 325
Types of Recruitment Research 326
Human Resource Planning for Recruitment Research 327
Learning Curve as a Tool for Recruitment Research 329
Cause and Effect Model in Recruitment Research 330
Recruitment Research at Organization Level 331
Cost Benefit Analysis and Recruitment Research 332
Predictive Analytics for Recruitment Research 333
Using Predictive Analytics for Recruitment Research 334
Predictive Analytics for Recruitment Research—Lessons from Organizations 335
Summary 336
References 340

INDEX **341**

Preface

In a competitive world, talent is increasingly becoming a major differentiator for organizations. Organizations today compete for talent; hence recruitment functions also encompass talent attraction. Even in mid-sized organizations, recruitment and selection has now become a specialized function. For small enterprises, owners themselves get directly involved with the recruitment and selection. In large organizations, it has now become an on-going process. People, and more specifically talented people, are now being the most sought after resources for growth and sustenance of the organizations; recruitment and selection has become strategic human resource management function. Although we have many self-help guides for recruitment, we do not have a text book to prepare students with appropriate theoretical and operational inputs, so as to create their base level knowledge to become successful in their future job endeavor. Information on industry practices are so varied, it really cannot be the sole basis for knowledge accumulation. Also such practices are very much organization specific, hence often such practices are consequentialist than universalist. Recruitment and selection is also offered as a standalone three credit course in many B-schools for HR specialization students. Students here hardly get the support of teaching materials, except their dependence on the faculty inputs, more in the form of experience sharing.

Given the above backdrop, this book has been designed and developed to aid the MBA/PGDBM students, particularly those who are doing HR specialization. Also the book is a self-help guide for the academia and professionals as in their respective job roles, they are often expected to recruit people for their organizations.

The book is mix of theories and operational knowledge inputs. Operational knowledge inputs are primarily crafted based on the industry practices, and the experiential knowledge of the author as recruitment consultant for many organizations, including IITs.

The book has been conveniently designed in twelve self-paced chapters. Each chapter starts with an opening case-let or vignette, provides snapshots on industry practices, and ends with a case study. Each chapter has both chapter-end general review and critical review questions.

Chapter-1 introduces the concepts of recruitment and selection, and also this initial chapter sets the pace of discussions in subsequent chapters. Chapter-2 covers discussions on human resource planning for recruitment and selection. In Chapter-3 we discuss job analysis and profile matching, and even introduce the concepts of job sculpting, job questionnaire, etc.

Chapter-4 outlines details on policies and procedures for recruitment, its importance and significance and alignment with the HR strategies and business goals.

In Chapter-5, strategic recruitment and selection issues are detailed, and also the processes of alignment of the recruitment and selection with the business plans and strategies are discussed.

Chapter-6 elaborates the tools and techniques for recruitment and selection with special emphasis on the latest recruitment tools like e-recruitment, digital recruitment, recruitment through social media, etc. The chapter also discusses various recruitment and selection models, usages of recruitment metrics and analytics, etc.

Chapter-7 encapsulates legal issues, including diversity inclusivity, equality in recruitment and selection, etc.

Chapter-8 focuses on ethical issues in recruitment and selection, emphasizing on ethical due diligence, gender mainstreaming and recruitment ethics, ethics compliant recruitment policy, social media and recruitment ethics, etc.

Chapter-9 outlines international recruitment and selection issues covering diversity and cross-cultural issues, training and development function for the international recruitees, their compensation and benefits design program, and performance management systems.

Chapter-10 discusses on-boarding program, its concepts, purposes and priorities, designing, branding, co-creating, process of gamification, etc.

Chapter-11 discusses career planning, career development and employees' succession; its relationships with the talent management practices and identification of potential talents, etc.

Chapter-12, the last chapter of the book, describes the techniques of research on recruitment and selection, its cost-benefit analysis for recruitment research, and its importance especially when predictive analytics is used.

ACKNOWLEDGEMENT

I gratefully acknowledge the support received from Cengage editorial team members, colleagues from both the academia and professions, friends and relatives, and his family members. I welcome all critical observations on the book, including suggestions for future improvement, to be emailed at dkb@ximb.ac.in or dkbhattacharyya@yahoo.co.in.

Prof. D.K. Bhattacharyya

Chapter 1

Essentials of Recruitment and Selection

LEARNING OBJECTIVES

After reading this chapter, you will be able to understand:

1 Recruitment and selection functions in an organization
2 Strategic importance of recruitment and selection
3 Process of recruitment
4 Policies and procedures of recruitment
5 Recruitment process outsourcing
6 Selection and interview process
7 On-boarding and induction program
8 Placement of employees after selection
9 Recruitment of generation Y and generation Z employees

Talent attraction: first thing Bosch India does in recruitment and selection

Bosch India has been operating in India since 1922. With €1.2 billion in sales revenue and headcounts of 28,000 associates (2014), spread across 11 manufacturing sites, Bosch India is a good example of an innovative multinational. The company believes their success in India is attributable to frugal innovation. The company is now developing products like single-cylinder pumps, multicylinder pumps, and mechanical distributor pumps through reverse innovation for global market. It is hiring trained graduates systematically in India, and in fact hiring in India was highest in 2015 compared to company's units in other countries. In India, the company recruits software developers and creative engineers.

As the company gives thrust on diversity inclusivity, they can attract a large number of women talents who feel more secured and valued (obviously for adherence to the principles of equity) than many other multinationals in India. Also the company attracts, in general, a large number of applicants for various job positions. One of the possible reasons for successful creation of such a brand value is company's own cultural identity, which ensures strong sense of pride in all employees. With the vision of "creating value—sharing value," the company provides employees with the entrepreneurial freedom and financial independence. With support to employees for different services at a very low price, the company helps employees to improve their quality of work life. This is part of company's "feel good workings at Bosch" program. Improved quality of work life is further reinforced by the company with liberal healthcare benefits, including preventive healthcare. Another important area of HRM practices in Bosch is company's employee development program through training and competence management. Employee development program focuses on both technical and business processes, including development of soft skills. Employees by developing their competence and performing better can pursue their career paths, selecting from multiple options. A declared career development policy for the company is "helping employees to make targeted progress all within an equitable system."

Obviously, all these have enhanced the brand value for Bosch India and transformed them to one of the most preferred employers in India.

INTRODUCTION

People are the major differentiators for any organization. Globally, it has now been proved that crux of organizational success lies on its people. Acquiring right people for the right job, therefore, becomes the most critical human resource management (HRM) function for any organization. Recruitment and selection is the manpower acquisition function of any organization. With global competition for talent, recruitment and selection function is obviously becoming more challenging. Attracting talent which has now become an integral part of recruitment and selection function of an organization requires more strategic thoughts and actions including organizational branding and enhancement of visibility. Again with attracting and acquiring the right fit for the jobs, recruitment and selection functions broadly do not get completed. It further extends to the entire process of on-boarding, developing, and retaining the people, so that organizations continue to enjoy competitive advantages with their competent human resources. High cost of manpower replacement is making recruitment and selection function for any organization more and more challenging. Another important challenge for the recruitment and selection function is to comply with a number of regulatory and institutional norms, while recruiting without, however, compromising the quality. Quota-based recruitment, demonstrated diversity, neutrality in recruitment process, ethical issues, merit-based and bias-free recruitment with transparency, etc., are some of the important issues which today's human resource managers are facing in organizations. Because of such complexities of recruitment and selection function, it requires thorough knowledge and professional skills in effective management of this function.

HR managers extend support to organizations in choosing the right candidates for the right jobs. Recruitment is one of the important strategic functions for organizations, as effective recruitment ultimately enables organizations to sustain competitive strength. For recruiting in various positions in the organization, it is necessary to go for external hiring, as redeploying existing manpower through job restructuring (internal recruitment) may not be adequate. External hiring process precedes human resource planning (HRP). Through HRP we can understand the extent of external hiring after adjustment of internal manpower (Bhattacharyya, 2013).

Thus, recruitment, selection, induction, and placement are important tools for procuring and effectively using human resources in an organization (Fig. 1.1).

While recruitment involves employing suitably trained workforce, selection helps in choosing the right candidate for the right job. Induction and placement is putting men to the right jobs. This chapter focuses on these four important organizational activities. Being the introductory chapter, it also sets the pace of discussion in subsequent chapters, introducing different areas of recruitment and selection functions. Chapter 2 discusses human resource planning for recruitment and selection, while Chapter 3 elaborates on job analysis and profile matching. Chapter 4 explains policies and procedures for recruitment. Chapter 5 deals on

FIGURE 1.1 Manpower procurement or acquisition.

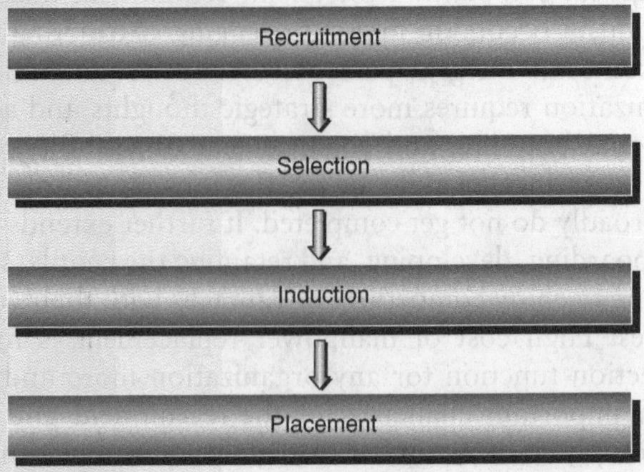

strategic recruitment and selection, followed by Chapter 6 on tools and techniques of recruitment and selection. Chapter 7 detailed on legal issues on recruitment and selection followed by Chapter 8 on ethical issues for recruitment and selection. Chapter 9 discusses international recruitment and selection, while Chapter 10 elaborates on on-boarding and Chapter 11 is on career planning and development. Finally, Chapter 12 highlights research in recruitment and selection.

Each chapter is self contained and adequately backed with theories and corporate practices.

DEFINITIONS AND CONCEPTS OF RECRUITMENT AND SELECTION

Definitions and concepts of recruitment and selection can be understood once some literatures on it are reviewed. For example, Rynes (1990) defined recruitment as all organizational practices and decisions which can influence the number and types of individuals who are willing to apply and accept a job. Importance of recruitment and selection process in any organization can be appreciated once we see how with the recruitment of competent individuals, organizational performance significantly increases. Research studies like Rynes, et al. (1980) and Arvey et al. (1975) can establish that effective recruitment and selection largely depends on organizations (more specifically the brand value of organizations), recruitment timing, nature of job, and various other job aspects. Effective recruitment and selection also depends on the quality of job analysis, recruitment strategy, and the selection method. The terms recruitment and selection may be defined as the process to identify sources of manpower to meet the requirements or the staffing schedule and employ effective measures for attracting that manpower in an adequate number to facilitate the selection of an efficient working force. As recruitment and selection are two distinct terms, even though operationally they are used interchangeably, we have to discuss these terms independently for better clarity.

RECRUITMENT

Recruitment functions in recent years have assumed importance for increase in organizational emphasis on human resources. Traditional approach to personnel management was to ensure routine human resources maintenance functions for organizations. But recently, radical changes in human resource management, i.e. perceiving human resources like other important resources (physical and financial) of an organization have developed new areas for personnel management. The human resources are the people who are part of the organization. Broadly speaking, they may be direct employees, the customers served, part-time persons, temporary employees or consultants or any person or persons with a variety of other relationships with the organization. Within the human resources area, there are two major activities. The first is concerned with the recruitment, selection, placement, compensation, and appraisal of the human resources (these are known as human resources utilization functions or personnel functions). The other functions are directed to work with the existing human resources for improving their efficiency and effectiveness. These are known as Human Resources Development (HRD) functions which are designed to enable existing human resources to learn activities for their effective functioning in the present jobs, future identifiable jobs, and so also for future undefined jobs.

For increasing importance of human resources, it is now imperative for all organizations to retain the manpower and at the same time to recruit and select best possible talents in the country. Most of the organizations are now facing technological changes resulting in radical change in the recruitment process. Such a technological change, inter alia, calls for hiring manpower having higher skills and knowledge. However, in case of recruitment of manpower for unskilled jobs, there seem to be no apparent problems for the organization, as these people are abundantly available in our country for obvious high rate of unemployment. For high technology literate employees, i.e., mostly those who are in managerial positions with professional skills, recruitment function is more complex and dynamic.

Recruitment and selection are considered two distinctly different tasks which completes the process of manpower acquisition. Operationally these two terms are used interchangeably in organizations. Some of the universally accepted definitions of recruitment have been listed below, and reviewing such definitions, we can conceptualize recruitment and understand how it differs from the selection.

- Flippo (1984) defined recruitment as a "........ process of searching for prospective employees and stimulating and encouraging them to apply for jobs in an organization." Flippo further explained recruitment process becomes positive when it can stimulate prospective job seekers to apply for jobs.
- Yoder (1972) again defined recruitment process is to "discover the sources of manpower to meet the requirements of the staffing schedule and employ effective measures for attracting that manpower in adequate numbers to facilitate effective selection of an efficient working force."
- Kempner (1971) defined recruitment as "... the first stage in the process which continues with selection and ceases with the placement of the candidates."

Reviewing all the above definitions it is clear that recruitment process comes first, followed by selection. Recruitment process considers

FIGURE 1.2 Recruitment process.

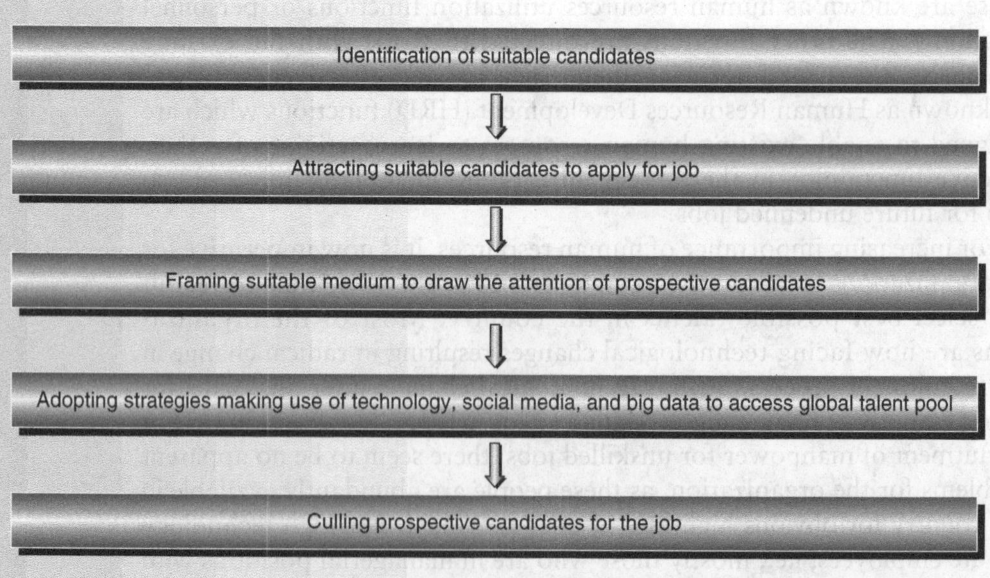

identifying suitable candidates for a job, attracts them to apply for the job, frames suitable medium to draw the attention of prospective job seekers, adopts strategies making use of technology, social media, and big data to get access to global talent pool and make them the prospective candidates for the job, etc (Fig. 1.2).

SELECTION

Like recruitment, some of the definitions of selection can be listed as follows:

Ivancevich (2003) defined selection as the process of choosing the person or persons who best meet the selection criteria for the job position from the list of candidates. According to Bohlander and Snell (2010), selection is a process of choosing the right candidates for filling a vacant or newly created job position. More appropriately, Bateman and Snell (2002) defined it as a process of choosing among qualified candidates to hire. More or less in the same line of thought there are definitions from Schermerhorn et al. (2003), who considered selection as a series of steps, and Stone (2005), who termed selection as a process of differentiating between applicants.

Selection process succeeds recruitment. While recruitment reaches the candidates, selection ensures best candidates are finally selected and placed in organizations. In selection process the candidates who apply for the job are interviewed and evaluated and then finally selected the best-fit for the job and offered the job. Selection being the process of elimination, it is important to carefully craft the selection process, so that best available talent is finally selected. During the process of selection, HR managers also require to comply with several legal, institutional, and social norms. Even for complying with such norms, HR managers need to ensure quality hire, so that organizations can grow and sustain.

Broadly speaking, selection is also considered the part of recruitment process. In a recruitment cycle, selection may require successive stages, so that proper candidates are ultimately recruited by the organization. For example, initial stage of selection may require HR managers to shortlist candidates applied for the job. Initial shortlisting further gets screened with job-profile matching, i.e., the job-person fit. Then there may be written examination, multistep interview including on-the-job interview, etc. However, all these depend on the job position and the nature of job.

Many organizations complete other formalities before asking the candidates to appear for face-to-face interviews. Rationality is that such shortlisted candidates should go through a robust screening process almost half-way through the selection process. Skype or phone screenings have now become important for any selection process before the interview. Even some organizations do the background checks.

PWC's selection process

PWC recommends prospective candidates to understand the company first, referring to their global core competencies. For selection the company advises the candidates to find answers to questions like: how one can contribute to team success, why one is applying to PWC, how one can personally contribute to client services, and finally what would be the preferred date to join. A prospective candidate for PWC job needs to complete the online application form first, then take the online tests, attend first interview, attend an assessment center, and then final interview. Once a candidate successfully completes all these successive hurdles, he or she is selected for the job.

Source: Adapted from http://www.pwc.com/m1/en/careers/student/application-process.jhtml, seen on June 10, 2015.

Difference Between Recruitment and Selection

Recruitment and selection as a staffing process is used in the organizations as one and the same. However, it has been already clarified that these two terms are distinctly different. Recruitment attracts and induces people to apply for the jobs, while selection determines who should be offered the job. Depending on the nature of the organization and the nature as well as level of job, recruitment and selections functions may be managed by either a single person or the same group of people, or may be separated. Many organizations outsource nonexecutive level recruitment and selection function, while involving them directly in recruitment and selection process of executives.

Recruitment and selection are two distinct phases of staffing process. Differences can be listed as given in Table 1.1:

TABLE 1.1 Differences between recruitment and selection

Recruitment	Selection
Identifying and attracting candidates to apply for the jobs	Following series of steps and screening to choose the best-fit for the job position

(*Continued*)

TABLE 1.1 Continued

Recruitment	Selection
It is a positive process, as it encourages more and more number of eligible candidates to apply for the job	It is a negative process, as it rejects a large number of candidates applied for the job and select among them the best-fit
Recruitment is not a contract, it is a relationship	Selection is a contract between the selected employees and the employers
Recruitment process does not follow any hurdles	Selection is a successive hurdle technique
With support of technology and big-data analysis time requirements for recruitment functions can be substantially optimized	Selection process being more elaborate, and as it requires close interaction with the prospective candidate, it is more time consuming
Purpose of recruitment is to create a talent pool	Purpose of selection is to select the appropriate talent for the job
Recruitment is a search process	Selection is a process of elimination

Despite the above-listed differences, as has already been said, both the terms are interchangeably used in organizations.

You cannot attract talent unless you follow the way IBM says

Companies like IBM always try to create their brand value to attract talent. For example, a company through its web-site declares that it values employees' passion, provides opportunities to learn new skills, and even provides customized professional development as well as leadership training. All such declarations are further reinforced by competitive benefit program, performance-based bonus, global innovation, diversity inclusivity, work–life balancing, etc.

Recruitment and Selection Functions

The first important task of recruitment functions is to frame a recruitment policy. Framing a recruitment policy calls for review of manpower requirement, i.e., it should be adequately supported by an effective manpower forecasting. Manpower planning and so also manpower forecasting of an organization depends on many important factors like present nature of work, possible change in the future working of the organization, the manpower records and information available in the organization for the present strength, the diversification plans and programs of the organization, the environmental change and the change necessary in the organization to respond to such environmental changes, etc. Most of the organizations, in principle, believe in recruiting the best possible manpower from outside the organization. However, recruitment policy of some organizations considers recruiting the employees based on the recommendation of the present employees or recruiting employees from the wards of the existing employees.

For example, in Tata organization, there is a system to recruit employees for unskilled/low-skilled jobs, both technical and nontechnical nature, from the wards of the existing employees. Such a policy of recruitment in Tata organization has been accepted on principle and Tata, in their manufacturing units, maintains a separate employment exchange record to enlist the names and other details of the employees' wards to offer them employment as and when vacancy arises. But such a type of recruitment policy is not followed while hiring manpower for managerial jobs. In such cases, companies are looking for best available talents. Thus, they go for either advertising the vacancies in leading newspapers and good professional journals of the country or recruitment of such managerial manpower by effecting campus interview, also going for retaining the services of recruitment consultants. Such recruitment consultants, having maintained a separate data bank for the prospective job seekers, can make available list of prospective managerial manpower to such companies. In addition to the framing of recruitment policy, each organization carries out regular forecasting of manpower recruitments for making its recruitment a scientific process of selection.

Internal Recruitment

In some cases, organizations also try to internally man higher managerial vacancies from their existing employees. In those cases, organizations need to have robust succession planning systems and focus on developing their existing manpower adopting suitable training and development functions. Training and development may not necessarily always ensure availability of the best talents internally. Organizations are then compelled to recruit from outside sources, mentioned above. Effective internal recruitment systems need to be strengthened by "promotion from within" policy. Internal recruitment is very effective for employee engagement, motivation and retention. Particularly for talent retention, organizations always prefer internal recruitment for sourcing future managerial manpower. Globally, most of the organizations are using this as their recruitment strategy.

However, some organizations, in the process of following the internal recruitment process, dilute the quality of selection. It is like fishing for talent in a small pool. Even employees of such organizations consider their automatic elevation to the leadership positions in a time scale. Hence, it is often recommended to go for hiring fresh talent from the market. However, considering the issues of employees' motivation and retention, a mixed approach is always considered better. Some organizations have fixed ratio between internal and external recruitment for certain job positions.

Recruitment Policy

Sound recruitment policy calls for adopting scientific process of recruitment, i.e., those techniques, which are modern and scientific. Recruitment policy also requires understanding of the high cost of managerial turnover. Unless a company adopts a suitable recruitment policy, it may not be possible for the company to select the right candidate for the right job. A sound recruitment policy, therefore, needs to (Fig. 1.3):

(1) identify, at the outset, the recruitment needs of the organization,
(2) identify the preferred sources of recruitment,
(3) frame suitable criteria for selection, and finally,
(4) consider the cost of recruitment.

Framing of recruitment policies

Companies frame their recruitment policies, often with some general statements, while details on policy implementation are laid down in their procedures. For example, Wipro ensures in their recruitment advertisements that they will not give preference to any type of applicants, unless it is necessary for genuine occupational reasons, in which case the company will disclose the reasons. If we carefully examine this, such declaration in the recruitment policy statements, in fact, supports Wipro's culture of diversity neutrality.

FIGURE 1.3 Components of recruitment policy.

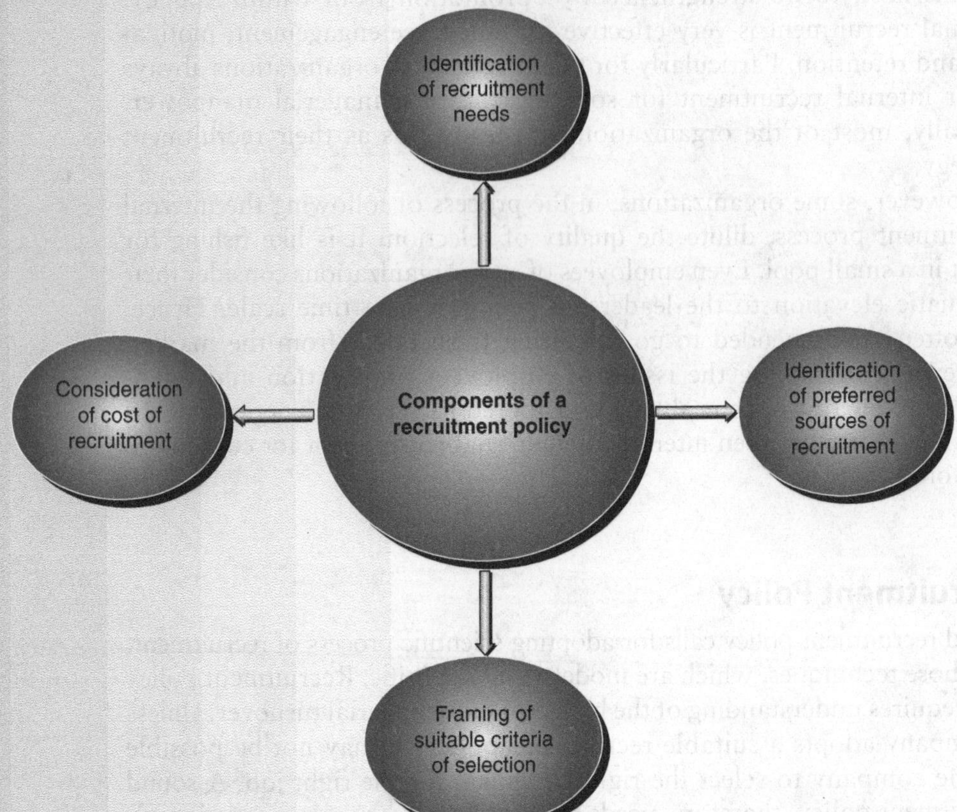

A template of recruitment policy is presented below.

Recruitment Policy of XYZ Company

Introduction

XYZ Company believes in attracting the best talent, and hence follows fair, efficient, and effective recruitment methods.

Purpose

This recruitment policy has been developed to provide opportunity to attract the best talents so that they can feel attracted and apply for the vacant job positions in the company. The policy also outlines the guidelines for employment of the employees.

Policy

(1) Ensure that all internal recruitment opportunities are properly explored by widely circulating notices and personal communication to eligible candidates (based on HR records).
(2) When vacancies are available, go for external recruitment after exploring the internal opportunities.
(3) For external recruitment, select medium of advertisements and other channels of communication, so that more number of eligible candidates feel attracted to apply.
(4) All eligible candidates must be directed to apply through company's web portal using the standard application blank.
(5) Initial screening of applications should be done with the programmable software.
(6) Automatic regret letters should be sent to those who are quarantined by the software.
(7) Screened profiles must be checked by the HR before asking the candidates to appear for an interview.

The above recruitment policy is an abridged version. Likewise, policy statements can be made more elaborately.

Along with such policy statements, it is also important to detail the procedures, so that effective policy implementation can be done.

Recruitment procedures

Recruitment procedures detail step-by-step actions required for implementing the recruitment policy. Let us take a look at one of our policy statements, i.e., policy statement number 7, which says, "Screened profiles must be checked by the HR before asking the candidates to appear for an interview." Now to implement this policy, step-by-step actions may be detailed in the recruitment procedures, which may be as under (Fig. 1.4):

(1) Screened profiles must be checked by more than one member.
(2) One of the members must represent the department which had requisitioned for the manpower.
(3) Diversity and legal issues must be conformed before the initial selection of the profiles.
(4) All the members must agree on the profile.

FIGURE 1.4 Recruitment procedures.

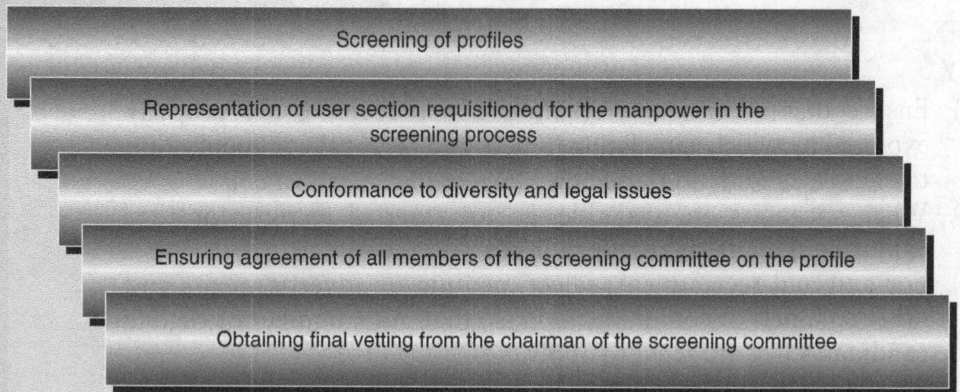

(5) In case of disagreement, the matter must be recorded and sent to the Chairman of the Selection Committee for final vetting.

Likewise for each policy statement, detailed procedures should be listed, so that it can help in guiding effective decision-making in recruitment and selection.

Recruitment and selection process

In this section, recruitment and selection has been considered one and same function in the organization, as it is in operational sense.

As has already been discussed, a particular organization may effect recruitment either from the internal sources, i.e., by promoting the existing employees for higher positions, or they may go for outside sources. Thus, internal and external sources of recruitment can be resorted to by any organization, subject to the convenience and feasibility. Recruitment is an art of attracting applicants, from whom the most suitable ones may be selected in a particular job or jobs. Internal recruitment may often avoid the unpleasantness, but it is not necessarily effective because it does not allow the organization to get many alternatives to select the best available talent. The external sources being open, it gives opportunity to an organization to tap the best or suitable candidates from widely dispersed areas. The requisition for recruitment contains brief description of the post, qualification and experience required, etc. Such requisitions are normally signed by the head of the Human Resource Department. External sources of recruitment are taken recourse to keeping in view the type of personnel required. The workmen may be recruited at the gate itself or from the employment exchange. Management trainees are taken from the institutes and universities based on campus interview. Senior executives are attracted through advertisements in leading newspapers and magazines. The major sources of recruitment for different types of personnel, therefore, are as follows:

(1) Employment exchanges,
(2) Consultants and private employment agencies,
(3) Advertisements in periodicals and newspapers, radio, and TV,
(4) Deputation,
(5) Universities and management institutes,
(6) From the source of existing employees,
(7) Trade unions,
(8) Internet/job site, etc.

The employment exchanges maintain register of candidates seeking various types of job. Under Compulsory Notification of Vacancies Act, 1955, the employers are required to notify certain types of vacancies to the nearest employment exchange and recruit candidates from the applicants registered with them. The skilled and unskilled workers and the clerical staff are mostly recruited through employment exchanges. Private consultants and agencies assist organizations in locating technical and managerial staff. They charge prescribed fees for their services to the organization.

Advertising in newspapers and magazines, radio, and TVs has now become most resorted practice for attracting the prospective candidates. It also helps in building the image for the organization because through such advertisements, the organization makes available certain information like their product, market share, turnover value, etc., to the public in general and target consumers in particular. Since written press insertions or verbal advertisements through audio and audio-visual methods give the first hand information to the prospective job-seekers, each organization is required to give as much factual information as possible regarding the job-expectations from the candidates, their age-group, qualifications and experience, salary and perks attached to the positions and important conditions of service, the time-limit and mode of applying, etc. There are some agencies that help organizations in drafting, publishing, and broadcasting advertisements.

Deputationists are mainly appointed in public sector undertakings. The civil servants are often deputed for many senior and mid-level positions for a specified time.

Recruitment from universities and management institutes is effected through campus interviews. Almost all good private organizations select their management trainees through such a method. Some organizations even sponsor the cost of prospective students during their learning to join them after completion of the course.

From the source of existing employees also, recruitment is done by many private organizations to ensure commitment and loyalty and to motivate the employees at the same time. Such type of recruitment however is restricted only to the clerical and unskilled jobs in most of the cases.

Trade unions also recommend candidates for clerical and unskilled jobs. This practice is not in vogue in many organizations. Only in technical training scheme, trade unions are found to influence the organizations to induct their recommended candidates as apprentices.

Recruitment through Internet/job sites also has now become very popular for its wide reach to focused job seekers, immediacy and cost effectiveness. Because of its global reach, an organization also gets the flexibility to attract the best talent. Many placement agents have now started this service to increase their business volume.

The next step in the selection procedure is to personify such attributes in candidates, i.e., developing a specification of persons to define the background education, training, personality, and characteristics of the candidates to suit the vacancy position. This in reality is an exercise to preportray an ideal candidate for a job.

Preliminary screening of applicants

Number of applications normally received against any advertised vacancy is usually more. This creates the problem of selecting the right persons from many. Moreover, conducting tests and interviews for all the candidates may not be always feasible and at the same time cost efficient. To obviate such problems, most of the organizations sort out unsuitable candidates before going ahead with the selection process. There are many different ways to do such preliminary screening. Some organizations conduct short tests for all the applications, while best method may be the checking of "Application Bank." Each organization before going for the selection process develops its own standards or potential attributes for the prospective candidates. This helps them also to define the rejection standards. For example, for the post of a Stenographer, a particular organization may define their rejection standards as follows:

(1) Those who are having shorthand speed below 100 words per minute and types speed below 40 words per minute

(2) Those who are not having any working experience
(3) Those who are above 35 years age.

By checking "Application Bank" of the candidates, an organization may reject a good number of applicants based on the above rejection parameters. All the above processes, therefore, enable an organization to short-list the candidates before going ahead with the subsequent stages of selection. The rejection standard like the ones stated above may also be mentioned in the advertisement itself so that the number of applicants is minimized.

Some organizations also adopt "successive-hurdles" technique as an effective screening process. This technique calls for arranging all selection factors in order of importance. For example, if for a particular post, aptitude test is considered most important; the first step should be to test the aptitude of the candidates, then other successive tests, like qualification, job experience, personality, etc. may be conducted provided the candidates qualify these hurdles one by one.

Review of application blanks The application **blanks** form is designed to have detailed information about the applicants. Some organizations have their own printed application blank while others ask the candidates to give their particulars in a standard format to elicit information like:

(1) Personal data and biographical information, i.e., name, address, telephone number, age, gender, marital status, children, nationality, education (school, college, university attended, degree/diploma passed, year of passing, subjects, grade or division obtained, etc.), professional qualification and membership of professional bodies, language known (ability to read, write, and speak), etc.
(2) Chronological employment history for all jobs (with joining and leaving dates in each case of employment change), employer's name, address and nature of business positions held and duties, reason for leaving (if any).
(3) Personal circumstances, when available, prepared to serve anywhere or not.
(4) Medical history, brief details of any serious illness, number of days absented during last few years (in case the applicant served earlier somewhere) on medical grounds, record of hospitalization (if any), disability, major operation, etc.
(5) Interest, hobbies, sports, and other activities.
(6) Anything else which the applicant may like to add in support of his candidature.

Several other items may be included in the application blank on the specific requirements of the organization and the job.

Weighted application blanks are also prepared by some organizations to record personal history items associated with the job success. For each item of the application blank, weight factors are predetermined. Importance of weight factors for different jobs also varies. For example, for unskilled laborers' job, education may be given less weight, while for executive positions, education receives higher weightage. Application blank, therefore, helps in comparing the applications.

Reference checking

Some organizations ask for references from the applicants in application blank itself to get information on candidate's character and antecedents. Such references are preferred from earlier employers and schools/colleges/universities that have some acquaintance with the candidates. Organizations try to verify candidates' antecedents from the references either over phone, through correspondence or personal visits. Most of the organizations send a brief questionnaire to such references alongwith a confidential note, requesting them to furnish such details.

Psychological testing

Generally, psychological testing is used for purposes like determining training needs and evaluation of training programs, selection and placement, transfer and promotion, counseling, etc. However, such testing is primarily used for selection and placement. These tests are of different types such as group or individual test, instrumental tests, aptitude or achievements tests, personality and interest tests, etc. Group tests are designed to test a group of candidates simultaneously. Individual tests are for individual candidates at a particular point of time. Instrumental tests can be group tests or individual tests. When it is an individual test, it makes use of different tools to study individual candidates' familiarity and skills. But, in case of its application for a group, it involves written test or paper–pencil test to study the written responses of the candidates. Aptitude tests are intended to assess the potentiality of the applicants to learn the job, while achievement tests enable assessing how effectively an individual can perform his job. Conventionally, aptitude tests are administered on freshers, i.e., those who are not having any past job experience, while achievement tests are intended for experienced candidates, which are having bearing with job performance. For marketing job and managerial as well as executive jobs such tests have much relevance. However, psychological tests are mostly designed to measure the aptitude and skills of successful job performers. For selection and placement, most of the organizations retain the services of consultants and experts on psychological testing. This minimizes the chance of error in selecting the wrong candidates for different job positions. Since psychological testing is a complex method and it has wide divergence, we have briefly introduced the concept of attitudinal measurement with simple example and illustrations together with some conceptual details about different types of measurement and scales.

Attitude measurement

Attitude is a mental state of an individual which tends to act or respond or is ready to respond for or against objects, situation, etc., with which his/her vested feeling or effect, interest, liking, desire and so on, are directly or indirectly linked or associated (Bhattacharyya, 2015). During our process of development we respond to objects, which gradually shape our attitude. This is why we also define attitude as a learned cognitive mechanism. Attitude being our psychic state, it cannot be observed directly. We need to measure it through our observations, inferences, prediction from behavioral data, administering various psychometric tools, etc. In recruitment, measurement of attitude is important, as through such measurement it is possible to understand how far the new incumbent would fit with the culture of the organizations, and whether such an incumbent can work with a team.

Interview

Interview is defined as a conversation with a purpose. Such a purpose is classified under three categories, i.e., obtaining information from the candidates, giving information to the candidates and finally to motivate the candidates. The first purpose is intended to get information from candidates regarding their background, experience, education, training, and interests to evaluate their suitability as per the requirements of the organization. The second purpose is to provide the candidates with information regarding the organization, its philosophy, personnel policies, etc. The third purpose is to establish a positive relationship to motivate the prospective candidates to join the organization. However, all these purposes being successive stages of interview, the subsequent stages are followed only when the interviewers are prima facie satisfied with the candidates in the first stage.

Human Resource Department of most of the organizations conducts preliminary interview for the candidates. However, for subsequent interviews, a committee of executive is formed to select the right candidates.

For managerial and executive positions, organizations prefer to retain the service of consultancy organizations with subject experts on the selection committee.

There are different types of interview as under:

(1) **The patterned interview:** This is also known as a structured or standardized interview. It is intended to assess the candidate's emotional strength and stability, industry, ability to get along well with others, self-reliance, willingness to accept responsibility, motivation, etc.

(2) **Indirect or nondirective interview:** This type of interview is meant for helping the candidates to feel relaxed and free to talk. Interviewers become listeners and allow the candidates to reveal their personality, in-depth knowledge in a free and relaxed atmosphere.

(3) **Direct planned interview:** It is a simple question–answer session to ascertain the suitability of the candidates.

(4) **Stress interview:** This interview assesses the candidates' emotional balance under a situation of tension and stress. Such tension is, therefore, deliberately created by interruptions, provocations, silence, and criticism or even by firing questions. Interviewers in such a situation deliberately become more unfriendly and even, at time, hostile. For selection of executives, who are required to work under stress, such a method is often adopted.

(5) **Group interview:** This method is intended to assess the leadership ability of the candidates. Generally, a topic is given to the candidates to discuss among themselves. The interviewers remain in the background to assess the best leaders, their initiative, poise, adaptability, awareness, interpersonal skills, etc.

(6) **Panel or board interview:** Several interviewers collectively interview a candidate to rate his/her attributes. Generally, such a panel consists of several experts and each of them interviews a candidate only in those areas on which they have the requisite expertise.

In Fig. 1.5, types of interview are explained. For conducting a successful interview, interviewers should be adequately competent and trained. The interview should be conducted in a suitable place. It should be well planned; job descriptions and information about the applicants should be adequately studied. Interviewers should be free from any conceivable prejudice. Interviewees should be allowed to feel relaxed. Beginning and ending of an interview should be made in a best possible friendly manner, etc.

The limitations of traditional selection process like failure to select the right persons for the right jobs and too much emphasis on written tests as well as interviews have resulted in development of psychometric method. This method enables quantifying the attributes, through which the candidates in order of their merit can be selected. Many organizations today are making use of this method to ensure proper selection of their employees (Fig. 1.5).

FIGURE 1.5 Different types of interviews.

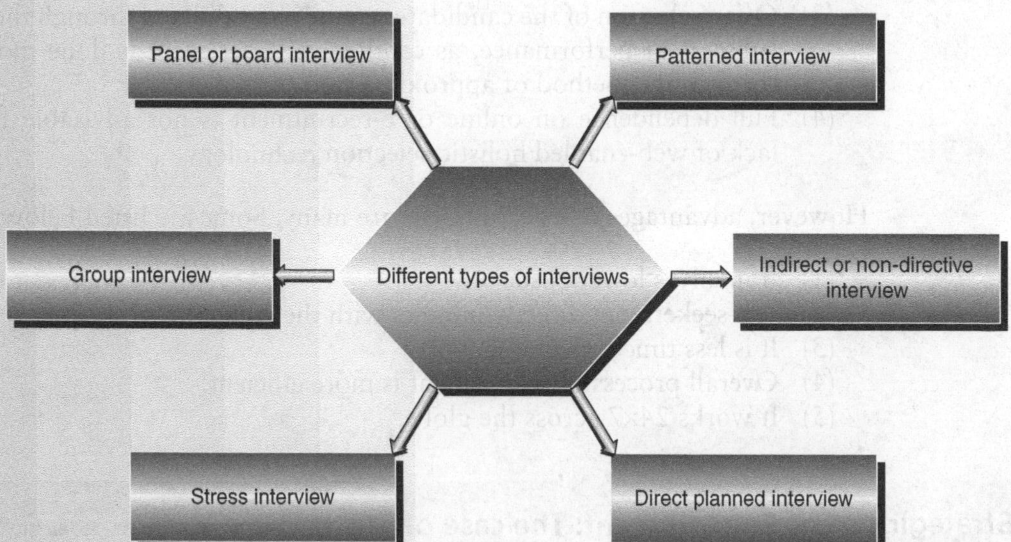

How shell conducts interview?

Shell conducts different types of interviews for different job roles. For commercial job roles, Shell conducts a business scenario interview. Here prospective candidates are given a business scenario and then asked to analyze the risk, action plans to mitigate the risk, and likely impact of such recommended action plans on the strategy. After 15 minutes for preparing the answer, candidates are interviewed for 20 minutes. Interview questions are mostly business related and competency-based. For a technical job profile, a similar interview process is followed, but usually after 15 minutes of presentation on the topic, technical interview continues for 30–40 minutes. Mostly, project-related questions previously handled by the candidates are asked in the interview. Here also the interview is competency-based.

E-recruitment

E-recruitment is also known as online recruitment. Although its use is rapidly increasing, it is not free from defects. Some of the shortcomings are:

(1) Online processing of the details of the job seekers is time consuming and also the results are debatable.
(2) Internet penetration and usage is yet to become a recognized method of job seeking.
(3) Often selection of the candidates cannot be validated through their subsequent performance, as candidates' assessment is done more through the method of approximation.
(4) Full dependence on online or e-recruitment is not advisable for lack of web-enabled holistic selection technology.

However, advantages of e-recruitment are many. Some are listed below:

(1) It involves lower costs.
(2) Job-seekers can directly interact with the company.
(3) It is less time consuming.
(4) Overall process of recruitment is more efficient.
(5) It works 24×7 across the globe.

Strategic use of E-recruitment: The case of Deloitte in Holland

For Deloitte, e-recruitment is a great challenge particularly in Holland, where percentage of job seekers is awfully low. The type of profiles Deloitte looks for is represented only by quality workforce, which itself is very small in number in Holland, and 10% of which only prefer to go for job change. Interestingly, a large number of people in Holland are in social media. To ensure Deloitte can preach them and attract them to be a Deloittian, the company went for a very innovative social media strategy. First, Deloitte focused on building strong employer brand identity so that they can attract the talent. Second, the company went for diverting traffic to their career sites. They organized their career web-site outside their corporate web-site. Thereafter, the company categorized the career web-site into three types, i.e., students, young professional, and professional. Such categorization helped Deloitte to organize contents as per preferences of different age-groups. In the social media Deloitte's recruitment staff created their profiles, and gradually formed communities. Systematic communication with the communities with their career web-site tag, and sharing of enriching content particularly on career choices, could help Deloitte create a crowd of their own. And, this was the potential source of talent for Deloitte in Holland.

Outsourcing

Recruitment through outsourcing vendors is gaining importance day by day. Business volatility day by day has made the manpower requirement of organizations more time independent than a well-planned function, if not for all jobs, at least for some. Information Technology (IT) and IT-enabled services (ITeS) organizations being execute project based assignments, depend mainly on outsourced manpower. For manufacturing industry, outsourcing is restricted to noncore activities, although many manufacturing organizations take the advantage of outsourcing for manpower cost optimization. Nationally and internationally, there are many manpower supply vendors who can make available people with any skill-set even for a very short period.

In addition to the above, it is observed that the recruitment process outsourcing (RPO) activities are increasing day by day. RPO is increasing in Indian companies. In abroad such practices have become common. In India, we have the example of Wipro. Wipro has outsourced its HR function to PeopleStrong Today, PeopleStrong looks after Wipro's hiring process including interview, candidate screening, and related functions. RPO as a sector is likely to grow in India in coming years. Some of the advantages enjoyed by the company when they outsource their recruitment functions are:

(1) Reducing cycle time of recruitment and help organizations in creating sustainable talent pipeline for meeting present and future needs of manpower.
(2) Making recruitment process more efficient and effective.
(3) Improving selection ratio.
(4) Helping organizations to focus on their core business
(5) Reducing manpower sourcing costs substantially.

Thus, the scope of outsourcing does not get limited to manpower outsourcing, i.e., engaging or hiring people from manpower vendors, usually for a shorter duration. It also extends to outsourcing of recruitment process to specialized agencies for making the recruitment process efficient.

Induction

After selection of employees, the first step is to orient them to organizational life. Induction or orientation program of an organization is a process to guide and counsel the employees to familiarize them with the job and the organization. This process helps an organization to clarify the terms and conditions of employment, specific job requirements and also to inculcate confidence in the minds of the new entrants.

Objectives

General objectives of such a program normally are:

(1) To introduce new employees with the organizational environment, exposing them to the mission, history and traditions of the organization, its achievements and future challenges, its personnel policy and expectations from the new employees.
(2) To create a positive attitude in the minds of the new employees.
(3) To create proper awareness in the new employees enabling them to understand the business of the organization.
(4) To provide opportunity to interact with other fellow employees and also with other managerial employees of the organization.

A good induction program should contain following areas which are conveniently distributed under organization's point of view and employee's point of view.

Organization's point of view:

(1) History, mission, objectives, and philosophy of the organization.
(2) Its product, production process, operations involved, state of technology.
(3) Its past achievements, present status, and future growth plan.
(4) Structure of the organization and the functions of different departments.
(5) Delegation of authority and decision-making process.
(6) Personnel policies, other miscellaneous policies, practices, and regulations.
(7) Job descriptions and responsibilities.
(8) Expectations from new employees.

Employee's point of view

(1) Job responsibilities
(2) Office procedures
(3) Grievance-handling procedures
(4) Salary and perks
(5) Service rules governing hours of work, overtime,
(6) Rules covering probation, confirmation, promotion opportunities, transfer, etc.
(7) Retirement and superannuation benefits.
(8) Employee services and welfare activities.
(9) Employee's participation in small group activities, question schemes.
(10) Performance evaluation.

Steps in Induction Program

An induction program essentially involves the following steps:

(1) **General orientation:** It includes guided tours in different departments of an organization; introduction with fellow employees, supervisors and executives; collection of information about the organizations' mission, philosophy, achievements, future plans, etc. Some organizations have their printed manuals, which they give to their new employees to orient them with their induction training programs for a week or so. The purpose of such general orientation program is to build a sense of pride in the minds of the new employees and also to create an interest in them about the organization.

(2) **Specific orientation:** This is intended to help new employees to get acclimatized with their new work environment. The supervisor or the departmental boss of an employee takes him on round to his place of work and impart vocational guidance for his particular nature of work. He is also told about the technology, environment, and other facilities available in the organization, prevailing practices and customs, and specific expectations from an employee. For executives and managerial employees, targets and key result areas for each of them are given to make them aware of what organization expects from them.

(3) **Follow-up orientation:** This orientation is conducted after some time of initial induction of an employee, i.e., preferably within a period of 6 months or so. The purpose of such orientation is to give guidance and counsel to the employees to ensure that they are reasonably satisfied and gradually settling with the organization.

Employees Socialization

Employee orientation and induction is also called an employee socialization process. Socialization, however, is a continuous process, today's organizations being dynamic. For the new employees Decenzo and Robins (1999) identified that socialization process involves three distinct stages as under:

(1) **Prearrival stage:** At this stage individual employee comes to an organization with certain values, attitudes and expectations. This exercise being undertaken at the selection stage to enable an employee to understand to what extent his perceived mapping gets with organizational culture and systems, it is the duty of the persons involved in the selection process to facilitate this.

Now-a-days because of availability of information about organizations through different media, including web-sites and internet, an enthusiastic individual may also have some preconceived ideas about the organization. Therefore, it is better to first understand from the individual about what he understands about the organization and then help him to synchronize this information with the reality. This helps the individual to take the right decision.

(2) **Encounter stage:** At this stage, perceptions earlier generated by an individual, are re-affirmed through a well-planned induction program. Any dichotomy between the employees' perceptions and organizational perceptions needs to be properly identified and removed through increased socialization process.

(3) **Metamorphosis stage:** At this final stage of socialization, employees understand the organizations and identify them with the organizations. Employees develop a sense of belongingness and become a contributor to achieving organizational goals and objectives.

However, as explained earlier, socialization is a continuous process as organizations are now required to go for restructuring and reengineering every now and then keeping pace with changing environment.

Placement

After the initial program is over, an employee is put to a specific job, for which he has been selected. Most of the organizations put new employees on probation for a specified period after which they are confirmed or made permanent, provided they match the organizational requirements. Personnel department periodically reviews the progress of such employees getting feedbacks on their performance from their controlling authority. Some organizations have also a system to extend probationary period, if the employees fail to match to the organizational expectations. Such second placement is known as 'differential placement'.

Placement is defined as assigning employees job for which they have been identified as suitable based on the selection techniques. But such definition would be meaningless, if a particular employee is recruited against a particular vacancy. Generally, the question of placement arises when a group of trainees are recruited. Organizations, to identify the true potentiality of an employee, in such cases, make provision for short-term placement, during which phase, employees are allowed to work on different jobs, through a systematic job rotation program. However, at a later stage, permanent placement is effected matching the employees' competence, knowledge, skill and job interest. Other forms of placement have been discussed in the chapter on transfer and promotion.

Importance of Induction and Placement

Common use of higher technology, increased level of knowledge and skills of the new job entrants, production restructuring and flexibility coupled with perceptive change about human resource, which is now considered as most important resource of an organization, have now transformed labor as an item for competitive sale and purchase. However, despite the problem of unemployment in India, there still exists dearth of knowledgeable and skilled workers and so also executives and managers. Recent economic liberalization program of the Government of India has now paved the way for entry of multinationals and foreign companies. Market globalization has further intensified the competition. Development of Total Quality Management philosophy, inter alia, is also demanding sea change in product and service-mix of an organization. All these together have now increased the scope for job-mobility for employees with knowledge and skills of appropriate type and degree.

Unfortunately, retaining employees after the recruitment and selection is an utterly neglected area in Indian corporate sector. Many organizations spend several lakhs of rupees in terms of job advertisement, conducting tests and interviews, hiring the services of consultants and psychologists etc., for selecting a managerial employee. Weak induction program, without adequate emphasis on building confidence and sense of belongingness in the minds of the new employees, result in quick separation, so also wastage of colossal sum of money for the organization. Such experience is quite common in public sector units. Very recently a leading Tata organization has lost a few hundreds of their young engineers and professionals who left en masse to join elsewhere.

Some organizations, on the contrary, do not review the progress of the new employees who become permanent automatically after completion of their probationary tenure, despite the reason that they are unproductive.

Thus, a good induction and placement program is required to ensure employees' retention by keeping their motivation high, while at the same time, getting rid of the unproductive employees within the organizations.

Onboarding

Induction process is also known as onboarding. Onboarding concept is more encompassing, as it emphasizes on adjusting new hires both to the social and performance aspects of jobs quickly and smoothly (Bauer, 2011). Effective onboarding program helps new hires to develop their positive attitude, acquire the required knowledge and skills, and learn proper behavior for their effective functioning in the organizations. Like induction, onboarding program also varies from organization to organization. Bauer has developed the best practices guideline for onboarding, wherein he has listed certain important things like implementing basics, making the first day special, design and implement formal orientation programs, create and use written onboarding plans, making it participatory, monitoring progress, and meeting with stakeholder.

Recruitment Matrices

Sullivan (2013) classified recruitment matrices in three types: historical, real-time and predictive. Historical matrices no more can help in strategic recruitment and selection decision, as with the passage of time, business scenarios also change. Real-time matrix has some utility, as using it HR managers can promptly alter or improve the decisions. These types of matrices are based on recent trend or recent recruitment performance. Third types of metrices are known as predictive matrices. These help HR managers to predict future problems and opportunities in recruitment and selection.

Based on Sullivan's analysis, some of the recruitment matrices may be discussed as under:

Historical metrices

(1) **Performance level of new hires:** Measures actual job performance of new hires.
(2) **Diversity inclusive recruitment:** Measures extent of diversity inclusion, like percentage of women recruitment, etc.

Real-time matrices

(3) **Missing of strategic opportunities for poor recruitment:** Delay in new product development and launching, delay in project, etc.
(4) **Delay in filling vacancy of key positions:** This is particularly for direct revenue generating jobs, like sales and marketing, etc.
(5) **Performance failure of new hires:** Usually measured after completion of a performance cycle.
(6) **Voluntary turnover of new hires:** Particularly evident in generation Y, and more relevant for software industries.
(7) **Percentage of innovators in new hires:** High percentage is a good indicator for organizational innovation.

Predictive matrices

(8) Forecast on availability of quality candidates
(9) Forecast on recruitment competition

(10) Forecast on the talent opportunity
(11) Forecast on unemployment rate
(12) Forecast on labor costs

These apart, there are certain routine matrices, using what organizations can think of achieving efficiency in their recruitment and selection functions. Most of these matrices are commonly used by the organizations.

(1) Rate of acceptance of job offer
(2) Quality of recruitment source
(3) Quality of the job applicants
(4) Satisfaction level with the recruitment process
(5) Recruitment performance
(6) Brand strength of employer

It is however for the organizations to decide to select the appropriate matrices for measuring their recruitment and selection function. A number of research studies, including a research study carried out by the Boston Consulting group could identify recruitment and selection, exerts highest impact on profit of the organization. Hence, it is advisable for organizations to choose the appropriate matrices for effective management of their recruitment and selection function.

Use matrices strategically: Learning from Marriott

Marriott International, the leading global hospitality company with US $13 billion revenue, faces great challenges in recruiting talent for the hospitality industry, across their various locations. Realizing the need for strategic focus for recruiting talents, the company has designed three indigenous recruitment matrices using which they can time to time calibrate their recruitment strategies. These are:

(1) Focused campaigns on key jobs (to attract job seekers to key roles)
(2) Leverage a database of potential candidates (for identifying candidates with precise skills for the jobs)
(3) Measure cost per hire

Using these three recruitment matrices, the company is successful in managing their recruitment and selection function.

Recruitment and selection decision-making process now also gets influenced by HR analytics. All decisions on human resources, be it on recruitment, performance management, succession planning, training, compensation design, and talent management now require more scientific approach. With big data such scientific approach to HR decision making process is possible using various predictive models. With less risk of decisional errors, therefore, HR analytics is becoming more effective tool for HR decision making process. To ensure fact based decision making process in recruitment and selection also, some organizations have started using HR analytics.

Recruiting Generation Y

Organizations today confront the challenge of recruiting generation Y which is also known as internet or dot.com generation. Characteristically, generation Y is different from its predecessors which have already been established through series or researches by scholars like Broadbridge et al., 2007a; Shaw and Fairhurst, 2008. Selection and recruitment process for Generation Y may be significantly different as asserted by Lindquist (2008). This therefore requires HR managers' greater understanding of generation Y in terms of their expectations and goals. Researchers agree that generation Y people are those who took their birth between 1977 and 1994 (Cennamo and Gardner, 2008; Glass, 2007; Martin, 2005; Oliver, 2006; Reynolds et al., 2008; Szamosi, 2006).

For effective recruitment, selection and framing of retention strategies, at the outset it is necessary to assess expectancy value and goal setting

For GE generation Y gets attracted for a purpose

GE is successful in attracting generation Y, as it believes in doing. Many organizations proclaim they are innovative, but they hardly embrace innovative practices in designing new products, processes and services. GE is the exception, as it believes in the culture of open innovation. With innovation GE today is a world class manufacturing and process solutions company. Its open innovation is reinforced by GE's culture of open collaboration. With the culture of experimenting, collaborating and learning, GE today can transform to a company of ideas. Simultaneous reengineering of culture, along with the business portfolio and the operation processes, could Experimenting, collaborating and learning are the three important areas which can sensitize the mind-sets of generation Y and so also generation Z, transforming GE the most sought after company for their learning, self-development and career growth.

norms of general Y people. These two considerations are categorized under process-related theories (Hertel and Wittchen, 2008). These theories help understand occupational motives, ideals and interests, i.e., the expectancy value of generation Y. At a given point of time a generation Y person can make a choice between different options based on his/her expectancy. Google's frequent calibration of employee benefits program is increasingly making the workplace filled with five star amenities, pacing with the changing expectancy value of their employees, which largely are part of generation Y is a good example. Like expectancy value for generation Y, goal-setting theory explains the way they focus on action goals.

As generation Y recruitment and selection process is critical, it is necessary to develop better clarity on the process-related theories, so that the best talents in different areas among generation Y can be attracted, recruited and retained. Expectancy-value percepts of generation Y is classified under cognitive-motivational theory. As per this theory, a motivated behavior is the outcome of positive or negative expectations and value assigned by an individual employee to attain any specific goal (Lynd-Stevenson, 1999; Petri and Govern, 2004). Expectancy-value theory has its roots to research of Vroom (1964) and subsequently to researches of Shepperd and Taylor, 1999, Brewer and Skinner, 2006, and Hertel and Wittchen, 2008. Vroom's expectancy model of motivation defines motivation as the product of 'expectancy (E) × (instrumentality (I) × valence (V). It is indicated as V × E × I. This theory assumes that behavior of employees is a conscious choice among different alternatives. Expectancy is individual employee's belief that his/her increased effort leads to increased performance. For generation Y expectancy is mediated by their feelings that organizations will make available required resources, groom them with appropriate skills and extend necessary support, so that they can do their job better. Instrumentality is the belief that with better performance, they would get valued outcome. Obviously, this requires organizations to showcase transparent compensation and reward program, so that employees can influence their belief that better performance would lead to valued outcome. Valence is the importance assigned by individual employees on the expected outcome. With positive valence only individual employee shows its preference to attain the outcome. Obviously, it requires organizations to design their compensation and benefit baskets as flexible as possible, so that employees and more particularly generation Y can make their conscious choice from different alternatives, and thus nurture the positive valence.

Goal-setting theory approach explains how individual employee frames its strategies to achieve goals, and direct its efforts accordingly. For generation Y, organizations need to frame meaningful goals, which are difficult, yet attainable (Brewer and Skinner, 2006). Generation Y people always believe that they are capable to do difficult tasks, hence when organizations fail to assign difficult and challenging job role, they feel demotivated. Such organizations, therefore, do not attract Generation Y, causing problems in recruitment and selection. Good example is high attrition rate in IT and ITeS organizations. These organizations recruit Generation Y people in a large number. After joining these organizations, these youngsters feel they are not able to utilize their skills. As a result, in earliest opportune moment they change their job or go for higher studies for more relevant career options in future.

Both these process related theories, i.e., expectancy-value and goal-setting, have significant influence on generation Y, while they select any organization for their career growth. Obviously, this requires organizations to guard against these two aspects for attracting and recruiting best talent in generation Y.

Think before you recruit generation Y

Former GE CEO Jack Welch said "Generation Y represents the most exciting people in the world. They have the propensity to do their own thing." Several studies have validated such observation of Jack Welch. Analyzing the workplace behavior of generation Y employees, it is observed that these employees believe in collaborative decision making. Being flexible they can accommodate with change, and finally they also challenge the status quo. These being the characteristics of generation Y, it is always desirable that organizations set their premises first, before they recruit generation Y.

Expectations of Generation Y from Their Organizations

It is difficult to generalize the expectations of generation Y from their organizations. However, based on many research results, it can be summarized those as under:

(1) Challenging and creative work with clear directions from managers who are attitudinally more positive (Broadbridge et al., 2007a; Martin, 2005)

(2) Eagerness to be a part of team represented by highly committed and motivated workers (Martin, 2005)

(3) Propensity to be more result oriented, hence feel the need to get empowered, desire multi-tasking, and job pressure (Shaw and Fairhurst, 2008)

(4) Do not like to be micromanaged, i.e., expect more autonomy in doing their job (Broadbridge et al., 2007a; Martin, 2005)

(5) Expect constant feedback and praise at work (Shaw and Fairhurst, 2008)
(6) Expect instructions to complete their job assignments (Glass, 2007)
(7) Value mentoring and training for their professional growth and transition from one job to another (Cennamo and Gardner, 2008)
(8) More influenced by technology for workplace interaction (Crumpacker and Crumpacker, 2007; Glass, 2007).
(9) More optimistic about future careers (Oliver, 2006; Wong et al., 2008).

Understanding such expectations of generation Y, HR managers can frame their strategies for attraction recruitment of talented job aspirants. Obviously, all these require organizations to bring necessary changes in their systems and policies.

Poor performance may not always dilute your brand value: Case of DuPont

With Monsanto grabbing market share, DuPont has substantially reduced its compensation budget, first by cutting the bonus payouts and secondly by delaying the salary increases. Ellen Kullman, the Chairman and CEO of the company admits that the company did not meet the targets. Along with such declaration, Kullman further announced series of cost control measures that the company has initiated. DuPont is an innovative company, which declares it a science company, and all along remained a preferred organization for engineering talent. To diffuse the mounting tension in the minds of the prospective job seekers, Kullman, however, focused on restoring the confidence, saying these are 'prudent decisions' considering the long-term sustainability of the organization. With Kullman's reputation as a CEO, DuPont's brand value hopefully will not get diluted, and the company will continue to attract talent.

Recruiting Generation Z

Generation Z, the Digital Generation, born between the year 1995–2010, is sweeping the workforce market. Already organizations like Yahoo, Apple, Samsung have started recruiting from generation Z. One research study indicates more than 60 percent of generation Z people would like to be entrepreneur, rather than working for others. Obviously, this would be the primary challenge for the organizations in future recruitment. Even those who could be recruited, their retention would be a great challenge, as they would be restless for leadership roles, like a natural entrepreneur.

Research studies indicate generation Z people show signs of being entrepreneurial. They are less influenced by money. They prefer in-person communication with managers. They want to get importance. Hence managers need to take them seriously, and finally they also like to work for an honest leader.

Generation Z people are referred as digital natives, social media junkies, multi-screen generation, etc. We use the term gamification, i.e., game-like behaviors, so that we can attract and retain generation Z talent in organization. Gamification refers to the use of game in non-game situations. It is not adding game in a recruitment process, rather it is used as dynamics of engagement, which facilitates engagement of both conscious and subconscious mind of generation Z people, and thus enable the HR managers to truly assess their degree of fit with the job and culture of the organization. A properly designed game can unearth multiple touch points, and help HR managers to make the selection process more effective.

A large number of generation Z people are engaged by Samsung, Facebook, and Google as apprentices.

Recruitment and Selection in India

In India recruitment and selection function is influenced by several factors. The first important issue is compliance with the legal norms. Legal norms come in terms of quota-based recruitment for some socially challenged communities, particularly for those jobs which require unskilled people. Similarly, there are some social norms, like recruiting people from the place where the organization situates. Here again, this is for the unskilled jobs. These apart, we have diversity issues. Organizations cannot discriminate in their recruitment and selection process on grounds of culture, race, gender, religion, language, etc. This aspect is enshrined by our Constitution. Time to time certain institutional mandates also influence recruitment and selection process in organizations. For example, recently Securities and Exchange Board of India (SEBI) mandated compulsory induction of at least one women board member in every listed company.

Apart from legal, social and institutional issues, Indian organizations are also facing certain compelling challenges in recruitment and selection. India has now become the global innovation hub, resulting rush for many multinational companies to start their innovation centers in India. Today, almost all large multinational companies (MNCs) have their innovation centers in India. These innovation centers attract and recruit the top talent, across all age-groups of people. More recruitment, however, is done from generation Y age-group. This apart, many MNCs have their manufacturing, processing and service units in India. MNCs like GE, Siemens, BASF, Bosch, LG, Samsung, Maruti, Toyota, Ford, etc, have their own manufacturing and processing units, and some even have their innovation hubs in India. Almost all global IT and ITeS companies also have their operations in India. All these organizations also compete for talents, causing enormous challenges for today's HR managers to strategically design their recruitment and selection functions. For adequacy of quality manpower, many global companies also source their manpower requirement from India for international job assignments. Realizing such importance, many organizations today renamed their recruitment and selection function as talent acquisition. Many Indian organizations are experimenting with innovative recruitment and selection strategies, coping with such challenges. For example, for recruiting talents from generation Y, employee referrals, as a sourcing strategy, are used by almost all organizations, largely, however, by IT and ITeS companies. This is followed by newspaper advertisements. Indian companies have also started re-emphasizing on internal recruitment through strategic succession planning. This obviously requires organizations to create career development opportunities for the employees, systematic training and development, job rotation, mentoring and coaching, etc.

SUMMARY

- Recruitment, selection, induction and placement are staffing functions. For any organization, human resources are considered most critical and important differentiator for growth and sustainability. This obviously requires organizations to be very strategic in managing the staffing functions.
- Human resource planning helps assessing the manpower requirement of any organization. After assessing the manpower requirement, HR managers first look into the internal source of hiring, i.e., recruiting people from within the organization. Thereafter, external sources of recruitment are explored.
- This chapter being introductory, the basics of recruitment and selection functions have been explained. Various tools for selection have also mentioned linking with the theories and concepts on the subject for better understanding.
- The chapter after introducing the concepts of recruitment and selection separately, and differentiating between them, these two terms have been used once again as one and the same in the corporate world.
- The chapter helps the readers to understand various aspects of recruitment and its processes from the organizational perspectives. Similarly, the chapter briefly discusses various tools of selection.

- The chapter suggests for recruiting generation Y and generation Z people in the organizations, which would henceforth be necessary. Appropriate strategies need to be framed, so that these people feel attracted to apply. In explaining these aspects, the chapter has elaborated on some corporate practices.
- For managing the recruitment and selection functions efficiently, the chapter suggests the need for framing suitable policies, and illustrated some template of policies and procedures.
- The chapter mentions that the cycle of recruitment and selection ends only after successful onboarding of new hires and their placement in the earmarked job positions.
- Using various recruitment matrices, HR managers can measure the efficiency and effectiveness of their recruitment and selection functions, take corrective actions to improve in future, and also calibrate their strategies.
- The chapter begins and ends with case studies and also sets the premises of our discussions on further chapters.

Key Words

Internal recruitment: Process of hiring from within the organizations.

Nondirective interview: Here interviewers become listeners and allow the candidates to feel relaxed and feel free to talk.

Follow-up orientation: This orientation gives guidance and counsel to the employees to ensure that they are reasonably satisfied and gradually settling with the organization.

Recruitment: Process of identification and attraction of candidates to apply for the jobs.

Recruitment procedures: Detailing of step-by-step actions required for implementing the recruitment policy.

Patterned interview: Structured or standardized interview.

Stress interview: This interview assesses the candidates' emotional balance under a situation of tension and stress.

Metamorphosis stage: This is the final stage of socialization to help employees develop a sense of belongingness and effectively contribute to organizational goals and objectives.

Selection: Process of following series of steps and screening to choose the best-fit for the job position.

E-recruitment: Online recruitment.

Review Questions

1. Explain the concept of recruitment. Also, discuss various recruitment functions, and explain why such functions are important for organizations?
2. Define internal recruitment. What are advantages and disadvantages of internal recruitment?
3. Explain why it is necessary for an organization to have a recruitment policy. List out some of the important points, which you may like to have in a recruitment policy of a manufacturing organization.
4. What are the different recruitment processes? Briefly state their merits and demerits.
5. Discuss the importance of selection process and mention the steps involved in such process.
6. Suppose you have been retained by an organization to select a few management trainees. What process do you think you should consider and why?
7. What is an induction program? Is there any difference between induction and onboarding? What are the important areas the need to be considered for an effective induction program?
8. Explain the steps involved in an induction program. Why is induction and placement important for organizations?
9. Define attitude. Why, in recruitment and selection, do we need to assess the attitude of candidates?
10. Explain why recruitment of Generation Y and Generation Z deserves special attention from organizations. In what way Generation Z is different from Generation Y?
11. Explain the concept of recruitment process outsourcing. Is it at all desirable for an organization?
12. What is e-recruitment? Explain with example how it can be successfully used by any organization.
13. Write short notes on:
    (a) Multiple career paths
    (b) Job rotation
    (c) Probationary period
    (d) Follow-up orientation
    (e) Stress interview
    (f) Application blank
    (g) Deputation
    (h) Successive hurdles
    (i) RPO
    (j) Digital Generation
    (k) Succession Planning

Critical Review Questions

1. You have to recruit management and engineering trainees visiting campuses. Design campus recruitment program, assuming that you have to give mandate selection on the sport.
2. Design some predictive recruitment metrics for a software developer with some rationality.

Multiple Choice Questions

1. Identify the incorrect statement:
   (a) Manpower acquisition function broadly encompasses talent management function in organization
   (b) Manpower acquisition function also involves talent attraction
   (c) Manpower acquisition succeeds human resource planning
   (d) Manpower acquisition also involves manpower redundancy planning
   (e) Manpower acquisition is part of recruitment and selection function in organization

2. Recruitment and selection function also involves:
   (a) Attracting talent in the organizations
   (b) Organizational branding
   (c) Enhancement of organizational visibility
   (d) Onboarding, developing, and retaining people
   (e) All of the above

3. Identify the incorrect statement:
   (a) Regulatory and institutional norms do not affect organizational recruitment decisions
   (b) Quota-based recruitment requires compromising with quality
   (c) Diversity neutrality is a regulatory requirement in recruitment and selection
   (d) Ethical recruitment practices enhance organizational brand image
   (e) Recruitment and selection is a strategic function

4. Effective recruitment and selection process enables organizations to:
   (a) Sustain competitive strength
   (b) Facilitate job restructuring
   (c) Rationalize external hiring after adjusting internal manpower
   (d) Design appropriate onboarding program
   (e) All of the above

5. Person job-fit is ensured by:
   (a) Recruitment
   (b) Selection
   (c) Induction and placement

(d) Placement
(e) All of the above

6. Indicate which is an incorrect statement:
   (a) Recruitment involves all organizational practices and decisions which can influence the number and types of individuals willing to apply and accept a job
   (b) Effective recruitment is measured in terms of selection of competent individuals and organizational performance
   (c) Brand value of organizations, recruitment timing and nature of job also contribute to effective recruitment function
   (d) Job analysis, strategy, and the selection method are not deterrent for effective recruitment
   (e) Recruitment and selection are two distinct terms

7. Indicate which is not a part of recruitment process:
   (a) Identification of suitable candidates
   (b) Attracting suitable candidates to apply for job
   (c) Framing of suitable medium to draw the attention of prospective candidates
   (d) Culling prospective candidates for the job
   (e) None of the above

8. Selection is a process which:
   (a) Best-fit according to job criteria
   (b) Involves series of steps
   (c) Differentiates between applicants
   (d) Follows a process of elimination
   (e) All of the above

9. Indicate which statement is wrong for recruitment:
   (a) Identifying and attracting candidates to apply for the jobs
   (b) Encouraging eligible candidates to apply for the job
   (c) Fostering relationships
   (d) Creating talent pool in organizations
   (e) Restricting search of potential candidates

10. Indicate which statement is wrong for selection:
   (a) Choosing the best-fit for the job position
   (b) It is a positive process
   (c) Essentially a contract between the selected employees and the employers
   (d) Apply successive hurdles technique
   (e) More time consuming

11. A recruitment policy does not:
   (a) Spells out the process of manpower planning
   (b) Considers internal recruitment process
   (c) Details preferred sources of recruitment

(d) Frames suitable selection criteria
(e) Considers cost of recruitment

12. Recruitment procedures do not consider:
(a) Detailing of actions required for implementing a recruitment policy
(b) Processing of candidates' profiles
(c) Complying with diversity and legal issues
(d) Clarifying that user sections' (who had requisitioned for the manpower) have no role in selection process
(e) None of the above

13. Application blanks are designed to have information on:
(a) Personal data and biographical information of job applicants
(b) Chronological employment history
(c) Medical history
(d) Hobbies
(e) All of the above

14. Indicate which is not a type of interview:
(a) Patterned interview
(b) Indirect interview
(c) Fitment trial interview
(d) Direct interview
(e) Stress interview

15. Indicate which is not an advantage of e-recruitment:
(a) It decreases costs
(b) Job-seekers can directly interact with the company
(c) It is less time consuming
(d) It automates total recruitment process
(e) It makes process of recruitment efficient

16. Advantages enjoyed by the company when they outsource their recruitment functions are the following excepting:
(a) Reduces cycle time of recruitment but cannot help organizations in creating sustainable talent pipeline for meeting present and future needs of manpower
(b) Makes recruitment process more efficient and effective
(c) Improves selection ratio
(d) Helps organizations to focus on their core business
(e) Reduces manpower sourcing costs substantially.

17. Identify the incorrect statement:
(a) Induction is a process of introducing new employees with the organizational environment
(b) Induction motivates people for work
(c) Induction creates positive attitude in the minds of the new employees

(d) Induction creates proper awareness in the new employees to understand organization
(e) Induction provides opportunity to interact with other fellow employees

18. Indicate which is not a stage of employee socialization process:
(a) Pre-arrival stage
(b) Post-arrival stage
(c) Encounter Stage
(d) Metamorphosis stage
(e) None of the above

19. Indicate which statement is more appropriate for onboarding:
(a) Onboarding and induction is same
(b) Onboarding is more encompassing than induction
(c) Onboarding process helps new hires to integrate both the social and performance aspects
(d) Onboarding process is more universal in nature
(e) Good onboarding program also focuses on stakeholders' meeting

20. Which type of recruitment metrics use people analytics:
(a) Historical
(b) On-going
(c) Real-time
(d) Talent management
(e) Predictive

21. Real-time Metrics helps in assessing the following excepting:
(a) Missing of strategic opportunities for poor recruitment
(b) Involuntary turnover of new hires
(c) Delay in filling vacancy of key job positions
(d) Performance failure of new hires
(e) Innovators in new hires

22. Predictive HR metrics can help in recruitment, excepting:
(a) Forecast on availability of quality candidates
(b) Forecast on talent opportunity
(c) Forecast on unemployment rate
(d) Forecast on labor costs
(e) Forecast on technological changes

Answers:

1. (d) 2. (e) 3. (a) 4. (e) 5. (e) 6. (d) 7. (e) 8. (e)
9. (e) 10. (b) 11. (a) 12. (d) 13. (e) 14. (c) 15. (d) 16. (a)
17. (b) 18. (b) 19. (d) 20. (e) 21. (b) 22. (e)

CASE STUDY

Recruitment and selection: lessons from Tesco

Tesco is one of the largest retailers of the world. With current turnover of £69.7 billion and headcounts of 5 lakh, Tesco now operates from 12 countries through its 7817 stores. The company's core purpose is making "... what matters better together." The value statement of the company is using "... scale for good." For Tesco scale indicates providing affordable, high quality food to people around the world, and creating value for customers. Like other retailers, Tesco also source their manpower globally with strategic recruitment ad selection process. Operating from 12 different countries, international sourcing of manpower for Tesco is a great challenge.

Recruitment and selection process in Tesco starts with their manpower planning, using which Tesco assesses the number of manpower required with different skill-sets at different locations, in different countries. To meet the operational manpower requirement, Tesco recruits regularly. These types of recruitment and selection are largely for manpower replacement against the attrition, and to meet the contingent manpower requirement, for increasing the scale of operation, due to business fluctuation. Manpower planning, therefore, is primarily for meeting the future manpower requirements.

Manpower planning process also considers job description for the future vacant jobs, with details on job title, duties and responsibilities for the jobs, requirements appropriate skill-sets and competencies, characteristics and attributes of the prospective candidates, etc. Once the process of manpower planning gets over, Tesco goes for advertising for the jobs, to ensure that job vacancy news reach to the potential candidates for the jobs. However, mode of job advertisements largely varies depending on the nature and level of job. As the company believes in both internal and external recruitment, the company looks for both internal and external talents. External talent sourcing process starts, once the company believes that best-fit talent in alignment with the job requirements may not be available within the organization. Tesco advertises their vacancies through websites, online media, television, radio, job-search websites, etc.

For its strong brand value, the company gets a large number of applicants for the advertised job positions, requiring robust section process. With thorough screening of the profiles of the job applicants, the company shortlists the candidates for interview, and invites them to appear for the same. After the initial interview of the company, qualified candidates are taken through the assessment center (to take the candidates through a number of individual and group exercises). Successful candidates through assessment center are again taken through second round of interview, and finally selections are made.

The entire process of recruitment and selection of Tesco, is so designed that the company ultimately ends up in recruiting the best talent for the job positions. For Tesco, recruitment and selection is a win–win process. This is because the company only recruits those who are the right-fit for the job and also who fits in the Tesco culture. Also from the candidates' point of view they feel they have made the right choice in joining Tesco for their long-term career growth opportunities.

Question: As a recruitment specialist, critically evaluate Tesco's recruitment and selection process.

REFERENCES

Arvey, R.D., Gordon, M., Messengill, D. and Mussio, S. (1975), "Differential dropout rates of minority and majority job candidates due to time lags between selection procedures", *Personnel Psychology*, 38: 175–180.

Bateman, T.S. and Snell, S.A. (2002), *Management: Competing in the New Era*, McGraw-Hill Irwin, Boston.

Bauer, T.N. (2011), "Onboarding new employees: Maximizing success", SHRM Foundation's Effective Practice Guideline Series, SHRM. http://www.shrm.org/about/foundation/products/pages/onboardingepg.aspx, accessed on 9 June 2015.

Bhattacharyya, D.K. (2013), *Human Resource Planning*, 3rd edition, Excel Books, New Delhi.

Bohlander, G.W. and Snell, S. (2010), *Managing Human Resources*, Cengage Learning.

Brewer, N. and Skinner, N. (2006), Work motivation, in O'Driscoll, M., Taylor, P. and Kalliath, T. (Eds), *Organisational Psychology in Australia and New Zealand*, Oxford University, Melbourne, Victoria.

Broadbridge, A.M., Maxwell, G.A. and Ogden, S.M. (2007), 13_2_30: "Experiences, perceptions and expectations of retail employment for generation Y", *Career Development International*, 12(6): 523–544.

Cennamo, L. and Gardner, D. (2008), "Generational differences in work values, outcomes and person organisation values fit", *Journal of Managerial Psychology*, 23(8): 891–906.

Crumpacker, M. and Crumpacker, J.M. (2007), "Succession planning and generational stereotypes: should HR consider age based values and attitudes a relevant factor or passing fad?" *Public Personnel Management*, 36(4): 349–369.

Flippo, E.B. (1984), *Personnel Management*, New York, McGraw-Hill.

Glass, A. (2007), "Understanding generational differences for competitive success", *Industrial and Commercial Training*, 39(2): 98–103.

Hertel, G. and Wittchen, M. (2008), Work motivation, in Chmiel, N. (Ed.), *An Introduction to Work and Organizational Psychology: A European Perspective*, Blackwell, Malden, MA, pp. 29–55.

Ivancevich, J.M. (2003), *Human Resource Management*, Tata McGraw-Hill, New Delhi.

Kempner, T. (ed., 1971), *A Handbook of Management*, London, Weidenfeld and Nicolson.

Lindquist, T.M. (2008), "Recruiting the millennium generation: the new CPA", *The CPA Journal*, 78(8): 56–59.

Lynd, Stevenson, R.M. (1999), Expectancy value theory and predicting future employment status in the young employed," *Journal of Occupational and Organizational Psychology*, March, 72: 101–106.

Martin, C.A. (2005), "From high maintenance to high productivity", *Industry and Commercial Training*, 37(1): 39–44.

Oliver, D. (2006), "An expectation of continued success: the work attitudes of generation Y", *Labour and Industry*, 17(1): 61–84.

Reynolds, L., Campbell Bush, E. and Geist, R. (2008), "The generation Y imperative", *Communication World*, 25(2): 19–22.

Rynes, S.L. (1990), Recruitment, job choice, and post hire consequences: a call for new research directions, in Dunnette, M. and Hough, L.M., *Handbook of Industrial and Organizational Psychology,* Vol. 2, Palo Alto, CA: Consulting Psychology Press.

Rynes, S.L., Heneman, H.G. III and Schwab, D.P. (1980), *Individual reaction to organizational recruiting: a review, Personnel Psychology*, 1980, 33: 529–542.

Schermerhorn, J.R., Hunt, J.G. and Osborn, R.N. (2003), *Organizational Behaviour*, 8th edition, New York, NY: John Wiley & Sons, Inc.

Shaw, S. and Fairhurst, D. (2008), "Engaging a new generation of graduates", *Education+Training*, 50(5): 366–378.

Shepperd, J.A. and Taylor, K.M. (1999), "Social loafing and expectancy value theory", *Personality and Social Psychology Bulletin*, 25(12): 1147–1158.

Stone, R. (1998), *Human Resource Management*, Brisbane, Wiley.

Sullivan, J. (2013), High-impact Strategic Recruiting Metrics for WOWing Executives, web-site: http://www.ere.net/2013/01/28/high-impact-strategic-recruiting-metrics-for-wowing-executives/, accessed on 8 June 2015.

Szamosi, L.T. (2006), "Just what are tomorrow's SME employees looking for?" *Education+Training*, 48(8/9): 654–665.

Torrington, D. and Hall, L. (1991), *Personnel Management*, Prentice Hall, Cambridge.

Vroom, V.H. (1964), *Work and Motivation*, Wiley, New York, NY.

Yoder, D. (1972), *Personnel Management and Industrial Relations*, Prentice-Hall of India.

Appendix-1

Name of the Post

Advertisement No.

Personal Data

<table>
<tr><th colspan="3">Full Name:
Ms/Mr</th><th colspan="2">Applicant's Photograph</th></tr>
<tr><td colspan="3">Date of Birth, State, Marital Status</td><td colspan="2"></td></tr>
<tr><td colspan="3">Nationally, Whether SC/ST</td><td colspan="2"></td></tr>
<tr><td colspan="3">Height: .... cm.
Weight: .... kgs.</td><td colspan="2">Vision:
Normal/Corrected
Spectacle Lens Nos.</td></tr>
<tr><td colspan="3">Address to which we should write:
Telephone No.</td><td colspan="2">Permanent Address
Telephone No.</td></tr>
<tr><td colspan="3">Father's/Husband's Name and Occupation:</td><td colspan="2"></td></tr>
<tr><td colspan="5">If you have any relative employed in/or on the Board of our company, please give details.
Details of previous employment in this company or its sister concerns, with reasons for leaving.
Details of previous employment elsewhere, with reasons for leaving</td></tr>
<tr><td>Languages:
Mother Tongue</td><td>Speak</td><td colspan="2">Read</td><td>Write</td></tr>
</table>

Education

Examinations	School/ College	Year From	Attend To	Major Subjects	Class, % of Marks and Ranks
Scholastic Achievements					

Examinations	School/ College	Year From	Attend To	Major Subjects	Class, % of Marks and Ranks
TRAINING					
Name of the Firm/ Institution		From	To	Details of Training	Stipend, if any
WORK EXPERIENCE					
Employer		From	To	Position held and nature of work	Salary p.m. Basic Total

Extra Curricular Activities

Types of activities	At School	At College	Elsewhere
Official Position held:			
Sports			
Participation			
Positions held			
Captain, Secretary/ Manager			
Have you ever been convicted? If so, give full details			
Have you had any major illness, operations or accidents?			
Any other information that you would like to furnish:			
Name and addresses of three persons other than relatives to whom we may write for reference:			
Name	Address		
Minimum Salary Expected:			
We appreciate your time and effort you have spent in completing this application. Would you please check your application to ensure that you have completely and accurately answered each and every question?			

<table>
<tr><th>Types of activities</th><th>At School</th><th>At College</th><th>Elsewhere</th></tr>
<tr><td colspan="4">I declare that the particulars given above, are to the best of my knowledge, correct and complete and undertake to advise the company immediately of changes, if any, in respect of my particulars given above. I confirm that there is no legal bar in my applying for and accepting the above-mentioned employment.</td></tr>
<tr><td colspan="2">Date</td><td colspan="2">Signature of the applicant</td></tr>
<tr><td colspan="4">I have verified the certificates and testimonials where necessary.</td></tr>
<tr><td colspan="2">Date</td><td colspan="2">Officer-in-Charge</td></tr>
</table>

Chapter 2

Human Resource Planning for Recruitment and Selections

LEARNING OBJECTIVES

After reading this chapter, you will be able to understand:

1. The process of manpower planning
2. Manpower planning tasks at the macro and micro levels
3. The manpower planning process in any organization
4. The importance of aligning manpower plan of an organization with their business goals
5. How manpower planning helps in recruitment and selection process

Human resource planning and recruitment: The Japanese way

Age-old Japanese human resource management practices, i.e., lifetime employment, seniority-based compensation, and company-wide labor union, even though got diluted for business complexities and competition, Japanese organizations still continue their traditional way of human resource planning and recruitment. Japanese organizations precede their human resource planning by need analysis. Through such need analysis, organizations envisage the nature of manpower they will be requiring in future, and then they frame their recruitment strategy. For existing manpower, organizations focus on developing them through systematic training and promotion. Employees who cannot be developed or when required man-hours are less than the available man-hours, organizations go for redundancy. However, such cases are not very frequent in Japanese organizations, unless otherwise there are compelling business reasons, as Japanese workers go through compulsory training and development reinforcement, which gradually make them more productive.

For its long-term focus, Japanese organizations envisage the future need for human resources much ahead. Under no circumstances they go for lateral recruitment to meet the manpower need, else they continue to recruit the young people right for the entry level job positions, and then groom them with training and learning reinforcement, so that such new recruits can meet the future need of the organization. Dangerous (Kiken), dirty (Kitanai), and hard (Kitsui) jobs in Japan are now managed by robots; hence these jobs are kept outside the scope of human resource plan. For other jobs recruitments are made strictly at the entry level, from young and inexperienced people.

INTRODUCTION

Human resource planning (HRP) integrates all HR activities and the strategic plans of an organization to coordinate recruitment and selection, succession planning, promotion, performance management systems, and training and development. It is also the primary level function of HR and precedes all other functions of HR. HRP balances the demand and supply of manpower, aligning with the strategies and business plans of the organizations. Rothwell and Sredl (2000) observed that HRP helps to analyze the environmental trends that may affect the HR supply chain and in the process narrow the gaps between present human resource supply and the forecasted human resource demand. To ensure strategic alignment of HRP with the company's business plans, they have recommended the need for developing an HR framework that can put more emphasis on results and measurable achievements. Rothwell and Sullivan (2005) also endorsed the similar views. In both the cases, the use of balanced score card as a tool has been suggested. Recruitment and selection function precedes HRP. Comparing present human resource to future human resource needs, the organization identifies skills and competency gaps and develops plans for building the existing human resources through succession planning and career development initiatives. Although this helps the organization to make their human resources future ready, along with this the organization also needs to plan for recruitment and selection, to ensure manpower availability never becomes a constraint for achieving the business goals and strategic intents.

Scope of HRP also extends to organizational pursuits to ensure that required competency is maintained in line with organizational mission, vision, and strategic objectives. HRP provides strategic basis for taking HR decisions, anticipating change. It is not merely concerned with manpower demographics, turnover projections, succession planning, etc. Therefore, HRP helps to plan for redundancies and manpower replacements, and changes in manpower competencies in a systematic manner. However, pacing with the need for this book, we will limit our focus explaining only on HRP's role as a support function for recruitment and selection.

IMPORTANCE OF HRP FOR RECRUITMENT AND SELECTION

Human resources of an organization are no longer considered important business constituent; it has now become almost inseparable from strategic and business planning issues. While the major part of human resource management issues focus on its best optimization through practices, the process starts after the acquisition of manpower; HRP issues are still not considered critical, either for lack of knowledge or for unwillingness to invest time and money (Bhattacharyya, 2013). Even then we find that systematic HRP is a necessity for the organization for the following reasons.

First, organizations are prone to face unpredictable attrition, for sudden change of top managerial level employees, viz., change of CEOs, COOs, CFOs, functional directors, etc. Such change in organizations succeeds in voluntary attrition of a large number of employees. We have many such instances in the corporate world. To ensure timely replacement, initiating recruitment, and selection, HRP helps.

Second, complexities of business legitimize inclusion of HRP with business and strategic plans of the organization. Business complexities are not attributable only to globalization and competition; it is often the results of internal pursuits of the organizations. Such internal pursuits are frequent process changes through technology support, and for emulating the best business practices of world-class organizations. Again customers' expectations are changing. They want quality goods and services at a competitive price. Many business excellence models suggest us the ways and means to achieve this. But all these require availability of quality manpower, which are competent and flexible enough to take up this challenge. Obviously, with HRP, we cannot ensure availability of quality manpower.

Third, various other environmental constraints like social, economic, and legal are also great influencers in HRP. We plan for business expansion, diversification, mergers and acquisition, or even for present business consolidation, but without HRP we are in haywire.

Finally, effective HRP when precedes recruitment and selection process, organizations can get the best manpower, who aligns with their values, culture, business goals, and strategies.

Realizing such importance, many organizations consider HRP from a long-term perspective and align the same with their strategies and business plan (Burack, 1986). A more recent study by Doving and Nordhang (2010) on 3877 organizations across 21 countries could identify the use of strategic human resource planning (SHRP) as an integral part of overall HRM strategies. However, HRP focus was found to be constrained by the resource support and the organizational endorsement. What is more astounding from their studies that organizations are unsure about the cost–benefit considerations for investment on HRP? Turner (2010) in his pioneering work published by CIPD, London suggests our renewed focus on manpower planning even in economic uncertainty from post-2008 period, changing its focus on organizational capacity planning. Turner argues that HRP is increasingly becoming a compelling need for the organization to deal with both expected and unexpected events. HRP can also help the organization to contain cost by up-skilling without damaging its competitiveness. Obviously for such reasons, HRP needs integration with strategy and business plans, with flexibility to balance both the long-term and short-term business focus. Let us see the generic SHRP model presented in Fig. 2.1.

SHRP is now what we legitimately argue is a necessity for organizations. SHRP requires alignment of organizational HRP with their business and strategies so that suitable manpower availability cannot become a deterrent factor in achieving the business results. Critical value of human resources in organizational sustenance and growth is now acknowledged. But such a critical value can only be harvested when the flow of human resources is ensured through SHRP.

FIGURE 2.1 Strategic human resource planning model.

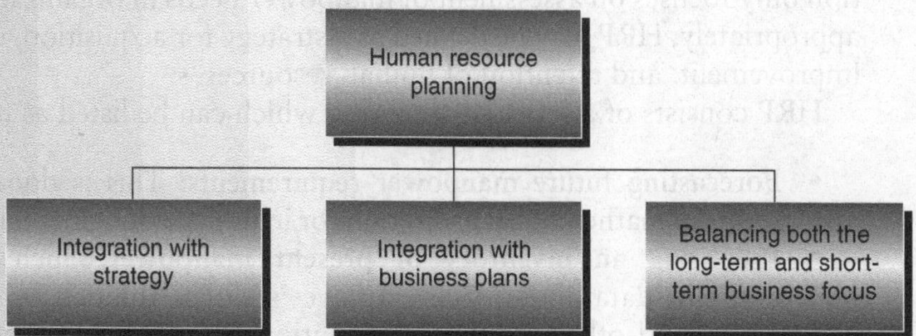

CHALLENGING ROLE OF HR PLANNERS

Designing human resource plans in alignment with the business goals and strategies is a challenging task. First thing that comes to our mind is that HRP is forecasting manpower requirements using various simulated models, along with the standard software packages to approximate the category-wise headcounts. With research inquisitiveness, HR professionals hardly do the HRP. Obviously for such reasons, decisional errors are many, and hire and fire is almost a regular practice in the corporate world. We invest a lot in emulating the best practice management, complying with the world-class systems and standards, technology, but not on the basic foundation of our knowledge on HRP. Another astounding observation is that most of the HRP researchers are from operations research discipline. They make models and plans scanning the organizational data, which many HR professionals thoughtlessly consider sacrosanct for their human resource requirements. Perhaps this simple area has been complicated for over cross-disciplinary interface, making it a mundane choice for the HR professionals. HR academics and professionals do not also like to understand the importance of this area, as the knowledge incompetency makes them depend on consultants or hunches and intuition. Managerial judgment or qualitative assessment of manpower planning is not bad, but complexities of business today demand testing our inferences with quantitative tools and techniques, at least to validate and reduce our decisional errors.

HRP ACTIVITIES

It is a planning process by which an organization can move from its current manpower position to its desired manpower position. Through

HRP organizations strive to have the right number and the right kinds of people at the right places at the right time. However, the above definition only focuses on assessment of manpower needs in organization. More appropriately, HRP may be defined as a strategy for acquisition, utilization, improvement, and retention of human resources.

HRP consists of a series of activities, which can be listed as under:

- **Forecasting future manpower requirements:** This is done either in terms of mathematical projections or in terms of judgmental estimates.
- **Preparing an inventory of present manpower:** Such inventory contains data about each employee's skills, abilities, work preferences, and other items of information. This helps in preparing the skill inventory, which helps in quick replacement decisions from employees within the organization, wherever crisis situation arises.
- **Anticipating problems of manpower:** Projecting present manpower into the future and comparing the same with the forecast of manpower requirements can do this. This helps in determining the quantitative and qualitative adequacy of manpower.
- **Meeting manpower requirements:** This can be achieved through planning recruitment and selection, training and development, induction and placement, promotion and transfer, motivation and compensation to ensure that future manpower requirements are correctly met.

Effective HRP activities not only envisage the need for human resources, but also it helps in planning for manpower redundancy.

To manage HRP activities effectively requires HR department to coordinate with the operating management for planning and establishing objectives. HR department has to collect data from overall organizational perspectives, pacing with the long-term objectives and the business goals, and so also with the strategies of the organization. Effective HR planning also requires regular measurement and monitoring of performance against the plan, and providing feedback to the management about the headcounts, in terms of both recruitment and redundancy. HR department only with research insights can align HR planning with organizational planning, and in the process can make HRP truly a business aligned function.

STEPS FOR HRP

Effective HRP requires the following number of steps. Although organization-wide such steps vary, here we have discussed such steps more from universal perspectives.

(1) **Job analysis:** Job analysis differentiates one job from the other. A job is the collection or aggregation of tasks, duties, and responsibilities, which are assigned to an individual employee. Job analysis provides following information:
- Job identification, which is done by providing a title or a code number for each job.
- Job characteristics, location, physical setting, hazards, and discomforts of a job.
- Job assignment, specific operation, and tasks, which make an assignment, its importance, simplicity, complexity, and the responsibility.
- Materials, tools, and equipment required for a job.
- Job performance, nature of operation (lifting, handling, drilling, setting up, etc.)
- Personal attributes, like experience, training, physical strength, mental capabilities, aptitudes, other skills, etc., required for efficient performance of the job.
- Job relationship, scope for advancement, patterns of promotions, direction or leadership form, etc.

Sources of job information: Information on a job is usually obtained from four principal sources as follows:
- From those who are supervising the job, e.g., supervisors and foreman.
- From professional job analysts (consultants), who may be retained to study a job?
- From technology vendors, who define jobs in their literatures?

Apart from HRP, job analysis serves the following important purposes of human resource management.
- Recruitment and Selection
- Wage and Salary Administration
- Job Reengineering
- Industrial Engineering Activity
- Employees Training and Management Development
- Performance Appraisal
- Health and Safety

(2) **Job descriptions and job specification:** After the job analysis process is over, job description and job specification are developed before going into the successive steps of HRP. Job description is recording of duties, responsibilities, and conditions needed for satisfactory performance of a particular job. Job description covers job content (conditions, tasks, and responsibilities) and job specification denotes job requirements (i.e., qualities necessary in the worker for satisfactory performance of the job). Thus, job specifications

translate job descriptions into human qualifications and attributes required for successful performance of a job.

(3) **Developing work rules:** Most of the organizations, after developing job descriptions and job specifications, develop work rules, which are some predetermined decisions about certain courses of action that may be taken when certain contingencies arise. Organizations develop such work rules in documented form and use the same as a control device to ensure predictability of behavior. Starting and stopping of work, rest periods, time-keeping, insubordination, fighting or drinking on the job, smoking, report of injuries, etc., are normally incorporated in such work rules.

(4) **Application of industrial engineering techniques:** Work study, method study, and work measurement techniques are also applied as a preceding step for HRP. These techniques provide opportunity for effective use of plant and equipment, effective use of human efforts, measurement of human work, better ways of doing things, developing predetermined standard time, etc.

(5) **Other factors:**

- **Layout:** Layout of a factory influences determination of manpower requirement. Some plants and equipment work in isolation (like Lathe, Drilling Machine, etc.), while some other works are performed in a group continuously (like excavators). When a group of machines work in union, one or more persons may attend the whole group. But when machines are not in continuous operation, a single person may look after more than one machine. Thus requirements of manpower may vary for the layout and machine arrangement in a shop floor or factory.
- **Statutory requirements:** For certain positions in mines, electrical installations, hazardous places (chemical plants, etc.), and welfare amenities need to be provided as per statutory regulations. Positions like welfare officers, safety officers, and medical officers fall under this category.
- **Shifts:** Number of manpower required also depends on whether the work would be carried out in general shift or in shifts. Number of working shifts will decide the requirement of manpower.
- **Leave reserve:** Since no one can work all the days for one reason or the other, certain allowances need to be given while working out manpower requirement. Apart from unpredictable leave of absence, workers are allowed leave systematically for a certain period in a year. Conventionally, 20% allowance for weekly off and leave reserves are allowed in factories while working out manpower requirements. In mines, however, rate of absenteeism being high, such allowance percentage is on much higher side.

OBJECTIVES OF HRP

Some of the important objectives of HRP are listed as under:

(1) To integrate planning and control of manpower with the organizational planning to ensure best possible utilization of all resources.
(2) To coordinate manpower policies of the organization. Recruitment and selection, training and development programs, placement and induction programs, promotion and transfer policies, decisions on remuneration and rewards, etc.
(3) To achieve efficiency of work in all spheres.
(4) To ensure cost minimization.
(5) To eliminate all types of wastages including waste of time.
(6) To maintain required levels of skill and competency, matching present and future needs of the organization.

Practice assignment

A multinational company engaged in manufacturing and selling of cements in India is following their own manpower planning system, assessing the manpower requirement based on their forecasted business plan. This required them to assess manpower, keeping in view their budgetary limit. In initial years of their operation, they did not face any problem. However, the problem mounted from successive years, when Indian cement majors like AV Birla (Grasim), ACC, Gujarat Ambuja, pegged competition by introducing value-added cement using the latest technology support. The MNC had to reduce their manpower strength to scale down their activities. This put them to tremendous opposition from local political leaders and trade unions.

You have been asked by this MNC to suggest them what approach they should follow in manpower planning to avoid such a situation in the future. Recommend your steps.

Manpower Demand Forecasting

Manpower demand forecasting is influenced by primarily two important factors, i.e., volume of output and the level of productivity. Manpower requirement may change due to change in output volume or mix, which calls for analysis of performance.

Similarly, as the level of productivity alters over time, it also affects manpower requirements. This calls for analysis of productivity.

(1) **Analysis of performance:** To derive the manpower demand, it is necessary to estimate the manpower requirements in relation to the workload. To start with, each unit of manpower (more conveniently defined in terms of man-hours or man-days) required for different categories of job to accomplish the job in its entirety is determined. After such determination the total workload is related to the manpower units of different categories and then finally the total requirement of manpower of different categories is determined. Such an analysis, therefore, calls for analysis of performance through either direct methods or indirect methods.

Direct analysis is to review past performance to derive a ratio between two variables (workload and manpower of certain category). This can be done either by relating to a particular point of time or by averaging figures over a period of time. To illustrate this, we may give the following hypothetical example:

Category A	Category B
Manufacturing 1 ton of saleable steel requires 10 skilled workers.	Manufacturing 1 ton of saleable steel requires 10 skilled workers
2 tons require 20 skilled workers	2 tons require 15 skilled workers.

Company A has a constant ratio, while Company B has a variable ratio, as it can double the rate of production, adding relatively less number of manpower and therefore, can achieve the economy of scale. The period over which such forecasts can be made depends on the organization.

Indirect analysis is based on the estimates made on past experience. Thus, it is less systematic than the direct analysis. However, for short-range forecasts, indirect analysis is more preferred, as experienced managers can make this analysis after putting considerable thought.

(2) **Analysis of productivity:** Productivity has two major components, technological change and manpower utilization. As technological change requires huge capital investment, organizations look for better manpower utilization to achieve increased productivity. With better human relations, productivity can be increased. Again

rates of productivity substantially vary the level of performance. Manpower demand forecasting can be made more effective, once we consider both the variables, i.e., the performance and the productivity. Most of the public sector enterprises are over-staffed, presumably for inadequate emphasis on both these two aspects simultaneously.

Macro and Micro Level HRP

Organization level manpower or human resource planning cannot be done in isolation of macro issues. In fact, primary reasons for rising importance of HRP are for both macro and micro level issues. At the aggregative or macro level, HRP is influenced by general environmental factors like employment–unemployment situation, demographic changes, legal control and institutional policies, policies on globalization and opening of market, etc. At organizational or micro level, HRP is more influenced by technology changes, organizational restructuring, skill and competency gap, strategic objectives, trade unions pressure (though it is dwindling over the years), lead time for manpower procurement, i.e., recruitment and selection, training and development, etc. Macro level issues are exogenous, i.e., uncontrollable, while micro level issues are endogenous and, therefore, controllable by an organization.

> Since 1983, United Airlines effectively uses the manpower planning techniques, both for their expansion plans and for routine operations. The company formed an in-house manpower planning group under one senior vice president. The internal team could develop a scheduling program, specific to the needs of the organization. Scheduling employees for Airline Company involves huge tasks, for obvious variety of manpower requirements with different skill sets, with little or no interchangeability. To start with the company first made use of scheduling technique for reservation office employees totaling 4000 in number. Compared to the manpower planning for the entire airline activities, the task of scheduling 4000 reservation office employees was not that troublesome for the company. With 20,000 decisional variables, the manpower planning model for United was a great success, resulting in huge savings on manpower costs.

HRP at Macro-Level

Development of human resources is one of the important objectives of any country for long-term economic growth. For a developing economy like

India such importance is far more. This is more visible from our economic planning, as the government over the years is giving increasing priorities to population planning and control, education, health, social security, housing, etc. All planned efforts are now being initiated to augment institutional support for developing human resources at the national level. Following are the major issues before our Government to develop human resources at the national level.

(1) **Population planning and control:** To enforce control over population explosion to avert economic imbalances, the government has initiated population planning and control measures. Unless such control is enforced in a planned manner, no amount of institutional support can sustain this, resulting in generation of unproductive population, who will remain a drain on our national resources.

(2) **Literacy and education:** To develop human resources at the macro level, the Government of India's National Policy on Education in 1986 provides a broad framework for complete eradication of illiteracy in the country by declaring basic primary level education up to standard V free and compulsory. To strengthen institutional infrastructure for education, the policy emphasizes on increased government and nongovernment expenditure. Allowing private participation in education is a right direction at this stage. From elementary education, the focus on secondary, university and higher education, technical and vocational education, adult education is also increasing.

(3) **Health and medical care:** Health sector reforms are another required initiative for developing human resources at macro level. In this respect, India has recorded disparity and regional imbalances. Although there is increased allocation for central sector health services, at state level, the situation is very depressive. Baring few positive changes in life expectancy ratio, infant mortality rate, child mortality rate, etc., we are still far away from improving general health indices for the nation. Core communicable and noncommunicable diseases like malaria, tuberculosis, leprosy, blindness, aids, cancer, etc., are still not under expected level of control. In other words, heath-related activities and achievements are also not at all its expected level to support total development of quality of life.

(4) **Housing:** In housing, the government has renewed its efforts by adopting the National Housing and Habitat Policy, 1998. The basic thrust of this policy is to achieve sustainable development of housing infrastructure through public–private partnership. Repealing of Urban Land Ceiling and Regulation Act, 1976 is also another positive direction in this respect. In building housing infrastructure,

Housing and Urban Development Corporation (HUDCO) is playing a crucial role. Although achievement is far falling short of requirement, positive attitude of the the government in this direction would definitely contribute to development of human resources and quality of life in the years to come.

In addition to above, centralized strategy for human resource planning and development, at state level, state planning boards and at district level, manpower planning generation councils have been set up. At the Apex level, planning commission is very active in HRP-related activities, which culminated the setting up of Institute of Applied Manpower Research (IAMR). So far, however, IAMR could come out with labor market information on planning and forecasting of scientific manpower.

Macro level HRP is a complex and dynamic process and it requires a longitudinal study to understand the results of various policy measures and actions. There still exists an imbalance in supply and demand for human resources at macro level. While, on one hand, the country is facing mounting burden of unemployment, on the other hand, it is still in shortage of skilled manpower. Large-scale migration of skilled manpower to other countries further aggravated the situation.

Macro-Level HRP Models

Macro-level manpower planning is reinforced through educational planning with the following two recognized approaches:

(1) The Manpower Requirement Approach (MRA)
(2) The Rate of Return Approach (RRA)

RRA is also known as cost–benefit analysis of human capital.

By establishing a linear relationship between the manpower category in different industry groups and their output, MRA helps us to project the demand for manpower at the macro level. For the educational planning at the national level, this approach is much in use in our country. Let us understand how it works:

(1) It establishes a liner relation between employment and output and then extrapolates manpower requirements in different categories for years to come.
(2) Initially category-wise manpower coefficients are computed based on past data, which then are applied on the hypothesized growth pattern of different industry groups.

(3) Thereafter, aggregate manpower requirement of different categories is worked out.
(4) These inputs are then converted into different types of educational requirements.

Even though it is a simple technique for macro-level manpower vis-à-vis educational planning, it is not a dynamic approach, as it does not cater for labor market flexibility. Perhaps this deficiency itself is responsible for critical skills shortage in our country, as our educational planning is reinforced by this approach. Similarly, technology–output relationship is considered stable under this approach, which in reality is not. Moreover, inter-occupational job mobility, man–machine substitution, costs, etc., are also not considered, while computing aggregate manpower requirement of different categories.

Rate of Return Approach (RRA)

RRA or cost–benefit analysis of human capital is applied to decide the aggregate investment requirement for different skill development. Cost and earnings of an individual over his productive life cycle are first computed and then their discounted value is estimated to assess the rate of return. However, aligning our national plans to such cost–benefit considerations alone may ignore the social cost benefit aspects of education. Non-availability of data, labor market flexibility, fluctuations in rate of return, etc., are the other major deficiencies of this approach.

However, despite such deficiencies in both the estimation tools of manpower at macro level, these can at least help in approximation in setting priorities in education and skill development. Certain deficiencies are due to our in-built system of compiling labor market information. At least on two important counts, these are visible. Indian Labor Year Book and Annual Survey of Industries are two major publications of the Government of India, which can streamline the information inputs required for macro level manpower planning. First, both the publications are not available on time. There still exists a time lag of 5–6 years in their publications. The system of data compilation in such publications is age-old and not in relation to requirements. Here, we will explain one major deficiency in Indian Labor Year Book of Labor Bureau, Shimla. This Year Book, among others, compiles data on trend of industrial disputes in India, with their distribution of casual factors, like wages and salaries, indiscipline and violence, bonus, etc., in percentage terms. There is no inter-relation with "Mandays Loss." Therefore, it is difficult for us to understand the severity of individual casual factor, as mere percentage distribution is a misnomer. The Institute of Applied Manpower Research over the years studied the manpower requirements of different categories in the country. They have made some sectoral and occupational requirement analysis of manpower for engineers, nurses, scientific manpower, etc.

Apart from the above, Labor Economics as a subject for study is not yet properly integrated with major labor–management related courses, which again restricts our knowledge input about labor market trend and its analysis.

Labor Economics

Labor Economics studies the demand and supply for the important factor of production, i.e., human beings. Marshall and Smith are the two pioneering economists who first recognized that the study of market for labor is not possible without understanding the social relations of production, long-term contractual arrangement, problems of motivation, institutions like unions and internal labor markets, etc. All these characteristic requirements differentiate the market for labor from other markets.

The most important development in the modern labor economics is the development of the concept of human capital. Human capital approach analyzes the individual decision making in regard to supply of labor and other behavioral areas, which are more related to sociology rather than economics. Before the development of the concept of human capital, labor supply decisions were considered more as an economic rationality. By making such a decision as in inter-relational variable of education, skill, investment, wages, working hours, etc., the subject of labor economics has been demarcated from the traditional economic analysis.

Like labor supply which depends on individual decision making, as an outcome of different inter-relational variables; labor demand and firms' behavior is influenced by internal labor markets, hiring, promotion, wage policies, and the structure of wages in various markets, etc. Most of the firms maintain computerized personnel records to analyze their demand for labor. There are many techniques for analysis of labor demand. For example, a firm may study the likely response of workers to a particular wage and personnel policy (which optimizes their profits). Some firms offer maximum compensation to match with the workers' expectations and then try to maximize the utility of workers, while other study examines the effect of deferred compensation, piece rates, and other systems of rewards. The Neo-classical model on study of labor demand examines the magnitude of elasticity and cross-elasticity of labor demand for worker of different skills and the effect of minimum wages on employment.

Similarly, elasticity of substitution and complementarities are also studied to analyze the labor demand.

In the area of labor institutions, effects of unions on wages, wages in unionized and nonunionized industries and occupations, difference between union and nonunion workers, etc. are studied.

Labor Markets

Demand, supply, and institutions interact in labor markets and labor economics studies the operation of labor markets considering all these issues. Analysis of labor markets is carried out for different occupational segments, viz., markets for blue-collar workers, markets for white-collar workers, markets for professionals, etc. Investigating markets for knowledgeable and skilled workers, differentiating supply and demand forces in the markets, geographic and industrial motilities, unemployment, wage pattern, etc., are the areas for studying the labor markets. Recently, however, macro changes in wages and unemployment over a given period of time, both within the country and across countries, are also studied to synthesize the facts of the labor markets with the basic principles of economics.

In India, the Indian Society of Labor Economics (ISLE) is institutionally carrying out pioneering studies in labor economics. ISLE organizes national-level conferences on different areas of labor economics and tries to develop this as a distinct discipline having importance in both the academic and professional research in understanding the trend of the most important factors of production, i.e., human beings. ISLE regularly publishes Indian Journal of Labor Economics, which is considered an international journal on the subject of Labor Economics.

HRP Micro Level

We have discussed the micro or organizational level HRP in our initial notes. Here, we will discuss about some of the techniques and tools used by an organization to do such planning.

Forecasting HR or manpower requirements: Organizations while forecasting manpower requirements use various quantitative tools. Apart from these there are some models. Since we are now at the nascent stage of learning HRM, we will restrict our discussions only on some widely used tools.

(1) **Analysis of workload factors:** To forecast the manpower requirements at different points of time, workload analysis is extremely important. Analysis of present and future workload depends on

possibility of quantifying the work content in every area of an organizational activity. Following steps help in workload analysis.

(a) **Classification of work:** Identifying the work or job content and time requirement for such job or work unit does classification of work. Work or job content classification helps in breaking jobs in different components, which together completes an operation. Deciding the standard time, using work measurement techniques, can do time requirement analysis for each such job component. In some cases, cycle time for each job component is mentioned in machine literatures. Extrapolating time requirement from such data can help in deciding time requirement. However, this may not help us for service jobs, like customers' query handling, administrative or managerial jobs, clerical jobs, etc. Approximation of time requirement for such jobs can be done for an existing organization, based on past experience and benchmarking (comparing with other organizations). There are certain limitations of job or work content analysis. Major problem is job quantification, as all jobs are not quantifiable. Deciding standard times of job scientifically requires rigorous time study, which is not only costly but also time consuming. Secondly, normal fatigue allowance is not considered while developing such time requirement. However, during the process of developing standard time through time study, such problems can be addressed. Thirdly with the pace of technological change, standard time required also varies, which means setting of job time at one point of time may not hold good subsequently. Moreover, technology also changes the job content and even the job family. For example, job of a turner, who is using a lathe machine, may change to an operator, when he/she uses a computerized machining center (CNC). Similarly, job of a clerk, who is doing the job manually, may change to a computer operator, when he/she is using computer systems.

Thus, classification of job content and analysis of time requirement for each job component is a dynamic process.

(b) **Forecasting number of jobs:** After classification of jobs and work content and its time requirement, in the next phase of workload analysis, job forecasting in quantitative terms for number of jobs is done for a time period. This is done based on the demand projection, i.e., aligning with the organization's business plan.

(c) **Converting the projected jobs in man-hours:** Multiplying the time requirement of each job with number of projected jobs, man-hours for jobs are computed.

(d) **Converting the man-hours into manpower requirement:** In the final phase of workload analysis, aggregate man-hours are converted into manpower requirements. This is done considering leave reserve, normal fatigue allowance, etc. Leave reserve accounts for absenteeism, while fatigue allowances account for the nonproductive time.

Example of workload analysis

Let us analyze workload factor to access manpower requirement in a given day of the Customer Service Department of an Automobile Battery manufacturer. The company enjoys highest market share but does not want to give any chance to their competitors for any possible deficiency in the customer services. The company operates six Battery Mobile Service Vans in Delhi, with some territorial mark for each van. Each van is having a wireless set and receives the complaint from stranded customers on roads while they log their complaints to customer service department on a real-time basis. Each van (depending on their area) rushes to attend a compliant within 10–15 minutes time limit and lifts the battery from a stranded car, puts a stand-by and informs the customer that they will be back with the battery after 24 hours, telephoning the customer. The company deploys the technicians in their service center based on projected workload in a particular day. Technicians are deployed from their manufacturing division, as skills required for battery servicing are interchangeable with battery manufacturing. This way, the company optimizes their manpower requirement in their service department.

(2) **Time series analysis:** Employment data over a time period (time series) are used under this method as the basis for manpower forecast. However, mere projecting the past into the future, without considering endogenous and exogenous changes, will increase the forecasting errors, which may be either under forecasting or over forecasting of manpower requirements.

(3) **Moving average method:** Under this method, average of the combined employment level data for the recent past is considered the forecasted employment level for the next period. This technique is useful to guard against random fluctuations. However, it requires careful selection of time periods, which may be a 6-period, 10-period, 12-period moving average. If time periods chosen are too few, we may get wide variability in our forecast. Therefore, considering more time periods, we get better results. Whatever time period we select for over forecast, it is necessary to continue the same number of periods for our computations. After each

period elapses, the figure for the oldest period is dropped and the figure for the newest period is added for our subsequent computation of manpower requirements.

EXAMPLE

Godrej has the following manpower data for their health care division for past 6 years:

Year	Manpower level/data (in nos.)
2001	500
2002	600
2003	800
2004	1000
2005	1100
2006	1300

You have been asked to forecast their manpower requirement in 2007 using a 6-period moving average.

Solution

$$F_m = \frac{500 + 600 + 800 + 1000 + 1100 + 1300}{6}$$

$$= \frac{5300}{6} = 883 \text{ Nos.}$$

If we are asked to use 4-period moving average to forecast manpower for 2007, then we require dropping the data of 2001 and 2002 and computing the forecasted manpower as under:

$$F_m = \frac{800 + 1000 + 1100 + 1300}{4}$$

$$= \frac{4200}{4} = 1050 \text{ Nos.}$$

From the above variation in results, we can well understand the danger of considering lesser time periods in manpower forecasting.

For achieving better results, weights may be assigned for different time periods at the discretion of the analyst. For example, manpower level of 2001, 2002, and 2003 may be less relevant; hence, for these years weights may be assigned as 1 each. For 2004, weight may be 2, for 2005, weight may be 3, while for 2006, weight may be 4. Now the forecasted manpower for the year 2007 would be as under:

$$F_m = \frac{1(500) + 1(600) + 1(800) + 2(1000) + 3(1100) + 4(1300)}{\sum w, \text{ i.e., } 12}$$

$$= \frac{500 + 600 + 800 + 2000 + 3300 + 5200}{12}$$

$$= \frac{12,400}{12} = 1033 \text{ Nos.}$$

(4) **Exponential smoothing:** In moving average method, we need to carry forward large volume of historical data. We can eliminate the need for such past records adopting this method. This method smoothens random errors by giving exponentially decreasing weights to historical data.

Such a weight factor is indicated by alpha (α), which is a smoothing constant, a nonlinear decimal value that lies between 0 and 1. The formula for the exponential smoothing model is

$$F_m = F_t + \alpha(A_{t-1} - F_{t-1})$$

where

F_m = forecasted manpower
F_{t-1} = forecasted demand for the previous period
α = smoothing constant
A_{t-1} = actual manpower required for the previous period

EXAMPLE

Assume that the forecasted manpower requirement for an organization was 700, while their actual requirement was 680. Considering alpha value of 0.4 (which the company feels would produce the best results), compute the manpower requirement for the current period.

Solution

$$700 + 0.4\ (680 - 700) = 692 \text{ Nos.}$$

Double exponential smoothing can also be done to get further cushion in manpower forecasting.

(5) **Manpower planning models:** The use of mathematical models for manpower planning dates back to 1779, when John Rowe developed an actuarial model for planning careers in the Royal Marines (Jones, 1964). Manpower systems can be described in terms of stocks and flows. Stocks are the number of staff in the organization at a given point of time. Stocks are divided into categories such as sex, age, length of service, etc. Flows are related to recruitment, promotion, wastage, transfers, demotion, etc. Some of the conventional models have already been discussed in this chapter. In this section, we will discuss some selected mathematical models, which require a fundamental knowledge of mathematics.

(a) **Markov models—hierarchical systems:** In hierarchical systems, the routes for the employees, which is the promotion ladder, are well defined. It means all employees can elevate themselves in the organization using a well-defined career path. Most employees start in an organization at the bottom rung and climb up the ladder one at a time. Any wastage is equivalent to falling off the ladder. Young and Almond (1961) devised a hierarchical manpower system by framing subgroups of employees on the basis of salary grade and length of service. The researchers have used the theory of Markov process to measure the long-term equilibrium distribution of employees among the subgroups.

The basic assumption of this model is that an employee in a particular grade or a status group has a fixed chance of promotion in a given year, independent of vacancy. Thus, the number of employees receiving promotion depends on the number of eligible staff in the grade. The promotions are, however, subject to fulfillment of eligibility criteria, such as seniority, qualifications, or experience.

The central equation for this model is

$$n\ (t+1) = n\ (t)\ P + R\ (t+1)r$$

where $n(t)$ is the vector of stocks at a given time t, i.e., the number of employees in each status group; P is the matrix of transition probabilities between each of status groups; r is the vector of probabilities of a recruit starting in particular status groups; $R(t)$ is the number of new recruits at time t.

If the number of employees $n(t)$ in each status group at a particular time is known, the equation may be used to predict the value of $n(t)$. In other words, the number of employees in each status group at a later time t can be calculated. This is, however, subject to the conditions that recruitment levels, $R(t)$, during the period $t = 0$ to $t = T$, are already known or specified. Alternatively, the total number of employees in the system which is $N(t)$ may be specified. The prediction equation, therefore, may be rewritten in the following form.

$$n\,(t+1) = n\,(t)\,q + m\,(t+1)\,r$$

This is the more usual form of Markov chain model than the earlier one. Here, $M\,(t + 1) = N\,(t + 1)$. It not only includes the transition within the organization but also the effects of wastage and recruitment to maintain the balance in the organization. Human resource planning using a Markov chain is considered more probabilistic. Moreover, Markov models allow too much fluctuation of the sizes of the status group, while in practice sizes are tightly constrained. To avoid such problems, the renewal theory of HRP was developed.

The objective of this model is to forecast the number of employees in each of the categories at equidistant points in time ($t = 0, 1, 2, \ldots$). In this model, the number of employees that makes a transition from one category to another category in a given period, is assumed to be a constant fraction of the size of the first mentioned category at the beginning of the period. These fractions are called transition fractions. The actual number of employees in all categories, the transition fractions, and the future recruitment in all categories has to be given. The future number of employees in all categories (the future manpower distribution) is forecasted. Markov models are also called push models. This is because transition fractions are given and the future distribution of manpower over the categories (called manpower distribution) is determined by the values of these transition fractions. Thus, the employees are pushed through the manpower system. Markov model is based on the steady-state distribution as it accounts for transition probabilities assuming in the long term forecasted numbers of employees in all categories are constant, if recruitments, promotions, and wastage fraction are constant.

(b) **Renewal models:** The objective of the renewal model is to forecast the manpower flows, given the number of employees in all categories. In renewal models the situation is observed at equidistant points in time. The actual manpower distribution, the desired manpower distribution in the future, and wastage fractions have to be known. The promotion flows and recruitment are determined by filling vacancies. Thus, renewal models are also called pull models. Renewal models too can have a steady-state distribution, when wastage fractions are constant. Renewal models concentrate on the basic assumption that requirements for employees are met by changes in promotions and recruitment rates. This model is useful when manpower requirements are known within reasonable limits.

The equation for the renewal model is as follows:

$$L(T) = f(T) + \int_0^t (t)\, L(T-t)\, dt$$

where $f(t)$ = frequency by length of service or leaving
$L(T)$ = leaving rate at time T

It is assumed that the post is filled at time 0.

(c) **Optimization models:** The optimization model matches the manpower availability with the manpower requirement. This model uses a finite horizon such as goal programming. The number of goals which the decision maker desires to achieve is determined. The goals may be minimum total salary costs, avoiding over employment, maintaining certain employment of minorities, etc.

Example of Markov Chain Model

Consider an example where the manpower system is made up of four levels:

- Management Trainee (MT)
- Assistant Manager (AM)
- Manager (M)
- Senior Manager (SM)

The progression from one level to another is straightforward and involves moving up the hierarchy. Obviously, not every employee moves up the ladder and the percentage of progression drops steadily as the levels go up.

Let us assume that there are two entry points in the system, one at the MT level and the second at the assistant manager level. There is an employee turnover at every level, although the percentage of turnover drops at every level as we go up the hierarchy level. The data for these employees is given in Table 2.1.

TABLE 2.1 Employee data at different levels

Particulars	MT	AM	M	SM
No. of employees	60	180	50	20
Employee turnover rates	22%	30%	10%	4%
New recruitments as a percentage of total recruitments	95%	5%	–	–
Percentage promoted to the next level (per annum)	78%	5%	2%	–

There are two assumptions that underlie the use:

(i) The employee in any group (for example, managers) has a fixed chance of promotion in any given year.

(ii) There is no requirement of vacancy to exist in the higher grade, and promotions will not get delayed because of competition from other employees.

The central equation used in this type of model is given below:

$$n(t+1) = n(t)\,P + R(t+1)\,r$$

where $n(t)$ is the vector of employees at time t, P is the matrix of transition probabilities between each pair of employee groups, r is the vector of probabilities of a new recruit starting in each particular employee group, and $R(t)$ is the number of new recruits at time t.

In the above example, the various figures would be as follows:

$$n(t) = \begin{matrix} MT & AM & M & SM \\ (60 & 180 & 50 & 20) \end{matrix}$$

	MT	0	0.78	0	0
$P =$	AM	0	0.65	0.05	0
	M	0	0	0.88	0.02
	SM	0	0	0	0.96
$r =$		(0.95	0.05	0	0)

We have deliberately used the rotation in explaining so that we can be clear how these numbers come into being. $n(t)$ is the actual number of employees in each employee's group, and r is the number of new recruits (95% in management trainee and 5% in assistant manager grade).

Let us try and understand the matrix P.

It can be seen from the table that 78% of employees at the management trainee level are promoted to assistant manager in the next year. So from MT on the left to AM, we find a figure of 0.78. Just below that is the figure of AM who remain at the same position. This figure comes from deducting the employee turnover figure (30% in this case) and promoted to the next grade figure (5% in this case) from a total of 100% (100 – 30 – 5 = 65%) = (0.65).

From MT to MT, figure is empty as there is no M, which remains as MT after a year (either he/she is promoted or he/she leaves). It can also be noted that there is no figure from MT to M or to SM because no jumps are possible.

Once we have the data in place, we can use the equation to calculate the number of employees in each grade for any number of years, provided our assumptions are fulfilled and the number of new recruits every year is known to us. Let us calculate the number of managers for the next year.

$$n\,(t+1) = n\,(t)\;P + R\;(t+1)\;r$$

$= 0.05 \times 180$ (5% of last year assistant managers who were promoted) $+ 0.88 \times 50$ (88% of current managers who remain)

$= 9 + 44 = 53$ managers

If we assume that we are going to take 60 new recruits every year for the next two years, we can calculate the number of employees in different grades.

It comes out to be

$$n(1) = (57 \quad 168.23 \quad 53 \quad 20.2)$$

It can be rounded off to,

$$n(1) = (57 \quad 168 \quad 53 \quad 20)$$

$$n(2) = (57 \quad 156.67 \quad 55.04 \quad 20.26)$$

It can be rounded off to,

$$n(2) = (57 \quad 157 \quad 55 \quad 20)$$

While the number of AM level employees will come down from the current 180 to 168 in the next year and to 157, two years from now; the number of managers will go up progressively.

This model helps us to see the effect of organizational policies. This can help human resource managers to plan accordingly for the future.

(d) **Cambridge model:** The Cambridge model concentrates on steady-state age distribution, i.e., staff distribution by age, which remains unchanged every year. Steady state is a stable equilibrium. Thus, if the system is affected, i.e., if it goes beyond equilibrium, it will tend to return to it. Everanuz (1975) developed the following models for steady-state age distribution.

(i) $A(j) = \dfrac{r(j)}{1+P}$

$$B(j) = \frac{1 - w(j)}{1 + P}$$

$$H_{jL} = A(j_L) + B(j-1) \text{ for } j = j_L + 1, j_L + 2, \ldots j_H$$

$$c = \frac{1}{\sum_{j=i_L}^{j=J_H} H_i}$$

$$g(j) = cH(j) \text{ for } j_L \ldots j_H$$

where $g(j)$ = proportion of staff in the steady-state age distribution aged j; $r(j)$ = proportion of recruits aged j, i.e., recruitment age distribution; $w(j)$ = wastage rate for staff aged j; P = long-term expansion rate; $(1 + P)$ = number of staff increases by a factor. If this is negative, it implies a contraction.

(e) **Simulation:** To simulate is to initiate. In general terms, simulation involves developing a model of some real phenomenon and then performing experiments on the model evolved. It is a descriptive, and not optimizing, technique. In simulation, a given system is copied and the variables and constants associated with it are manipulated in most artificial environment to examine the behavior of the system. Using simulation, an analyst can introduce the constants and variables related to the problem, set up the possible courses of action and establish criteria, which act as measures of effectiveness. The benefit of simulation, from the viewpoint of the analyst, stems from the fact that the results of taking a particular course of action can be estimated prior to its implementation in the real world. Instead of using hunches and intuition to determine what may happen, the analyst using simulation can test and evaluate various alternatives and select the one that gives the best results.

Broadly, there are four phases of the simulation process. They are:

- Definition of the problem and statement of objectives
- Construction of an appropriate model
- Experimentation with the model constructed
- Evaluation of the results of simulation

Monte Carlo Simulation

It is also known as a probabilistic simulation method. It can be described as a numerical technique that involves modeling with the objectives of predicting the system's behavior. The chance element is a very significant feature of Monte Carlo Simulation and this approach can be used when the given process has a random, or chance component.

Illustration

A hotel keeps a record of the number of staff requirement of various categories. Information relating to 200 days' requirement is as under:

	Demand								Total
No. of staff	5	6	7	8	9	10	11	12	
No. of days	4	10	16	50	62	38	12	8	200

Develop a simulation model to predict the demand of staff for 10-day period.

Solution

Firstly: Derive the probability distribution of demand for the staff, expressing each of the frequencies in terms of proportions. Dividing each of the values by 200, i.e., the total frequency does this. The resultant distribution would, therefore, be as follows:

No. of staff	5	6	7	8	9	10	11	12
No. of days	0.02	0.05	0.08	0.25	0.31	0.19	0.06	0.04

Secondly, determine random numbers using any mechanism of random number generator. There are various ways in which random numbers can be generated. These could be result of some device like coin or die, published table of random numbers, etc. However, the most convenient method is to make use of the published table of random numbers, published by the Rand Corporation of USA.

An assignment has to be worked out so that the interval of random numbers corresponds to the probability distribution. Since the probabilities have been calculated to two decimal places, which add up to 1.00, we need 100 numbers of two digits to represent each point of probability. Thus, we take random numbers 00 through 99 to represent them. Now, as the probability of 5 staff is equal to 0.02, we assign two random numbers 00–01 to this demand level; the probability of 6 staff being equal to 0.05, the next five numbers 02–06 would be assigned to this level. In a similar manner each of the demand levels would be assigned appropriate intervals as given:

Demand (No. of staff)	Probability	Cumulative probability	Random number interval
5	0.02	0.02	00–01
6	0.05	0.07	02–06
7	0.08	0.15	07–14
8	0.25	0.40	15–39
9	0.31	0.71	40–70
10	0.19	0.90	71–89
11	0.06	0.96	90–95
12	0.04	1.00	96–99

Cumulative probabilities column analyzes the assigned numbers to correspond to the same probability range for each event.

Thirdly, once the random number intervals are determined, we select a tracking pattern for drawing random numbers from the random number table. We may start with any column and row of the table and read the values in any set manner—horizontally, vertically, or diagonally. Using the pattern, we draw the random numbers and match them with the assigned events.

Let us assume for the purpose of this problem, we have decided to take every third value horizontally, starting with the fifth column and fourth row of the table of random numbers. The random numbers according to this patterns are 61, 74, 24, 03, 59, 16, 84, 92, 52, 07, etc. (for 10-day demand period). We draw as many random numbers as the number of days' demand required to be simulated.

The first number, i.e., 61 lies in the interval 40–70 corresponding to the demand level of nine staff. Thus, the simulated demand for the first day is nine staff members. In a similar manner, we can obtain the demand for each of the day. For the 10-day period, we have the following demand:

Day	1	2	3	4	5	6	7	8	9	10
Number	61	74	24	03	59	16	84	92	52	07
Demand of staff	9	10	8	6	9	8	10	11	9	7

EXERCISE

A caterer keeps reserve cooks during marriage season. Previous experience indicates the daily demand of cooks is as under:

Daily demand	0	10	20	30	40	50
Probability	0.01	0.20	0.15	0.50	0.12	0.02

Consider the following sequence of random numbers:

48, 78, 19, 51, 56, 77, 15, 14, 68, 09

Using this sequence, simulate the demand for the next 10 days. Find out the reserve situation if the owner of the caterer decides to maintain on payroll 30 cooks every day. Also estimate the daily average demand for the cooks on the basis of simulated data.

Solution

Demand	Probability	Cumulative probability	Random number interval
0	0.01	0.01	00
10	0.20	0.21	01–20
20	0.15	0.36	21–35
30	0.50	0.86	36–85
40	0.12	0.98	86–97
50	0.02	1.00	98–99

The simulated demand for the cooks for the next 10 days and the stock position for various days when decision is to make available 30 cooks a day would be as given:

Determination of Demand and Stock Levels

Day	Random number	Demand	Stock
1	48	30	–
2	78	30	–
3	19	10	20
4	51	30	20
5	56	30	20
6	77	30	20
7	15	10	40
8	14	10	60
9	68	30	60
10	09	10	80

Expected demand = 220/10 = 22 cooks per day

Advantages and Disadvantages of Simulation

Advantage: The chief merit of the simulation technique is its capacity to lend itself to problems that are cumbersome, or impossible to handle mathematically using analytical methods. Not only this, the technique allows the analyst to experiment with the system behavior without subjecting it to the risks that would be inherent in experimenting with the real system, it also compresses time to enable the manager to visualize the long-term effects in a quick manner. Besides, simulation is often used to test proposed analytic solutions as well.

Disadvantage: It does not represent a methodology for derivation of optimal solutions to the given problems. This approach is designed merely to provide characterization of the behavior of the system in question for a given set of inputs. Furthermore, the simulation approach is not precise in the sense that it yields only estimates, which are subject to sampling error. Of course, increasing the sample size can reduce the sampling error.

Another drawback is that it may not prove economical, as it requires a lot of efforts to develop a suitable model.

It is a tool of solution evaluation and does not generate problem solution. Thus, the analyst has to develop the proposed solution; then simulation can be used to test the relative desirability of those solutions.

(f) **Replacement theory:** A replacement is called for whenever new equipment offers more efficient or economical service than the old existing one. For example, the old equipment might fail and work no more, or is worn out and needs higher expenditure on its maintenance. The problem, in such situations, is to determine the best policy to be adopted with respect to replacement of the equipment. The replacement theory provides answer to this question in terms of optimal replacement period.

We consider the question of replacement in the following situations:

In respect of equipment/assets that deteriorate in performance over a time, they may be restored in whole or in part by expanding maintenance costs. Thus, the existing assets might be good technically, yet on economic considerations, it may not be worthwhile continuing with them and hence replacement may be called for. Machinery, equipment, buildings fall in this category.

In respect of units that perform adequately until sudden complete failure. The length of their service until failure varies randomly over some predictable range. Car bulbs, tubes, some electronic components, etc., are the items that are considered in this category.

In respect of replacement of staff of an organization which diminishes gradually due to death, retirement, retrenchment, and other reasons.

Staff Replacement

The staff of an organization calls for replacement because people leave the organization for several reasons. For planning a suitable recruitment policy, historical data are collected to estimate the likely stay of individuals with the organization through time. Here also, the stay of an individual employee may be a random variable but the characteristics of the group of employees are likely to be fairly stable.

EXAMPLE

Using the above information, answer the following questions:

What recruitment level per annum would be necessary to maintain this strength?

Year	1	2	3	4	5	6	7	8	9	10	11	12
Percentage expected to leave by end of period	5	18	35	45	62	75	88	90	95	96	99	100

If 15 of the sales persons are to be promoted to the next higher post, for which length of service in the organization is the primary criterion and at what average length of service can a new entrant expect to be promoted?

Solution

With an intake of 100 sales people every year, the distribution of the length of service of the sales force when equilibrium has been reached will be as follows:

Year	No. of people continuing
0	100
1	95
2	82
3	65
4	55
5	38
6	25
7	12
8	10
9	5
10	4
11	1
12	0
	Total = 492

Recruitment of 100 sales people every year would thus give a total strength of 492. To maintain and strength of 80 sales people, we need to recruit then:

$$\frac{80\times100}{492}=16.26\text{, say 16 persons}$$

With 80 persons in the sales team, the distribution of the completed length of service would be as follows:

Year	No. of Persons
0	16
1	15 (95%, of 16)
2	13 (82% of 16)
3	11 (65% of 16)
4	9 (55% of 16)
5	6 (38% of 16)
6	4 (25% of 16)
7	2 (12% of 16)
8	2 (10% of 16)
9	1 (5% of 16)
10	1 (4% of 16)
11	0
12	0

Since 15 sales people are to be promoted and the promotion would be on the basis of their length of service, the cumulation of the frequencies in this distribution reveals that a sales person can expect to be promoted after 5 years of service.

This is ascertained by counting backward, i.e., from 12th year onward. After the 5th year the total number of persons left is 16. Thus, promotion after the 5th year is considered better, if 15 people are required to be promoted on length of service.

PREDICTIVE STATISTICS FOR ORGANIZATION LEVEL HUMAN RESOURCE PLANNING

Regression Analyses

Information such as the number of people employed by rival organizations is often used by companies for human resource planning. In such cases, the HR planners can select random samples of employees and their productivity levels. The means of these samples can be used to predict the number of employees required by the organization. However, this technique is not full-proof as experience, performance levels, size of the organization, salary, revenues, etc., play important roles in manpower determination.

Regression analyses allow us to consider all these factors in deciding the requirement of manpower in an organization. Linear regression allows us to make predictions of any dependent variable (y) based on any independent variable (x). Multiple regressions allow us to make predictions of any dependent variable (y) based on several independent variables (x).

Linear Regression

In linear regression, we first make use of straight-line model. This model makes use of variables by plotting the x value on the x-axis (horizontal line), and each y value on the y-axis (vertical line). Each x value and its related y value make up the coordinates of each point. After all the points have been plotted on a graph, the result is known as a scatter diagram, as shown in Fig. 2.2.

FIGURE 2.2 Scatter diagram.

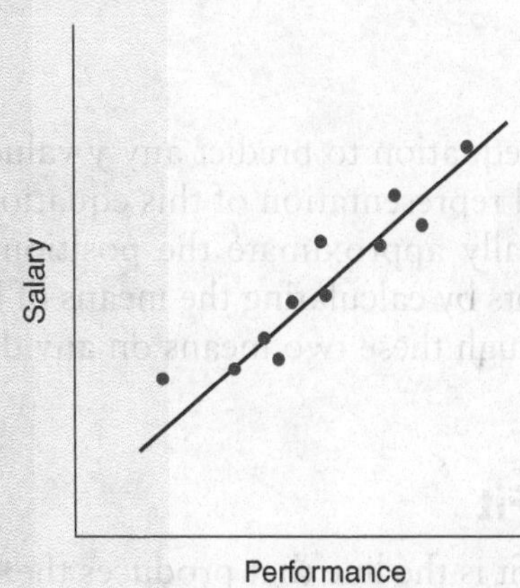

In this case, we are considering whether salary level significantly changes performance in an organization or not. Thus, a scatter diagram helps us to visualize the relationship, if any, between the x and y variables. Since this relationship is linear (x and y) it is possible to predict values of y from various values of x. This prediction comes from finding the straight line that best fits the data.

Least-Squares Model

The least-squares method is used to find the straight line that best fits the data. It is based on the principle that a line of best fit, or the one that describes a relationship between two variables best, is a line for which the sum of the squares of the deviations or differences between values on the straight line itself and the actual values will be at a minimum. Only one line of the infinite number available may be drawn to meet this requirement. The line of best fit must be computed mathematically, and it will always pass through the average of the x and y data.

The equation for this line is best expressed as

$$Y = \beta_0 + \beta_1 X_1 + \beta_2 X_2 + \ldots + \beta_p X_p$$

In this equation, β_0 is the regression coefficient for the intercept and the β_i values are the regression coefficients (for variables 1 through p) computed from

where

y = Dependent variable
x = Independent variable or predictor (used as a predictor of y)
β = Random error or residual (actual y value—mean of y)
β_0 = y-intercept
β_1 = Slope

We can use this equation to predict any y value when we know the value of x. A graphical representation of this equation is presented in Fig. 2.3.

One can visually approximate the position of a line of least squares through data plots by calculating the means of both axes. Regression lines always pass through these two means on any data plot.

Line of Best Fit

The line of best fit is the line that produces the best estimate of y based on any given value of x. One way to decide quantitatively how well a line fits

FIGURE 2.3 A graphical representation of the least square line.

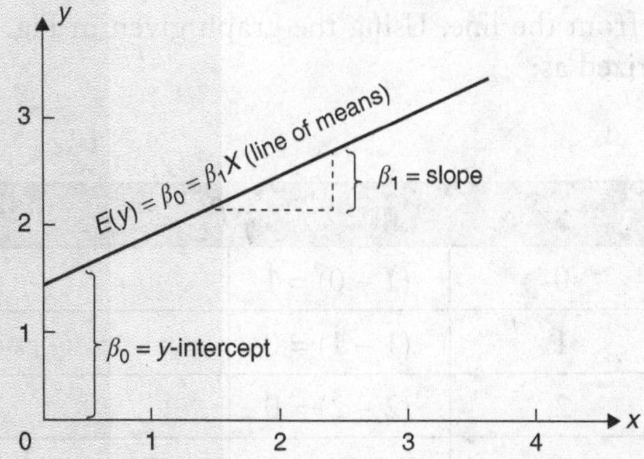

the data points is to calculate the extent to which the data points deviate from the line. This deviation or error is the vertical distance between the data point and the line. If we take the deviation or error for each of the data points, square them, then add them together, we have a sum of squared errors (SSE). The line that produces the smallest SSE is the line of best fit (Fig. 2.4).

FIGURE 2.4 A graphical representation of the line of best fit.

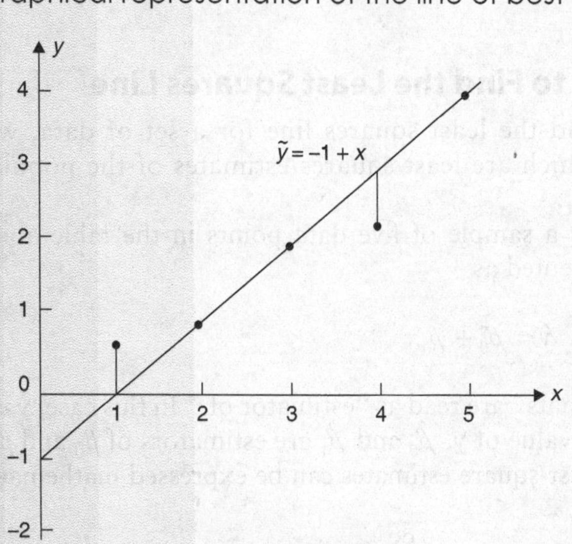

$\tilde{y}$ denotes the value of y predicted from the visually fitted model.

The best-fit line is the line with the smallest sum of squares of the errors (SSE), which is a measure of the extent to which the data points deviate from the line. Using the graph given in Fig. 2.4, the data can be summarized as:

x	y	$\bar{y} = -1 + x$	$(y - \bar{y})$	$(y - \bar{y})^2$
1	1	0	$(1 - 0) = 1$	1
2	1	1	$(1 - 1) = 0$	0
3	2	2	$(2 - 2) = 0$	0
4	2	3	$(2 - 3) = -1$	1
5	4	4	$(4 - 4) = 0$	0
			Sum of errors = 0	Sum of squared errors (SSE) = 2

The sum of errors equals 0, and the sum of squares of the errors (SSE) equals 2. Drawing different lines through the above graph would result in different values for the sum of errors and the SSE. Only the line with the smallest SSE would be the above regression line with an SSE of 2.

How to Find the Least Squares Line

To find the least squares line for a set of data, we must find $\hat{\beta}_0$ and $\hat{\beta}_1$, which are least squares estimates of the population parameters β_0 and β_1.

For a sample of five data points in the table above, the fitted line is represented as

$$\hat{y} = \hat{\beta}_0 + \hat{\beta}_1 x$$

The "hats" are read as "estimator of." In this case, $\hat{y}$ is the estimator of the mean value of y. $\hat{\beta}_0$ and $\hat{\beta}_1$ are estimators of β_0 and β_1.

Least-square estimates can be expressed mathematically as

$$\textbf{Slope: } \hat{\beta}_1 = \frac{SS_{xy}}{SS_{xx}} \qquad \textbf{y-intercept: } \hat{\beta}_0 = \bar{y} - \hat{\beta}_1 \bar{x}$$

where

$$SS_{xy} = \sum_{i=1}^{n} x_i y_i - \frac{\left(\sum_{i=1}^{n} x_i\right)\left(\sum_{i=1}^{n} y_i\right)}{n}$$

$$SS_{xx} = \sum_{i=1}^{n} x_i^2 - \frac{\left(\sum_{i=1}^{n} x_i\right)^2}{n}$$

n = Sample size
SS = Sum of squares

It should be noted that the higher the correlation (r) between x and y, the better the line will fit the data. The purpose of regression is to extract all possible information from the data. The regression model should explain as much as possible about the underlying process. However, due to real-world uncertainty, no model can explain everything. The information in the data that is not explained by the regression model is the error component, also known as residuals.

Managerial Judgment

A manager has to make a judgment about the future employment levels. Such a judgmental decision is based on his past experience, which he or she relates to past occurrences of some events and its effects on manpower plans. Managers have to use their judgment considering contingencies. Combining quantitative tools with managerial judgment can yield better results. There are, however, certain pitfalls in our assumed variables. In the following paragraphs, we have examined such pitfalls, which may lead to inaccurate manpower forecasts.

Difficulties in Manpower Forecasts Using Quantitative Tools

(1) When productivity data is considered an available tool to decide about manpower requirement, it is important to understand that productivity rise cannot always be attributable to increased human effort. Thus, increase in productivity due to changes in technology or sum total operational and managerial efficiency (total factor productivity approach) are the factors, which need to be integrated while doing manpower forecasts. But developing manpower planning models integrating the above two productivity variables is not so easy for obvious computational difficulty.

(2) It is difficult to get units of output in the same form for all jobs. For example, maintenance jobs are difficult to quantify. Moreover, maintenance problem is time independent. Planning for maintenance staff is one of the difficult tasks for manpower planner. Obviously for this reason, most of the organizations prefer to subcontract their maintenance function. Similar quantification problem is there for customer relationship management (CRM). Even with CRM solutions, quantification is difficult.

(3) Relationship between output and manpower is not always straightforward. Increase in output may lead to economies of scale and resultant cost efficiency and rise in productivity, which may not be attributable to manpower productivity.

(4) Effects of factors to improve productivity, i.e., new technology, incentive schemes, etc., may not be consistent over a time period. Therefore, projecting manpower requirement, considering effects of such factors may be inaccurate.

(5) Effect of different factors may not always be linear. Inter-relationship of different factors complicates forecasting of manpower. Although we have statistical techniques like multiple regression analysis, factor analysis, etc., their computational rigors often dissuade the manpower planners to use such tools.

(6) Uncertainty about the future is again a major problem for the manpower planner. Thus, extrapolating on past data may lead to a major inaccuracy in manpower estimation.

(7) Data on past workload factors may not be available, creating difficulty in emulating the same.

(8) Integration of manpower planning with corporate plans may not exist in an organization, creating problems for enterprise-wide manpower plans.

(9) Employees cannot always be related to output in a direct way.

(10) Human resource information systems (HRIS) may not exist in an organization. Lack of such information support system leads to inaccurate estimation of manpower.

For obvious constraints, explained above, managerial judgment along with statistical tools is often considered the best option for manpower

Practice assignment

A particular organization follows time series analysis for manpower planning. Over the years they found that forecasting errors for planning their manpower using this method is too high. Suggest the organization about how to guard against such forecasting errors.

planning. Often, it is said that planning for manpower within a given cost constraint, without bothering for past practices, leads to a better estimation.

Use of Qualitative Models for Better Managerial Judgment

Delphi technique

The word "Delphi" has come from Greek. In Athens of Greece during ancient times, it was a convention to consult an oracle representative of God Apollo who was believed to have contact with God. The priest could only interpret advice of the Oracle that time.

In modern times, this method is essentially a group process to achieve a consensus forecast. This method calls for selection of a panel of experts either from within or outside the organization, whose comments are crystallized from a series of questionnaire responses and then used as the basis to forecast. Series of questionnaire are prepared from the responses received from a prior set of questions in a sequencing manner. At every stage, information obtained from previous questionnaire is shared among the participating members, without, however, disclosing majority opinion; this otherwise may have peer-group influence on minority opinion.

The procedure of Delphi Technique may be enumerated as follows:

(1) To start with, it requires selection of a coordinator and a panel of experts both within and outside the organizations.
(2) The coordinator then circulates questions in writing to each such expert.
(3) The experts then write their observations.
(4) The coordinator then edits those observations and summarizes, without, however disclosing the majority opinion in his summary.
(5) On the basis of his summary, the coordinator then develops a new set of questionnaire and circulates those among experts.
(6) Experts then answer such a new set of questions.
(7) The coordinator repeats the process till such time he is able to synthesize from the opinion of the experts.

The success of the process again depends on the following factors:

(1) Experts should be so chosen that they have the requisite knowledge and skills to give the best answers.
(2) Questions should be relevant to the objective.
(3) Criteria for evaluating responses should be consistent, unbiased, and befitting with the objectives. Although there is no universal set

of criteria for evaluating responses, it is often considered necessary to follow the under-mentioned guidelines:

(a) Consider the assessment made by the experts in terms of their knowledge in the area.
(b) Consider the assessment in terms of feasibility, objectives, time, and resource requirement.
(c) Consider the assessment in terms of desirability.
(d) Consider the assessment in terms of extraneous factors.

Nominal group method

Like Delphi Method, Nominal Group Method also involves a panel of experts. However, the major difference between the two is that while under Delphi Technique, experts are not allowed to discuss among themselves, for assessing the questions, under Nominal Group Method experts are given the opportunity to discuss among themselves. Under this method, the coordinator assumes the role of a facilitator, allowing the experts to sit together to discuss their ideas and records of such discussions are made on a flip chart. After this, in round-table discussions on ideas, experts are asked to rank their ideas according to their perceived priority. The group consensus is then derived mathematically in terms of individual rankings. The process, therefore, affords creativity and facilitates scientific group consensus unlike consensus by qualification (as the coordinator ultimately decides the best course of action) under Delphi Technique.

SUMMARY

- Business complexities, demographic shifts in population, changes in technology, intensified competition even from global organizations, etc., have now made human resource planning a strategically important function for effective recruitment and selection in the organization. HR planning in the context of recruitment and selection requires us to consider business goals and strategies of the organization. It helps organization in deciding the manpower requirement in terms of skills, knowledge, competencies, etc.

- Human resource planning process considers both macro and micro level issues. Without proper human resource planning, organizations would continue to take manpower redundancy decision on short-term operational results. HRP process follows certain well-defined stages. At each such stage, it is necessary for the organization to collect data (both macro and micro), analyze those, and then plan for manpower. There are various tools for such analysis; some of these have been discussed, with examples, wherever necessary. However, quantitative tools and models may not be effective, when used in isolation. Combination of quantitative and qualitative techniques yields better results. Basic concern of HRP is to identify skill and competency gaps, subsequently developing plans for development of deficient skills and competencies in manpower to remain competitive. It has now become an important enterprise-wide strategic function to not only achieve goals and objectives but also sustain present level in a globally competitive environment.

Key Words

HRP: Human Resource Planning to assess manpower requirement in an organization.

Competency: Set of skill, knowledge, and attributes along with the behavioral requirements for a particular job.

Skill fap: Gap between desired skill and available skill of an employee.

RRA: Rate of return approach, followed in macro level manpower planning.

Exponential smoothing: Manpower forecasting technique by smoothening the random errors by giving exponentially decreasing weights to historical data.

Job analys: Performed to analyze the content of a job.

Internal recruitment: Recruitment for vacant positions from employees within an organization.

HRP: Human Resource Planning both at macro level and micro level. One of the most strategically important functions in an organization.

Job description: Process of naming a job to ensure that the nature of job is traceable with the job title.

Layout: Physical arrangement of factory and office space to reduce unnecessary movement of people and to gain the benefit from reduced fatigue.

Leave reserve: Accounting for absenteeism and assessing manpower requirement accordingly.

MRA: Manpower requirement approach followed in macro level manpower planning.

Application blank: Structured employment application format developed by a company to ensure uniformity in employee profiles.

Placement: Process of putting an employee into a job and followed by recruitment and induction.

Psychological testing: Performed to understand the matching of employees with their jobs.

Job description: It is recording of duties, responsibilities and conditions needed for satisfactory performance of a particular job.

Competency gap: Difference between identified set of competencies and available set of competencies in employees. Organization has to meet this gap through proper HRD interventions to avoid manpower redundancy.

Skill gap: Difference between required set of skill and available skill set in employees. This is done by developing skill inventories.

Markov chain: Young and Almond (1961) devised this hierarchical manpower system farming sub-groups on the basis of salary grade and length of service.

MACBETH model: MACBETH (MACro Computer Based Employment Heuristic) model is a recursive simulation model of the labor market and the evolution of occupational mismatches.

Cohort analysis: Cohort means homogeneous groups. Cohort analysis takes into account the length of service, which is important variable of wastage analysis.

Stability index: This index indicates stable workforce percentage for a given time period.

Layout: Physical arrangement of facilities and services of an organization, including arrangement of work stations/shop floors. This is done not only for efficient space utilization but also economizing movement of employees.

Leave reserve: Absenteeism rate considered for assessing organizational level manpower requirement, particularly for low skill jobs. For ten cars, provision for drivers should be more than ten.

Cambridge model: This model concentrates on steady-state age distribution, i.e., staff distribution by age, which remains unchanged year to year. Steady state is a stable equilibrium.

RRA: This is based on the calculation of the net returns on educational expenditure (ILO, 1984). It is measured considering the increase in net income that an individual will be able to earn in relation to the income that an individual would have earned had the individual not reached a given educational level.

Wastage analysis: Manpower wastage is an element of labor turnover. It is not labor turnover, per se. Wastage is severance from the organization, which includes, voluntary retirement, normal retirement, resignations, deaths and dismissals.

Labor turnover index: This index indicates number of levers as percentage to average number of employees. Average number of employees employed in a given time period is decided by adding the employees at the beginning and end and then dividing the same by two.

Review Questions

1. Discuss the importance of Human Resource Planning Process for Indian organizations.
2. What are the different stages of HRP process? Why is it important for us to consider the time scale of HRP forecasts?
3. Discuss the process of HRP forecasts using workload analysis and time series analysis.

4. What are the difficulties on manpower forecasts using quantitative tools? Do you think such difficulties can be removed by using qualitative tools?
5. What are the different methods of manpower wastage analysis? Do you think such methods are foolproof?
6. Discuss with examples different manpower planning models with a critical note about their limitations.
7. Define manpower planning. What are the activities involved in manpower planning?
8. What is optimum manpower planning? You have been retained by an organization to develop manpower planning system, what factors would you recommend them to consider for effective manpower planning?
9. Explain importance of macro-level manpower planning in India.
10. Discuss about different models of macro-level manpower planning.
11. Explain how organizational level manpower planning is carried out in an organization. Mention about some quantitative and qualitative tools used in organization level manpower planning.

Critical Review Questions

1. Your organization has made available their future production plan with specific time element analysis for various skill categories. You have been asked to develop a manpower plan, detailing requirement of employees in various categories. You have also been asked to suggest the nature of recruitment for these identified categories. Detail your action plan and steps. Also justify, why you feel these steps are essential.
2. In doing Markov Chain Analysis for doing manpower planning, what are your important areas of considerations? Do you think this approach can give you a foolproof result, when your underlying considerations are met? Justify your answer.

Multiple Choice Questions

1. Which function of HR is not coordinated by human resource planning:
   (a) Recruitment and Selection
   (b) Succession Planning
   (c) Employee Relations
   (d) Performance Management Systems
   (e) Training and Development
2. Indicate which is the most appropriate statement on human resource planning:
   (a) Human resource planning integrates all HR activities
   (b) Human resource planning integrates strategic plans

(c) Human resource planning assesses demand for manpower in organizations
(d) Human resource planning assess supply of manpower in organizations
(e) Human resource planning balances demand and supply of manpower aligning with the strategies and business plans of the organizations

3. Identify the incorrect statement:
   (a) Recruitment and selection function succeeds HRP
   (b) Recruitment and selection function precedes HRP
   (c) HRP compares present human resource to future human resource needs
   (d) HRP considers skill and competency gaps
   (e) Succession planning and career development are also integral part of HRP

4. Which of the following statement is not applicable for HRP"
   (a) HRP helps ensuring timely replacement of employees who suddenly leave the job
   (b) Business complexities fail to appreciate inclusion of HRP with the business and strategic plans of the organization
   (c) Social, economic, and legal environment influence HRP
   (d) Effective precedes recruitment and selection process
   (e) HRP follows a long term perspective

5. Identify the wrong statement:
   (a) HRP is a compelling need for the organization to deal with both expected and unexpected events
   (b) HRP can help organization to contain cost by up-skilling without damaging its competitiveness.
   (c) HRP needs integration with strategy and business plans, with flexibility to balance both the long-term and short-term business focus
   (d) HRP acknowledges critical value of human resources in organizational sustenance and growth
   (e) HRP cannot ensure flow of human resources in organizations

6. HRP activities involve:
   (a) Forecasting of future manpower requirements
   (b) Preparing inventory of present manpower
   (c) Anticipating problems of manpower
   (d) Meeting manpower requirements
   (e) All of the above

7. Indicate which information cannot be provided by job analysis:
   (a) Job characteristics
   (b) Job assignment
   (c) Materials and tools requirement for a job
   (d) Job pricing
   (e) Job relationship

8. In addition to HRP, job analysis helps in:
   (a) Jon re-engineering
   (b) Training and development requirements
   (c) Deciding on performance standards
   (d) All of the above
   (e) None of the above

9. Job description is recording of:
   (a) Duties, responsibilities and conditions needed for satisfactory performance of a particular job
   (b) Covers job content (conditions, tasks and responsibilities)
   (c) Succeed job specification
   (d) All of the above
   (e) None of the above

10. Indicate which is not an objective of HRP:
    (a) Integrate planning and control of manpower with organizational planning
    (b) Ensures capacity utilization
    (c) Ensures best possible utilization of all resources
    (d) Coordinates with manpower policies of the organization
    (e) Coordinates with promotion and transfer policies

11. Effective manpower planning cannot:
    (a) Achieve efficiency of work in all spheres
    (b) Ensure cost optimization
    (c) Eliminate wastage of time
    (d) Match present and future needs of manpower of the organization
    (e) None of the above

12. HRP is influenced by general environmental factors, excepting:
    (a) Employment-unemployment situation
    (b) Demographic changes
    (c) Legal control and institutional policies
    (d) Business cycle
    ((e) None of the above

13. Micro level HRP is influenced by following factors, excepting:
    (a) Change in technology
    (b) Organizational restructuring
    (c) Skill and competency gap
    (d) Uncontrollable environmental issues
    (e) Strategic objectives of organizations

14. National level human resource development also requires consideration of:
    (a) Population planning and control
    (b) Literacy and education

(c) Health and medical care
(d) Housing
(e) All of the above

15. Manpower requirement approach (MRA) works following approaches as under, excepting:
(a) Establishing a liner relation between employment and output and then extrapolating manpower requirements in different categories for years to come
(b) Computing category-wise manpower coefficients based on past data, and then hypothesizing growth pattern of different industry-groups
(c) Working out category-wise aggregate manpower requirement
(d) Using above inputs for assessing the educational requirements
(e) None of the above

16. Workload factor analysis cannot be performed by:
(a) Classification of work
(b) Classification of hierarchies
(c) Forecasting of number of jobs
(d) Converting projected jobs in man-hours
(e) Converting man-hours into manpower requirement

17. Simulation used for manpower planning considers following phases, excepting:
(a) Classification of problem
(b) Definition of the problem and statement of objectives
(c) Construction of an appropriate model
(d) Experimentation with the model constructed
(e) Evaluation of the results of simulation

18. Indicate which is not a difficulty in manpower forecasting using quantitative tools:
(a) When productivity rise cannot be attributed to increased human effort
(b) When it is difficult to get units of output in same form for all jobs
(c) When relationships between output and inputs are straightforward
(d) When effect of different factors on manpower forecasting is not linear
(e) When uncertainty about the future is high

19. Indicate which is not a qualitative model for better managerial judgement:
(a) Oracle Model
(b) Delphi Model
(c) Nominal Group Model
(d) Only (b)
(e) Only (c)

20. To evaluate responses received through application of Delphi model requires:
(a) Consideration of the assessment made by the experts in terms of their knowledge in the area
(b) Consideration of the assessment in terms of feasibility, objectives, time and resource requirement

(c) Consideration of the assessment in terms of desirability
(d) Consideration of the assessment in terms of extraneous factors
(e) All of the above

Answers:

1. (c)	2. (e)	3. (b)	4. (b)	5. (e)	6. (e)	7. (d)	8. (e)
9. (d)	10. (b)	11. (e)	12. (e)	13. (e)	14. (e)	15. (e)	16. (b)
17. (a)	18. (c)	19. (a)	20. (e)				

CASE STUDY

Deutsche Post and DHL Group: Challenge of Manpower Planning and Recruitment

For Deutsche Post (DP) and DHL Group, the world's largest conglomerate in logistics (industrial supply chain) and communications, with 4.9 lakh headcounts, spread across 220 countries, human resource planning is a strategic task. DP and DHL could successfully create a performance-driven work culture. The group acknowledges contributions from all cross-sections of employees and embraces an inclusive culture of talent management practices. With the practice of job mobility between different job verticals, employees get matured and can rise through the career ladders. Total rewards approach ensures not only systematic training and career development, even extends to work–life balancing, and improvement of quality of work life. Employees' children are provided scholarships. That the group believes in respect, recognition, and equal opportunities is evident from awards and accolades from different organizations and agencies for their activities in different countries. In 2015, Aon Hewitt conferred best employer award to DHL Express in Taiwan and Korea.

In Germany, the group essentially provides postal service, whereas globally the group is more visible as Logistics Company. For continuous focus on improvement of service quality through innovation, the group requires recruitment of talents. The group envisages by 2020 that they would be the "provider of choice for customers, an attractive investment for shareholders and the employer of choice for staff."

Employees after recruitment are helped to uncover their talents, supporting their aspirations for reaching their career goals. All employees have access to training and professional development opportunities, which also include a wide range of competency-building and talent management programs.

Because of their global spread and headcounts of 4.9 lakhs, the group faces challenge in manpower planning and recruitment. Such problems are often country-specific. In developed countries, including Germany, which is the headquarter of the group, problem is more aging workforce. In developing and emerging economy countries, problem is deficiency of knowledge, skill, and competencies. The group determines their medium-term manpower requirements, considering age distribution, rate of attrition, projected business growth, and expected changes in productivity. Also for effective manpower planning, the group simulates various scenarios to predecide manpower requirements in the future. This helps them to make their existing manpower future ready.

Question: Analyze the case of DP and DHL Group. As an HR expert what would be your prescribed solutions to source talent across the globe.

REFERENCES

Bhattacharyya, D.K. (2013), *Human Resource Planning,* 3rd edition. New Delhi. Excel Books.

Beer, S. (1979), *The Heart of Enterprise*. Chichester: Wiley.

Burack, E.H. (1986), "Corporate Business and HRP Practices: Strategic Issues and Concerns", *Organizational Dynamics*, 15(1): 73–87.

Doving, E. and Nordhang, O. (2010), "Investing in Human Resource Planning: An International Study", *Management Revue,* 21(3): 292–30.

Rothwell, W.J. and Sredl, H.J. (2000), *The ASTD reference guide to workplace learning and performance: Present and future roles and competencies* (3rd ed., Vols. 1–2). Amherst, MA: HRD Press, Inc.

Rothwell, W.J. and Sullivan, R. (Eds.) (2005), *Practicing organization development: A guide for consultants* (2nd ed.). San Francisco: CA: Pfeiffer.

Turner, P. (2010), *Reflections on workforce planning: From manpower planning to capacity planning—why we need workforce planning*. London, The Chartered Institute of Personnel and Development (CIPD).

Chapter 3

Job Analysis and Profile Matching

LEARNING OBJECTIVES

After reading this chapter, you will be able to understand:

1 Definitions and concepts of job analysis

2 Definitions and concepts of profile matching

3 PAQ and other job analysis methods

4 Job questionnaire

5 Job sculpting

6 Personality-based job analysis

7 Personality and career choice

8 Transaction analysis and personality

Multinational steel major after starting its mega steel plant in eastern India today faces the biggest problem of recruiting people, matching with their requirement. Although existing job portals had many promising service offers, the company could observe, even after screening 1000 candidates they get hardly one or two who match with their job requirements. Sourcing people from Korea, where the multinational is headquartered, would be expensive, as relocation expenses and head-quarter-based pay will be high. The CEO of the company is from South Korea, and he is very familiar to Indian culture and social systems. To ensure more people can be recruited, the company decided to reach to a larger pool of young people in India, installing multilingual profile-matching software. This software is capable of extending the scope of profile matching from key word search to automated comparison of job profiles with candidates' profiles, considering multiple factors, like industry experience, job family, skills, education, competencies, etc., which are associated with the job. These online recruitment solutions could not only enable the company for better reach to the profiles of the potential candidates, with scientific bent of analysis, but also draw list of more numbers of right-fit candidates. As a result, the company could address their recruitment problems through automated profile-matching software.

Some of the advantages, highlighted by the CEO of the company, are preparing a more accurate list of shortlisted candidates, simultaneous searching from social media, job boards, and various other databases through semantic matching, user-friendly interface, bidirectional matching (ability to match jobs to candidates and candidates' profiles to jobs), etc.

INTRODUCTION

Job analysis helps us to examine a job and then prepare the job description and job specification. In recruitment and selection process, job analysis helps us to prepare the desired profile structure of the candidates, who can match with or fit in the job. In addition, job analysis also helps in managing human resources, in improving quality and productivity, and in designing the compensation and benefits program. Traditionally, in organizations, we perform job analysis through observation and data collection. This can only give us closely similar job profiles. However, we often require defining the jobs in specific terms. Several tools like job sculpting, position analysis questionnaire (PAQ), common metric questionnaire (CMQ), work profiling systems (WPS), functional job analysis (FJA), Multipurpose

Occupational Systems Analysis Inventory-Closed Ended (MOSAIC), etc., are now used for better understanding of the job profiles and then taking recruitment decisions. In this chapter, we will discuss those tools which are commonly used.

PROFILE MATCHING

Profile matching is an employee selection process based on certain predetermined attributes for a job position. Commonly, profile matching is done matching with the personality characteristics. Now, however, we consider that profile matching is congruence to desired multitraits for a job position. Thus, profile matching is a technique used in personnel hiring where an applicant's characteristics are compared to those of the ideal or typical employee in the position they are applying for. Each characteristic of the template is assigned weights using a 5-point scale. Such characteristics or set of competencies widely vary from job to job. Let us examine the following characteristics of a desired job profile of an HR manager.

TABLE 3.1 Template of desired job profile.

Characteristics/competencies	Level of importance	Points assigned
Leadership	High	5
Communication ability	High	5
Interpersonal relations	High	5
Adaptability to change	Above average	4
Decision making ability	High	5
Strategic planning	Below average	2

Table 3.1 speaks on the template of a desired profile. However, for assessing to what extent the candidates' profile matches with the template, we need to come out with questionnaire (using 5-point scale) for each characteristic or set of competencies. In such cases, we have to include the points obtained by a prospective candidate, when questionnaire was used for assessing the degree of compatibility. With high degree of compatibility, the candidate will merit for selection. Let us assume that Mr. Sharma is a prospective candidate for the HR manager position in our organization. We have used the above questionnaire to measure compatibility of Mr. Sharma

with our desired profile. Using a questionnaire, we have measured the above characteristics of Mr. Sharma, and in Table 3.2 we are documenting the points obtained by Mr. Sharma.

TABLE 3.2 Points obtained by Mr. Sharma.

Characteristics/ competencies	Level of importance	Points assigned	Points obtained by Mr. Sharma
Leadership	High	5	5
Communication ability	High	5	5
Interpersonal relations	High	5	4
Adaptability to change	Above average	4	5
Decision making ability	High	5	5
Strategic planning	Below average	2	1

Now looking at the profile of Mr. Sharma, we find that he meets most of the profile requirements, barring mismatch of his score with desired level of interpersonal relations and strategic planning. Now, the company may decide whether with such minor deviation in competencies requirements, Mr. Sharma will merit selection or not.

POSITION ANALYSIS QUESTIONNAIRE (PAQ) AND OTHER JOB ANALYSIS METHODS

A structured Position Analysis Questionnaire (PAQ) can quantify the job analysis. Developed by McCormick, Jeanneret, and Mecham (1972), PAQ can study as much as 195 job elements, including human behavior requirements, and thus is capable of measuring human characteristics with job characteristics in a more comprehensive manner. Human behavior involved in work activities is first categorized into six types, and then for each category separate questionnaires are developed and responses are measured by the analyst on a scale of 0 to 5. For all these categories, 189 behavioral items are measured. Such categories are information input, mental process, work output, interpersonal relationships, work situation and job context, and other job characteristics. Apart from these, it also requires the study of tools and equipment required for job performance, physical and perceptual requirements of job, mathematical requirements, communication requirements, decision-making and responsibility-decisions about methods, order of work, standards, job conditions, and perceived job characteristics.

Among all, PAQ is considered the most powerful tool for job analysis and it is also used extensively by organizations across the world.

However, some other common tools for job analysis are explained later.

The Common Metric Questionnaire (CMQ) developed by Harvey (1991) is defined as worker-oriented job analysis instrument and is applicable for different nature of jobs. This questionnaire has different sets of questions on job characteristics under five major sections. These sections are background, physical and mechanical activities, work setting, contacts with people, and decision making. For each questionnaire item, responses are measured in terms of frequency, criticality, consequences of error, etc.

The Fleishman Job Analysis Survey (F-JAS), commonly known as ability requirements scales (Fleishman & Mumford, 1991), helps us in understanding a job measuring 52 cognitive, physical, psychomotor, and sensory abilities. This scale actually measures or rates the level of ability as functioning requirements for a job. Using this scale, occupational database has been created, which serves as a reference information for different occupations.

Functional job analysis (FJA) of Fine and Wiley (1971) also suggested seven scales to measure what workers need to do in a job. These are (1) things, (2) data, (3) people, (4) worker instructions, (5) reasoning, (6) math, and (7) language. Each scale has multiple levels indicating specific behavioral statements and illustrative tasks.

The MOSAIC (Multipurpose Occupational Systems Analysis Inventory-Closed Ended) is an occupation-specific database prepared by the U.S. Office of Personnel Management (OPM). For different sets of occupations, each job analysis inventory collects data on tasks and competencies. Tasks are measured in terms of importance, while competencies are measured in terms of importance and entry-level requirement. Although its basic purpose was to create occupational databases for government jobs, today it also serves as good reference information for job analysis.

Occupational analysis inventory (OAI) is again another important job analysis tool, which measures as high as 617 work elements, covering almost all occupational requirements. Work elements here are measured in terms of five categories, i.e., information received, mental activities, work behavior, work goals, and work context. Respondents here measure each job element using four rating scales, i.e., part-of-job, extent, applicability, or a scale specific for a particular job element.

Another commonly referred job analysis tool is work profiling system (WPS) of Saville and Holdsworth (1990). This job profiling system helps in effective planning of career development, employee selection, and job description. WPS has been designed as occupation specific, like separate WPS for managerial, service, and technical occupations. With structured questionnaire it measures ability, personality attributes, hearing skills, sight, taste, smell, touch, body coordination, verbal skills, number skills, complex management skills, personality, and team role. Aggregating the responses, databases are created, which can serve as reference points for the employers.

Job Questionnaire

A job questionnaire is a special tool for consolidating job information. It is a printed form, in which essential information about the job may be listed either by the employee or by his supervisors. The major advantage of the job questionnaire is that it uses the knowledge of those who are proximate to the job. In addition, it gives each employee an opportunity to participate and contribute by giving responses to the questionnaire, which facilitates immediate compilation of job information.

Another important advantage of job questionnaire is that compiled information can be used as job descriptions. This, therefore, eliminates the requirement of further writing of job descriptions. Moreover, by using a job questionnaire, organizations also get the benefit of communicating the up-to-date job information to the employees.

However, the major disadvantages associated with job questionnaire are that, its success depends on the understanding and writing ability of individual employees and supervisors. For perceptual incongruence, inconsistencies in the response pattern may arise. Such inconsistencies in the response pattern may multiply further when more cross-sections of people participate in the questionnaire response/survey. In addition, compiling job information from the questionnaire response again may suffer from the problem of exaggeration. These are the inherent problem of information quality through job questionnaire.

To eliminate such inherent problems of compiling job information through job questionnaire, it is always better to compile the information through a combination of direct observation and job questionnaire. This approach may be time consuming and involve huge cost, but more scientific as it eliminates the chance of error by both accounting the perceptive differences between what they perceive and what they do.

Job Sculpting

Traditionally, in organizations, we perform job-fit analysis, based on the profile, education, and previous job experience of the new recruitees.

Expectation is here employees will fit into the job in this process. Job sculpting is opposed to this concept of job-fit analysis, and suggests designing job profile in line with the interests of the employees. In their seminal work on job sculpting, Butler and Waldrop (1999) suggested the need for job sculpting for appropriate job-person-fit, so that people unnecessarily do not require leaving their jobs, as the jobs are not in line with their interests. It has been observed that in many organizations people leave their jobs despite being well paid, enjoying good work environment, good career development opportunities, opportunity for work–life balancing, and good quality of work life. A good example is the propensity among new talents to prefer job offers of RMSI Private Limited, an innovative geospatial and software solutions and services company of India. In terms of compensation and reward, the company nowhere matches with other peer group companies, or even with other technology and knowledge-intensive organizations. Even then people prefer to work for this company, as they feel they would be able to do their jobs that they like. This IT services company has only headcounts of 842 (2015).

Creating a job profile through job sculpting helps the employees to sensitize their deeply held interests, which they even try to fulfill through their jobs. It is like feeling satisfied while doing jobs. Butler and Waldrop (1999) recommended eight different life interests of employees, of which presence of at least three in jobs can make the job more interesting. In other words, effective job sculpting requires ensuring presence of at least three of the under-mentioned life interest issues in the job profile. These are presented below:

(1) Technology application—to what extent employees can make use of technology while they do their work.
(2) Quantitative analysis—opportunities for employees to make use of quantitative analysis while they do their jobs. Future jobs are increasingly being becoming analytics driven.
(3) Scope for theory development and conceptual thinking—helps in aligning their academic knowledge with the work, and in the process makes the jobs more interesting.
(4) Creativity—opportunities to employees to be more creative and innovating while doing their jobs. Most of the technology majors today embedded the culture of innovation in their workplaces.
(5) Counseling and mentoring—employees always like to play the role of a counselor and mentor. Hence giving such opportunities in their jobs can make it more interesting.
(6) Scope for managing people and relationships—this also enhances job interests.

(7) Scope for organizational control—presence of such opportunities in job also makes it more and more interesting.
(8) Opportunities of using their language and ideas—this again is liked by some people, and for them presence of such opportunities contributes to their happiness and they start liking the jobs (Fig. 3.1).

FIGURE 3.1 Ways of job sculpting.

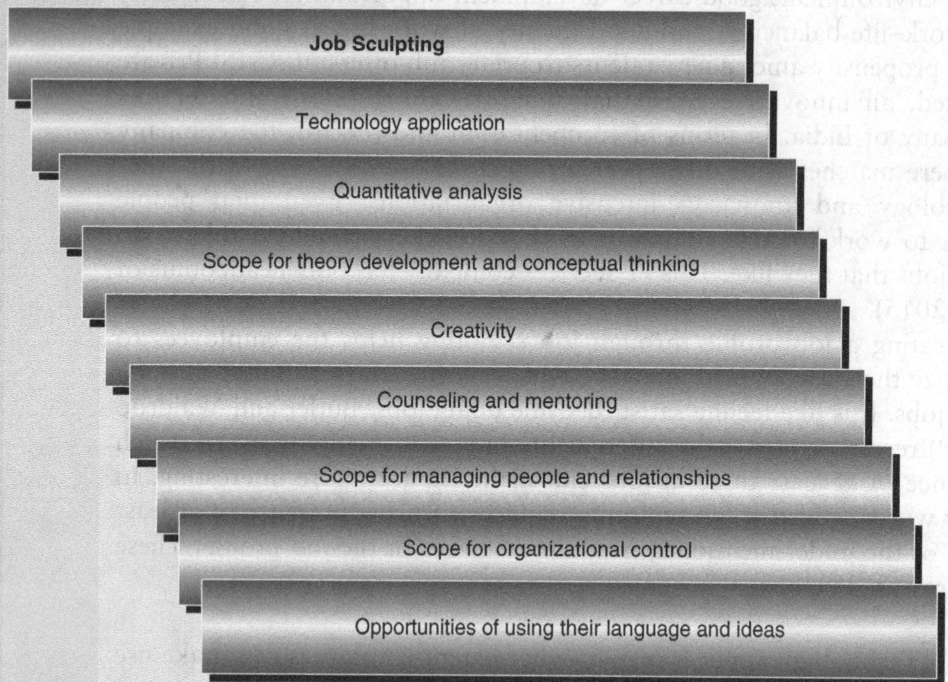

For organizations, effective job sculpting would depend on developing job profile, sensitizing at least three of the above job attributes, pacing with the areas of interests of the employees. Because people autonomously like their jobs, job sculpting will not only contribute to creating a performance-driven work culture, but also ensure talent retention and increased level of employee engagement. Effective job sculpting also depends on deeper understanding of the psychology of work satisfaction of the employees. "Deeply embedded life interests" of employees are their "topical enthusiasms," passions, and when they get opportunities to satisfy these through their jobs, they start liking their job, and give their best efforts.

Therefore, job sculpting is a process of matching people to jobs based on their "embedded life interests." Although matching people with jobs, in line with their skills, knowledge, and competencies, as a conventional practice still exists, it may not be liked by the people, as job may not be in congruent with their "deeply embedded life interests."

Culture Job-Fit

Culture as an important construct for people's choice of desirable jobs and occupations has been studied by many researchers (Lareau and Weininger, 2003). Success of recruitment and selection largely depends on congruity of culture of the employers or the organizations and the new hires. One study by Bourdieu (1984) could identify cultural similarities of employers and the employees in terms of shared tastes, experiences, leisure pursuits, and self presentation styles. With high degree of similarities employees will prefer job offers from such organizations. Subsequently, legitimacy of culture-fit recruitment and selection process was acknowledged by Elliot and Smith (2004), citing recruitment is not just economic stratification, it is also a social closure. Culture and recruitment fit can be best achieved with employee hiring matches with the organizational characteristics, job demands, and skills of the job seekers (Tilly and Tilly, 1998).

Culture-job fit has been defined by noted organizational psychologist Furnham as the "congruence between the norms and values of the organization and those of the person." Person-organization-fit can be better achieved when organizations attract, retain, and motivate employees who embrace similar values, norms, and beliefs (Kristof, 1996). Degree of person-organization-fit can be better achieved when it is mediated by culture.

For culture-person fit for recruitment, it is necessary for organizations to have their own clarity about their culture and values. Such understanding of the culture of organizations would be possible when we analyze the way they work. For example, if the culture of the organization is innovative and performance driven, while hiring we will expect employees to have the same cultural constructs. To assess such fit the following set of questions can be used.

Here are some questions that can help in assessing culture fit in an interview:

(1) What type of culture do you thrive in? (Does the response reflect your organizational culture?)
(2) What values are you drawn to and what's your ideal workplace?
(3) Why do you want to work here?

(4) How would you describe our culture based on what you have seen? Is this something that works for you?
(5) What best practices would you bring with you from another organization? Do you see yourself being able to implement these best practices in our environment?
(6) Tell me about a time when you worked with/for an organization where you felt you were not a strong culture fit. Why was it a bad fit?

Some organizations also assess the cultural constructs of prospective new hires putting them into a vicarious work situation, and then studying their interactions with others.

Personality-Based Job Analysis

Job analysis primarily helps us to understand more accurately which characteristics, like knowledge, skills, abilities, attitudes, personalities, etc., play important roles in different job positions in organizations. For different job positions all these characteristics are important, but its degree of requirements may vary. Even though personality characteristics *per se* are important for all job positions, its use in job analysis along with other job analysis instruments is still restricted. Researchers such as Goldberg (1983), Raymark, Schmit and Guion (1997), Smith (1994), Brannick and Levine (2002) recommended use of personality-based job analysis (PBJA), along with other traditional job analysis instruments for better understanding of a job. The purpose of job analysis is to divide the job into several smaller units, and then to document job-specific characteristics, which are essential for successful execution of a job. In selection decisions, job analysis plays the most pivotal role, as selection of candidates without it may render the selection improper. Moreover, for many organizations, selection process has legal implications. In such cases, job analysis document with the embedded personality characteristics to a great extent can validate the selection decisions of the organizations. Personality-based job analysis can also help us to predecide the personality traits required for execution of a job or jobs, and in the process can make our selection process more fool-proof.

Personality and Recruitment

In recruitment and selection, individual personality is important because personality of individual employees consists of their dynamic mental structures and coordinated processes of the mind, which determine their emotional and behavioral adjustments to the organization. Personality is dynamic because mental structures of individual employees continuously develop over their lifetime. Personality and individual behavioral pattern of employees become an important construct to adjust and succeed in work situations. Particularly in a changing business environment, to get the right fit, employers make use of personality tests in selection and recruitment decisions. Apart from this, personality assessment is also important for cultural transformation in an organization. With the understanding of cognitive and emotional bases of human behavior, personality assessment has gained further importance.

Reviewing all the theories on personality, it is, therefore, evident that personality testing in recruitment is our attempt to capture or summarize an individual's "essence." Personality is the science of describing and understanding persons. Clearly, personality is a core area of study for psychology. Individual intelligence also influences different aspects of personality in many different ways. In fact, intelligence is sometimes considered to be a part of personality.

Measurement of Personality Traits

Many psychologists have tried to reduce the many traits to a few essential ones. Among the best known essential trait approaches that we follow in measuring personality traits are:

- Murray 1938 (20+ "needs")
- Cattell (16 traits): 16 personality factors questionnaire
- Eysenck (3 traits): Eysenck Personality Questionnaire (EPQ)—Extraversion, Neuroticism, and Psychoticism
- Costa and McCrae (5 traits): NEO—Neuroticism, Extraversion, and Openness to Experience, Agreeableness, and Conscientiousness

Murray's theory observes that our behavior is driven by an internal state of disequilibrium. In other words, we lack something and this drives us, or we are dissatisfied and we desire for something. According to Murray, our personality is driven by our secondary needs: achievement, dominance, affiliation, and nurturance.

Cattell (1905–1998) viewed language as a useful source of information about personality. He had identified 16 personality factors (16 PF) as under:

- reserved versus warm
- concrete reasoning versus abstract reasoning
- reactive versus emotionally stable
- deferential versus dominant

- serious versus lively
- expedient versus rule-conscious
- shy versus socially bold
- utilitarian versus sensitive
- trusting versus vigilant
- practical versus imaginative
- forthright versus private
- self-assured versus apprehensive
- traditional versus open-to-change
- group-oriented versus self-reliant
- tolerates disorder versus perfectionist
- relaxed versus tense

Eysenck (1916–1997) designed the Eysenck Personality Questionnaire (EPQ). He believed that people could be described in terms of two super traits on biological basis:

- Introversion–extraversion (continuum of sociability, dominance, liveliness, etc.)
- Emotionality–stability (neuroticism) (continuum of upset and distress)
- Psychoticism was added later. But this aspect is less researched. This was a predisposition toward becoming either psychotic or sociopathic (psychologically unattached to other people). It also indicated a tendency to be hostile, manipulative, and impulsive.

Other studies on primary personality traits are Mayers–Briggs Type Indicator (MBTI) and the Big Five Model. MBTI is essentially a 100-question personality test to understand people's feelings and actions in a given situation. The responses are then classified into four major types, such as extroverted versus introverted, sensing versus intuitive, thinking versus feeling, and judging versus perceiving. These were then combined into 16 personality types—ESTJ, INFP, ESFP, INTJ, ESFJ, INTP, ENFP, ISTJ, ESTP, INFJ, ENFJ, ISTP, ENTJ, ISFP, ENTP, and ISFJ. Further for each personality type, specific attributes were identified. For example, a person with ESTJ type personality is practical, organized, and logical. Contrarily, INFP-type persons are more focussed on their inner world and driven by thoughts and emotion. Logical decision-making attribute is more evident in person with INTP-type personality. Software programmers, operations managers, HR managers may be more effective in their workplaces with INTP personality.

The Big Five Model is often considered the better alternative to MBTI. The five big personality factors are:

- Extroversion
- Agreeableness
- Conscientiousness
- Emotional stability
- Openness to stability

The five-factor model is commonly measured by Neuroticism, Extraversion, and Openness (NEO) given by McCrae and Costa (1995) to categorize personality as under:

- Neuroticism (emotional stability)
- Extraversion (introversion)
- Openness to experience (closeness to experiences)
- Agreeableness (disagreeableness)
- Conscientiousness (lack of conscientiousness)

Personality and Employment Testing

Use of personality testing for selection decisions has historical roots. Initially, many psychologists were against the use of personality testing. The use of cognitive ability tests in recruitment received wide acceptance, as it was construed as a more valid predictor for acquisition of job skills, and to some extent, even job performance. Managers also used to discard personality testing in recruitment decisions, alleging it unreliable and invalid. In fact, human resource management professionals initially emphasized on the use of personality scores for selection.

Personality testing became more prominent when disciplines like psychology, engineering, and management eventually merged to solve the organizational problems. Similarly, personality as a predictor of performance did not get acceptance, as numerous studies could not establish this. But there exists more or less common agreement that managers possess some set of personality traits. Some of the research studies in modern times, however, could show results about the role of personality testing in employee selection.

Validity and Reliability of the Selection Tests

Psychological tests need to be valid. The degree of validity of a test measure widely varies with respect to circumstances, use of specific tools, and its application. Primarily, the validity of a selection test depends on how the characteristics of the measurements relate to the selection test for the given job requirements. We consider selection test scores as valid, when there is a link between the test score and job performance. The degree of validity is understood in terms of employment selection tests, when results of one test can predict job performance behavior related by others. Reliability, on the other hand, tells us to what extent our test measure is reproducible, when we conduct a retest.

For selecting employees, we use validity on three counts: criterion-related, content, and construct. Criterion validity shows the correlation or other statistical relationships between the selection test score (predictor) and job performance (criterion). With high test score, if one performs high, we call it high criterion validity. Content validity indicates that content of the test reflects some important job-related behavior and the measurement of knowledge and skill for the said job-related behavior. Construct validity measures constructs or abstract job characteristics, which are crucial for the performance of the job. In most of the psychological tests used for selection, criterion-related validity is considered.

Test of Intelligence as Employability Test

Intelligence is mental capacity that, among other things, involves the ability to reason, plan, solve problems, think abstractly, comprehend complex ideas, learn quickly, and learn from experience. Intelligence is not merely book learning or a narrow academic skill. It reflects a broader and deeper capability for comprehending our surroundings.

A popular theory of intelligence is based on psychometric testing, i.e., intelligence quotient (IQ) test. However, as some researchers were dissatisfied with traditional IQ tests, they developed alternative theories of intelligence suggesting that intelligence results from independent capabilities that uniquely contribute to human intellectual performance. Measuring the IQ of a large population, we can arrive at a normal distribution. The approach toward understanding intelligence over a long period of time is based on psychometric testing. Such intelligence quotient (IQ) tests define general intelligence.

Some of the widely accepted IQ tests measures are Stanford–Binet, Raven's Progressive Matrices, the Wechsler Adult Intelligence Scale, and the Kaufman Assessment Battery for Children.

PERFORMANCE INTELLIGENCE TEST

After conducting IQ tests, we can obtain two separate IQ scores for a person. These are verbal IQ and performance IQ with individual scores for each subset within the verbal and performance categories.

- Digit symbol: Mental flexibility with random symbols
- Picture completion: Ability to notice differences between two pictures
- Block design: Mentally construct printed designs in your head
- Picture arrangement: Arrange pictures in a logical order
- Object assembly: Place the correct part in relationship to a whole

Both of these scores (verbal + performance) can then be combined to give an overall IQ score.

Emotional Intelligence (EI)

Emotional dimensions of behavior of people are still not considered by many organizations, as we still believe only in verbal and cognitive intelligence. We, however, develop our thought process through interaction. Gradually, it has been recognized that our emotions carry some sensible meanings, and it requires understanding. It was Daniel Goleman (1995) who had institutionalized the adoption of emotional intelligence measures in organizations, particularly during recruitment. Goleman's approach could help us in understanding the relation between reason and emotion. In organizations, we integrate emotional intelligence, personality, and intelligence quotient for achieving excellence in employees' performance. To recruit the right fit also, we make use of such an integrated approach.

Goleman (1995) defined emotional intelligence as the "capacity for reorganizing our own feelings and those of others, for motivating ourselves, for managing emotions well in ourselves and in our relationships." Thus, Goleman's basic argument is that our rational thinking alone cannot predict success. Even with high intelligence quotient (IQ), people may fail. Obviously for this reason, organizations always endeavor to develop leadership skills and competencies among employees for enhancing their emotional intelligence.

Two aspects of EI

To be successful, we require the effective awareness, control, and management of one's own emotions, and those of other people. This is the essential premise of Emotional Quotient (EQ). Thus, EQ embraces two aspects of intelligence:

- Understanding self, goals, intentions, responses, behavior, and
- Understanding others and their feelings

The Five Domains of EQ

Goleman identified the five "domains" of EI as follows:

- Knowing your emotions
- Managing your emotions
- Motivating yourself
- Recognizing and understanding other people's emotions
- Managing relationships, that is, managing the emotions of others (Fig. 3.2)

FIGURE 3.2 Domains of emotional intelligence.

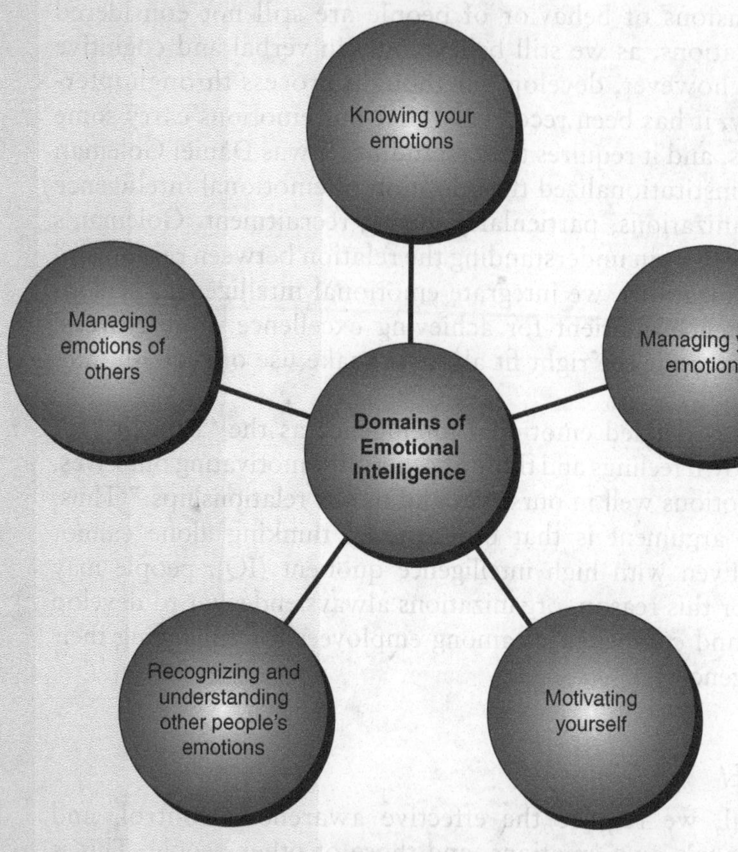

Emotional Intelligence has relationship with other behavioral studies like neuro-linguistic programming (NLP), transactional analysis, and empathy. By developing our Emotional Intelligence in these areas and the five EQ domains, we can become more productive and successful at what we do and also help others to be more productive and successful.

Employees' training on emotional intelligence can significantly help organizations to achieve group cohesion, team work, culture of collaboration, etc.

ETHICAL GUIDELINES FOR PSYCHOLOGICAL TESTING

Ethical guidelines on the use of psychological testing mandate to provide feedback to the persons who participate in such assessment in terms of general assessment/issues, reliability and validity, norm groups, feedback to the applicant, etc.

To apply psychological testing in job interviews, it is important to consider the following issues:

- Process of identification of constructs for a particular job
- Process of reporting the test results
- Previewing of test information before administration
- Process of integrating psychological test scores and interview results
- Norms for providing hiring recommendation (Fig. 3.3)

FIGURE 3.3 Ethical guidelines for psychological testing.

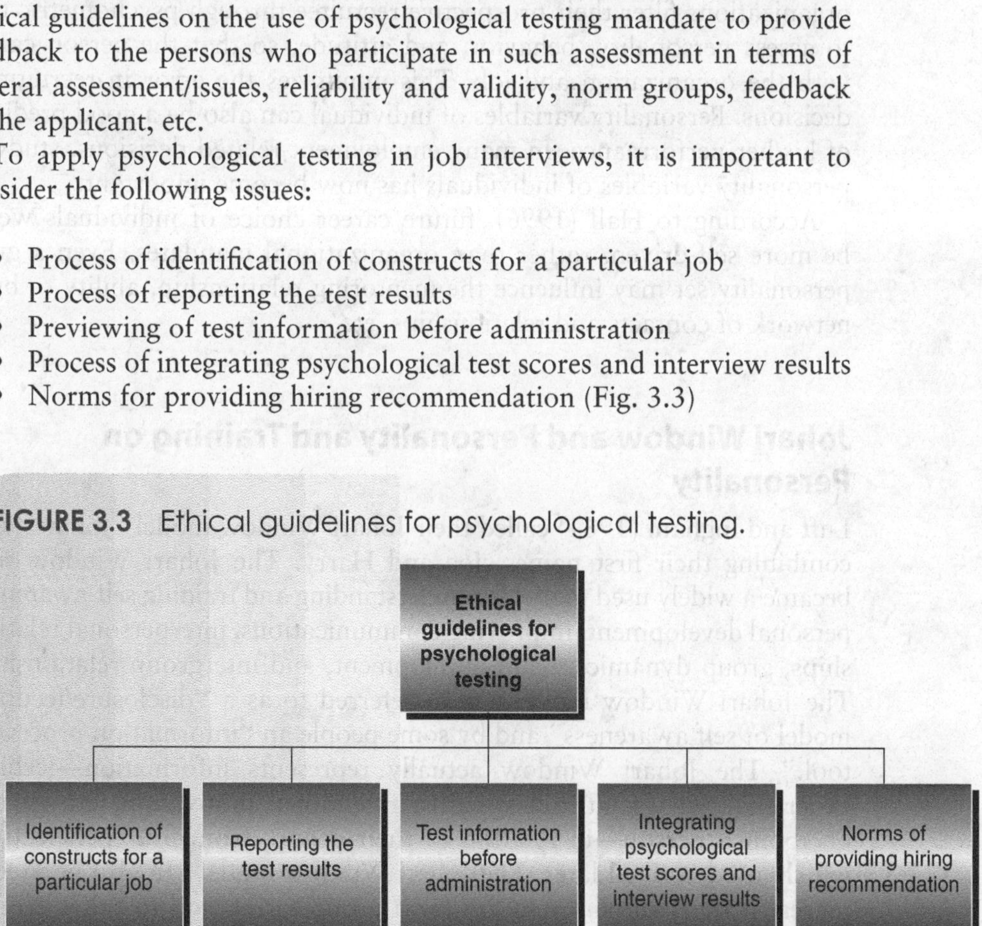

Personality and Career Choice

Personality is the reflection of the most dominant characteristics of our behavior. Personality can influence the career choice and also the performance of people in their chosen careers. This is why personality is also considered an integral part of vocational psychology (Borgen and Harmon, 1996). Relationship between personality and vocational psychology was also evident from Holland's (1997) research. Kristof (1996) could observe the compatibility between people and organization with respect to personality variables. Likewise, relationship between personality and organizational climate and culture has also been observed by researchers such as Bowen et al. (1991). Hence in recruitment decisions also we require the personality assessment reports of individuals. Many organizations filter their prospective recruitee through psychometric tests to assess personality, behavior, and attitude, so that the person can fit with the organization and job. This minimizes the error in recruitment decisions. Personality variables of individual can also be a good predictor of his/her performance. In many employment-related decisions, studying personality variables of individuals has now become important.

According to Hall (1996), future career choice of individuals would be more self-driven, rather than organizational mandates. Even a given personality set may influence the mentoring relationship, ability to build network of contacts and relationships, etc.

Johari Window and Personality and Training on Personality

Luft and Ingham (1961) called their Johari Window model "Johari" after combining their first names, Joe and Harry. The Johari Window soon became a widely used model for understanding and training self-awareness, personal development, improving communications, interpersonal relationships, group dynamics, team development, and intergroup relationships. The Johari Window model is also referred to as a "disclosure/feedback model of self awareness" and by some people an "information processing tool." The Johari Window actually represents information—feelings, experience, views, attitudes, skills, intentions, motivation, etc—within or about a person—in relation to their group, from four perspectives, which are described later. The Johari Window model can also be used to represent the same information for a group in relation to other groups. Johari Window terminology refers to "self" and "others": "self" means oneself, i.e., the person subject to the Johari Window analysis. "Others" mean other people in the person's group or team.

The Johari window has four regions, and each region indicates

- what is known by the person about him/herself and is also known by others—open area, open self, free area, free self, or "the arena"

- what is unknown by the person about him/herself but which others know—blind area, blind self, or "blindspot"
- what the person knows about him/herself that others do not know—hidden area, hidden self, avoided area, avoided self, or "façade"
- what is unknown by the person about him/herself and is also unknown by others—unknown area or unknown self

The diagram of the model is presented in Fig. 3.4.

FIGURE 3.4 Johari Window.

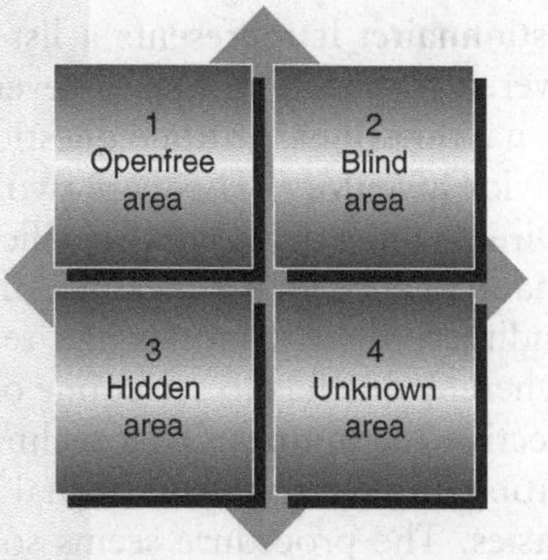

Luft and Ingham observed that there are aspects of our personality that we are open about, and other elements that we keep to ourselves. At the same time, there are things that others see in us that we are not aware of.

- **The public area** contains things that are openly known and talked about—and which may be seen as strengths or weaknesses. This is the self that we choose to share with others.
- **The hidden area** contains things that others observe that we do not know about. Again, they could be positive or negative behaviors, and will affect the way that others act toward us.
- **The unknown area** contains things that nobody knows about us—including ourselves. This may be because we have never exposed those areas of our personality, or because they are buried deep in the subconscious.
- **The private area** contains aspects of our self that we know about and keep hidden from others.

Personality Assessment

Assessment of individual personality constructs is important for us to map the differences in terms of certain measurable dimensions. Zanden (1987) suggested certain methods of personality measurement as under:

(1) **Interview method:** This consists of the formal method in which organized questions are asked face to face and the informal method which is used when obtaining information for maladjusted people.

(2) **Rating scales:** This is the useful method for learning what impression an individual has made on persons with whom he comes into contact in respect to some specified trait as honesty, punctuality, and emotional stability.

(3) **Questionnaire:** It represents a list of statements which are to be answered by checking one of several possible answers. There are personal questions, attitude questions, and interest questions.

(4) **Behavior inventory:** There are two kinds:
   - Direct which deals with specific information and no efforts are made to conceal the meaning of the questions.
   - Indirect which conceals the real purpose by giving a choice whereby one has to select one of two alternatives.

(5) **Projective techniques:** This technique represents an ambiguous situation into which the individual reads his own wishes, fears, and fantasies. The procedure seems so impersonal that the examinee often projects his real self and unraveled motives without knowing.

Do it yourself

As a training manager, which method of personality you recommend for a customer relations executive of a consumer durable company, and why?

"Personality change" can have at least three meanings: first, it can denote adjustment, whereby the change consists of exterior modifications and is temporary in nature. An individual may adopt a particular behavior forced by a certain situation, which is not congruent with his general pattern of behavior. This is not what is meant by personality change in this essay. Second, it can indicate a "quantum change." This is marked by a sudden and significant change where the individual's traits are totally transformed. This type of change, as we will discuss later, is not likely. The third meaning of personality change, which we adopt in this essay, could be referred to as "plasticity." This is a gradual change without the loss of the core material, presupposing some form of continuity. In this sense, personality change can also be understood as personality integration (Mischel, Shoda, & Smith, 2004).

Transactional Analysis (TA) and Personality

Transactional Analysis (TA) is a personality and psychotherapy for personal growth. Dr. Eric Berne, the originator of TA, considers a transaction as the unit of social intercourse. A transaction consists of a transactional stimulus (TS) and a transactional response (TR). TS is the behavior (verbal or nonverbal) produced by one person in acknowledgement of the presence of others when two or more people encounter each other. TR is the response to TS by another person.

Eric Berne (1961) founded Transactional Analysis. It is now widely applied in organizational communications. The basic premise of Eric Berne's Transaction Analysis is Sigmund Freud's contribution to human psyche. Berne advocated that while we communicate, we reflect our state of mind, which translates into child ego, adult ego, or parent ego. It is possible for a person to reflect all the three ego states simultaneously while communicating with others. Every ego state carries some different meaning.

The three distinct states called the ego states are the parent ego state, the adult ego state, and the child ego state. The parent ego state is produced by the play-back of recordings in the brain of unquestioned or imposed external events perceived by the person before his social birth, i.e., before the age of 5 years. This ego state consists of Nos, Don'ts, How – Tos and the facial expressions, tone of voice, manners, etc., of the person's parents. In other words, this ego state consists of the *"taught—concepts"* of life.

The child ego state is the response the little person produced to what he saw, heard, felt, and understood. Most of these are feelings because the child has not developed verbal responses at that time. In other words, this ego state may be considered the collection of *"felt-concepts"* of life.

The parent ego state begins with the biological birth of the individual and extends up to an age of five years. The child ego state also starts with the physical birth and continues to develop until the social birth (around the age of five).

The adult ego state develops after both the parent and the child ego states have begun to develop. This state begins to develop from about ten months of age. The function of this state is to update both parent data and child data by continuous examination of these data with respect to actual reality. Thus, only those taught concepts and felt-concepts applicable and appropriate to the present are accepted. Thus, the adult state is said to be the *"thought-concepts"* of life.

Berne defined ego states as "coherent systems of thought, feeling, manifested by corresponding patterns of behavior." Some authors, however, consider the term body language than behavior, because behavioral impulses may not be always evident, rather it is internal-felt experiences. According to Berne, each ego state is a distinct system of interacting feelings, thoughts, and potential behavior. Transactional analysis is extensively used in organizational development, to develop the right change premise, eliminating dysfunctional organizational behaviors.

SUMMARY

- Measurement of personality and understanding the personality lag of individual employees is very important for organizations. Training can help in addressing the personality lag, and holistically develop the individual employees and managers. Hence, there is a need for personality development training in organizations.
- HR managers make extensive use of various psychological tests before finalizing the selection of a prospective candidate for the job. The importance of psychological testing is understood from the fact that employees' ability to work extends beyond cognitive abilities and acquired knowledge and skill and includes personality and work behavior.
- HR managers help in employee selection by helping organizations to assess the employees' potential capabilities in job assignment. They also help in personality assessment to ensure that employees become the right-fit for the job.
- More rigorous understanding of the holistic person requires HR managers to make use of testing of IQ, EI, etc. More advanced tools like NLP can also help in accurate understanding of the likely behavioral pattern of employees.
- Use of psychological tools and techniques alone cannot serve the purpose. HR psychologists need to ensure their reliability and validity. Also complying with the ethical norms is considered extremely important.

Key Words

Rational Emotive Behavioral Therapy (REBT): Developed by Albert Ellis and it begins with ABC; A is for activating experiences, such as family troubles, unsatisfying work, early childhood traumas, and all the various things we point to as the sources of our unhappiness. B stands for beliefs, especially the irrational, self-defeating beliefs that are the actual sources of our unhappiness. And C stands for consequences, the neurotic symptoms, and negative emotions such as depression panic and rage that come from our beliefs.

The socializer: Type B personality people of this type love to be part of groups and organizations. They become the center of attention. They love excitement, are often impatient and demanding, and possess high-energy levels. As they want to be in the limelight they do very well in sales, advertising, marketing, public speaking, party planning, travel, and other similar positions. They are supportive of subordinates and enjoy being around, while they perform.

Perceptual set: Perception is the generic term for the complex sensory control of behavior. It is inferred from a hypothetical internal event of unspecified nature, controlled largely by external stimulation and variables such as habit and drive. Therefore, it is appropriate to state that "people tend to perceive what they expect to perceive." This is the primary reason why different individuals perceive the same situation in different ways.

Operant conditioning: Developed by B. F. Skinner. The organism is in the process of "operating" on the environment, which in ordinary terms means that it is bouncing around its world, doing what it does. During this "operating," the organism encounters a special kind of stimulus called the reinforcing stimulus, or simply the reinforcer. This special stimulus has the effect of increasing the operant—that is, the behavior occurring just before the reinforcer.

Phenomenological perspectives: Believes people "introspect," that is, concentrate on and report on subjective conscious experience. Introspection was seen as lacking in scientific rigor and as not having any particular application. Then psychoanalysis which emphasized the unconscious mind came along and become more dominant.

Decision making process: Due to difference in individual personality, perception, attitude, and thinking, the decision-making process differs from manager to manager. For obvious behavioral significance in decision making, we need to understand the behavioral implications and the differences in information processing which ultimately leads to decision making.

Review Questions

1. Define the term personality and explain its various characteristics.
2. Explain the various theories of personality and distinguish between descriptive and predictive theories.
3. Explain the influence of behavior and personality on decision making.
4. What is perception? Explain the factors influencing the perceptual process.
5. Explain the significance of organizational behavior. What are the main variables of organizational behavior?

6. Write short notes on:
   (a) Perception
   (b) Perceptual set
   (c) Individual behavior vs. organizational behavior
   (d) Lens model

Critical Review Questions

1. For recruitment of customer care executives for an automobile manufacturing organization riddled with customer complaints, you have been asked to suggest some personality assessment tools. Accordingly, select some personality assessment tools and also recommend how use of such tools will benefit the recruitment and selection process keeping in mind the unique nature of this job.
2. Many organizations still believe individual behavior of the people in the workplace largely gets influenced by group norms. One such organization, engaged in software development, recruited the best talent from different campuses. The selection process was based on technical tests and innovativeness of the applicants. The company being one that develops ERP solutions, every programmer requires to collect inputs from different cross-functional team members. Of late, the company identified gap areas in coordination between different cross-functional team members, resulting in delay in developmental work. Understand this situation and comment on how the company can avoid such a situation, duly addressing personality issues.

Special activity for recruitment managers

Like most of the organizations, your company also does recruitment validation through performance review of new recruiters within six months of their induction. Your boss has given you the assignment of follow-up induction training program for some performance laggards, who have been recruited six months before. Also your boss has asked for assessing their personality constructs and matching the results with their current job assignment. Design your courses of action.

Multiple Choice Questions

1. Indicate which is not part of job analysis:
   (a) Examining a job
   (b) Preparing job description and job specification
   (c) Prepare desired profile structure of the candidates
   (d) Helps in managing human resources
   (e) None of the above

2. Indicate which is not a job specification tool:
   (a) Job sculpting
   (b) Position analysis questionnaire (PAQ)
   (c) HR metric questionnaire (HRMQ)
   (d) Work profiling systems (WPS)
   (e) Functional job analysis (FJA)

3. Multipurpose Occupational Systems Analysis Inventory-Closed Ended (MOSAIC) is used for:
   (a) Better understanding of the job profiles
   (b) It helps in taking recruitment decisions
   (c) It is used for job evaluation
   (d) It describes a job
   (e) None of the above

4. Indicate more appropriate statement for profile matching is done:
   (a) Based on certain pre-determined physical and mental attributes for a job position
   (b) Based on benchmarking with competitors' job profiles
   (c) Based on matching with the personality characteristics of a job
   (d) Based on achieving congruence to desired multi-traits for a job position
   (e) Based on discretion of HR manager

5. PAQ was developed by:
   (a) McCormick, Jeanneret, and Mecham
   (b) Mintzberg
   (c) Peter Drucker
   (d) Henri Fayol
   (e) F.W. Taylor

6. Indicate which is a correct statement about CMQ:
   (a) CMQ measures emotions of workers
   (b) CMQ measures physical attributes of a job
   (c) CMQ was developed by McCormick
   (d) CMQ measures job characteristics under five major sections
   (e) CMQ is not a tool for assessing supervisory jobs

7. The Fleishman Job Analysis Survey (F-JAS) measures following job elements, excepting:
   (a) Physical
   (b) Cognitive
   (c) Psychomotor
   (d) Sensory
   (e) None of the above

8. OAI measures following job elements, excepting:
   (a) Job control
   (b) Mental
   (c) Work behavior
   (d) Work goals
   (e) Work context

9. WPS essentially focuses on:
   (a) Career development
   (b) Employee selection
   (c) Job description
   (d) All of the above
   (e) None of the above

10. Indicate which is not a job sculpting:
    (a) Job-fit analysis
    (b) Designing of job profile in line with the interest of organization
    (c) Designing of job profile in line with the interests of the employees
    (d) For achieving appropriate job-person fit
    (e) Only c and d

11. Indicate which is not a part of deeply held interest of an employee which we do not consider in job sculpting:
    (a) Theory development and conceptual thinking
    (b) Quantitative analysis
    (c) Working in silos
    (d) Creativity
    (e) Counseling and mentoring

12. Indicate which question(s) is/are more appropriate for culture-job-fit analysis:
    (a) What best practices would you bring with you from another organization
    (b) Why do you want to work here
    (c) What values are you drawn to and what is your ideal workplace
    (d) All of the above
    (e) None of the above

13. Indicate which is not helping us to measure personality traits:
    (a) Murray 1938 (20+ 'needs')
    (b) Cattell (16 traits): 16 personality factors questionnaire
    (c) Eysenck (3 traits): Eysenck Personality Questionnaire (EPQ)—Extraversion, Neuroticism and Psychoticism
    (d) Costa and McCrae (5 traits): NEO—Neuroticism, Extraversion, and Openness to Experience, Agreeableness and Conscientiousness
    (e) Sigmund Freud's Psychoanalysis

14. Which is not a domain of EI identified by Goleman:
  (a) Managing your emotions
  (b) Motivating yourself
  (c) Recognizing and understanding other people's emotions
  (d) Managing relationships, that is, managing the emotions of others
  (e) None of the above

15. Ethical guidelines for psychological testing address following issues excepting:
  (a) Process of identification of constructs for a particular job
  (b) Process of reporting the test results
  (c) Previewing of test information before administration
  (d) Process of integrating psychological test scores and interview results
  (e) Discretionary recruitment decisions

16. The Johari window has following regions excepting:
  (a) What is known by the person about him/herself and is also known by others—open area, open self, free area, free self, or "the arena"
  (b) What is unknown by the person about him/herself but which others know—blind area, blind self, or "blindspot"
  (c) What the person knows about him/herself that others do not know—hidden area, hidden self, avoided area, avoided self or "façade"
  (d) Confidential area
  (e) What is unknown by the person about him/herself and is also unknown by others—unknown area or unknown self

17. Individual personality constructs can be measured by:
  (a) Interview
  (b) Questionnaire
  (c) Rating scale
  (d) Projective technique
  (e) All of the above

18. Concept of transactional analysis was proposed by:
  (a) Eric Berne
  (b) Sigmund Freud
  (c) Thomas Harris
  (d) B.F. Skinner
  (e) David Hare

Answers:

1. (a) **2.** (c) **3.** (c) **4.** (d) **5.** (a) **6.** (d) **7.** (e) **8.** (a)
9. (d) **10.** (e) **11.** (c) **12.** (d) **13.** (e) **14.** (e) **15.** (e) **16.** (d)
17. (e) **18.** (a)

CASE STUDY

Social networking sites—can these be the best way for profile matching and sourcing manpower?

Social networking sites as potential source to collect and compile information about the potential candidates have not become very common. Particularly for recruitment of executives and managerial-level employees such trend is very common. Social networking sites not only allow the candidates to put their profile, but also allow organizations to collect information about the candidates. With analytics, scope of information gathering has now extended beyond such basic search, i.e., collecting information about potential candidates' preferences, likes and dislikes, interests, type of people they like to associate, how frequently use such sites to share information about him/her, and even information on topical events, etc.

LinkedIn is now considered one of the important social networking sites for job recruitment. This has been acknowledged by several researchers. LinkedIn is essentially a professional networking site since 2003. Since then, it has built its large memberships in more than 200 countries. Also companies in large number are now professional members of LinkedIn. HR professionals almost to the extent of 90% today are member of LinkedIn. Like LinkedIn, Facebook and Twitter also are other two important social networking sites, which can help in getting the potential candidates for various jobs. However, many companies use these social networking sites for information compilation on potential job candidates, side by side continuing with their traditional practice of recruitment. This group of HR professionals believes that in this way they can make their recruitment decisions more holistic and efficient. Adjudging the candidacy of potential candidates based on their social networking profiles may not be always a foolproof method, because people tend to have their cool social identity. For such reasons, it is important to simultaneously continue with the traditional process of profile matching and recruitment.

With increased number of cases of deceptive use of social media for job soliciting, companies are still not very convinced about its potential benefits, and truly cannot base their profile selection and recruitment decisions based on this information.

Question: Identify some companies making use of social networking sites for recruitment. List their experiences (both good and bad).

REFERENCES

Allport, G.W. (1937), *Personality: A psychological interpretation*. London: Constable.

Allport, G.W. (1961), *Pattern and growth in personality*. New York: Holt, Rinehart and Winston.

Bandura, A. (1977), *Social Learning Theory*. New York: General Learning Press.

Brannick, M.T. and Levine, E.L. (2002), *Job analysis: Methods, research, and applications*. Thousand Oaks, CA: Sage.

Berne, E. (1961), *Transaction Analysis in Psychotherapy: A systematic individual and social psychiatry*, New York, Grove Press.

Borgen, F.H., Harmon, L.W. (1996), "Linking interest assessment and personality theory: an example of convergence between practice and theory", in Savickas, M.L. and Walsh, W.B. (Eds), Handbook of Career Counseling and Practice, Davies-Black, Palo Alto, CA, pp. 251–66.

Bourdieu, P. (1984), *Distinction: A Social Critique of the Judgment of Taste*. Cambridge, MA: Harvard University Press.

Butler, T. and James, W. (1999), "Job Sculpting: The Art of Retaining your Best People", Harvard Business Review, 77(5): 144–152, 186.

Carver, C.S. and Scheier, M.F. (2000), *Perspectives on Personality* (4th ed.), Simon and Schuster, Needham Heights, MA.

Costa, P.T. and McCrae, R.R. (1992), Revised NEO Personality Inventory: Professional A manual. Florida: Psychological Assessment Resources.

Costa, P.T. and McCrae, R.R. (1994), "Set like plaster? Evidence for stability of adult personality", In Heatherton, T.F. and Weinberger, J.L. (Eds.) Can personality change? (pp. 21–39). Washington: APA.

Cunningham, J.W., Boese, R.R., Neeb, R.W. and Pass, J.J. (1983), Systematically derived work dimensions: Factor analyses of the Occupational Analysis Inventory. *Journal of Applied Psychology*, 68: 232–252.

Elliot, J. and Ryan, S. (2004), Race, Gender, and Workplace Power. American Sociological Review, 69: 356–386.

Eysenck, H.J. (2006), The Biological basis of personality. London: Transaction Publishers.

Fine, S. and Wiley, W. (1971), An introduction to functional job analysis: Methods for manpower analysis. Kalamazoo, Mich.: Upjohn Institute for Employment Research, (Methods for Manpower Analysis #4).

Fleishman, E.A. and Mumford, M.D. (1991), Evaluating classifications of job behavior: A construct validation of the ability requirement scales, Personnel Psychology, 44: 523–575.

Furnham, A. (1997), The Psychology of Behavior at work: The individual in an organization, Psychology Press, East Sussex, U.K.

Goldberg, L.R. (1993), The structure of phenotypic personality traits. American Psychologist, 48(1): 26–34.

Goleman, D. (1995), Emotional Intelligence, Bantam Books, New York.

Hall, D.T. (1996), Protean Careers of the 21st Century, The Academy of Management Executive, 10(4): 8–16.

Harvey, R.J. (1991b), The common-metric questionnaire (CMQ): A job analysis system (1st edition). San Antonio, TX: The Psychological Corporation.

Hersey, P., Blanchard, K.H. and Johnson, D.E. (2008), *Management of Organizational Behavior*, 9th edition, Upper Saddle River, NJ, Pearson Education.

Holland, J.L. (1997), Making Vocational Choices: A Theory of Vocational Personalities and Work Environments, 3rd ed., Psychological Assessments Resources, Odessa, FL.

Jackson, N. and Carter, P. (2000), *Rethinking Organizational Behavior*, Harlow, England, Financial Times/Prentice Hall.

Jung, C. (1923), *Psychological Types*, London, Routledge and Kepan Paul.

Keirsey, D. (1998), Please Understand Me II. Prometheus Nemesis.

Kristof, A.L. (1996), "Person-organization fit: an integrative review of its conceptualizations, measurement, and implications", Personnel Psychology, 49: 1–49.

Lareau, A. and Elliot, W. (2003), "Cultural Capital in Educational Research: A Critical Assessment", Theory and Society 32: 567–606.

Luft, J. (1961), "The Johari Window", Human Relations Training News, 5(1): 6–7.

Luthans, F. (1973), *Organizational Behavior*, New York, McGraw-Hill.

Maddi, S.R. (2006), "Taking the theorizing in personality theories seriously", American Psychologist, 61: 330–331.

Maslow, A.H. (1954), *Motivation and Personality*, New York, Harper.

Mayers, I.B. and Mc-Caulley, (1985), "A Guide to the Development and Use of Mayers-Briggs Type Indicator", Palo Alto: CA, Consulting Psychologist Press.

McCrae, R.R. and Costa, P.T. (1995), "Trait explanations in personality psychology", European Journal of personality, 9: 231–252.

McCormick, E.J., Jeanneret, P.R. and Mecham, R.C. (1972), "A study of job characteristics and job dimensions as based on the Position Analysis Questionnaire (PAQ)". *Journal of Applied Psychology*, 56(4): 347–368.

Mischel, W., Shoda, Y. and Smith, R.E. (2004), *Introduction to personality: Toward Integration*. Hoboken, NJ: J. Wiley & Sons.

Murray, H.A. (1938), *Explorations in Personality*, New York, Oxford University Press.

Myers, I.B. (1962), The Myers-Briggs Type Indicator. California: Consulting Psychologists Press.

Raymark, P.H., Schmit, M.J. and Guion, R.M. (1997), "Identifying potentially useful personality constructs for employee selection", Personnel Psychology, 50: 723–736.

Rorschach, H. (1998), *Psycho diagnostics: A Diagnostic Test Based on Perception* (10th ed.). Cambridge, MA: Hogrefe Publishing Corp.

Rotter, J.B. (1966), "Generalized expectancies for internal versus external control of reinforcement", *Journal of Consulting and Clinical psychology*, 41: 297–405.

Saville and Holdsworth Ltd. USA, Inc. (1990), *Work Profiling System Manual*. Boston: Saville and Holdsworth Ltd. USA, Inc.

Smith, M. (1994), "A theory of the validity of predictors in selection", *Journal of Occupational and Organizational Psychology*, 67: 13–31.

Tilly, C. and Charles, T. (1998), Work under Capitalism. Boulder, CO: West view Press.

Zanden, J. (1987), *Social Psychology*, New York: McGraw-Hill.

Chapter 4

Policies and Procedures for Recruitment and Selection

LEARNING OBJECTIVES

After reading this chapter, you will be able to understand:

1 Concepts of recruitment and selection policies
2 Importance and significance of recruitment and selection policies
3 Process of developing recruitment and selection policies
4 Aligning recruitment and selection policies with HR strategies and business goals

When recruitment through social media is your policy: lessons from L'Oreal

L'Oreal, more than a century-old global cosmetics major, operates from 130 countries. With 78,600 headcounts (2014) and 22.53 billion Euros turnover, the company is consistently growing. L'Oreal employees represent 156 different nationalities. The France-based company has successfully embraced the global culture, in terms of both workforce-mix and their product portfolio. With innovation as the key driving force, the company, like others, also competes for talent. This makes recruitment and selection function of L'Oreal more challenging. The company today makes extensive use of social media for attracting talent. Even for recruitment in India, the company today has embraced the policy of recruitment through social media. The career site of the company connects to Facebook, Twitter, Linkedin sites, which have been carefully designed by the company to attract more and more new talents to the organization. For example, they have L'Oreal Talent Recruitment Facebook Page, L'Oreal LinkedIn Page, L'Oreal Luxe TalentTube Facebook Page, @LOrealCareers Twitter, etc. The company even designed such social media recruitment sites, pacing with country-specific culture and recruitment needs, viz., facebook.lorealusa.jobs, twitter.lorealusa.jobs, linkedin.lorealusa.jobs, etc. The company proclaims such recruitment policy through social media could substantially reduce their recruitment costs in each location, from where they operate. Also this could substantially increase their talent pool, as through social media, they could reach to large cross-sections of target employees. With more than 59% women employees, and 44% of women on executive committees, the company today is a success story in creating a culture of innovation and diversity inclusion. Using social media as their prime source of recruitment, the company's talent reach today has become global.

INTRODUCTION

Policies are documented guidelines for decision-making. With policies organizations can delegate functions to people down the hierarchical chain. Of course this requires additional support of procedures. Procedures detail the steps and actions necessary for implementing policy. For their routine, repetitive, and operational functions, organizations prefer to make their decision-making process policy-bound. This helps consistency in decision-making process, and it also can ensure legal compliance. Legal compliance issue is particularly more relevant for human resource management policies, including policies on recruitment and selection. In framing policies, organizations comply with all legal provisions, so that employees can avoid all possible violations, and make their decision-making process compliant with legal, social, and cultural issues and norms.

With policies and procedures, organizations clarify what to do and how to do. Such clarity ensures decisional consistency. Policies need to be developed, pacing with business goals and strategies of the organizations also. Often, we observe organizations face the constraint of policies to achieve their strategic intents. For example, new market development strategy of any organization may get deterred for a recruitment policy that does not allow lateral hiring. Similarly, a compensation policy of an organization may be rigid on pay equity, dissuading new talents to feel attracted to the job positions.

Policies need to be written in a clear unambiguous way, so that it can only carry one meaning. Ambiguous policy statements get interpreted in several ways, resulting confusing actions by the people down the hierarchical chain. As these are the important guiding principles for decision making, many organizations compulsorily take their employees through awareness sessions to clarify their doubts in policy interpretations. It is recommended to first outline the activities for the function on which organization intends to develop policy statements. Identify which types of activities are strategic and which are routine. We do not require policy statements for strategic activities, as strategic decisions are flexible, and require wider considerations of multiple variables. Moreover, strategic decision-making is not delegated to people down the hierarchical chain. Policies are developed for routine decision-making process, which is delegated. With adequate consideration of scope of activities involved in recruitment and selection process, organizations can design policy statements, which are both business goals aligned and strategic-fit.

Along with the policy statements, we also need detailing of procedures that explain who will do what, what would be the steps, and what are the forms and documents required, etc. For each policy statement, we detail procedures in short and specific terms, more in the form of instructions. We can detail procedures with flowcharts also.

Organization-wise recruitment and selection policies vary widely or obvious difference in the values, culture, business goals, and strategies. Therefore, we cannot have any universal template on recruitment and selection policy. However, in this chapter, we have detailed some policy templates, based on which HR managers can develop recruitment and selection policies in their own organizations.

RECRUITMENT AND SELECTION POLICY

A recruitment and selection policy of an organization requires consideration of following facts:

- What are the nature of activities organization is engaged in
- How the organization is planning to recruit people for such activities
- What type of people the organization will recruit
- What process the organization will follow in recruitment and selection
- How the organization is planning to attract the best talent
- How the organization is meeting legal, cultural, and social needs while recruiting
- How recruitment and selection policy is aligned with business goals and strategies
- How the organization ensures fair recruitment and selection
- How recruitment and selection process of the organization is diversity inclusive
- How the organization validates recruitment decisions and calibrate the recruitment and selection policies

Some organizations see recruitment and selection functions are two distinct activities, and therefore may like to have two separate policies. In Chapter 1, although we have defined these two terms separately, but as has been said, operationally in most of the organizations, these two functions are seen as one and the same. Thus, while framing a recruitment policy for an organization, we also bring selection process in its scope, merging both recruitment and selection in one set of policy statements or documents.

Nike's policy changes on recruitment and selection

At any given point of time Nike, the global major in sports shoes and sports ware, needs about 100–120 people for their various job positions. With conventional recruitment and selection process, the company could get 800 applications for the prospective jobs in a month. Realizing such problem in manpower sourcing, more particularly in attracting the talent, the company embraced e-recruitment policy. For Nike each job applicant is also a customer or potential customer, hence responding to job applicants appropriately is a great challenge. Obviously, this requires huge contingent of people, who are capable of analyzing the applications, and arranging for the interview of people who are identified as possible talent for the organization. With e-recruitment solutions, the company could manage their recruitment and selection functions more efficiently. Also in the process the company could achieve cost-effectiveness in recruitment and selection.

In most of the organizations, recruitment and selection policies form important part of their HR policy documents. Primary intents of recruitment and selection policy are to follow a standard process for filling the vacant job positions in organizations. This ensures significant reduction in recruitment bias, and recruitment of the right-fit for the organization, which helps in building the talent pipeline.

At the outset, such policy outlines the hiring process. Depending on the nature of job positions, the company should go for recruitment through campus visits, or advertise the job vacancies in reputed newspapers, or retain consulting organizations, or engage recruitment process outsourcing (RPO) agencies, etc. While identifying possible sources for hiring, the company also considers objectives, finding answers to the purpose of their recruitment initiatives. One of the important objectives of recruitment is also attracting the talent, so that organizations can engage talent and sustain in competition. While for organizations, which are already identified as high brand value, potential employees feel attracted, for other organizations that are equally good and that offer challenging career, also use of social media, as explained in both the cases of L'Oreal and Nike, could be a solution. Such initiatives, of course, require policy support. With consideration of different aspects, mentioned above, organizations can come out with suitable recruitment and selection policy. Once developed such policy needs periodic review, pacing with the changing business goals, strategies, and the market conditions.

Importance and Significance of Recruitment and Selection Policy

As evident from our previous discussions, organizations frame their recruitment and selection policy, outlining certain principles that they follow while conducting the recruitment and selection process. Primary purpose is to ensure hiring of quality manpower, aligning with the business goals, strategies, values, and the culture of the organizations. Other important purposes are legal compliance, unbiased selection process, transparency, etc.

Importance and significance of recruitment and selection policies can be listed as under:

(1) It helps organizations to follow a transparent and efficient recruitment and selection process.
(2) It helps in sourcing appropriate talent to meet the strategic business needs of the organization
(3) It helps in complying with legal, social, and cultural norms
(4) It contributes to organizational brand building
(5) It ensures consistency in recruitment and selection process

(6) It facilitates in making recruitment process credible, thus avoiding any litigation
(7) It can ensure valuing of diversity and ethical norms
(8) It can ensure equality in recruitment decisions
(9) It can delegate the job of recruitment and selection, wherever it is necessary
(10) Through appropriate profile matching, it can facilitate in putting the right man for the right job.

However, the above list is not exhaustive. Indirectly also we can see the importance of such policy, when organizations take policy-bound recruitment and selection decisions. For example, appropriate selection of employees ensures reduced attrition rate, and so also reduced cost of training and supervision. With brand building, organizations can attract talent and strengthen their talent pool. It also can promote a culture of efficient productivity and performance.

Developing Recruitment and Selection Policies

We already know the scope of recruitment and selection policy for any organization need to be defined first to list the possible areas on which we may require policy statements. Depending on the understanding of such a scope, we need to develop our policies, and so also detail the procedures to implement policies to make sure that the recruitment process in the organization is to the extent compliant with the legal, social, and cultural mandates. Let us first understand what could be the scope of recruitment and selection function of an organization. For a typical large organization, recruitment and selection cycle extends to multiple activities. Some of the common activities are listed as follows:

(1) **Assess the need for and establish the purpose of the position**
(2) **Perform a position analysis**—emphasizing on creating a job profile
(3) **Prepare the position description**—in alignment with the organizational goals. It includes job title, working conditions, procedures, and conditions of employment, performance expectations, etc.
(4) **Forming recruitment committee**—members of such committee are empowered to take recruitment and selection decisions, conducting search for the potential candidates, arranging for the interview, selection, and recommend sending the offer of employment. In many organizations, search committee is represented by cross-functional team members, in addition to HR, and depending on the level of job position, even outside experts are involved.

(5) **Preparing detailed outline for the job position requirements and arranging for advertisement for sourcing**—job position outline contents information on expected contributions from the potential candidates, knowledge, and experience requirements, employment conditions, etc. Advertising for the job positions and possible source of identifying the potential manpower depends on the position levels and specific policies of the organization.

(6) **Screening of the applicants**—done through the process of profile matching.

(7) **Arranging for the interview**—with the screened list of the short-listed candidates, interview process is first decided (say, should it be first telephone, over Skype, or face to face, etc.), and then interview schedule is drawn by the selection committee, ensuring each interview panel is represented by not only the subject matter experts, but also cross-functional experts, so that appropriate identification of talent can be done, and only the best-fits are finally selected. A structured approach for the interview and ranking of interview scores as per the predecided criteria to a great extent can ensure fair selection process.

(8) **Drawing the list of selected candidates**—with consideration of interview scores, experience, education, age, health status, etc.

(9) **Outlining process of reference checks**—instead of doing on their own, some organizations prefer to outsource this function hiring some professional agencies.

(10) **Sending offer of employment**—the final stage of recruitment and selection cycle with complete details of information about the salary, probationary period, induction programs, career advancement information, etc.

In addition to the above, some organizations even include induction and onboarding processes in recruitment and selection cycle. In such cases, we need appropriate detailing of the policy statements covering such functions.

Even though researchers and practitioners have long urged organizations to make basic changes in the recruitment and selection process when implementing quality management practices (Bowen and Lawler, 1992), very few organizations implementing quality management pay requisite attention to these suggestions even today (Snell et al., 2000).

Why recruitment and selection policies are important can be understood from the contributions of Kilibarda and Fonda (1997), who had observed that organizations fail in differentiating between good practice and common practice in recruitment and selection, and adopt a rational approach. Such a problem can be mitigated substantially once organizations develop their recruitment and selection policies, emulating the best practice of world-class organizations. Similarly, Anderson and Shackleton (1986) indicated that the quality of new recruits depends upon an organization's recruitment practices, and that the relative effectiveness of the selection phase is inherently dependent upon the calibre of candidates attracted. Indeed, Smith et al. (1989) argue that the more effectively the recruitment stage is carried out the less important the actual selection process becomes. When an organization makes the decision to fill an existing vacancy through recruitment, the first stage in the process involves conducting a comprehensive job analysis. This may already have been conducted through the human resource planning process, particularly where recruitment is a relatively frequent occurrence. Once a job analysis has been conducted, the organization has a clear indication of the particular requirements of the job, where that job fits into the overall organization structure, and can then begin the process of recruitment to attract suitable candidates for the particular vacancy.

According to the institutional theory (DiMaggio and Powell, 1983), organizations adopt certain practices based on the pressures from their internal or external environments. These may be "coercive" pressures like laws regulating certain employment practices in organizations, "mimetic" pressures like the use of practices that seem to be effective in competitors, or "normative" pressures like practices inspired by shared professional values among HRM professionals. Compared to small organizations, larger organizations are more prone to institutional isomorphism. They will feel stronger coercive pressures since many laws place extra requirements on organizations employing more than a certain number of people. They will have more mimetic pressures since large organizations will require more accountability from the managers on decisions that they have made and many managers will take the tried and tested methods used by others in the market. They will have more normative pressures since larger organizations are more likely to employ more HRM staff who will try to bring their professional values to the organization. On the other hand, small organizations are not under the same levels of pressure as large organizations. They develop their own practices that are suitable for their culture and organization. Some empirical studies depict that informal recruitment methods produce workers who stay with the organization longer than those recruited by other methods (Taylor, 1994; Breaugh, 1981). In addition to lower turnover, some researchers have investigated the relationship between recruitment methods and job performance of recruits. Taylor and Schmidt (1983) found that employees who were recruited through informal methods received higher appraisals from their supervisors compared to those who were recruited through other methods.

For many organizations recruitment and selection policy is a standard procedural guideline. Ingersoll Rand, the century-old industrial conglomerate, follow certain principles for their recruitment and selection policy. These principles include informing job applicants on the application procedure and vacancy details, nature of information required to assess the suitability of the applicant, confidentiality of job applicants' information, and answering to written complaints of job applicants on the selection process.

Aligning Recruitment and Selection Policies with HR Strategies and Business Goals

Recruitment and selection process is the most important value-adding activity of any organization. With people, organizations can differentiate them from their competitors, can create an innovative and sustainable performance-driven workplace, and can sustain and grow. Obviously, this requires our careful thoughts to align recruitment and selection functions with the HR strategies and business goals, which we ensure right from the beginning, by designing the appropriate HR framework, which can help in measuring the results. Many organizations use balanced scorecard for this purpose.

Essentially, recruitment and selection function of any organization integrates all HR activities, HR strategies, and the business goals. With appropriate recruitment and selection, organizations can do effective succession planning for grooming in-house talents for future leadership roles, develop appropriate employee promotion policies, performance management systems and training and development. As it is a primary level HR function, and success of an organization largely depends on the quality of people hired, while designing the policy, organizations need to ensure that it supports in achieving the strategic intents and the business goals. Wherever policies become a constraint or a deterrent in achieving the strategic intents, organizations may review and if required even bring changes in such policies.

All organizations draw their annual business plans. They brainstorm, set their planning premises, and then go for drawing the plans. Recruitment and selection plays the most critical role in business plans. It requires divisional and unit heads to understand the available competencies in the organization to sustain the new business plans. When we do not have a competency-based HR system, at least we look for the skill inventories that can talk about the potentiality of our available manpower. When we observe the gap, we think first the potentiality of new hiring. Are these people available on hire? In many new skill-sets we may have the difficulty to get the people, or even if we get the people, compensation cost may not commensurate with the benefits. For new hires again we have to invest on training, and also allow the time to deliver results. Apportioning the costs of training and the costs of under performance during the period of settlement, we can understand how it affects our business plan. This is why we often go by the conventional approach of leveraging our core competencies for expanded business plans.

But our business plans may also require truncating some activities, or reducing the business volume, for unfavorable market conditions. In such cases, we think about our redundancy plans. Cost of employees' separation may be enormous for our bottom line. Side by side with our plan for redundancy, we have to go for redeployment plan for our surplus employees also, if required, even at the cost of skill-change training. But all employees may not be redeployed in or within the same job family, for obvious skill and knowledge mismatch. We may have to put them in different jobs, which may or may not be accepted by them. In most of the cases, companies manage to adjust such surplus employees in those jobs which are presently outsourced by them. Although the change management issues are critical here for employees' resistance, things can yet be manageable with employees' education depending on its necessity.

It is advisable to prepare a detailed checklist to test our alignment of business plan with recruitment and selection policies.

Similarly, we draw strategies to realize results of our business plans. Strategies that way give us direction. While we frame strategies, we consider the scope of our organization (to dissuade ourselves to take any strategies that may not be endorsed by our vision), thinking on resource allocation (through optimization of competing needs), and thinking on its abilities to cope with the situation of uncertainty. With such primary level understanding, we align our strategies with the recruitment and selection policies. For alignment with HR strategies, we need to consider one more important aspect of our organization, i.e., the structure. Human resource requirements widely vary with our organization structure. In a hierarchical or tall structure with narrow span of control, we need more manpower. With wide span of control, manpower requirement reduces. Again, hierarchical structure may not hold good for our new strategies. We may require matrix or strategic business unit (SBU) form of organization. Globally, many organizations experimented with matrix structure for manpower optimization. But dual reporting systems often dilute the purpose. The success rate is not encouraging. Matrix structure even though a breakthrough from the traditional hierarchical organization, but for augmented command and control, it suffers from the problems of conflict of interests, ultimately defeats the purpose of manpower optimization.

Again matrix structure requires more multi-skilled manpower with exposure to multiple products, services, and functions of the company. Even deployment of people from one matrix to another, in the same function, may require different skill sets, for difference in the work processes. It means sustaining a matrix structure requires more matured and experienced human resources who understand the dynamics of the organization.

To achieve our strategic intents, we may be requiring SBUs, so that each product or service vertical gets dedicated support. But running profit centers by SBU heads requires them to possess holistic skills and knowledge.

Thus, in either way, we need to consider the structure–strategy nexus along with our recruitment and selection. We already have a standing debate which comes first—structure or strategy. In this era of business complexities, structure must not stand against strategy. It means we need to make our structure as flexible as possible, to realize our ever-changing strategies. This obviously makes recruitment and selection function a more challenging function in organizations.

As in the case of alignment with business goals, for appropriate alignment of recruitment and selection policies with HR strategies, we also require appropriate checklist.

SUMMARY

- Recruitment and selection policies facilitate in appropriate hiring of quality manpower for achieving organizational strategies and business goals. It ensures consistency in recruitment and selection decisions, brings transparency, makes such decisions un-biased, and ethics and culture-fit. Also suitably designed recruitment and selection policy can align with the social and cultural norms and legal requirements.
- Because of strategic relevance, organizations while developing such policies consider their core objectives, and then assess to what extent such objectives can be achieved through such policy guidelines.
- Although we may not have any universal template for recruitment and selection policies, as it widely varies with the organizational needs, the template given in this chapter can serve as an important guide in preparing the policy documents.

Key Words

Recruitment policy: Documented guidelines for recruitment and selection decision-making.

Recruitment procedures: Detailing of steps to be followed in implementing the recruitment policy.

Recruitment committee: A search committee represented by cross-functional team members, in addition to HR. Depending on the level of job position, even outside experts are involved.

Screening of the applicants: Done through the process of profile matching.

Review Questions

1. What is a recruitment policy? How recruitment policy is different from recruitment procedure?
2. Discuss the importance and significance of recruitment and selection policy in organizations.
3. What steps do organizations need to follow while developing their recruitment and selection policies?
4. Explain how recruitment and selection policies can be aligned with HR strategies and business goals of organizations.
5. Write short notes on:
   (a) Institutional theory
   (b) Procedural guideline
   (c) Nimetic pressures
   (d) Normative pressures
   (e) RPO

Critical Review Question

1. Visit recruitment and selection policies of a large manufacturing organization. Explain how this organization could align such policies with their HR strategies and business goals.

Template of Recruitment and Selection Policy

Policy statement

This policy of recruitment and selection of XYZ Company commits to provide equal access of employment opportunities to all cross-sections of people of our society, so that we can select the best person in terms of knowledge, skills, experience, and aptitude for respective job positions.

Policy purpose

This policy sets out guidelines on:

- Job Descriptions

- Person Specifications
- Advertising Job Vacancies
- Application Procedures
- Short Listing Procedures
- Reference Checks
- Offers of Employment
- Management of Panels
- Unsuccessful Candidates

This policy should be applied whenever a position becomes available within XYZ.

Scope

This policy applies to all recruitment and selection activities of the organization, both on permanent payroll and contractual for all levels of employees, including executives and managers, except for the senior managerial level employees. All divisional heads and managerial employees have access to this policy document. Any selection in violation of the policy documents will make the person liable for disciplinary action, and such selection decision will be void.

Policy overview

Vacancy review

Whenever a post is declared vacant, HR head needs to review existing manpower position within the organization, and wherever possible HR head will try to explore the possibilities of filling such vacancies through internal manpower restructuring. Else HR head will clear the vacancies for external hire.

Sending of recruitment requisition

With clearance from HR head for external hiring, divisional heads will send the recruitment requisition to HR with information details, like job position(s), vacancies in each job category, job specifications and descriptions, specific skill-sets and competency requirements, preferred level of recruitment, duration of requirement, etc. Such detailing must be as wider as possible, so that appropriate sourcing initiatives can be taken by the HR.

Job advertisement

Any job vacancies, except at senior managerial level, must be advertised in national newspapers/job portals/company's website with as clear information as possible. Application blanks would be made available on company's career site, and all applicants would be advised to apply through the given web-links. Instant shortlisting of the candidates would be done electronically, and an autogenerated regret letter would be sent to those whose profiles are not selected.

Shortlisting

Shortlisted candidates would be informed with more details of the job positions and the schedule of the selection interview.

Interviewing and selection

For all interviews of nonexecutive job positions at least two persons form an interview panel, of which one must be the representative from the concerned department, where the job vacancies exist. For executive and managerial level job vacancies, the interview panel additionally should also have two more representatives, one from other department, and the other external functional expert.

Aggregating the interview scores, selection panel will be drawn and the panel will send their recommendation to HR head for further action.

Reference checking

HR will compulsorily conduct reference checking of all selected candidates, irrespective of their levels of appointment, retaining the services of empanelled recruitment process outsourcing (RPO) vendors. Any negative information will be taken seriously and the concerned candidate would be kept outside the scope of final selection.

Final approval from CEO

Final approval from CEO must be taken by the HR head before sending the formal offer letter to the finally selected candidates.

Sending of formal offer letter

Finally selected candidates will be sent a formal offer letter with details of contract note, with an advice to sign as a token of acceptance of employment offer and sending back to the HR department within a given time schedule.

Along with this policy documents, XYZ has also developed a procedural document.

Recruitment and Selection Procedure

Statement of purpose

This recruitment and selection procedure helps in implementing the recruitment and selection policies, detailed in a separate document. These procedures outline actions to be taken against each policy, so that conformity with the policy requirements and adherence to the values and culture of the organization gets maintained.

Job description

After the occurrence of the job vacancy, a detailed job description is prepared covering following aspects:

- Job title
- Location of the position
- Job reporting
- Job purpose
- Key activities
- Specific activities

Job/person specification

This includes specific requirements of:

- Knowledge
- Skills
- Competencies
- Education
- Experience
- Other attributes essential for the job performance

Job advertisement

Advertisements for the job positions are made in national newspapers/job portals and company's websites. Following information is essential for job advertisements:

- Job title
- Brief job description
- Job location
- Essential and desirable qualifications and experience requirements
- Nature of employment
- How candidates can apply for the job
- Closing date of job application
- Contact details for further information (for managerial employees only)

Job application processing and shortlisting

Refer to the policy documents.

Selection process and interviewing

Refer to the policy documents.

Reference checking

Refer to the policy documents.

Sending of offer letter

Refer to the policy documents.

Multiple Choice Questions

1. Indicate which is not a valid statement for policies
   (a) Policies are documented guidelines for decision making
   (b) Policies help in delegating functions to people down the hierarchical chain
   (c) Policies are implemented with the help of procedures
   (d) Policies can facilitate strategic decision making process
   (e) None of the above

2. Ambiguous policy statements:
   (a) Carry more than one meaning
   (b) Get interpreted in several ways
   (c) Leads to confusing actions by the people down the line
   (d) All of the above
   (e) None of the above

3. For strategic activities we require:
   (a) Separate policies
   (b) We require corporate policies
   (c) We require operational policies
   (d) We require policies on organizational control
   (e) None of the above

4. Along with the policy statement we also need detailing of ....:
   (a) Strategies
   (b) Culture
   (c) Norms
   (d) Procedures
   (e) Legal provisions

5. A recruitment and selection policy of an organization requires consideration of following facts, excepting
   (a) How the organization is planning to recruit people for such activities
   (b) What type of people organization will recruit
   (c) How organization can benchmark with competitors
   (d) What process organization will follow in recruitment and selection
   (e) How organization is planning to attract the best talent

6. Importance and significance of recruitment and selection policies can be understood in terms of the following, excepting:
   (a) It helps organizations to follow a transparent and efficient recruitment and selection process.
   (b) It helps in sourcing appropriate talent to meet the strategic business needs of the organization
   (c) It helps in complying with legal, social, and cultural norms
   (d) It contributes to organizational brand building
   (e) None of the above
7. Recruitment and selection policies ensure consistency in recruitment and selection process by:
   (a) Facilitating recruitment process credible, thus avoiding any litigation
   (b) It can ensure valuing of diversity and ethical norms
   (c) It can ensure equality in recruitment decisions
   (d) Through appropriate profile matching, it can facilitate in putting right man for the right job.
   (e) All of the above
8. Which is not activity in developing recruitment and selection policies:
   (a) Assessing the purpose of the job position
   (b) Carrying out position analysis
   (c) Process of screening of the applicants
   (d) Job outsourcing
   (e) Forming of recruitment committee
9. Identify the incorrect statement:
   (a) Recruitment and selection policies do not consider issues pertaining to the arrangement of interview
   (b) Process of drawing the list of selected candidates
   (c) Process of reference checking
   (d) Process of sending employment
   (e) None of the above
10. Indicate which statement(s) make(s) recruitment and selection functions more important in organizations:
   (a) People differentiate organization from their competitors
   (b) People can create and innovate
   (c) People can create sustainable performance driven workplace
   (d) People can help organizations to sustain and grow
   (e) All of the above

Answers:

1. (d) 2. (d) 3. (e) 4. (d) 5. (c) 6. (e) 7. (e) 8. (d)
9. (e) 10. (e)

CASE STUDY

Policy impediment for a clogged talent pipeline: experience of ABC limited

For ABC hiring strictly conforms to their policies on recruitment and selection. As a start-up in e-marketing, for initial 5 years ABC's hiring decisions were taken by their founder chairman-cum-CEO Mr. Arvind. However, with business expansion, more particularly for cross-border markets, Mr. Arvind now engaged a new CEO and team of professionals to manage ABC, confining his role in framing long-term strategies for the organization. With such structural change, Arvind felt the need for having detailed policy guidelines on recruitment and selection. He did form a team under the chairmanship of the newly appointed CEO to look into this matter and come out with a well-thought policy document in alignment with the strategies and business goals of ABC.

After reviewing the current business portfolio, ABC's business goals, and strategies, the team came out with the policy statements on recruitment and selection. As a policy the team agreed that recruitment for the managerial employees will only be made at the entry level. Each newly appointed management trainee will be taken through a structured induction program for two weeks. After such induction, they will be rotated around different jobs of ABC, and final placement would be given in the preferred job position of such new recruits. To ensure that talent pipeline does not get clogged, ABC has developed a structured career progression path for management trainees. Each management trainee has to complete some fixed years of service, before their case of promotion is considered. Rising through the career ladder, in addition to the completion of mandated years' of service in a particular grade, also requires management trainees who consistently perform at "above expectation level," for the targets assigned to them by their immediate seniors.

ABC, however, observed that such management trainees who are hired from campuses of renowned business schools, and engineering institutions, almost to the extent of 50% leave their jobs within three years. It means such a huge number of management trainees do not even wait for their next promotion opportunity, else prefer to join with a competing organization. Such high rate of attrition created a vacuum in ABC's talent pipeline. The CEO of the company decided to go for lateral hire, but divisional heads are more in favor of accelerated promotion for the smart performers, even though they have not completed their stipulated years' of service in the job.

Mr. Arvind now has to intervene in this matter.

Questions: What would be the line of action for Mr. Arvind?

REFERENCES

Anderson, N. and Shackleton, V. (1986), "Recruitment and selection: a review of developments in the 1980s", *Personnel Review*, 15(4): 19–25.

Breaugh, J.A. (1981), "Relationships between recruiting sources and employee tenure, absenteeism, and work attitudes", *Academy of Management Journal*, 24: 142–7.

Bowen, D.E. and Lawler, E.E. III (1992), "Total quality-oriented human resources management", *Organizational Dynamics*, 20(4): 29–41.

Dimaggio, P.J. and Powell, W. (1983), "The Iron Cage revisited: institutional isomorphism and collective rationality in organizational fields", *American Sociological Review*, (48): 147–60.

Kilibarda, P. and Fonda, N. (1997), "Random selection", *People Management*, December, pp. 36–9.

Smith, M., Gregg, M. and Andrews, D. (1989), Selection and Assessment ± A New Appraisal, Pitman, London.

Snell, S.A., Lepak, D.P., Dean, J.W. Jr and Youndt, M.A. (2000), "Selection and training for integrated manufacturing: the moderating effects of job characteristics", *The Journal of Management Studies*, 37(3): 445–66.

Taylor, M.S. and Schmidt, D.W. (1983), "A process oriented investigation of recruitment source effectiveness", *Personnel Psychology*, 36: 343.

Taylor, S. (1994), "The relationship between sources of new employees and attitudes toward the job", *The Journal of Social Psychology*, 134(1): 99–111.

Chapter 5

Strategic Recruitment and Selection

LEARNING OBJECTIVES

After reading this chapter, you will be able to understand:

1 Definitions and concepts of strategic recruitment and selection
2 Dimensions of recruitment and selection strategies
3 Features of recruitment and selection strategies
4 Importance of recruitment and selection strategies
5 Steps for recruitment and selection strategies
6 Connecting recruitment and selection with strategies and business goals

For NTPC attracting talent in power plants is a big challenge

In NTPC people work to enjoy and enjoy to work. Obviously, this is the prime reason why this public sector company attracts 1.6 lakh applications for filling their vacancies of 300–400 engineers every year. What is strategic recruitment and selection approach of the company which attracts the best engineering talent in the country? Company's chairman feels that this is attributable to the best training facilities, which the young talent wants. Other reasons obviously are the competitive pay package, which is comparable with the private sector, work–life balancing, open work culture (hardly any power distance even up to the level of Chairman-Cum-Managing Director), functional autonomy, opportunity to implement new learning, diversity inclusion, etc. The 1975 company with 25,230 (2015) headcounts and gender ratio of 1:15 (female to male) is one of the best examples of a company with high brand value. Most of the power plants of NTPC are located in remote areas, even then people enjoy working, as in work sites NTPC provides the best quality of work life, like Wi-Fi township, best English medium schools for children, shopping malls, medical facilities, etc.

INTRODUCTION

Organizations can get sustainable competitive advantage only through human resources (Bhattacharyya, 2014; Buderi, 2000; Nahapiet and Ghoshal, 1998; Grant, 1996). Obviously, futuristic organizations will continue to nurture their long-term vision, assuming that they would be able to get quality human resources who can facilitate in the creation of knowledge and develop unique competence, which can differentiate them from their competitors. Attracting, developing, and retaining quality human resources, or for that matter talent management (Bhattacharyya, 2015), requires strategic management of recruitment and selection function. Strategic recruitment and selection ensures availability of quality human resources. It assumes through recruitment of quality human resources, organizations can achieve both long-term and short-term strategic goals. Hence, recruitment and selection strategies can be defined as the process of developing specific recruitment and selection plan in line with organizational strategy, with adequate detailing on specific job requirements. This way strategic recruitment and selection can help in achieving the overall organizational strategic and business needs. Assumptions are quality human resources will contribute toward achieving the strategic intents. In fact while recruiting people, operationally, organizations limit their strategic focus only on those who are their key employees and who would be driving the organizational growth, and in the process will be helping the organization to achieve its strategic intents. Also strategic recruitment and selection function extends to the process of developing human resources, balancing the mix of human resources, provisioning for contingent manpower, etc. A good example on the need for balancing human resources can be cited, interpreting the trend of recruitment in Indian public sector banks, which is increasingly becoming top-heavy. More managerial-level employees than clerical-level employees could create an important structural problem in the future in Indian public sector banks.

This chapter discusses various strategic issues in recruitment and selection process with proper emphasis on theoretical, conceptual, and operational issues along with the examples from the corporate world.

DEFINITIONS AND CONCEPTS

Human resources are the major differentiators in organizations. Hence, attracting talent, recruitment, and selection function now requires a strategic focus. Strategic recruitment and selection denotes prima facie focus on those key job positions, which are able to anchor the business growth, bring desired changes, and drive a culture of performance. This obviously calls for differentiating between strategic and tactical recruitment and selection. For example, P&G, the global FMCG major, meet their contingent manpower requirement retaining the services of Manpower Group globally. This is, however, one way to look into the strategic recruitment and selection. The more holistic way to explain it as management of recruitment and selection function strategically. From the operational point of view, strategic recruitment and selection means attracting talent and finally selecting them for critical job positions, so that they can cope with situation of uncertainty, give proper direction to the organization, drive change, and transform the organization for long-term sustainability and growth. Obviously, it involves selection of appropriate recruitment channels, taking required initiatives, aligning recruitment and selection process with the business needs of the organizations, retaining the new recruits, focusing on their continuous development, and also optimizing the cost of recruitment. From the organizational point of view only 5% of the job positions may be strategically important.

What constitutes strategic recruitment and selection function? Perhaps the best answer to this is whatever organizations feel important to achieve long-term and sustainable competitive advantages. Evenden

(1993) could see that ensuring quality of workforce is the most important strategic recruitment and selection function of any organization. Koch and McGrath (1996) could relate strategic recruitment and selection process to the use of different channels or sources to ensure a larger pool of applicants. Snell and Dean (1992) considered strategic recruitment and selection process involves human capital development, and use of various recruitment inducements, so that quality manpower feels attracted to the job positions. From a broader perspective, strategic recruitment and selection process also involves critical decisions on balancing between organization-specific skills and general skills, with appropriate mix of manpower availability from within the organization and from the internal or external market sources. More appropriately, Snell et al.'s (1999) suggestions are valid here. Their suggestions are to characterize human resource capabilities from two dimensions, which contribute to firm specific value, and which are unique in nature. Obviously, at organization level, we ensure this balancing at hiring through both internal and external sources.

Also recruitment and selection strategies largely depend on the size of the organization. For example, large organizations may have their strategies to design compensation and benefits program above market rate to attract talent from their competiting organizations. Small organizations may not be able to pay more, but strategically focus on other issues, like job sculpting, innovative work culture, more functional autonomy, etc., to attract talent. Job sculpting is designing of job profile in line with the interests of the employees. In their seminal work on job sculpting, Butler and Waldrop (1999) suggested the need for job sculpting for appropriate job-person-fit, so that people unnecessarily do not require leaving their jobs, as the jobs are not in line with their interests. Job sculpting practices in organizations also attract new talents to organizations.

Based on the introductory discussions, we can think of strategic recruitment and selection from the following perspectives (Fig. 5.1):

(1) Understanding of organizational strategy and resource demands
(2) Reviewing of employees' skills
(3) Manpower planning for the future
(4) Developing recruitment strategy in alignment with business goals
(5) Implementing recruitment strategy through right-fit recruitment process
(6) On-boarding
(7) Developing and retaining talent

In other way, we can see it as design of recruitment and selection process, which can attract talent to the organization, consider strategically

FIGURE 5.1 Perspectives of recruitment and selection.

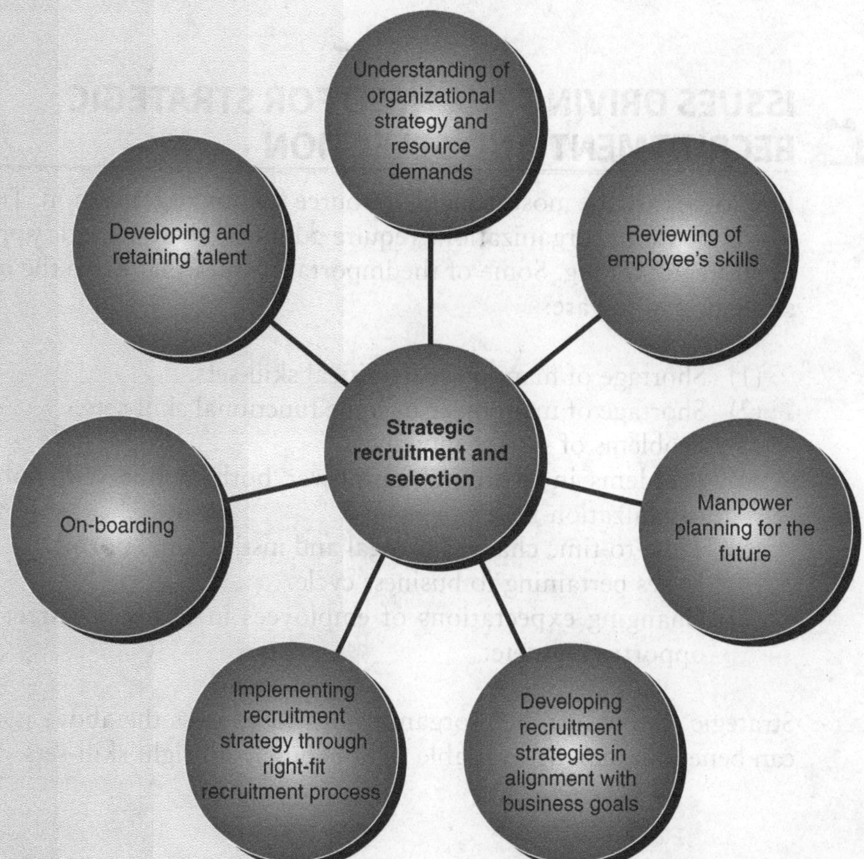

recruitment channels and methods, ensure employer's value proposition, align with the organizational and human resource strategies, and develop suitable action plans for retention of development of talent, after the recruitment and selection process.

Strategic recruitment and selection process analyses the possible implications of recruitment and selection on the strategic, tactical, and operational plans of the organizations. It encompasses even the other related HR functions like onboarding, employee development, promotion, transfer, redeployment, attrition, retention, etc. However, such scope of strategic recruitment and selection will vary from organizations to organizations depending on the strategic, tactical, and operational plans, as based on such plans, critical HR issues vary. From this perspective, we cannot have any universal approach to strategic recruitment and selection.

ISSUES DRIVING THE NEED FOR STRATEGIC RECRUITMENT AND SELECTION

Employees are the most valuable resource for any organization. To sustain in competitions, organizations require adoption of systematic approaches to strategic staffing. Some of the important issues that drive the needs for strategic staffing are:

(1) Shortage of manpower in critical skill-sets.
(2) Shortage of manpower in some functional skill-sets.
(3) Problems of skill redundancy.
(4) Problems in sourcing manpower both in line with job-fit and organization-fit.
(5) Time-to-time changes in legal and institutional norms.
(6) Issues pertaining to business cycle.
(7) Changing expectations of employees in terms of career growth opportunities, etc.

Strategic staffing can help organizations to address the above issues, and can benefit in making available right people with right skill-sets.

IMPORTANT COMPONENTS OF STRATEGIC RECRUITMENT AND SELECTION

Some of the important components of strategic recruitment and selection can be listed as under:

(1) It is process for defining and addressing the staffing implications of an organization's strategic and operational plans.
(2) It is a long-term context for short-term activities.
(3) It focuses on critical issues.
(4) It manages employees' movement in and out of an organization, encompassing recruitment, selection, promotion, transfer, redeployment, attrition, and retention.
(5) It focuses on all human resource management activities that support strategic staffing mission of the organizations. These include employee development, career planning, succession plans, etc.

PURPOSE OF STRATEGIC RECRUITMENT AND SELECTION

Based on our understanding of strategic recruitment and selection functions, including understanding the important components of this function, we can see essentially strategic staffing and recruitment functions serve the following two purposes.

(1) To define and integrate recruitment and selection actions with the long-term strategy and business goals of the organizations.
(2) To identify and develop talent pipeline to meet the changing needs of the organization.

BENEFITS OF STRATEGIC RECRUITMENT AND SELECTION STRATEGY

Recruitment and selection strategy can benefit organizations in many ways. Some of these benefits are listed as follows:

(1) Recruit, develop, and deploy the talent as may be required to meet the present and future demands of organizations.
(2) Calibrate manpower needs meeting changing business needs.
(3) Ensure better utilization of human resources.
(4) Retrain or redeploy employees pacing with the changing needs of the organizations.
(5) Assess nature of future manpower requirements, and accordingly help employees to choose their career anchors and focus on their development plans.
(6) Make effective use of human resources addressing diversity issues and institutionalizing culture of diversity inclusivity.
(7) Help in developing manpower for meeting contingent and tactical human resource requirement.

In addition to business and competitive advantages issues, strategic staffing approach could ensure more inclusivity in terms of diversity, social and ethical norms, legal mandates, etc. Hence, it balances both business and responsibility management aspects in organizations.

To ensure strategic recruitment and selection, practices are institutionalized in organizations. Torrington and Taylor (2002) recommended the need for adequate job analysis and sharing of the job requirements as transparently as possible with the prospective candidates, followed by rigorous selection methods. Selection methods need to ensure screening of abilities and traits of the job applicants, and their compatibility with the organization.

DIMENSIONS OF RECRUITMENT AND SELECTION STRATEGY

Based on our above discussions, it can be said that dimensions of recruitment and selection strategy can be understood in the context of size of an organization. This denotes that depending on the size of the organization, strategy on recruitment and selection would vary. However, for better understanding of dimensions, at the outset we need to get answers to questions, like whom, how, and where to recruit. For example, organizations have to make a choice between recruiting less skilled or better skilled people. While better skilled people may churn out better performance results, organizations may face the challenge of loyalty and high rate of attrition from this category of manpower. Less skilled people with training can be transformed to quality manpower, and their cost of hiring will be lower. The same logic also applies to organizational recruitment decisions visiting campuses of top institutions, vis-à-vis picking up quality students from less known institutions; also hiring of young people so that they can be trained and developed based on organizational changing requirements time to time versus lateral hiring of senior people. Similarly, "whom to recruit" issue also decides between the challenge of internal hiring or hiring from existing employees versus hiring from external sources.

The second dimension, i.e., "how to hire" again requires organizations to adopt different methods of internal and external recruitment. In case of external recruitment, this requires strategic selection of recruitment channels, which can attract more potential talents as candidates for the job positions. Also this dimension requires organizations to strategically decide on manpower vendors for availability of temps and contractual employees, as we have many legal provisions associated with this.

The third dimension on "where to recruit" is more on selection of appropriate labor markets for strategic recruitment of human resources. For example, many multinational companies, while sourcing their manpower in workstations, located in other country (host country), strategically choose people from third country nationals, instead of people from the host country (HCN) (Fig. 5.2).

Yet, in another way, dimension of recruitment and selection strategies also encompasses issues like nature of the organizational activities, organizational spread, level of technology used in the organization, culture of the organization, etc.

FIGURE 5.2 Dimensions of recruitment and selection strategy.

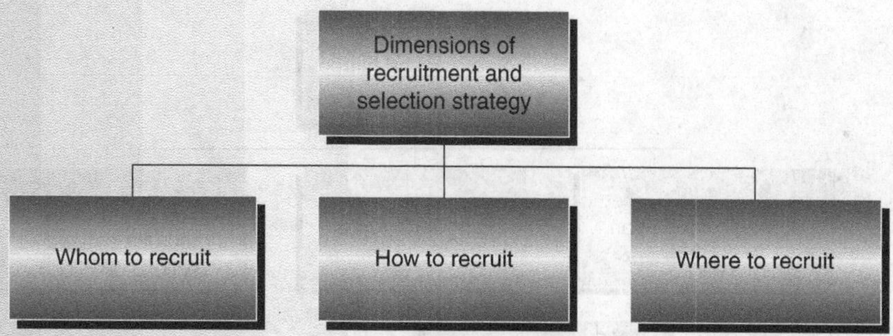

FEATURES OF STRATEGIC RECRUITMENT AND SELECTION

Dimensions of strategic recruitment and selection vary with the nature of organizations. However, features of strategic recruitment and selection are universal in nature. With literature support, this aspect can be authenticated. For example, Sparrow and Hiltrop (1994) identified three interdependent features of strategic recruitment and selection, like integration with organizational strategy, long-term focus, and cascading of organizational strategies to strategic recruitment and selection. These common features primarily acknowledge the need for integration of recruitment and selection process in any organization with the organizational strategy with mandates on alignment of employees' behavior. Idea behind is achievement of overall strategic intents through the process of strategic recruitment and selection process. Yet, in other way, we can understand the features of strategic recruitment and selection as a process of alignment with the vision, mission, goals, and objectives. It is expected that potential people who are selected through the recruitment process would be able to integrate them with such requirements so that organizations can sustain in a globally competitive environment. Miller (1984) viewed features of strategic recruitment and selection as talent identification and attraction, so that best-fit people are recruited for addressing organizational strategic needs. Obviously, this requires not only organizational strategic plans, but also design of suitable recruitment and selection programs to identify the right-fit.

Organizations go for strategic recruitment and selection process to build their capabilities to cope with future uncertainties (Millmore, 2003). In a sense strategic recruitment and selection process helps organizations

FIGURE 5.3 Features of recruitment and selection strategy.

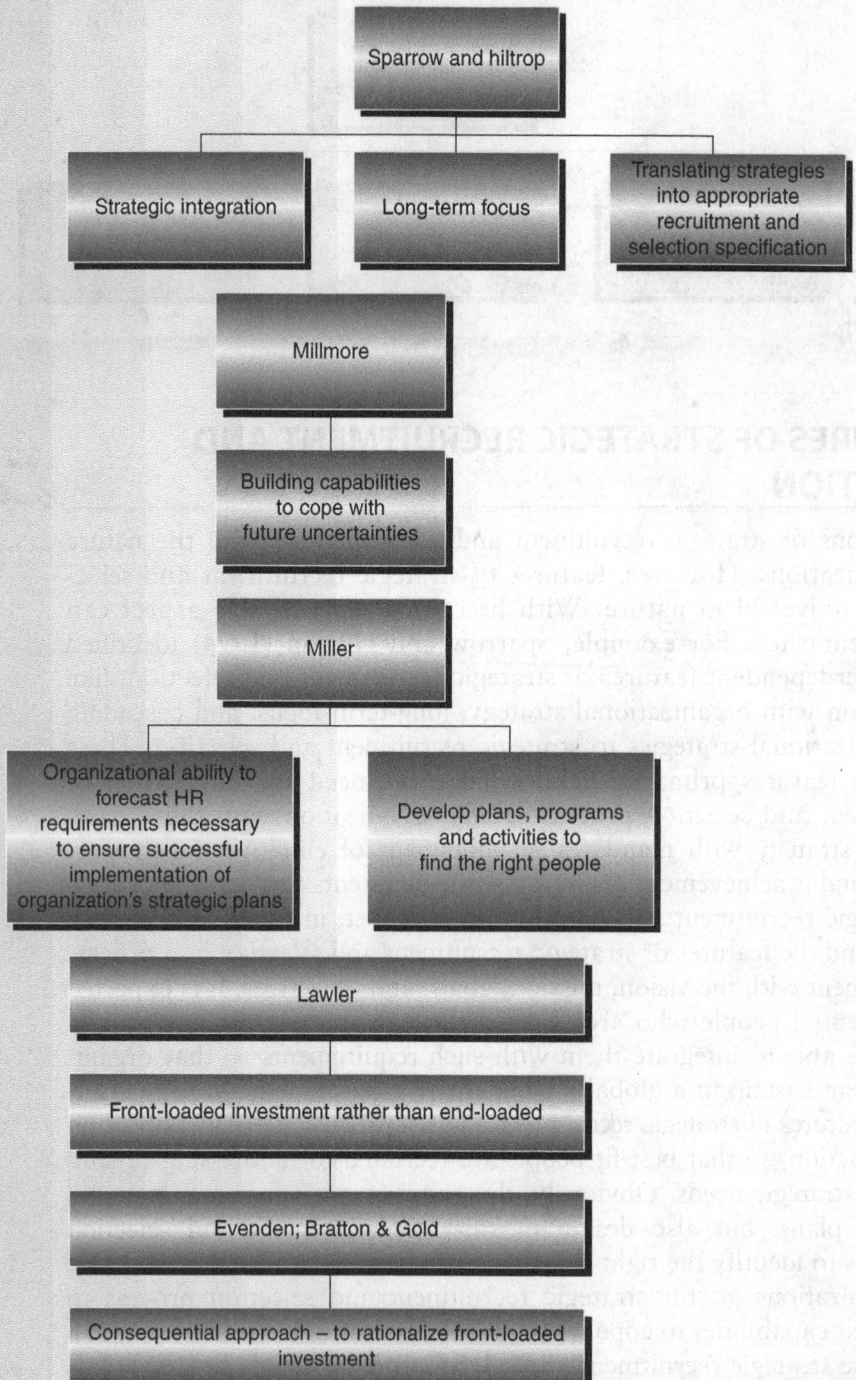

to make them future ready. Lawler (1994) suggested the need for evaluating the respective merits and demerits of strategic recruitment and selection process in terms of front-loaded or end-loaded investment strategies. Many organizations adopt front-loaded investment strategies in recruitment and selection, so that they can select top talent right in the beginning by even offering best compensation and benefits and total rewards program; while some organizations strategically go for end-load recruitment and selection, focusing on potential talent and even suffering from losses in immediate future in terms of poor performance, and high cost of training and development. Evenden (1993), Bratton and Gold (1999) recommended the need for rationalizing front-loaded investment in terms of long-term sustainability and growth of the organizations. Also such decisions must also take into account multi-stakeholders perspectives. Storey and Sisson (1993), however, suggested front-loaded investment in strategic recruitment and selection, rather than risking future investment for nurturing and developing talent (Fig. 5.3).

IMPORTANCE OF STRATEGIC RECRUITMENT AND SELECTION

Organizations focus on strategic recruitment and selection for multiple reasons. Although such importance or reasons are not universal in nature, we can see some degree of commonalities in organizations. These are:

(1) **Planning for the future:** Strategic recruitment and selection process is not just important for filling up of jobs. Many organizations even source best talents, when they are available, expecting their utilization in the future. For example, Apple's entry into retail business was the idea of late Steve Jobs; Tim Cook, current CEO, could make it bigger vertical strategically, recruiting Angela Ahrendts for retail operation with a front-loaded investment approach, i.e., offering higher compensation and benefits packages than many other senior-level employees. Therefore, for effective planning for the future, strategic recruitment and selection is of utmost importance.

(2) **Strategic tie-ups with manpower vendors:** Organizations worldwide are now embracing lean management practices, reducing their current headcounts on permanent payroll to optimum level, and depending on a large number of contingent workers. This requires selecting the appropriate manpower vendors and having strategic tie-up with such vendors, so that such vendors can cater to flexible requirements of organizational manpower. Some manpower

vendors can also help organizations to source talents for recruitment on permanent payroll (Rothwell and Kazanas, 2003). Both P&G and Unilever make use of Manpower Group for meeting their requirements of contingent workforce. For example, Gurgaon-based recruitment process outsourcing (RPO) company People Strong is the manpower vendor for WIPRO.

(3) **Meaningful contribution to HR functions:** Finally, strategic recruitment reinforces HR strategy and in the process helps organizations in achieving their business goals. This is possible as strategic recruitment process can analyze and meet the talent need of the organization in the long run; time-to-time coordinating with the HR departments, sharing information with HR, and giving feedback to HR on availability of critical talent-sets.

STEPS FOR DEVELOPING EFFECTIVE RECRUITMENT AND SELECTION STRATEGIES

To develop effective recruitment and selection strategies, it is important for organizations to follow a structured approach. This need not be based on any established model or models. Depending on specific organizational needs, we require thorough understanding of organizational manpower needs, assess availability of such manpower, make use of metrics and analytics, and then decide our effective recruitment and selection strategies. In these processes, some organizations also create their own recruitment models. Based on these approaches, we can list some of the important steps for recruitment and selection strategies (Fig. 5.4):

(1) **Review of the existing manpower inventory of the organization:** Availability of a structured manpower or skill inventory of an organization provides information on competency levels, skills, qualifications, previous training, education, knowledge, performance records, etc. This helps in framing effective recruitment and selection strategies for the organization.

(2) **Understanding of employment trend within the industry:** This helps in exploring the challenges of predication of critical manpower shortages assessing availability of such manpower from the labor market and so also from competing organizations, etc. Also such research information can help in calibrating compensation and benefits structure for better retention of existing employees in the organization.

(3) **Understanding existing employees' demographic details:** For assessing when the organization may face the challenge of large-scale

manpower replacement, what would be retirement plans of existing employees, would these employees be interested to continue with their job, or are likely to leave, etc.

(4) **Collect inputs from best practice organizations:** This is required to respond to both the nimetic and normative pressures, i.e., the pressure from competing organizations (nimetic) and best practice organizations (normative). This can also be facilitated by reading business journals and strategically deploying research staff to collect such information and feed the same to the organization.

(5) **Collecting labor data and statistics:** For better interpretation of labor market situation, this is helpful.

(6) **Time-to-time calibration of succession plans:** This facilitates in maintaining the talent pipeline.

FIGURE 5.4 Steps for developing effective recruitment and selection strategies.

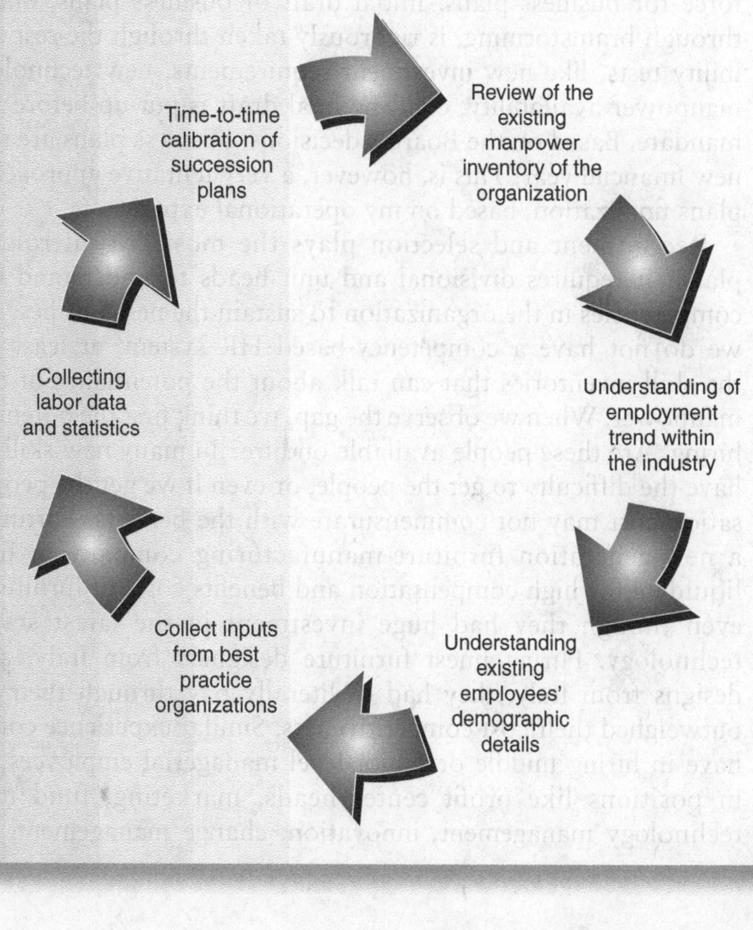

Therefore, effective recruitment and selection strategies require organizations first to create a long-term strategic plan for understanding the strategic direction. This needs to be followed by a series of other activities line setting the strategic criteria for each job, deciding on strategic selection criteria, understanding a good-fit recruitment process, etc.

CONNECTING RECRUITMENT AND SELECTION WITH BUSINESS PLANS

All organizations draw their annual business plans. They brainstorm, set their planning premises, and then go for drawing the plans. It is the usual practice for the business houses to take their key persons out for a trip and spend two/three nights to sign off their business plans. Also they invite some outsiders to give them some ideas, more in the form of a pep talk, to collect input on new ideas. Such outside experts, however, do not participate in framing the business plans; they just act as igniting force for business plans. Initial draft of business plans, once developed through brainstorming, is rigorously taken through the resource compatibility tests, like new investment requirements, new technology support, manpower availability, etc. The final draft is put up before the Board to mandate. Based on the Board's decisions, business plans are sealed for the new financial year. This is, however, a very tentative approach to business plans finalization, based on my operational experience.

Recruitment and selection plays the most critical role in business plans. It requires divisional and unit heads to understand the available competencies in the organization to sustain the new business plans. When we do not have a competency-based HR system, at least we look for the skill inventories that can talk about the potentiality of our available manpower. When we observe the gap, we think first the potentiality of new hiring. Are these people available on hire? In many new skill-sets we may have the difficulty to get the people, or even if we get the people, compensation cost may not commensurate with the benefits. Fortune Furnitech, a new-generation furniture-manufacturing company in India, has to liquidate for high compensation and benefits costs of furniture designers, even though they had huge investment in the latest state-of-the-art technology. Hiring finest furniture designers from Italy, and sourcing designs from Italy, they had to literally pay through their nose, which outweighed their cost competitiveness. Similar experience companies may have in hiring middle or senior-level managerial employees, particularly in positions like profit center heads, marketing, fund management, technology management, innovation, change management, and even in strategic HR functions. Sealing business plans without considering these aspects may be a day-dreaming for the companies.

For new hires again we have to invest on training, and also allow the time to deliver results. Apportioning the costs of training and the costs of under performance during the period of settlement, we can understand how it affects our business plan. This is why we often go by the conventional approach of leveraging our core competencies for expanded business plans.

But our business plans may also require truncating some activities, or reducing the business volume, for unfavorable market conditions. In such cases, we need to think about our redundancy plans. Cost of employees' separation may be enormous for our bottom line. Side by side with our plan for redundancy, we have to go for redeployment plan for our surplus employees also, if required, even at the cost of skill-change training. But all employees may not be redeployed in or within the same job family, for obvious skill and knowledge mismatch. We may have to put them in different jobs, which may or may not be accepted by them. In most of the cases, companies manage to adjust such surplus employees in those jobs which are presently outsourced by them. Although the change management issues are critical here for employees' resistance, things can yet be manageable with employees' education depending on its necessity.

At operations level, we may have the flexibility to outsource. But here again we have to develop our vendors, including manpower service providers strategically. If we go for job outsourcing in volumes, it is always better to develop our own dedicated vendors, if required, even with our own investment. This will not dilute our quality and services. Remember the case of EMC, the storage device company of world repute, who had to suffer for poor quality of vendors' supplied items. When we go for managing our operations with outsourced manpower, ensure that they are under strict supervision and control, and our work processes are adequately simplified.

CONNECTING RECRUITMENT AND SELECTION WITH STRATEGIES

We draw strategies to realize results of our business plans. Strategies that way give us direction. While we frame strategies, we consider the scope of our organization (to dissuade ourselves to take any strategies that may not be endorsed by our vision), thinking on resource allocation (through optimization of competing needs), and thinking on its abilities to cope with the situation of uncertainty. With such primary-level understanding, we align our strategies with the recruitment and selection.

Let us first explain how strategies connect with recruitment and selection process. Suppose our business plans envisage for an incremental change of 20% in your business volume. We are not introducing any new product verticals. We have taken the strategies to achieve this incremental business volume 10% through existing customers, and 10% through new market development. We have to take stock of our marketing and sales team. Increased sales from our captive customers require us to focus on customer relationships management (CRM). CRM is a specialized area. Do we think our existing marketing and sales team are capable to boost CRM activities to achieve the results? Else we need to hire. Similarly, new market development requires professionals who know the tricks. What are our strengths in this area? When we go for augmenting our market share through new product verticals, we require specialized product managers.

Again to align strategies with recruitment and selection, we need to consider one more important aspect of our organization, i.e., the structure. Human resource requirements widely vary with our organization structure. In a hierarchical or tall structure with narrow span of control, we need more manpower. With wide span of control, manpower requirement reduces. Again, hierarchical structure may not hold good for our new strategies. We may require matrix or strategic business unit (SBU) form of organization. Globally, many organizations experimented with matrix structure for manpower optimization. But dual reporting systems often dilute the purpose. The success rate is not encouraging. Matrix structure even though a breakthrough from the traditional hierarchical organization, but for augmented command and control, it suffers from the problems of conflict of interests, ultimately defeats the purpose of manpower optimization. Again, matrix structure requires more multiskilled manpower with exposure to multiple products, services, and functions of the company. Even deployment of people from one matrix to another, in the same function, may require different skill-sets, for difference in the work processes. It means sustaining a matrix structure requires more matured and experienced human resources who understand the dynamics of the organization.

To achieve our strategic intents, we may be requiring SBUs, so that each product or service vertical gets dedicated support. But running profit centers by SBU heads requires them to possess holistic skills and knowledge.

Thus, in either way, we need to consider the structure-strategy nexus along with our recruitment and selection process. We already have a standing debate which comes first—structure or strategy. In this era of business complexities, structure must not stand against strategy. It means we need to make our structure as flexible as possible, to realize our ever-changing strategies. This obviously makes recruitment and selection a more challenging function in the organization.

SUMMARY

- Recruitment and selection function is now a strategic function for organizations. It means organizations need to manage this function strategically. However, many organizations are yet to recognize their strategic and business importance, and still continue to consider this as a routine operational function. Recruitment and selection function integrates all HR activities and the strategic and business plans of any organization. It coordinates human resource planning, succession planning, promotion, performance management systems, compensation and benefits plan, and training and development. Broadly, it is considered a part of talent management function. Strategic recruitment and selection narrows the gaps between present supply and demand of human resources for any organization.
- Legitimacy for inclusion of recruitment and selection as strategic and business-aligned function in any organization is primarily attributable to complexities of business. Such complexities are not just limited to global competition; it even extends to the need for internal restructuring for frequent change in technology and business processes. Obviously, these affect the human resources, coping which organizations embrace the strategic and business-aligned approaches for recruitment and selection. Through strategic recruitment and selection, organizations ensure availability of quality manpower who are competent and flexible enough to take up challenges.
- Also strategic recruitment and selection process balances the social, economic, and legal requirements with the organizational need for business expansion, diversification, mergers and acquisition, and even in present business consolidation.

Key Words

Strategic recruitment and selection: It denotes prima facie focus on those key job positions, which are able to anchor the business growth, bring desired changes, and drive a culture of performance.

Strategic staffing: It is a process for defining and addressing staffing implications of strategic and operational plans. Staffing, in this context, includes all managed movement into, around, and out of an organization (e.g., recruitment, hiring, promotion, transfer, redeployment, attrition, retention, etc.).

Review Questions

1. Define strategic recruitment and selection. What are its important dimensions?
2. Explain features of recruitment and selection strategies.
3. What is the importance of recruitment and selection strategies? Why organizations need to have well-defined recruitment and selection strategies?
4. For framing recruitment and selection strategies for an MNC spread across 180 countries, what steps would you recommend and why?
5. How recruitment and selection strategies can be connected with business plans and overall strategies of organizations? Give some examples from the corporate world to elaborate your answer.
6. What are the dimensions of strategic recruitment and selection?
7. Explain the purposes and benefits of recruitment and selection strategies.
8. Write short notes on:
   (a) Tactical recruitment and selection
   (b) Contingent manpower
   (c) External sources of recruitment
   (d) Front-loaded investment model

Critical Review Questions

1. Study recruitment and selection strategies of any organizations and assess how such strategies could help the organization to achieve its business goals. Develop your answer interpreting at least last three years' business results.

Multiple Choice Questions

1. Strategic management of recruitment and selection function is important because of following reason(s):
   (a) To get quality human resources
   (b) To nurture long-term vision of the organization
   (c) To ensure effective talent management
   (d) All of the above
   (e) None of the above

2. Identify incorrect statement(s):
   (a) Strategic recruitment and selection focuses only on key job positions
   (b) For those job positions which can anchor business growth
   (c) For all job positions
   (d) For those job positions who can drive desired changes
   (e) For those job positions which can create and sustain a performance driven work culture

3. Indicate which statement(s) best-fit for strategic recruitment and selection:
   (a) Management of recruitment and selection function strategically
   (b) Identification of manpower vendors
   (c) Decisions on outsourcing
   (d) Deciding on time-frame of recruitment
   (e) All of the above

4. Organizations follow strategic recruitment and selection process for:
   (a) Achieving long-term and sustainable competitive advantages
   (b) To ensure selection of quality workforce
   (c) To use different channel or sources to ensure larger pool of applicants
   (d) To create talent pipe line
   (e) All of the above

5. Indicate which is not a perspective of strategic recruitment and selection:
   (a) Understanding of organizational strategy and resource demands
   (b) Benchmarking with competitors' recruitment and selection strategies
   (c) Implementing recruitment strategy through right-fit recruitment process
   (d) On-boarding
   (e) Developing and retaining talent

6. Indicate which issue(s) drive(s) strategic recruitment and selection:
   (a) Shortage of manpower in critical skill-sets
   (b) Changing legal and institutional norms
   (c) Problems related to skill redundancy
   (d) Issues pertaining to business cycle
   (d) All of the above

7. Important components of strategic recruitment and selection are as follows, excepting:
   (a) Focusing on operational issues
   (b) Focusing on critical issues
   (c) Focusing on employee development
   (d) Focusing on redeployment
   (e) None of the above

8. Strategic recruitment and selection benefits organizations in following ways, excepting:
   (a) Recruit, develop, and deploy the talent as may be required to meet present and future demands of organizations
   (b) Calibrate manpower needs meeting changing business needs
   (c) Ensure better utilization of human resources
   (d) Retrain or redeploy employees pacing with the changing needs of the organizations
   (e) None of the above

9. Inter-dependent features of strategic recruitment and selection are:
   (a) Integration with organizational strategy
   (b) Long term focus

(c) Cascading of organizational strategies to strategic recruitment and selection
(d) Only a and b
(e) a, b, and c

10. Steps for effective recruitment and selection strategies are as under, excepting:
(a) Review of existing manpower inventory of the organization
(b) Understanding employment trend within the industry
(c) Restricting focus on peer-group companies
(d) Collecting labor data and statistics
(e) Periodic calibration of organizational succession plans

Answers:

1. (d) 2. (c) 3. (a) 4. (e) 5. (b) 6. (e) 7. (e) 8. (e)
9. (e) 10. (c)

CASE STUDY

My God! I pay the best still my top talents are leaving

Organizations across the globe compete for talent. To recruit and select the talent, organizations tend to offer attractive compensation. In India, we find government jobs do not attract talent, obviously for less competitive compensation and benefits. However, central public sectors are now able to attract and retain the talent, as government has unshackled the control from these organizations. These organizations are more Memorandum of Understanding (MOU) driven. MOUs are signed between the Department of Public Enterprises and the respective Chairman of such organization. MOU spells out clearly the financial and nonfinancial targets, with distinct weights on specific parameters.

While designing compensation, the first issue for the organization is to consider how effectively it can hire and retain the desired talent. But again the organization has to see in that process internal and external pay equity issues are not compromised. Another important aspect in compensation design is to consider how it can exert impact on individual and organizational performance.

It is now empirically proved that with higher compensation and benefits, organizations can enhance both the number of applicants and quality of applicants. However, this depends on the nature of job. For example, in India, bank jobs do not attract quality manpower obviously for systemic risk factor. Systemic risk here denotes the risk one bank employee (even in the lower rung) has to face for any wrong decision, which added to nonperforming assets (NPA). Therefore, even with competitive compensation and benefits, Indian banking industry has failed to attract talent, causing serious talent-crunch for the banks.

Again even with better compensation and benefits, employee retention may not always be possible. Generation Y and Generation Z always make meaningful connotation of their work. They want freedom: feel empowered, decision-making role, and positive support from their boss. They feel that boss must indulge them in work. Such indulgence they expect more in terms of support, more like the way a responsible parent treat their erring kids, even get the job done. We have good example of HUL. People leave the job not for compensation and benefits which is eventually the best in the country, and even internationally comparable, people leave them because they feel a typical organizational plateauing syndrome. They interpret their jobs are becoming unchallenging, as their organization is already the best. It means established organizations may lose their talent to start-ups.

Now as an HR manager how can you address these issues? While you design your compensation and benefits packages, first thing you need to understand how strategic you are. Could you see how well your compensation plan fits with other issues? Make a list of all other issues and then comment as an HR manager how you are going to ensure those?

REFERENCES

Bhattacharyya, D.K. (2014), "Talent Development Process of CPSEs: A Reflection on Practices and Requirements", *The Journal of Institute of Public Enterprise*, Vol. 37 (3 and 4): 91–99.

Bhattacharyya, D.K. (2015), "Sustainable Business Through Human Resource Management Practices: A study on two century old family-managed organizations in India", 4th Asian Management Research Case Conference (AMRC), 2015. Presented in USM, Penang, Malaysia with joint participation of IIM, Bangalore, and University of Lahore.

Bratton, J. and Gold, J. (1999), *Human Resource Management – Theory and Practice*. 2nd edition. Palgrave Macmillan, New York.

Buderi, R. (2000), *Engines of Tomorrow: How the World's Best Companies are Using their Research Labs to Win the Future*. New York: Simon & Schuster.

Butler, T. and Waldrop, J. (1999), "Job Sculpting: The Art of Retaining Your Best People", Harvard Business Review, September–October, pp. 41–63.

Evenden, R. (1993), "The strategic management of recruitment and selection", in R. Harrison (ed.), *Human Resource Management: Issues and Strategy*, Wokingham: Addison-Wesley, pp. 219–45.

Grant, R.M. (1996), "Towards a Knowledge-based Theory of the Firm", *Strategic Management Journal*, 17(Winter Special Issue): 108–22.

Koch, M.J. and McGrath, R.G. (1996), "Improving Labor Productivity: Human Resource Management Policies Do Matter", *Strategic Management Journal*, 17(5): 335–54.

Lawler, E.E (1994), "From Job-Based to competency-Based Organisations", *Journal of Organisational Behaviour*, Vol. 15, pp. 3–15.

Miller, E. (1984), "Strategic Staffing, in D.J. Fombrun", N.M. Tichy, and M.E. Devanna (eds.), *Strategic Human Resource Management*, New York: John Wiley, pp. 57–86.

Millmore, M. (2003), "Just how extensive is the practice of strategic recruitment and selection", *Irish Journal of Management*, 24(1): 87–108.

Nahapiet, J. and Ghoshal, S. (1998), "Social Capital, Intellectual Capital and the Organizational Advantage", *Academy of Management Review*, 23(2): 242–66.

Rothwell, W.J. and Kazanas, H.C. (2003). *Planning and Managing Human Resources: Strategic Planning for Human Resource: Strategic Planning for Personnel Management*, 2nd edition, Amherst, MA: Human Resource Development Press, Inc, p. 350.

Snell, S.A. and Dean, J.W. (1992), "Integrated Manufacturing and Human Resource Management: A Human Capital Perspective", *Academy of Management Journal*, 35(3): 467–504.

Snell, S.A., Lepak D.P. and Youndt, M.A. (1999), "Managing the Architecture of Intellectual Capital: Implications for Strategic Human Resource Management", in G.R. Ferris (ed.), *Research in Personnel and Human Resources Management*, London: JAI Press, pp. 175–93.

Sparrow, P.R. and Hiltrop, J.M. (1994), *European Human Resource Management in Transition*, Hemel Hempstead: Prentice-Hall.

Storey, J. and Sisson K. (1993), *Managing Human Resources and Industrial Relations.* Milton Keynes: Open University Press.

Torrington, D., Hall, A. and Taylor, S. (2002), *Human Resource Management*, 5th edition, Harlow, Prentice-Hall.

Chapter 6

Tools and Techniques for Recruitment and Selection

LEARNING OBJECTIVES

After reading this chapter, you will be able to understand:

1. Understanding tools and techniques of recruitment and selection
2. Recruitment through social media
3. E-recruitment/digital recruitment
4. Selection interviews
5. Personality assessments
6. Use of assessment centers for recruitment
7. IQ tests and test of emotional intelligence
8. Models of employee selection
9. Recruitment metrics and analytics

Use of psychometric tools is not only restricted to recruitment and selection decisions in organizations. These tools can even help HR managers to develop their program for counseling employees in their career transition process. During recessionary trends, companies face the challenge of manpower redundancy. Employees who lose their jobs feel the need for support from their companies so that they can make their career transition process successful. Using psychometric tools at this crisis situation, it is possible to understand the extent of employees' willingness to switch their job, and accommodate them in new job and work environment. Results of psychometric tests help in providing counseling support, with focus on enhancing confidence level of employees, and equipping them to leverage their strengths so that they can make their career transition process smooth enough. Using MBTI some companies could get good results. Some companies however also reinforce the confidence level of employees building their capabilities through specialized training, so that they find them more demanding in competitive job market.

INTRODUCTION

Recruitment is a strategic human resource management function (Liviens & Chapman, 2010) with primary objective to identify and attract potential employees (Barber, 1998). The traditional, i.e., paper-based, recruitment of external candidates from job advertising is a linear process with consecutive tasks. It usually starts with the identification of required applicants, their location and placement in the labor market, and proceeds with activities designed to attract and persuade qualified applicants to apply. Job applications are then received, screened, and sorted, leading to the drawing up of a shortlist. The process ends with communicating the prescreening results to applicants.

A typical recruitment process is treated as a business process (Reynolds, 1995), which in line with Davenport and Short (1990) can be defined as a set of logically related tasks performed to achieve a defined business outcome for internal or external recipients. A business process occurs across or between organizational subunits and is independent of a formal organizational structure. In the case of recruitment, this process is normally performed for either internal customers—line managers and executives from various parts of the organization—or external ones, e.g., clients, resulting in a shortlist of candidates which customers can choose from.

The recruitment process can vary in complexity and degree of difficulty depending on the recruitment objectives and the recruitment sources chosen. The most commonly used sources for external recruitment are newspaper ads, private and public employment agencies, Internet job boards, corporate websites, employee referrals, colleges and universities, search firms, job fairs, Internet-related sources, e.g., corporate websites, etc.

Tools and techniques used for recruitment and selection include interview, ability testing, personality assessment tests, assessment centers, competency-based recruitment, reference checking, and job offers.

TRADITIONAL RECRUITMENT TOOLS

Traditional recruitment tools are those that are time-tested and are used by organizations for several decades. Such tools are still being used by organizations, even side by side with the modern recruitment tools like e-recruitment or recruitment through social network sites. Such tools are range of pre-employment assessments, tests, and tools that can strengthen the hiring process. We have many traditional recruitment tools, but it is always advisable for organizations to use appropriate mix of the right tools for specific job roles. This can significantly reduce the risk of wrong hires. Some of the traditional tools, which are used by organizations extensively for their recruitment process, are:

(1) **Interviews:** It is one of the most reliable and extensively used recruitment and selection tools. Depending on the job profile various types of interview methods are followed. Essentially, however, phone interviews and face-to-face interviews form the core part of recruitment process. It involves asking appropriate questions, following consistent process all along without any bias in selection, etc.

(2) **Skills testing:** This is particularly useful for those job positions that essentially require certain set of competencies. Such competencies and skills are essentially testable; hence with skills testing, HR managers can take their recruitment decisions because of person job-fit.

(3) **Personality/Psychometric assessments:** Some job roles require assessment of team-fit, motivation, and work styles, and so also some specific behavioral traits for some job roles. Using personality/psychometric assessment tools, HR managers can make their recruitment decisions for such job positions.

(4) **Aptitude and competency-based assessments:** Some jobs may also require some specific aptitude, viz, numerical aptitude for

accounting functions, analytical aptitude for managerial decision making, etc. Obviously for such job positions, HR managers prefer aptitude and competency-based assessments.

(5) **Reference checks:** After taking the recruitment decisions using appropriate mix of the above tools, it is always desirable to go for reference checking, so that previous managers can vouch for the candidacy of the selected individuals. Such reference checking can validate recruitment decisions, more particularly in terms of skills and attitudes of the new recruits.

(6) **Police verification:** Such verification authenticates that our selected candidates are free from any criminal records, and therefore can be the appropriate fit with the job positions in the organization.

There can be many other tools available, ranging from conventional and time-tested methods like newspaper advertisements to social media networking. However, whatever tools selected by organizations, it is always desirable to select the appropriate tools, so that right-fit are appointed for specific job roles. For external recruitment, advertising, employee referrals, headhunting, social networking, participation in job fairs, etc., are some of the most common recruitment tools used by organizations.

MODERN RECRUITMENT TOOLS

Modern recruitment tools are those that are more technology-enabled, and that can facilitate in searching and sourcing potential talents for organizations without any geographical jurisdiction. People today are prepared to relocate, once they understand their career choices are more challenging. Also the race for global talent hunt makes organizations to mine for candidates from any possible locations in the world. All these have made modern recruitment functions more challenging and technology-enabled. Recruitment through social network sites, e-recruitment, or digital recruitment are more popular as modern recruitment tools. For the purpose of this book, we however emphasized on the use of the term e-recruitment, as the more encompassing and interchangeable term for recruitment through social networking sites (SNS), digital recruitment, and Internet-based recruitment or e-recruitment, as a whole.

E-RECRUITMENT

E-recruitment, recruitment through social networking sites (SNS), or digital recruitment have now become important medium for strategic hiring in today's organizations. Reasons for sudden shift to such hiring strategy are primarily for reaching to a large pool of suitable applicants who otherwise would have been a difficult reach for organizations. With the spurt of Internet, today's job seekers make extensive use of SNS, and for them the main contact points for organizations are SNS like Facebook, LinkedIn, Twitter, etc. Organizations also find it convenient to put their organizational profile, career news, and much other relevant news for the prospective candidates, interpreting which prospective candidates can make their informed choice on the job profile, organizational culture, and their career growth opportunities, which make them gradually mentally adept and organization-fit right from their day of joining. Several research studies indicated that SNS can attract large pool of candidates, facilitate organizations for scientific screening of candidates' profiles, etc. Also through SNS-based recruitment, organizations can take adequate cognizance of candidates' antecedents, and ensure better legal compliance. Since the late 1990s, such mode of recruitment is gaining importance and now it has emerged as the multipurpose individual and business tools (Boyd & Ellison, 2008). Almost all organizations that continuously source manpower today have created their own Facebook page, LinkedIn profile, and/or a Twitter account. All these organizations are driven by a common goal to reach as many prospective talents as possible so as to make them more visible and recognizable among those talents who are available for hire. Company's recognition is absolutely important as prospective talents, i.e., those who are available for hire, tend to prefer those companies, which they recognize (Greengard, 2012). With new technology support SNS-based recruitment processes today have become much wider in scope in terms of locating and attracting talents, reference checking, and even cost effectiveness. Therefore, reasons for such trends of e-recruitment are easy and quick access to wide pool of workforce with diverse skills and competencies (Doherty, 2010), cost-effective recruitment strategies, quick information processing, and for making the overall recruitment process more efficient. Finally, prospective talents who are hired from SNS or through e-recruitment process are also expected to be more computer-friendly or tech-savvy. All these are viewed as the positive outcomes of e-recruitment.

Despite such advantages, some companies are hesitant to embrace such recruitment options primarily for their unwillingness to switch over from their existing traditional recruitment practices. Such reasons are attributable to lack of expertise, unfamiliarity, and even to some extent fearing ethical and legal restrictions.

SNS-based or e-recruitment is a description of the process that companies follow to discover and recruit talented individuals from the Internet (Allden & Harris, 2013). Minton-Eversole (2007) explains that e-recruitment is a fast-growing method of hiring employees as more and more individuals post their résumés online in search for a better future. The success of e-recruitment mainly derives from the fact that now companies have the ability to reach a larger potential applicant pool, since the geographical constraints are nonexistent (Cappelli, 2001, cited in Tong & Sivanand, 2005), and individuals are more willing to travel overseas for employment. Today, there are two types of online recruiters: the corporate recruiters that are ordinary companies seeking employees online, and the third-party recruiters that are companies offering expert services. The third-party recruiters act as a medium between the pool of potential applicants and the companies. They collect all the résumés posted online in a database and then provide to client companies those who are most relevant to the position available.

Benefits and Risks of E-Recruitment

SNS-based or e-recruitment process has now changed the dimension of recruitment practices in organizations. Some of its benefits are substantial reduction of recruitment costs, reduction of cycle time for recruitment, wider reach to prospective pool of talents across the globe, more effective employee referrals, etc. It is now proved that e-recruitment can substantially reduce the cycle time for hiring, reducing the intervening time required for hiring, like reduction of intervening time for job posting, receiving of applications from prospective job applicants, filtering the profiles, contacting the shortlisted candidates, collecting relevant information about the candidates for detailed checking of the antecedents, etc. Also, it can significantly reduce the cost of recruitment. Both these have been cited as prime benefits of e-recruitment. Doherty (2010) also could observe the benefit of e-recruitment in terms of explaining and building brand value of organizations, which could influence prospective talents to feel attracted with the company. Obviously, this benefits organizations in getting larger pool of prospective talents, from whom companies can hire those who are the right-fit. Even e-recruitment facilitates in initial screening of prospective talents through some one-line questionnaire and psychometric tests. Despite such benefits, SNS-based or e-recruitment also has multiple risks, which are explained later.

SNS-based or e-recruitment cannot be the only way of recruiting talents in organizations. In many organizations, for many job positions, traditional methods of recruitment may still be important, as all prospective talents may not like to make effective use of Internet for seeking their candidacy for the jobs. Another important bottleneck of SNS-based or e-recruitment may be the requirement of huge investments for building the appropriate platform. It may also enhance the cost for new software and monitoring systems for tracking job applications, need more training reinforcements for HR professionals, who will be required to perform the recruitment function, along with documentation of job descriptions, job specifications, maintenance of company's web-site, e-accounts, etc. Also companies require selecting appropriate recruitment web-sites, balancing information sharing, guard against all legal issues, etc.

Finally, SNS-based or e-recruitment encompasses three important dimensions like use of social media to attract applicants, use of social media to screen applicants, and compliance with legal and ethical issues. It no doubt ensures wider reach to larger pool of talents, spread across the globe, but again it has to be used cautiously, and perhaps as an additional tool, rather than a standalone tool for recruitment in organizations.

SNS-Based or E-Recruitment Tools

SNS-based recruitment denotes recruitment through social network sites. With the increase of SNS-based or e-recruitment, recruitment processes in organizations have now become more strategic and technology-enabled, requiring organizations to go for tech-savvy and innovative to ensure increased flow of talented candidates. With the advancement of technology-enabled recruitment process, organizations now have multiple tools for best recruitment.

However, for all job positions, organizations may not make use of all such recruitment tools. Some of the known recruitment tools are discussed below:

(1) **Profile tracking/applicant tracking systems:** This system enables organizations to track suitable profiles for the job positions from large pool of applicants. With active participation in SNS-based recruitment process, organizations receive regularly a large number of applications for different job positions, even when such applications are unsolicited. This obviously makes HR department's tasks complicated to shortlist desired profiles. With Profile Tracking/Applicant Tracking Systems, such tasks become much easier, as such in-built systems can track suitable candidatures, while can quarantine those profiles that are not matching with organizational job requirements. Many software vendors now provide standard systems for this purpose.

(2) **Mobile recruiting tools:** With powerful smartphones and tablets, mobile recruitment of late started gaining importance. Several

research studies indicate job seekers in large numbers look for jobs on their mobiles. Mobile recruiting requires HR managers to focus on their communication, engagement, and recruitment of talent. Such tools require use of QR (quick response) codes, text alerts, apps, and even mobile-optimized web-sites. Here also many software vendors provide standard software solutions.

(3) **Gamification:** It involves application of game mechanics to nongame environments, like recruitment with primary focus on studying how people get motivated and change their behavior. Gamified applications as front end of the recruitment process serve as attraction and engagement tool for the candidates, and facilitate in identification of right talent for specific job positions. Gamification developers like ConnectCubed and Peoplefluent provide assessment games, and also work as talent management software.

(4) **Collaborative tools:** Such tools are used to share and exchange information and interact. It helps in integrating HR and recruitment function with the rest of the organization and in the process eliminates the silo approach for making the recruitment process more effective.

(5) **Location technology:** It helps in tracking the real-world geographic position of the job applicants from their mobile phone or computer device, primarily based on Internet protocol (IP). Such location tracking can enable organizations to automatically provide job applicants details of job vacancies with other relevant information specific to their location.

(6) **Video interviewing:** This tool is increasingly becoming important for video-conferencing for conduction of interviews. Video interviewing can facilitate in picking up subtle emotional clues and body language of the job applicants and in the process can replace the need for face-to-face interviews. For this tool also we have many standard solutions available in the market.

(7) **Automatic internet sourcing:** Such a tool is used for advanced searching of rare talent through numerous professional networks. With keyword searches, using such a tool, potential talents can be tracked, and then contacted for job positions in organizations.

Success of SNS-based or e-recruitment therefore largely depends on effective use of above tools (Fig. 6.1).

While building an SNS-based or e-recruitment process, organizations need to ensure that such a process is efficient, cost-effective, churn out more suitable candidates, and can ensure ethical and legally compliant recruitment decisions. E-recruitment tools and techniques require customization as per the requirements of the organizations.

FIGURE 6.1 Tools to support SNS-based recruitment.

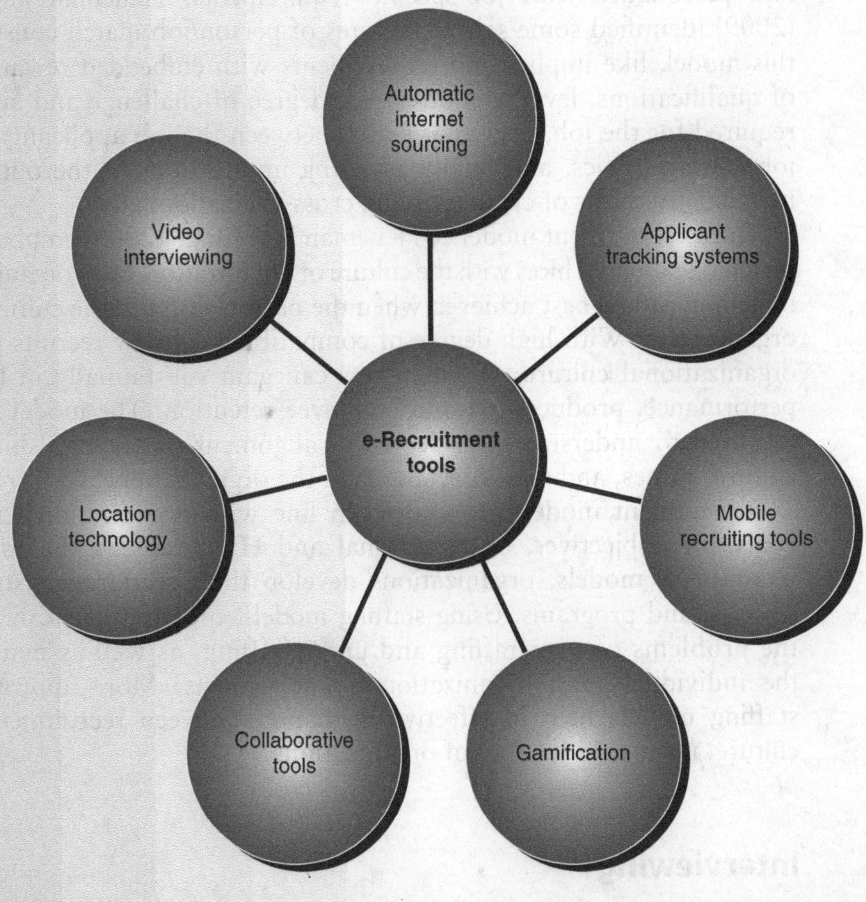

RECRUITMENT MODELS

Use of recruitment models, both for maintaining appropriate recruitment levels, matching with organizational work demands, and so also for attracting and retaining suitable talents in organizations, has become popular now. Most of these models are prescriptive, developed based on empirical research. For example, Staffing Quantity Levels, widely used staffing model, help organizations matching the recruitment level with the work requirements. Pioneered by Heneman and Judge (2009), this model *prima facie* can match with projected staffing availability with the projected staffing requirements, and in the process can balance between overstaffing and understaffing.

Another recruitment model, commonly known as staffing quality person/job match, helps organizations to match individual talents, skills, and personality with job-specific requirements. Heneman and Judge (2009) identified some salient features of person/job match constructs of this model, like implicit job requirements with embedded rewards, level of qualifications, level of motivation, degree of challenge and autonomy required for the job, degree of match between the job applicants and the job characteristics, and finally assessing implications of the outcome of matching in terms of cross-training, cross-utilization, etc.

Third recruitment model of Heneman and Judge (2009) emphasizes on matching potential hires with the culture of organization. Such organizational matching can be best achieved when the person fits with the culture of the organization. With high degree of compatibility of new recruits with the organizational culture, organizations can gain substantially in terms of performance, productivity, and employee retention. The model suggests the need to understand the degree of alignment of potential hires with culture, values, and the expectations of the organization.

Recruitment models are crafted in line with organizational mission, goals, and objectives, organizational and HR strategies. Based on the recruitment models, organizations develop their recruitment strategies, policies, and programs. Using staffing models, organizations can mitigate the problems of overstaffing and understaffing, as well as match with the individuals and organizational requirements. More appropriately, staffing models help in effective mediation between recruitment, jobs, culture, norms, and values of organizations.

Interviewing

Interviewing is a process of eliciting information from the job applicants to assess suitability of their candidacy for the job positions. Effective interviewing requires specialized skills of the HR managers. Through interview process, HR managers, at the outset, establish rapport with the job applicants to make them feel at ease, and then seek the truth attentively listening and evaluating responses against the questions. Successful conduction of interview precedes drawing of an interview sequence plan or an interview plan.

Success of interview process primarily depends on the prevalent physical and psychological factors. Physical factors include selection of appropriate ambience, free from noise and interruptions with comfortable settings. Psychological factors are avoidance of fear, excitement, and intimidation, which are major impediments for success of any interview process. With negative psychological factors, answers to the questions to the interviewees may get distorted and may even raise the problem of reliability.

Good interview practices also require expertise in framing interview questions. Interview questions are raised by the interviewers to assess the candidature of the job applicants, including seeking clarification on their profile, antecedents, etc. Free narrative or open-ended questions are more preferred than direct questions or questions for cross-examination. Cross-examination questions are often asked by the interviewers to assess the accuracy of interviewees' responses.

Good interview practices also require appropriate selection of a topic, matching with the goals and objectives of the interview process. Interviewers at the outset introduce themselves, define the interview purpose for better clarity to the job applicants, and in the process set the tone of the interview.

Interviewers need to understand the rights and privileges of the interviwees, and accordingly avoid questions that are sensitive in nature and infringe upon the privacy of the job applicants. Phase-wise structuring of the interview process, like introduction, building of rapport, questioning, and summarizing, to a great extent helps the interviewers to manage the interview process effectively.

Effective Interviewing

Effective interview needs careful plan so that job applicants' attributes that can help in successful job performance can be tracked, his/her communication abilities can be assessed, information about his/her educational qualifications, work experiences can be meticulously studied, knowledge, skills, and competencies can be studied, and final selection decisions can be taken on merit. Depending on the levels of recruitment, four different styles of interviews, i.e., situational, personality-based, stress, and behavioral interviews, can be conducted. Situational interview determines how a job applicant responds to real work situations, which can be measured through hypothetical, role play, or actual problem-solving situations. The personality profile evaluates traits important to the success of the individual in the job position. Stress interviews measure applicants' abilities in dealing with highly stressful situations. The behavioral interview bases questions on past performance, assuming that individuals will do at least as well in a new position as they did in their previous job positions.

Like interview styles, interviews can be structured or unstructured. Structured interview approach requires interviewing candidates with preplanned questions, while unstructured interview approach sets the pace of interview based on the candidates' ease. Some organizations also follow semistructured interview process, where some questions will be standard and common to all, while some other may be flexible, pacing with the ease of the candidates.

While interviewing, it is also important to keep pace with the time allotment. Depending on the job positions, actual interview timing may vary between 30 and 60 minutes. Similarly, it is important to set the interview environment, which can ensure candidates' privacy, distractions, and can help in eliciting information naturally. A standard format of interview plan could be greeting with small talk essentially for rapport building, orientation to explain to the candidates the way interview may continue, information on work experience and education, other activities and interests, discussions on strengths and weaknesses, and finally closing of the interview.

Types of Interview

The two main types of interviews conducted in employee recruitment and selection process are structured and unstructured.

The unstructured informal interview is normally conducted as a preliminary step primarily for building the rapport with the job applicants. Such interviews are entirely informal and are not controlled by a specific set of detailed questions. Rather, the interviewer is guided by a predefined list of issues. These interviews amount to an informal conversation about the subject.

Informal interviewing is not concerned with discovering "how many" respondents think in a particular way on an issue (this is what the final survey itself will discover). The aim is to find out how people think and how they react to issues, so that the ultimate survey questionnaire can be framed along the lines of thought that will be most natural to respondents.

The respondent is encouraged to talk freely about the subject, but is kept to the point on issues of interest to the interviewers. The respondent is encouraged to reveal everything that he/she feels and thinks about these points. The interviewer must note (or tape-record) all remarks that may be relevant and pursue them until he/she is satisfied that there is no more to be gained by further probing. Properly conducted, informal interviews can help in assessing the candidacy of the job applicants. Often in job interviews focus group type of interview process is followed.

Structured Standardized Interview

A structured interview follows a specific questionnaire in a set order and in a set manner to ensure no variation between interviews. Responses are recorded on a questionnaire form (usually with prespecified response formats) during the interview process, and the completed questionnaires are then analyzed quantitatively to decide on the interview score. The structured interview usually denies the interviewer the opportunity to either add or remove questions, change their sequence, or alter the wording of questions.

Depth Interviews

Depth interviews are one-to-one encounters in which the interviewer makes use of an unstructured or semistructured set of issues/topics to guide the discussion. The objective of the exercises is to explore and uncover deep-seated emotions, motivations, and attitudes. They are most often employed when dealing with sensitive matters and respondents are likely to give evasive or even misleading answers when directly questioned. Depth interviews make use of psychoanalysis. Also it requires specialized expertise of the interviewer.

Telephone Interviews

Telephone interviews are conducted, where face-to-face interviews may be expensive, and even at times are time consuming. In some cases, organizations use telephone interviews as a mode of preliminary screening of the candidatures of the job applicants. Compared to personal interviews, telephone interviews may not give any specific advantages for the recruitment process, except saving of cost and managing the recruitment process at speed (Fig. 6.2).

FIGURE 6.2 Types of interview.

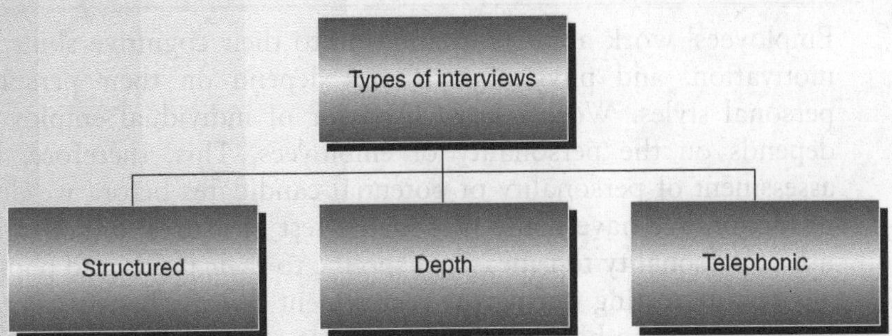

PSYCHOLOGICAL TEST FOR RECRUITMENT

In recruitment and selection understanding, the personality and personal style of candidates can help interviewers to minimize the risk of wrong hiring. It requires following structured approach in assessment of prospective hires, particularly in terms of their fit with organizations. This degree of fit indicates not only addressing competency issues; even it considers prospective candidates' personality, so that they feel more compatible with their jobs and organizations. In broader sense, personality matching also helps in matching with the organizational culture, and work environment. In addition to recruitment and selection, understanding personality and personal styles of potential hires help in succession planning, career planning and career development, counseling, etc.

Assessment of personality and personal styles of candidates answers the following questions of interviewers:

(1) Who are the best fit for the jobs and the organizations?
(2) Do they have potential talent that can be harnessed by the organizations?
(3) Do they have prerequisite emotional intelligence for effective managerial work?
(4) What could be the appropriate career path for these potential hires?
(5) What would be the interpersonal behavior of these potential hires?
.

We also call this process as psychological testing, psychological profiling, psychometric assessment, etc. Despite criticism, in recruitment and selection, organizations globally still continue to use personality and personal style assessment of potential candidates, for achieving effectiveness in hiring decisions.

TEST OF PERSONALITY FOR RECRUITMENT

Employees' work abilities in addition to their cognitive skills, expertise, motivation, and physical attributes depend on their personality and personal styles. Work-related behavior of individual employees largely depends on the personality of employees. This, therefore, legitimizes assessment of personality of potential candidates before we decide them to recruit. We have many personality test measures; organizations make use of personality test measures specific to their needs and choices. Thus, personality testing during the recruitment process benefits organizations in predicting the behavioral propensities of potential candidates and the degree of its replication in actual work environment.

Personality of potential hires indicates their social image, as it reflects their most dominant behavioral characteristics. In recruitment and selection, assessment of personality is important as it helps in assessing potential candidates' dynamic mental structures and their coordinated mental processes. Such inputs help in recruitment and selection decisions in terms of understanding potential candidates' emotional and behavioral adjustments to the organization. Personality is dynamic because mental structures of individual employees continuously develop over their lifetime. Personality and individual behavioral pattern of employees become an important construct to adjust and succeed in work situations. Particularly in a changing business environment, to get the right-fit, employers make use of personality tests in selection and recruitment decisions. Apart from this, interest in personality assessment is also important for cultural transformation in an organization. With the understanding of cognitive and emotional bases of human behavior, personality assessment has gained further importance.

Study of personality can be made from different perspectives such as those listed here (Fig. 6.3):

FIGURE 6.3 Different perspectives of personality.

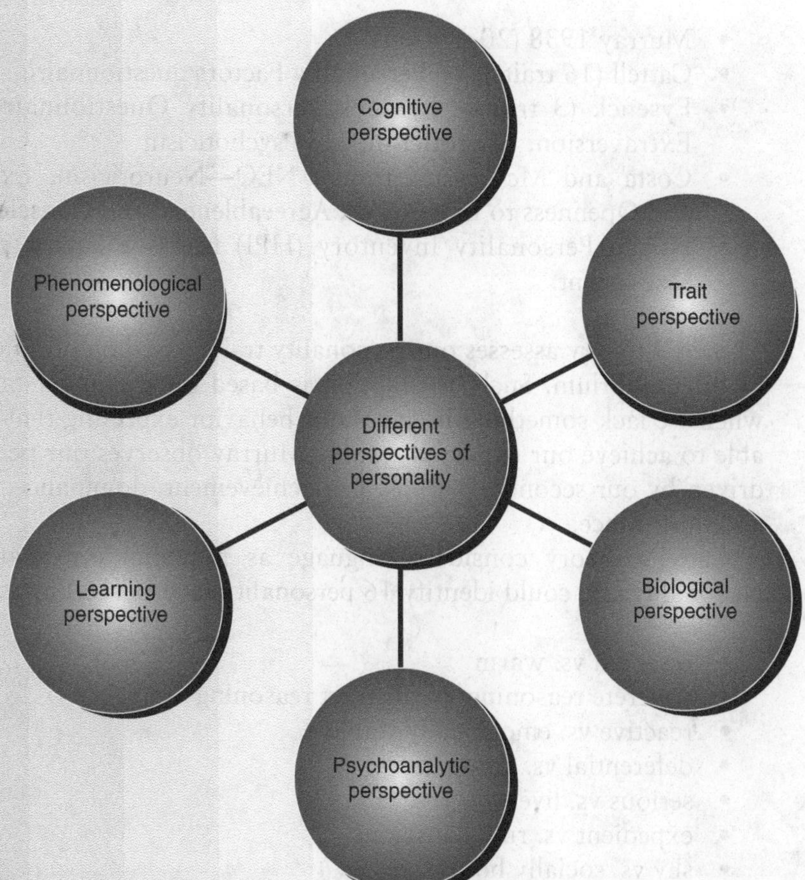

- Trait perspective
- Biological perspective
- Psychoanalytic perspective
- Learning perspective
- Phenomenological perspective
- Cognitive perspective

Measurement of Personality Traits

Personality traits are many. It is difficult to list personality traits that are universal, rather evident in all types of people. Psychologists also widely differ in their arguments on personality traits. However, using the following personality traits measurement tools, we can classify personality of individual employees into some common traits, which can influence their work behavior.

- Murray 1938 (20+ "needs")
- Cattell (16 traits): 16 Personality Factors questionnaire
- Eysenck (3 traits): Eysenck Personality Questionnaire (EPQ)—Extraversion, Neuroticism, and Psychoticism
- Costa and McCrae (5 traits): NEO—Neuroticism, Extraversion, and Openness to Experience, Agreeableness, and Conscientiousness
- Hogan Personality Inventory (HPI) for Five Factor personality assessment.

Murray's theory assesses our personality traits based on our internal state of disequilibrium. Such assumption is based on the understanding that when we lack something it drives our behavior expecting that we will be able to achieve our expected results. Murray observes our personality is driven by our secondary needs, i.e., achievement, dominance, affiliation, and nurturance.

Cattel's theory considers language as potential information about personality. He could identify 16 personality factors (16 PF) as under:

- reserved vs. warm
- concrete reasoning vs. abstract reasoning
- reactive vs. emotionally stable
- deferential vs. dominant
- serious vs. lively
- expedient vs. rule-conscious
- shy vs. socially bold
- utilitarian vs. sensitive
- trusting vs. vigilant

- practical vs. imaginative
- forthright vs. private
- self-assured vs. apprehensive
- traditional vs. open-to-change
- group-oriented vs. self-reliant
- tolerates disorder vs. perfectionist
- relaxed vs. tense

Eysenck's theory believes that people can be described in terms of two super traits, and accordingly we can classify personality of people based on biological basis. Eysenck classifies our personality as under:

- Introversion–extraversion (continuum of sociability, dominance, liveliness, etc.)
- Emotionality stability (neuroticism) (continuum of upset and distress)
- Psychoticism added later: less researched. This was a predisposition toward becoming either psychotic or sociopathic (psychologically unattached to other people). Also, a tendency to be hostile, manipulative, and impulsive

To measure above personality traits, Eysenck designed the Eysenck Personality Questionnaire (EPQ).

Other studies on primary personality traits are Meyers-Briggs Type Indicator (MBTI) and Big-Five Model. MBTI is essentially a 100-question personality test to understand from people their feelings and actions in a given situation. The responses are then classified into four major types, such as extroverted vs. introverted, sensing vs. intuitive, thinking vs. feeling, and judging vs. perceiving. These were then combined into 16 personality types—ESTJ, INFP, ESFP, INTJ, ESFJ, INTP, ENFP, ISTJ, ESTP, INFJ, ENFJ, ISTP, ENTJ, ISFP, ENTP, and ISFJ.

Attributes of some of the types are as under:

ESTJ—Practical and organized on a logical basis.

INFP—More focused on their inner world and driven by thoughts and emotion.

ESFP—These people derive their energy from the external sources and not within the organization.

INTJ—This type of people derive energy from their inner world and they are more emotion driven.

ESFJ—This type of people believe on facts and take decisions based on their personal values.

INTP—This type of people take decisions on the basis of logic.

The Big Five Model

This model is often considered the better alternative that MBTI. The big five personality factors are—

- Extroversion
- Agreeableness
- Conscientiousness
- Emotional stability
- Openness to stability

The five-factor model is commonly measured by the NEO (Neuroticism, Extraversion, and Openness) by McCrae and Costa (2003) to categorize the personality as under:

- Neuroticism (Emotional stability)
- Extraversion (Introversion)
- Openness to experience (Closeness to experiences)
- Agreeableness (Disagreeableness)
- Conscientiousness (Lack of conscientiousness)

Hogan's Personality Inventory (HPI) is another five-factor personality assessment tool that consists of a detailed questionnaire item with 206 true–false items. HPI is considered more like a business-focused personality assessment tool, developed based on socio-analytic theory, and this can predict occupational success. This captures dominant behavioral tendencies that are relevant to social life. Primary scales in HPI measure adjustment, ambition, sociability, interpersonal sensitivity, prudence, inquisitiveness, and learning approach. Occupational scales measure service orientation, stress tolerance, reliability, clerical potential, sales potential, and managerial potential. Based on these two different scales, HPI generates data report, career builder report, management builder report, and leadership forecast challenge report, etc. Further HPI can also be used in Hogan Development Survey (HDS) to measure motives, values, preferences inventory, etc.

Personality and Employment Testing

Use of personality testing for recruitment and selection decisions was initially discarded by the industrial psychologists alleging such practices are unreliable. However, human resource management practioners started accepting personality scores as the basis of selection, and gradually personality testing became more prominent with the convergence of psychology, engineering, and management disciplines for interpretation and solution of organizational problems. Although initial focus was on the use of cognitive ability tests, as organizations used to construe its results better predictor of skill and performance of potential hires; gradually personality tests have also been accepted as predictor of performance. With such acceptance, personality testing gradually is in practice in organizations for employees' selection.

Validity of the Psychological Tests

Any psychological tests need to be valid. The degree of validity of a test measure widely varies with respect to circumstances, use of the specific tools, and its application. Primarily, the validity of a selection test depends when the characteristics of its measurements relate to the job requirements selection test. We consider selection test scores as valid, when there is a link between the test score and the job performance.

The degree of validity is understood in terms of employment selection tests, when one test result can predict others' job performance behavior. For employees' selection we use criterion-related validity, content validity, and construct validity. Criterion validity shows the correlation or other statistical relationships between selection test score (the predictor) and the job performance (the criterion). With high test score, if one performs high, we call it high criterion validity. Content validity indicates content of the test reflects some important job-related behavior and the measurement of knowledge and skill for the said job-related behavior. Construct validity measures constructs or abstract job characteristics, which are crucial for the performance of the job.

In most of the psychological tests used for selection, criterion-related validity is more considered.

Validity of selection tests is essential for any organization using psychological tools. Those organizations that use criterion-related validity basically use two core strategies: (i) concurrent validation study that collects predictor test scores from the current job performance measures, and (ii) the second strategy for a predictive validation study in which predictor test scores are obtained from job applicants at the time of hire. However, job performance measures are obtained only when new employees could get sufficient time to learn the job, and there exists the correlation between the predictor test and job performance scores.

Another aspect of validity study is that the specific job for which the test is done is similar to the job for which the test was originally developed. Such determination of similarity can only be ensured when the organization systematically undertakes the job analysis to identify the tasks, duties, responsibilities, and work condition of job and the knowledge, skills, and abilities that are essential for the successful performance of the job.

Further, to understand validity of psychological tests for recruitment, we determine the validity correlation coefficient, which is the correlation coefficient between an employee's selection test score and one or more relevant measure of job performance. With higher validity coefficient, we get more valid test score.

Predictive validity is the most important property of employee selection. Such validity has the ability to predict job performance, learning, and success.

Characteristics differences of samples create problem for validity study. It is known to us that different demographic groups of people tend to perform differently, while they all are taking the same tests.

Validity and Reliability

Validity and reliability are the two important constructs for any psychological tests. Through validity and reliability we get precision in our measurement of test scores. Validity represents how well is our variable measurement in relation to what actually we supposed to get. Reliability, on the other hand, tells us to what extent our test measure is reproducible, when we conduct a retest.

To minimize threats to validity, we focus on designing the psychological test measures scientifically. We do it logically, so that through cross-verification we can understand its reliability. In other words, reliability helps us to minimize eventual errors in validity.

Test of Intelligence as Employability Test

Intelligence is a very general mental capability that, among other things, involves the ability to reason, plan, solve problems, think abstractly, comprehend complex ideas, learn quickly, and learn from experience. Intelligence is not merely book learning or a narrow academic skill. It reflects a broader and deeper capability for comprehending our surroundings.

A popular theory of intelligence is based on psychometric testing, i.e., intelligence quotient (IQ) tests; however, for some researchers' dissatisfaction with traditional IQ tests prompted their developing alternative theories of intelligence suggesting that intelligence results from independent capabilities that uniquely contribute to human intellectual performance. Measuring the IQs of a large population, we can conform to a normal distribution. The approach to understand intelligence over a long period of time is based on psychometric testing. Such intelligence quotient (IQ) tests define general intelligence.

Based on the results of a series of studies Spearman concluded that there was a common function (or group of functions) across intellectual activities including what he called intelligence which helps us in sensory discriminations. This common function became known as "g" or general intelligence. To objectively determine and measure general intelligence, Spearman invented the "s" factor using the mathematical proof. This resulted in the development of Two-Factory Theory of Intelligence. The Two-Factor Theory of Intelligence holds that every test can be divided into a "g" factor and an "s" factor. The g-factor measures the "general" factor or common function among ability tests. The s-factor measures the "specific" factor unique to a particular ability test.

Intelligence tests are now widely used in recruitment and selection decision making. Very common intelligence test is known as verbal intelligence test measures, which consider measuring following aspects (Fig. 6.4):

- Information: a person's level of general knowledge
- Comprehension: how well one can understand questions and grasp concepts.
- Arithmetic: a person's mathematical abilities.
- Similarities: measures abstract thought.
- Digit Span: measures attention span.
- Vocabulary: measures a person's knowledge of different meaning of words.

FIGURE 6.4 Common intelligence test.

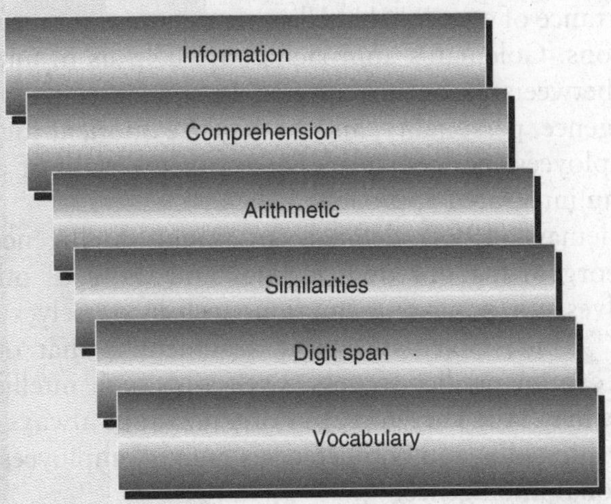

Intelligence or IQ tests of above 100 score is considered above average level of intelligence, who may contribute better in performance. Some broad classification of people in terms of their intelligence can be made as under:

- With score under 70, we say people are mentally retarded
- 70–80: borderline retarded
- 80–90: below average
- 90–110: average
- 110–120: above average
- 120–130: superior
- Above 130: very superior

Using IQ test scores as the sole basis for recruitment and selection is not recommended, as people with high IQ scores may have other negative attributes, which may make them poor performer and less interactive, so also poor in interpersonal relationships.

Emotional Intelligence

With over emphasis on verbal and cognitive intelligence, we often ignore the importance of emotional dimensions of human behavior. In organizations interpersonal relations, interaction with people are important. Our thought process gets influenced with such interaction and interpersonal relations; hence our emotions have meanings. For this reason, understanding emotions help us in interpreting behavioral dynamics, and in recruitment and selection we can take more matured decisions. Daniel Goleman (1998) for the first time recommended the importance of emotional intelligence as important measures for recruitment decisions. Goleman's approach could help us in understanding the relations between reason and emotion. In organizations, we integrate emotional intelligence, personality, and intelligence quotient for achieving excellence in employees' performance. To recruit the right-fit also we make use of such an integrated approach.

Goleman (1998) defined emotional intelligence as the "capacity for reorganizing our own feelings and those of others, for motivating ourselves, for managing emotions well in ourselves and in our relationships." Thus, Goleman's basic argument is that our rational thinking alone cannot predict success. Even with high intelligence quotient (IQ), people may fail. Therefore, our organizations always endeavor to develop leadership skills and competencies among employees for enhancing their emotional intelligence.

Emotional Intelligence—Two Aspects

This is the essential premise of EQ. To be successful we require the effective awareness, control, and management of one's own emotions, and those of other people. EQ embraces two aspects of intelligence:

- Understanding self, goals, intentions, responses, behavior and
- Understanding others and their feelings.

EMOTIONAL INTELLIGENCE—THE FIVE DOMAINS

Emotional Intelligence has relationship with other behavioral studies like NLP (Neuro-Linguistic Programming), Transactional Analysis, and Empathy. By developing our emotional intelligence in these areas and the five EQ domains, we can become more productive and successful at what we do, and also help others to be more productive and successful.

Neuro-Linguistic Programming (NLP)

Neuro-Linguistic Programming (NLP) is an interpersonal communication model to establish relationship between desired behavioral patterns and the pattern of our thought process, and thus helps us to increase the self-awareness among people transforming them to a mentally and emotionally matured person. Richard Bandler and John Grinder (1975), the founders of NLP, through their studies could observe that there exists connection between neurological processes ("neuro"), language ("linguistic"), and behavioral pattern; hence through programming we can organize the same to achieve specific goals of life. Initially, focus of NLP was to use it for psychological therapy, as it could help in understanding the phobias, depression, habit disorder, psychosomatic illness, and learning disorders. Gradually, use of NLP has been accepted in recruitment and selection decisions also.

Ethical Guidelines for Psychological Testing

Ethical guidelines on the use of psychological testing mandate to provide feedback to the persons who participate in such assessment in terms of general assessment/issues, reliability and validity, norm groups, feedback to the applicant, etc.

To apply psychological testing in job interview, it is important to consider the following issues:

(1) Process of identification of constructs for a particular job.
(2) Process of reporting the test results.
(3) Previewing of test information before administration.
(4) Process of integrating psychological test scores and interview results.
(5) Norms for providing hiring recommendation.

Recruitment Metrics as Recruitment Tools

Sullivan (2013) classified recruitment metrics into three types: historical, real-time, and predictive. Historical metrics no more can help in strategic recruitment and selection decision, as with the passage of time, business scenarios also change. Real-time metrics have some utility, as using it HR managers can promptly alter or improve the decisions. These types of metrics are based on recent trend or recent recruitment performance. Third types of metrics are known as predictive metrics. These are future focused and help HR managers to predict future problems and opportunities in recruitment and selection.

Based on Sullivan's analysis, some of the recruitment metrics may be discussed as under:

(1) **Historical metrics:** Performance level of new hires, diversity inclusive recruitment.
(2) **Real-time metrics:** Missing of strategic opportunities for poor recruitment, delay in filing vacancy of key positions, performance failure of new hires, voluntary turnover of new hires, percentage of innovators in new hires, etc.
(3) **Predictive metrics:** Forecast to availability of quality candidates, forecast on recruitment competition, forecast on the talent opportunity, forecast on unemployment rate, forecast on labor costs, etc.

These apart, we have certain routine metrics, using what organizations can think of achieving efficiency in their recruitment and selection functions. Most of these metrics are commonly used by organizations.

(1) Rate of acceptance of job offer
(2) Quality of recruitment source
(3) Quality of the job applicants
(4) Satisfaction level with the recruitment process
(5) Recruitment performance
(6) Brand strength of employer

It is, however, for organizations to decide to select the appropriate metrics for measuring their recruitment and selection function. Number of research studies, including a research study carried out by the Boston Consulting group, could identify recruitment and selection exerts highest impact on the profit of the organization. Hence, it is advisable for organizations to choose the appropriate metrics for effective management of their recruitment and selection function.

Recruitment Analytics

Recruitment analytics refer to the use of big data for predictive recruitment decisions. It can facilitate in recruitment marketing, filtering of prospective candidates, identifying outliers, planning appropriate interview questions, and finally selecting the appropriate candidates, who can fit with the job and the organization and also who can be retained over a long period. It is important to remember that recruitment decisions are critical for organizational success; hence, analytics-driven recruitment can immensely benefit organizations in selecting appropriate candidates for the job positions. Some of the advantages of analytics-driven recruitment decisions are streamlining of hiring policies, focusing on recruitment marketing to evoke better qualitative and quantitative responses, objective evaluation of skills and competencies of the job applicants, and finally adopting proactive hiring approaches. However, many researchers suggest exclusive use of recruitment analytics for taking recruitment decisions may not be always desirable. It is important to make use of recruiters' experience, knowledge, and expertise along with the recruitment analytics for better recruitment decisions.

Ability Tests for Recruitment

Many organizations make use of standardized ability tests tools to measure knowledge, physical, mental, mechanical and clerical abilities of job seekers, so that right-fit recruitment can be made possible. Traditionally, ability tests are basic aptitude tests, also known as achievement tests, which help in measuring the level knowledge, which a prospective candidate acquired through his or her previous job experience, or previous knowledge. Some of the standard ability tests tools are:

- Intelligence test measures developed by Binet and Simon for assessment of the mental age of the job seekers
- Stanford-Binet Intelligence Scale
- Stanford-Binet Otis self-administering test if mental ability, etc.

Mental ability test tools measure several distinct abilities of the job applicants, and using the total scores obtained by a particular candidate, appropriate selection decisions can be taken by organizations. Some of the important mental ability constructs are memory span, figural classification, numerical fluency, spatial orientation, verbal comprehension, visualization, conceptual classification, intuitive reasoning, semantic relations, ordering general reasoning, figural identification, conceptual foresight, and logical evaluation.

Mechanical Ability Tests help in assessing job characteristics with machines and equipment. It tests manual performance, written problems, spatial visualization, perceptual speed and mechanical information. Similarly, for assessing clerical aptitude, Minnesota Clerical Test is also popular.

The use of various ability tests depending on the job characteristics has now become more popular as such tests can significantly predict the job performance.

SUMMARY

- Traditional recruitment and selection process is linear and it involves consecutive tasks. However, with the change in dynamics of business, recruitment and selection function has now become a business process. This requires use of various tools and techniques of recruitment and selection so that organizations can recruit only the right-fit in terms of performance, integration with the culture of organizations, and who can be developed and retained.
- After explaining various tools and techniques of recruitment and selection, the chapter explains concepts and processes of e-recruitment/digital recruitment, recruitment through social network sites, various personality assessments tools, use of assessment centers, IQ tests and test of emotional intelligence, and models. Modern recruitment tools like emotional intelligence, neuro-linguistic programming, and use of metrics, and analytics have also been discussed. The chapter also briefly discussed ethical issues in using psychological testing.

Key Words

Modern recruitment tools: Modern recruitment tools are those which are more technology-enabled, and which can facilitate in searching and sourcing potential talents for organizations without any geographical jurisdiction.

E-recruitment: Recruitment through social networking sites (SNS) or digital recruitment, which have now become important medium for strategic hiring in today's organizations.

Profile tracking/Applicant tracking systems: This system enables organizations to track suitable profiles for the job positions from a large pool of applicants.

Murray's theory: It assesses our personality traits based on our internal state of disequilibrium. Such assumption is based on the understanding that when we lack something it drives our behavior, expecting we will be able to achieve our expected results. Murray observes our personality is driven by our secondary needs, i.e., achievement, dominance, affiliation, and nurturance.

Recruitment analytics: It refers to the use of big data for predictive recruitment decisions. It can facilitate in recruitment marketing, filtering of prospective candidates, identifying outliers, planning appropriate interview questions, and finally selecting the appropriate candidates, who can fit with the job and the organization and also who can be retained over a long period.

Gamification: It involves application of game mechanics to nongame environments, like recruitment with primary focus to study how people get motivated and change their behavior.

Neuro-Linguistic Programming (NLP): It is an interpersonal communication model to establish relationship between desired behavioral patterns and the pattern of our thought process, and thus helps us to increase the self-awareness among people transforming them to a mentally and emotionally matured person.

Review Questions

1. Discuss some of the contemporary tools of recruitment and selection.
2. What is SNS-based recruitment? How SNS-based recruitment can help organization to attract talent?
3. What are different types of interviews? For selection of managerial level employees which types would be more relevant?
4. Why do we assign importance on personality assessment before selection? How personality factor can have effect on job performance?
5. Discuss the importance of assessment center-based evaluation for recruitment and selection.
6. IQ and EQ test scores are important in selection! Do you agree with this? Discuss with logic.
7. Briefly discuss different models of recruitment.
8. Explain how recruitment and selection functions can be managed effectively with metrics and analytics?

9. Write short notes on:
   (a) Digital recruitment
   (b) Unstructured Interviews
   (c) Stress interviews
   (d) NLP
   (e) Ability tests
   (f) Predictive analytics
   (g) Hogan's personality test
   (h) Employability Test

Critical Review Question

1. Identify some of the recent cases of top level recruitment in organizations. Critically comment on such cases of recruitment.

Multiple Choice Questions

1. Identify incorrect statement:
   (a) Recruitment is a strategic human resource management function
   (b) Primary objective of recruitment is to identify and attract potential employees
   (c) Paper-based recruitment is a nonlinear process with consecutive tasks
   (d) Recruitment activities are designed to attract and persuade qualified applicants to apply
   (e) A typical recruitment process is treated as a business process

2. Commonly used recruitment sources are the following, except:
   (a) Employee referrals
   (b) Social media
   (c) Manpower vendors
   (d) Corporate web-sites
   (e) None of the above

3. Tools and techniques used for recruitment and selection do not include:
   (a) Interview
   (b) Job-fitment trial
   (c) Personality assessment tests
   (d) Assessment centers
   (e) Competency-based approach

4. E-recruitment represents:
   (a) Recruitment through social networking sites (SNS)
   (b) Digital recruitment
   (c) Recruitment through Facebook, LinkedIn, Twitter
   (d) Internet-based recruitment
   (e) All of the above

5. SNS-based recruitment is a fast-growing method of hiring as:
   (a) More and more individuals post their resumes online in search for a better future
   (b) It increases ability of organizations to reach a larger potential applicant pool
   (c) It eliminates geographical constraints
   (d) Only (a) and (b)
   (e) Both (a), (b), and (c)

6. Indicate which is not a benefit of e-recruitment:
   (a) Reduction of recruitment costs
   (b) Reduction of cycle time for recruitment
   (c) Facilitate recruitment on merit
   (d) Facilitate wider reach to prospective pool of talents across the globe
   (e) All of the above

7. SNS-based recruitment tools are:
   (a) Profile tracking/applicant tracking systems
   (b) Video interviewing
   (c) Gamification
   (d) All of the above
   (e) None of the above

8. In recruitment gamification involves:
   (a) Application of game mechanics to nongame environments
   (b) Study how people are motivated and change their behavior
   (c) Attracting and engaging job applicants
   (d) All of the above
   (e) None of the above

9. Identify the incorrect statement:
   (a) Staffing Quantity Level is a recruitment model
   (b) Staffing Quality Level is a recruitment model
   (c) Candidates-fit with the culture of the organization is a recruitment model
   (d) Based on selection of recruitment models organizations develop their recruitment strategies
   (e) Staffing models cannot help in mediating, overstaffing, and understaffing in organizations

10. Indicate which is not a requirement of good interview practices:
   (a) Expertise in framing interview questions
   (b) Appropriate selection of a interview topic
   (c) Understanding of the rights and privileges of the interviewees
   (d) Flexible interview process
   (e) Phase-wise structuring of the interview process

11. Type(s) of interview can be:
   (a) Standardized interview
   (b) Depth interview
   (c) Telephone interview
   (d) All of the above
   (e) None of the above

12. Personality assessment cannot help in understanding:
   (a) Who could be the best-fit for the jobs and the organizations
   (b) Who could be a potential talent
   (c) What could be the interpersonal behavior of the potential hire
   (d) What could be the negotiation skill of the potential hire
   (e) What would be the appropriate career path for the potential hire

13. Study of personality can be made from different perspectives, except:
   (a) Cognitive perspective
   (b) Phenomenological perspective
   (c) Learning perspective
   (d) Training perspective
   (e) Learning perspective

14. Using NLP, we can understand the following, except:
   (a) Interpersonal communication model
   (b) Helps in understanding desired behavioral pattern
   (c) Pattern of thought process
   (d) Connects between neurological and language processes
   (e) Connects between neurological process, language process, and behavioral pattern

15. Ethical guidelines on the use of psychological testing mandate do not consider:
   (a) Process of reporting the test results
   (b) Process of identification of constructs for a particular job
   (c) Process of reporting test results
   (d) Process of integrating psychological test scores and interview results
   (e) Process of recruitment on political recommendation

16. Indicate which is not the correct answer for the standard ability tests:
   (a) Intelligence test measures
   (b) Stanford-Binet Intelligence Scale
   (c) Stanford-Binet Otis self-administering test
   (d) Standard Likert Scale
   (e) None of the above

Answers:

1. (c) 2. (e) 3. (b) 4. (e) 5. (e) 6. (a) 7. (d) 8. (d)
9. (e) 10. (d) 11. (d) 12. (d) 13. (d) 14. (d) 15. (e) 16. (d)

CASE STUDY

For Hyatt recruitment is more business focused

Hyatt, the global hospitality chain, always endeavors to recruit the best, as their core philosophy is to make a difference in the lives of the guests with their authentic hospitality services. With close to a lakh of employees, the company operates in 45 countries through their subsidiaries and franchise. Biggest challenge for Hyatt is to align their leadership with corporate goals. Such process starts right from the beginning; first by selecting people who can be well aligned with the company's vision and service orientation and culture, and second focusing on development of these people so that they can align with the corporate goals and contribute to ongoing success. Thus, both in employee selection and development, the company intended to achieve excellence. Making use of relationship-based selection methods with clarity on expectations from leadership positions, the company could come out with smart hiring and so also developing of hired employees, aligning with their business needs.

With strong talent pipeline, the company could actually source 80% of their managerial talents internally. For sourcing of rest 20% of managerial talents, the company uses word-of-mouth and internal referrals. This apart the company selects from large pool of external candidates' college graduates at entry level managerial positions. With core emphasis on top quality development of selected employees for future leadership positions in alignment with the business objectives, the company focuses on selection tools that can not only measure a potential hire's capabilities to face customers, but also can ensure that such potential hires can be retained, better engaged, and contribute to business success on a sustainable basis.

The company could come out with their customized recruitment solutions with support from consultants, factoring job observations, job analysis, testing through validation, culture-fit analysis, etc. Hyatt's recruitment and selection tools therefore are more inclusive, all encompassing, and result-oriented.

Question: Critically evaluate Hyatt's recruitment process. Do you think using this process Hyatt could really succeed in talent retention?

REFERENCES

Allden, N. and Harris, L. (2013), "Building a positive candidate experience: Towards a networked model of e-recruitment", *Journal of Business Strategy*, 34(5): 36–47.

Bandler, R. and Grinder, J. (1975), The Structure of Magic: A Book About Language and Therapy. Palo Alto: Science and Behavioural Books.

Barber, A.E. (1998), *Recruiting Employees*, Thousand Oaks, CA: Sage Publications.

Boyd, M.D. and Ellison, B.N. (2008), "Social network sites: Definition, history, and scholarship", *Journal of Computer-Mediated Communication*, 13(1): 210–230.

Cappelli, P. (2001), "Making the most of on-line recruiting", *Harvard Business Review*, 79(3): 139–146.

Davenport, T.H. and Short, J.E. (1990), "The new industrial engineering: Information technology and business process redesign", *Sloan Management Review*, 31(4): 11–27.

Doherty, R. (2010), "Getting social with recruitment", *Strategic HR Review*, 9(6): 11–15.

Greengard, S. (2012), "Picking—and keeping—the cream of the crop: Smart strategies are needed for both recruitment and retention of talent", *Human Resource Management International Digest*, 20(3): 26–29.

Goleman, D. (1998), *Working With Emotional Intelligence*, Bantam Books, New York.

Heneman, H.G. and Judge, T.A. (2009), *Staffing Organizations*, 6th Edition. McGraw-Hill/ Irwin. Boston, MA.

Hogan, R. (1997), *Handbook of Personality Psychology*, San Diego: Academic Press.

Lievens, F. and Chapman, D. (2010), *Recruitment and Selection*, in Wilkinson, A., Bacon, N., Redman, T. and Snell, S. (eds). The Sage Handbook of human resources management. London, Sage.

Minton-Eversole, T. (2007), "E-recruitment Comes of Age, survey says", *HR Magazine*, 52(8): 34.

Murray, H.A. (1938), *Explorations in Personality*, New York: Oxford University Press.

Reynolds, G.W. (1995), *Information systems for managers* (3rd. ed.). St. Paul, MN: West Publishing Company.

Sullivan, J. (2013), "How Google is Using People Analytics to Completely Reinvent HR", http://www.eremedia.com/tlnt/how-google-is-using-people-analytics-to-completely-reinvent-hr/. Seen on 27-12-2015

Tong, Y.K. and Sivanand, C.N. (2005), "E-recruitment service providers", *Employee Relations*, 27(1): 103–117.

Chapter 7

Legal Issues in Recruitment and Selection

LEARNING OBJECTIVES

After reading this chapter, you will be able to understand:

1 Conceptual understanding of legal issues in recruitment and selection
2 Benefits of legal-compliant recruitment and selection process
3 Diversity and equal employment opportunities
4 Equality in compensation design
5 Ethical issues in recruitment and selection

Country-Specific Legal Compliance Is a Necessity: Case of *Nimita*

In recruitment and selection, legal compliance issues precede companies' values and expectations, understanding of the key activity, determining the key hires, and then developing recruitment and selection process. *Nimita*, an international NGO, engaged in global childcare recently started operation in Noida, India. Being headquartered in the United States, *Nimita* thought they will continue to follow the same legal compliance in recruitment and selection, as the US laws pertaining to employment practices are more stringent than those in India. Based on this assumption, *Nimita* engaged one international-level manpower vendor, which is also headquartered in the United States and has operation in India. The multinational manpower vendor asked *Nimita* to comply with Indian Labor laws, which will avoid any possible litigation related to recruitment and selection in the future. However, *Nimita* argued this may enrage the donors who are Americans and who may not like *Nimita's* functions getting constricted by Indian Labor laws. However, to ease this problem, the manpower vendor came out with a detailed policy document, well within the Indian laws, and then made it transparent, detailing their hiring process on their website. This was further strengthened with series of frequently asked questions, so that prospective candidates for *Nimita* get adequately informed before they decide to compete for job positions. *Nimita* shared this document with their headquarter team and finally got the vetting and also the word of appreciation. With such documentation and its publication on their website, *Nimita* today functions without any legal constriction in their recruitment and selection process, and also in their overall human resource management practices.

INTRODUCTION

Recruitment and selection process in any organization has also ethical and legal dimensions. We have separately discussed on ethical issues. In this chapter, we will be focusing on legal issues, which may have potential effect on recruitment and selection process in Indian organizations. The potential effect of legal issues is not just limited to public sector organizations; it also encompasses the private sector. However, better understanding of the legal issues would be possible when we consider social and ethical norms in employment practices in India. Indian Constitution through series of Articles enshrined the need for diversity inclusivity, equity, and fair employment practices. Such compliances not only benefit the company in terms of avoiding litigation, but also help in building organizational brand identify.

Legal issues of recruitment and selection in India have potential effects on the nature of employment relationships, diversity management issues, and equal employment opportunities, child labor issues, contract labor issues, issues pertaining to compensation management, promotion, redeployment, etc. Not that in all these cases we have specific mandates on legal requirements. For example, promotional decisions in organizations do not come under any legal enforcement, but it is expected that employers will be fair and objective in their promotional decisions. Similarly, engaging contract workers in organizations is not in technical sense banned, but is used in a regulated manner. In this chapter, discussions have been made on important legal provisions, which organizations must adhere for their recruitment and selection process. Also the chapter highlights on those social norms of recruitment and selections, for which we may not have any legal mandates, but organizations need to demonstrate more inclusivity in their practices. Good example is diversity management practices.

Although in India we have more than 400 labor laws (including labor laws at State level), which is often viewed by foreign investors as the major deterrent for their investment; operationally, we find many Indian companies including some of the multinationals are not adhering to the provisions of labor laws in their employment practices. In India, we do not have effective machinery or institutional support systems to enforce labor laws. However, any good organization needs fair and legally complaint employment practices, including following of legally compliant recruitment and selection processes.

BENEFITS OF LEGAL-COMPLIANT RECRUITMENT AND SELECTION PROCESS

Instead of considering legal provisions as deterrent to quality hiring decisions, organizations in India need to adopt a more inclusive approach. Legal compliance in recruitment and selection to a great extent can help organizations achieve strategic intents. Some of the known benefits of legal-compliant recruitment and selection process can be listed as under:

- Can enhance brand value of organization—with increased brand value, organizations can attract and retain talent. Also organizations enjoy social recognition, which in the long run cascades to customers' confidence and increase in market share.
- Can enhance quality in recruitment and selection process—as organization gets more potential job applicants for their job positions, enjoying the opportunity to select the right-fit.

- Can facilitate unbiased recruitment and selection decisions with practice of fairness.
- Can create culture of fair and ethical practices as employees also feel that organization is truly ethical in their employment practices.
- Can abolish unfair employment practices, like engagement of child labor, engagement of contract workers in violation of Contract Labor (Regulation & Abolition) Act, 1970, etc.
- Can promote diversity inclusivity through diversity neutral recruitment and selection process.

Thus, legal compliance in recruitment and selection process needs to be seen more from inclusive perspective, realizing that it can benefit organization in many ways.

In India, Article 309 of the Constitution governs the recruitment and conditions of service of persons working under the Union or a State. As a result, recruitment and selection process in the Central and the State Government establishments are regulated. Time to time rules regulating the recruitment and selection, and so also the conditions of service are framed to govern the employment relationships. Recruitment rules in such establishments provide detailed information on eligibility criteria, service conditions, promotion, deputation, etc.

SNAPSHOTS ON LABOR LAWS GOVERNING RECRUITMENT AND SELECTION

Diversity Inclusivity in Recruitment and Selection

Workplace diversity issues have now generated enormous activities in organizations. Diversity management practices are positively seen by the stakeholders, and also contribute to organizational value-stream. Worldwide through various government actions, discriminatory employment practices based on race, color, religion, age, disability, gender, culture, and ethnicity have now been prohibited. With diverse workforces, culture of organization becomes complex. Hence, organizations need to change to accommodate the principles of valuing diversity. Among others, this requires focus on changing employees' attitudes and eliminating discriminatory behaviors.

Theoretical percepts of organizations emphasize convergence issues like collective goals, objectives, issues, problems, and results, which require people to come together irrespective of their religion, caste, race, gender, etc. Organizations need to integrate different diverse entities to pursue common goals. Managing diversity requires strict conformance to the principles of uniformity. A truly diverse organization is capable of achieving efficiency and competitiveness, pooling the collective efforts of diverse workforce. Diversity also ensures innovation. Diversity must be carefully and constantly nurtured. Diversity management is the attempt to bring together competing interests into a single whole. Without productive diversity, culture of the organization can suffer from the problems of lack of new initiatives, innovation, and responsiveness to change (Bhattacharyya, 2014).

Globally employment landscape is fast changing. Organizations now believe in gender inclusivity and cultural diversity of workforces. Definition of diversity is not, however, limited to gender and cultural issues; it even now encompasses ethnicity, race, age, religion, education, socio-economic background, etc. In Indian organizations, we, however, face the challenge of managing gender diversity (Bhattacharyya, 2010). Most of the Indian organizations are focused on managing gender diversity in workplaces to avoid the legal issues. But such perspectives cannot help organizations to gain from the diversity-neutral workplaces. This requires institutionalization of diversity-inclusive work culture. Again, there is a subtle difference between uniformity and diversity. When diversity neutrality is practiced in organizations to avoid eventual legal complications, we call it uniformity (Olsen & Martins, 2012). Contrarily, when diversity is embedded in organizational DNA, we call it diversity inclusive workplace (Jordan, 2011). Therefore, with uniformity in diversity management practices, we achieve legal compliance, but with diversity-inclusive work culture, we can gain organizational effectiveness.

Different Approaches to Diversity

Diversity inclusion and competitive advantage of organizations could be linked by Fleury (1999), based on study of Brazilian organizations. Fleury defined diversity as mixture of people within the similar social system. Therefore, diversity is an inclusive approach, encompassing race, gender, age, color, physical disability, ethnicity, etc. (Kundu & Turan, 1999). With encouraging results for practicing diversity neutrality and embracing diversity inclusion, organizations across the world started aligning diversity issues with their strategy (Hayes & Mandez, 1997; Palich & Gomez, 1999) to get the benefit of efficiency and effectiveness in terms of achieving higher productivity and improving quality (Morrison, 1992), etc. With these gradually diversity management practices have been acknowledged as necessity in the corporate world. Cox (1993) defined diversity management as organizational systems and practices making use of potential advantages of diversity. To ensure diversity inclusion and neutrality, the first thing that organizations need to do is following the principles of equal employment opportunities. For this, organizations first document their policies on diversity issues, and then try to institutionalize the culture of diversity inclusion through series of interventions. Such interventions may be periodic diversity management audit, aligning adherence to diversity policies with performance management systems, periodic training reinforcements on diversity, etc. In organizations human resource management department plays the critical role in institutionalizing diversity management practices.

Diversity management has now become a business imperative for organizations. However, approaches to diversity management vary from organizations to organizations with respect to deficiency, discrimination, and differentiation (Glastra, 1996) (Fig. 7.1).

Deficiency approach to diversity management restricts focus on individual-specific deficiencies in knowledge, competencies, and skills. Individual-specific deficiencies are assessed in terms of some preset organizational standards (Glastra, op. cit.). For example, performance standards of an organization may be predecided, based on certain parameters. Now when an individual employee is unable to reach the required performance standards, organizations can differentiate the compensation logically.

Discrimination approach is prejudiced diversity exclusion employment practices (Glastra, op. cit.). This is more purposive and deliberate employment practices of organizations to generate more profit through workplace inequality. At times, ill effects of discriminatory approach may not be for the reasons that this is endorsed by the organizations; rather it may be individual employees' choices and preferences. This obviously requires training reinforcement to bring desired attitudinal changes in employees.

Differentiation approach is attributable to cultural diversity (Glastra, op. cit.). Culture binds people together. Hence, in any workplace when

FIGURE 7.1 Approaches to diversity management.

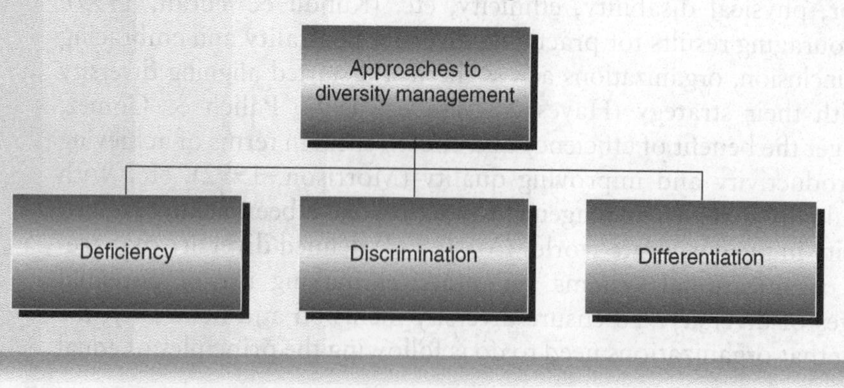

employees are represented by people from different culture, the organization needs to be more culture-inclusive, i.e., embedding cross-cultural issues in their workplaces. Otherwise, the said organization is bound to suffer from the problems of culture incongruence. Here again, learning on collective cultural differences is considered important (Trompenaars, 1993; Pinto, 1994; Pinto, et al., 2014; Hofstede, 1980; Hofstede, 2011).

Gender Diversity

Indian organizations are largely influenced by gender inequality. Gender diversity is a strategic imperative. Valuing gender diversity, organizations can balance their male and female workforce requirements, and create the workplace where all cross-sections of people can perform their best. Some researchers also observe gender diversity benefits organizations in marketing. With women in leadership positions, organizations can attract the female talent pool for their long-term sustainability and growth.

Gender diversity can best be achieved through macro level initiatives, viz., empowerment of women. Social inclusion of women in economics and politics can pave the way for organizational propensity to embed the gender mainstreaming, as part of their workplace practices. The term gender mainstreaming is more inclusive than gender diversity. Gender mainstreaming in workplace not only eliminates gender discriminations, providing equal opportunities to men and women, but also creates a level playing field for women employees, giving them space to balance their work-life. Thus, by valuing gender diversity, organizations not only gain, with economic empowerment, the society also benefits (Booth & Bennett, 2002; ILO, 2010).

However, creating equal opportunities both for men and women is not so easy at the organization level. At the outset it requires agreement to the philosophy of gender diversity by the top management of the organizations. Embracing gender diversity as a necessity, rather than a legal compulsion, can create the required platform for gender mainstreaming culture. This is followed by series of actions, including developing of policies, its implementation, and checking of conformance.

Having gender-sensitive staff policies, conforming to both regulatory requirements and social norms, and adherence to such policies in managing the organizations, is considered to be the most important step after agreement to the philosophy of gender diversity by the top management. For example, reflection of gender-sensitive staff policies can be better understood from the recruitment and selection process of the organizations. Unless the job specifically requires the male members, organizations should be neutral between male and female employees. Degree of such neutrality can be understood by calculating the number of female employees recruited from the number of female applicants for the job, and comparing the same with the recruitment of male employees. In many cases, organizations in their advertisements for job declare women to be unsuitable. Such declaration in job advertisements clearly indicates organizational approaches to gender diversity issues. Again many organizations have their policies for gender mainstreaming, but in practice still lack spontaneouity. Good examples are discrimination between male and female employees in giving annual increments, discrimination in promotion, overt and covert pressure on whistle blowing for sexual harassment, bias in performance reviews, etc.

Therefore, at organization level, gender mainstreaming not only requires embracing diversity-inclusive policies and programs, but also requires adequate monitoring mechanism for its strict adherence. Employees of the organizations also will start cooperating, once they are convinced on its benefits to the organizations. However, it requires systematic training and awareness programs.

Gender Diversity in India

Inclusive approach to gender diversity in India is enshrined in the Constitution. Series of Constitutional amendments have subsequently reaffirmed this. Even India has gone to the extent of enactment of Women's Reservation Bill in 2010. All these are expected to bring changes in the women employment and gender diversity in Indian organizations. After globalization, with the entry of multinational organizations, gender diversity issues in India have also been accentuated. On gender diversity issues, some of the multinationals have even gone beyond our Constitutional mandates, as in their respective countries, diversity issues are more valued. Indian organizations including public sectors over the years have shown more affirmative action to comply with the reservation policies of socially challenged communities. Such approach gradually overlooked the need for gender diversity issues. Articles 15 and 16 of the Indian Constitution, among others, also emphasized on the gender diversity issues. In addition, we had also series of debates, discussions, activities, workshops, seminars, emphasizing on the need for valuing gender diversity. Despite all such initiatives, share of women employment in organized sector in India is just 20.4% (2010). Share of women employment in public sector, however, is just 17.4% (2009).

To ensure compliance with the gender diversity norms, Securities and Exchange Board of India (SEBI) recently enforced that all stock exchange listed companies in India should at least have one women director in the Board of the companies. Even though compliance for this mandate was given by SEBI with a deadline of March 31, 2015, till today we find enormous list of defaulters. Some of the Indian companies complied with such mandate, appointing their wife, daughter, relative, or trusted female employee as Director to represent in the Board of the companies. This list also includes some of the Fortune 500 listed companies in India. Today, we observe in India in the Board of the companies women representation is limited to 4.7%. Contrarily in many countries like Norway, Finland, France, Sweden, the United States, Britain, and even in some developing countries, representation of women in the companies' Board is as high as 30%. Among the list of defaulting companies in India in terms of appointment of women directors in the Boards of the companies, we find even some government-owned or public sector companies. Such a scenario explains that in India we are yet to imbibe the culture of gender inclusivity.

Interestingly, however, many empirical studies, at both the national (India) and international levels, confirm valuing gender diversity, companies can achieve efficiency and effectiveness. This, therefore, negates out age-old perception that with gender diversity we dilute the quality of the organizations. Again viewing the gender diversity issues more for legal compliance, and, hence, getting rid of this problem appointing friends and relatives in the Board are not the solution. What is important is to acknowledge the fact that with gender diversity our organizations can add value to their business.

To understand India's position in terms of valuing gender diversity in organizational practices, in Table 7.1, we have shown the share of women employment in organized sector for the period from 1900 to 2010.

It is evident from the table that growth of women employment in organized sector, during this period, has almost remained stagnant, and even in some cases, such growth trend has decelerated.

Equality in Recruitment and Selection

Equality in recruitment and selection denotes adoption of practices respecting race, culture, ethnicity, language, disability, gender, religion, belief, and age. In all these matters, organizations need not only to be neutral, but even have more inclusive approaches. Good organizations always have documented policies on these issues. Right to Equality in public employment is a fundamental right as per Indian Constitution. This is enshrined in Article 16 of The Constitution of India. Right to Equality broadly refers to the equality in the eyes of law, discarding any unfairness on grounds of caste, race, religion, place of birth, and sex. It also includes equality of prospects in matters of employment, abolition of untouchability, and abolition of titles. Articles 14, 15, 16, 17, and 18 of the Constitution of India highlight the Right to Equality in detail. Hence from these perspectives, equality in recruitment and selection practices

TABLE 7.1 Share of women employment in organized sector.

Share of Women Employment Out of Total Employment in Organized Sector in India (1990 to 2011)									
									(Figures in '000)
Year	Public sector			Private sector			Total		
	Women	Total	% of Women	Women	Total	% of Women	Women	Total	% of Women
1990*	2256	–	–	1390	–	–	–	36.46	–
1991*	2347	–	–	14.34	–	–	–	37.81	–
1992	2467.0	19209.6	12.8	1522.7	7846.1	19.4	3889.8	27055.7	14.4
1993	2476.7	19326.1	12.8	1549.7	7850.5	19.7	4026.3	27176.6	14.8
1994	2564.6	19444.9	13.2	1589.3	7929.9	20.0	4153.9	27374.8	15.2
1995	2600.4	19466.3	13.4	1627.5	8058.5	20.2	4227.9	27524.7	15.4
1996	2634.5	19429.3	13.6	1791.9	8511.6	21.1	4426.4	27940.9	15.8
1997	2727.6	19559.1	14.0	1909.4	8685.5	22.0	4637.0	28244.5	16.4
1998	2762.7	19417.8	14.2	2010.9	8747.9	23.0	4773.6	28165.8	17.0
1999	2810.7	19414.8	14.5	2018.4	8698.2	23.2	4829.2	28113.1	17.2
2000	2857.0	19313.7	14.8	2065.8	8646.0	23.9	4922.8	27959.7	17.6
2001*	2859.2	19137.5	14.9	2090.1	8651.7	24.2	4949.3	27789.2	17.8

(continued)

TABLE 7.1 Continued

Share of Women Employment Out of Total Employment in Organized Sector in India (1990 to 2011) (Figures in '000)									
Year	Public sector			Private sector			Total		
	Women	Total	% of Women	Women	Total	% of Women	Women	Total	% of Women
2002*	2886.7	18773.4	15.4	2048.7	8432.1	24.3	4935.4	27205.5	18.1
2003*	2904.7	18579.7	15.6	2063.7	8420.7	24.5	4968.4	27000.3	18.4
2004*	2890.0	18196.7	15.9	2044.4	8246.0	24.8	4934.4	26442.7	18.7
2005*	2921.0	18006.6	16.2	2095.3	8452.3	24.8	5016.2	26458.6	19.0
2006*	3002.8	18188.3	16.5	2117.7	8805.1	24.1	5120.5	26993.3	19.0
2007*	3017.5	18002.2	16.8	2294.4	9274.0	24.7	5311.9	27276.2	19.5
2008*	3040.4	17674.0	17.2	2472.2	9875.0	25.0	5512.0	27548.0	20.0
2009*	3091.1	17790.0	17.4	2488.8	10307.0	24.2	5580.0	28098.0	19.9
2010*	–	–	–	–	–	–	5859.0	28708.0	20.4
2011*	–	–	–	–	–	–	5954.0	28999.0	20.5

Note: * : As on March 31.

Source: Ministry of Statistics and Programme Implementation Govt. of India. (ON212) & Ministry of Labour and Employment, Govt. of India. (ON318)

even extend to private sector employment. Private sector organizations in India, however, limit their focus on those issues, which are governed by explicit legal mandates.

Practice of equality in recruitment and selection enables organizations to attract larger pool of candidates, and in the process facilitates selection of quality manpower, who can benefit organizations in achieving their strategic and business goals. Practicing equality not only requires policy support, even calls for adequate training of manpower so that they can enforce such practices in organizations. To ensure organizations are successfully practicing equality in employment, particularly, in their recruitment and selection process, adverse impact analysis is done. For example, for the same job, there may be applicants from different groups of people. Let us assume we are differentiating applicants in terms of disability, gender, and ethnicity. Distribution of 1000 applicants for a job position in the above categories, number of persons selected from each category, and percentage of selection has been made as presented in Table 7.2:

TABLE 7.2 Details of applicants.

Details	Applicants with disability	Female applicants	Male applicants	Ethnic applicants	Total
Nature of applicants	100	300	500	100	1000
Percentage of applicants in each category	10	30	50	10	100
Selected applicants	10	20	75	5	110
Percentage of selected applicants in each category	100	66.66	150	50	Total will not add to 100

If we analyze the pattern of recruitment and selection, based on the above, we can apparently see the adverse impact in cases of selection of female and ethnic candidates. However, companies may have predetermined policies on quota-based selection, in line with government-announced reservation systems.

Adverse impact analysis can be done for individual category of applicants in terms of applied, shortlisted, and appointed. For example, we can analyze candidates in terms of disabled and not disabled, ethnic and non-ethnic, etc. Good organizations time to time analyze such data to assess whether they are following equality in true sense.

Theoretically, adverse impact in recruitment and selection denotes discriminatory selection practices, which prejudice the interest of the protected group. Adverse impact analysis can be done in all areas of employment practices, like recruitment and selection, succession planning, compensation decision, promotion, training, transfer, and also performance appraisal. Negative effect of recruitment decisions on protected group often may not be felt by the organizations, i.e., when decisions are unintentional. In India for protected group of people, we have host of legislation and rules, violation of which while taking recruitment decisions, whether intentional or unintentional, may be vulnerable to discriminatory employment practices. In recruitment and selection decisions, adverse impact analysis is done taking into consideration the selection rate with respect to gender, race, ethnic group, culture, language, caste, religion, or disability. Organizations need to have clear policy guidelines on these issues. Although for private organizations, we do not have any legal mandates, but their employment practices can be questioned by the protected group, when they feel discriminated.

Equality in Compensation Design

Equality issues are not just limited to initial hiring decisions. It extends to compensation design. While designing compensation for every job position, public sector organizations strictly follow equity principles. Merit issues, however, are taken care of through performance-related pay (PRP). For public sector companies, PRP is regulated by memorandum of understanding (MOU) by Department of Public Enterprises (DPE). Such MOU is like key performance areas (KPAs) with detailing on every performance indicator (KPI). PRP is a variable component of compensation, solely linked to the performance, and with the earning of more variable pay one can earn higher than his or her peer in the same job. However, base pay and other fixed components of pay would remain the same for a specific job position. In private sector, merit-based pay systems being followed, pay variation in the same job position is not unlikely. Some private sector organizations, however, value equity, and reward good performers through PRP. They align their KPAs with the business goals and strategies. Good private sector organizations time to time go for pay calibration, so that they can ensure competitive compensation for their employees. This helps them to retain talent, substantially reducing the rate of attrition. Internally also they go for pay calibration, time to time measuring equity/inequity in pay using compa-ratio.

For external equity, Salary Range Midpoints and Market Reference Points (MRPs) represent the market average pay for positions. An employee's salary compa-ratio indicates how his or her salary compares to the market. Salary compa-ratios should reflect employee work experience, skills, and performance. Compa-ratios are used to measure an employee's pay relative to the market average pay for his or her position and to facilitate salary equity analyses among groups of employees. For internal benchmarking or calibration, we take an employee's Annual Salary and divide it by the Salary Range Midpoint associated with the grade level of the employee's position, or the MRP if the position has one. Then multiply the result by 100. This produces a salary compa-ratio, or the employee's salary as a percentage of the midpoint/MRP. A compa-ratio of <1 (or less than 100%) means that the employee is paid lower than his or her band's midpoint (average).

To enforce pay equity within an organization, first we calculate compa-ratio and then decide for the same level of performance, what should be our rate of increment. Therefore, the amount of increase awarded to an employee is usually dependent on the employee's performance and compa-ratio. Let us consider the following case:

Employee	Salary	Midpoint	Compa-ratio	Performance
Mr. X	42,500	50,000	0.85	Excellent
Mr. Y	56,000	50,000	1.12	Excellent

An employee who is an excellent performer with a compa-ratio of 0.85 should receive a larger raise than an excellent performer with a compa-ratio of 1.12. Calculating compa-ratios is a simple process that provides complex information to compensation specialists. When your compa-ratio—the ratio of your pay to the market rate for your job—significantly exceeds 100%, your employer is extremely generous, or your job is in great demand, or you are ready for a promotion.

Most organizations provide a recommended course of action to take if the compa-ratio falls within a certain percentile range. For example, if the ratio percentage falls between 0 and 33%, the result is a grade demotion. If the ratio falls between 34 and 66%, the result is a lateral movement and if it falls between 67 and 100%, the action is a promotion.

Similar concern for equality in employment practices like promotional decisions is very important. As an extended part of recruitment and selection, employee promotion systems influence organizational hiring, both in terms of internal and external recruitment. One promotional decision at the senior level will have rippling effect on subsequent levels, resulting vertical movement. Fair and transparent promotion is not only viewed by the employees as good practice, it also adds to the organizational brand value. Often organizations make their promotional decisions discretionary, prejudging others' interests who are also eligible to get promoted. Discretionary promotional decisions may not be legally untenable, but prejudiced employees can question such decisions, and even can solicit court intervention. Therefore, in taking promotional decisions, it is always essential to adhere to the principles of equity.

Legal Briefing on Recruitment and Selection in India

For employment practices as a whole, we have couple of legal and constitutional provisions, compliance with which has now become important for organizations. We have seen most of legal and constitutional mandates require strict conformity in public employment. However, against private organizations, protected group of people can frame charges, when they feel their interests are getting prejudiced. For recruitment and selection, private organizations are expected to frame their own set of rules within the ambit of the law of land. It is a good example diversity issues. Like public sectors, private organizations are also expected to embrace diversity inclusivity, so that diversity gets embedded with the strategies and business practices.

Various acts and provisions that encompass recruitment and selection decisions in India are discussed below.

The Child Labor Prohibition and Regulation Act prohibits the employment of children below 14 years and 15 years in certain specified employment. Subsequently, the Union Cabinet cleared amendments to the child labor law to allow children below the age of 14 to work in select non-hazardous family enterprises. These norms are also applicable to entertainment (excepting circus) and sports industry. The new Child Labor (Prohibition and Regulation) Bill, 2012 now recommends ban on child labor unless they finish elementary education. Even International Labor Organization (ILO) considers child labor issue as the most important international labor standard issue, violation of which may debar organization from international trade by the World Trade Organization (WTO). For using child labor, WTO imposed restriction on international trade on Bangladesh garment manufacturers, Indian carpet manufacturers, etc. Almost 2% of Indian workforces are children.

Like this we also have Employment Exchanges (Compulsory Notification of Vacancies) Act, which calls for notification of all vacancies in employment exchanges to get the list of prospective candidates for the non-executive/non-managerial level job positions. We have Apprentices Act, Interstate Migrant Workmen Regulation of Employment and Conditions of Service Act, The Factories Act, The Mines Act, Equal Remuneration Act, The Contract Labor (Regulation and Abolition) Act, numerous constitutional provisions for reservations in services, policies, rules and regulations, etc. which encompass the recruitment and selection process in organizations.

In the United States, we also see numerous legal provisions, which regulate recruitment and selection processes in organizations. What is important to see some specific Acts in the United States regulate directly the recruitment and selection processes, for example, The Age Discrimination in Employment Act, Uniform Guidelines in Employee Selection Procedures, The Immigration Reform and Control Act, The Americans with Disabilities Act, The Genetic Information Nondiscrimination Act, etc. We also find similar trend in many European countries like Australia, Japan, etc.

Constitutional provisions in India that regulate recruitment and selection process have already been discussed above. Such important provisions are Article 14, which harps on equality before law, Article 15 that focuses on prohibition of discrimination on grounds of religion, race, caste, sex or place of birth, etc. We also find similar provisions in Article 16, which guarantees equality of opportunity in matters of public employment, abolition of untouchability, protection of certain rights regarding freedom of speech, Article 23 that prohibits traffic in human beings and forced labor, Article 24 prohibiting employment of children in factories, Article 43 for living wage for workers, etc.

Internationally, now the concept of fair employment practices emerged, which call for recruitment and selection of employees based on merit, sensitivity toward age, race, gender, religion, marital status, family responsibilities, or disability. Good example of practicing fair employment practices by a multination company is GE. GE is committed to fair employment practices prohibiting any form of illegal discrimination and provides equal access and fair treatment to all employees on the basis of merit. Wherever GE goes, the company adheres to all applicable laws in their employment practices. GE particularly emphasizes on adhering to the laws pertaining to freedom of association, privacy, and recognition of the right to engage, collective bargaining, prohibition of forced, child, and elimination of any improper employment discrimination. With such fair employment practices more than 200 year old conglomerate GE continues to grow.

SUMMARY

- Indian Constitution, Labor Laws (both central and state), social norms, and culture influence recruitment and selection process in India. For public employments all these requirements are sacrosanct. For private organizations, however, not all requirements, except the labor law provisions, and partly constitutional provisions, need to be met compulsorily. However, complying with such requirements ensures good employment practices, and enhances organizational brand identity.
- Compliance with diversity issues is increasingly gaining importance. Most important constituent of diversity issue is gender inclusivity. Although we have constitutional provisions for employment equity, on gender issue, organizations still continue their practices more as legal compliant rather than taking an inclusive approach, recognizing the importance of engaging female employees for innovation and business growth.
- To ensure recruitment and selection function complies with the entire constitutional, legal, social, and cultural requirements, organizations time to time calculate the adverse impact ratio, based on which they calibrate their process.
- Well-designed and all-compliant recruitment and selection process benefits companies in terms of attracting and retaining talent, as companies enjoy high brand value.

Key Words

Recruitment rules: Recruitment rules provide detailed information on eligibility criteria, service conditions, promotion, deputation, etc.

Managing diversity: It integrates different diverse entities to pursue common goals, and thus requires strict conformance to the principles of uniformity.

Diverse organization: A truly diverse organization pools the collective efforts of diverse workforce, ensures innovation, and achieves efficiency and competitiveness.

Diversity neutrality: Practice of avoiding legal complications on diversity issues in organizations. We also call it practice of uniformity.

Diversity inclusivity: Process of embedding diversity in organizational DNA and creating a diversity-inclusive workplace.

Deficiency approach: Practice of focusing on individual-specific deficiencies in knowledge, competencies, and skills. Individual-specific deficiencies are assessed in terms of some preset organizational standards.

Discrimination approach: Prejudiced diversity exclusion employment practices.

Review Questions

1. Discuss why legal issues are important in India for recruitment and selection decisions.
2. What are the benefits of a legal-compliant recruitment and selection process?
3. Briefly discuss on labor laws in India which can exert influence on recruitment and selection decisions.
4. What is diversity inclusivity? How diversity inclusivity can help an organization in recruitment and selection?
5. Explain status of gender diversity practices in Indian organizations.
6. Explain the principles of equality in recruitment and selection and in compensation design.
7. Write short notes on:
   (a) Constitutional provisions for recruitment and selection process
   (b) Child Labor Prohibitions and Regulations Acts
   (c) Principles of Equality in Compensation Design
   (d) Diversity inclusivity
   (e) Differentiation approach in diversity
   (f) Gender diversity
   (g) Gender mainstreaming

Critical Review Questions

1. Visit any organization (it can be a virtual visit also). Study their diversity management practices. Comment whether such practices can institutionalize diversity inclusivity in your selected organization?
2. The Government of India is going for major labor law reforms. Critically review impact of such reforms on recruitment and selection practices in Indian organizations.

Multiple Choice Questions

1. Legal issues of recruitment and selection in India have potential effects on the following, except:
   (a) Nature of employment relationships
   (b) Diversity management issues
   (c) Equal employment opportunities
   (d) Child labor issues
   (e) Skill development issues

2. Identify incorrect statement:
   (a) Promotional decisions in organizations do not come under any legal enforcement
   (b) It is expected that employers will be fair and objective in their promotional decisions
   (c) Engaging contract workers in organizations not in technical sense banned, but used in a regulated manner
   (d) Diversity inclusivity includes gender mainstreaming
   (e) None of the above

3. Legally-compliant recruitment and selection can benefit organizations in following ways, except:
   (a) Can enhance brand value of organization
   (b) Can enhance quality in recruitment and selection process
   (c) Can facilitate unbiased recruitment and selection decisions with practice of fairness
   (d) Can hinder recruitment and selection on merit
   (e) Can create culture of fair and ethical practices as employees also feel that organization is truly ethical in their employment practices

4. Identify the incorrect statement on diversity inclusivity:
   (a) Diversity inclusivity practices are positively seen by the stakeholders
   (b) Diversity inclusivity contributes to organizational value stream
   (c) Diversity inclusivity means embedding culture of diversity in workplace practices
   (d) Diversity inclusivity and diversity neutrality can be treated as one and the same
   (e) Diversity inclusivity helps in avoiding discriminatory employment practices

5. Approaches to diversity management are the following, except:
   (a) Deficiency
   (b) Discrimination
   (c) Differentiation
   (d) Cultural diversity
   (e) Diversity neutrality

6. Gender diversity in organizations can best be achieved through:
   (a) Empowerment of women in workplaces
   (b) Inclusion of women in team
   (c) Increasing representation of women in management of organizations
   (d) Providing equal opportunities to men and women
   (e) All of the above

7. In addition to gender diversity equality in recruitment and selection denotes adoption of practices respecting:
   (a) Race
   (b) Culture
   (c) Ethnicity
   (d) Language

8. Adverse impact analysis in recruitment and selection helps us in understanding:
   (a) Discriminatory selection practices
   (b) Measure equality in recruitment and selection decisions
   (c) Understanding whether recruitment and selection decision of organization prejudiced the interest of the protected group
   (d) Selection rate with respect to gender, race, ethnic group, culture, language, caste, religion, or disability
   (e) All of the above

9. Identify incorrect constitutional provisions in India that regulate recruitment and selection process:
   (a) Article 14
   (b) Article 15
   (c) Article 23
   (d) Article 24
   (e) Article 44

10. Fair employment practices in recruitment and selection denote:
   (a) Recruitment and selection based on merit
   (b) Diversity inclusive recruitment and selection
   (c) Avoidance of improper employment discrimination
   (d) Refraining from engagement of child labor
   (e) All of the above

Answers:

1. (e) 2. (e) 3. (d) 4. (d) 5. (d) 6. (e) 7. (e) 8. (e) 9. (e) 10. (e)

CASE STUDY

Exxon Mobil

ExxonMobil, the global energy company, has embraced diversity inclusivity in their workplaces. The company believes this could enhance their competitive advantages. The global diversity framework of the company focuses on:

- Attracting, developing, and retaining the diverse workforce to meet global business needs.
- Fostering productive work environment respecting individual and cultural differences.

- Identifying and developing leadership capabilities in a variety of international and cultural environments.

Company's standard business conduct covers all human resource management practices, including recruitment and selection; with commitment to equal employment opportunities, prohibition of harassment and discrimination in the workplace, alignment with applicable laws and regulations of respective countries of operation. Gender identity issues have been recognized by the company much before federal law in the United States. The company believes harassment in any form directly conflicts with the company policy and hence should not be tolerated. To ensure fair employment practices, the company educates and trains all employees worldwide. With 75,000 headcounts the U.S. headquartered energy major today sets example before others.

Being committed to professional development of employees with long-term career-oriented approach to support their career goals, and being committed to ongoing employee coaching and continuous performance improvement, today the company has become one of preferred employers of the world.

ExxonMobil today is a glaring example whose fair employment practices could make them one of the best practice organizations for others to emulate.

Question: Emulating ExxonMobil way, i.e., diversity inclusivity, organizations can benefit in terms of talent attraction. Support your answer with evidences from other organizations.

REFERENCES

Bhattacharyya, D.K. (2014), *Organizational Behaviour* (2nd ed.). New Delhi: Oxford University Press.

Bhattacharyya, D.K. (2013), "Performance-Related Pay: Evidence-Based Studies in Indian Central Public Sector Enterprises", *Compensation and Benefits Review*, 45, 215–222.

Bhattacharyya, D.K. (2010), *Cross Cultural Management*. New Delhi: PHI.

Bolman, L.G. and Deal, T.E. (2003), *Reframing organizations: Artistry, Choice, and Leadership*. San Francisco: Jossey-Bass.

Booth, C. and Bennett, C. (2002), "Gender Mainstreaming in the European Union: Towards a New Conception and Practice of Equal Opportunities", *European Journal of Women's Studies*, 9, 430–446.

Bryan, J.H. (1999), "The Diversity Management", *Executive Excellence*, 16, May, pp. 6.

Cox, T.H. Jr. (1993), *Cultural Diversity in Organizations: Theory, Research and Practice*. San Francisco: Berrett Koehler.

Ely, R.J. and Thomas, D.A. (2001), "Cultural Diversity at Work: The Effects of Diversity Perspectives on Work Group Process and Outcomes", *Administrative Science Quarterly*, 46, 229–73.

Fleury, M.T.L. (1999), "The management of culture diversity: Lessons from Brazilian companies", *Industrial Management and Data systems*, 99, 58–59.

Glastra, Folke, J. (1996), "Intercultural Management and the Calculation of Difference", *Opleiding and Ontwikkeling*, 9, 13–20.

Hayes, R. and Mendez, R.A., (1997), *The Diversity Directive*. New York: McGraw Hill.

Hofstede, Greet (1980), *Culture's Consequences: International Differences in Work-Related Values*. Beverly Hills, London: Sage.

Hofstede, G. (2011), "Dimensionalizing cultures: The Hofstede Model in Context", *Online Readings in Psychology and Culture*, 2(1). Retrieved February, 10, 2015, from http://dx.doi.org/10.9707/2307-0919.1014.

International Labour Organization (2010), Gender Mainstreaming Strategies in Decent Work Promotion: Programming Tools. *GEMS Toolkit*/ILO Regional Office for Asia and the Pacific, Bangkok. Retrieved February, 2015, from http://www.ilo.org/wcmsp5/groups/public-asia/ro-bangkok/sro-bangkok/documents/publications/wcms143849.pdf.

Jordan, Hudson, T. (2011), Moving From Diversity to Inclusion, *Profiles in Diversity Journal*. Retrieved February 10, 2015, from http://www.diversityjournal.com/1471-moving-from-diversity-to-inclusion.

Kundu, S.C. and Turan, M.S. (1999), "Managing cultural diversity in future organizations", *The Journal of Indian Management and Strategy*, 4, 61–72.

McMillan-Capehart (2005), "A Configurational framework for diversity – Socialization and culture", *Personnel Review*, 34, 488–503.

Morrison, A.M. (1992), *The new leaders: Guidelines on leadership diversity in America*. San Francisco: Jossey-Bass.

Olsen, J.E. and Martins, L.L. (2012), "Understanding organizational diversity management programs: A theoretical framework and directions for future research", *Journal of Organizational Behavior*, 33, 1168–1187.

Palich, L.E. and Gomez-Meija, L.R. (1999), "A theory of global strategy and Firm Efficiencies: Considering the effects of Cultural Diversity", *Journal of Management*, 25, 587–606.

Pinto, D. (1994). *Intercultural communication*. Bohn, Stafleu: Van Loghum.

Pinto, F.C., Serra, R.F. and Ferreira, M.P. (2014), "A Bibliometric Study on Culture Research in International Businesses", *BAR, Rio de Janerio*, 11, 340-363. Retrieved February, 15, 2015, from http://dx.doi.org/10.1590/1807-7692bar201430p.

Rao, A., Stuart, R. and Kelleher, D. (1999), *Gender at Work: Organization Change for Equality*. Connecticut: Kumarian Press.

Richard, W.J. (1997), Workforce 2020: Work and Workers in the 21st Century. Washington, D.C. Hudson Institute.

Rodrigue, Fontaine (2007), "Cross-cultural Management: Six perspectives", *Cross Cultural Management – An International Journal*, 14, 125–135.

Thomas, A. (1991), "Provision for Social Welfare: Employer Participation", *Social Work*, 27, 44–49.

Thomas, D. and Ely, R. (1996), "Making Differences Matter: A New Paradigm for Managing Diversity", *Harvard Business Review*. September–October. 79–91.

Trompenaars, F. (1993), *Riding the Waves of Culture: Understanding Cultural Diversity in Business*. London: Nicholas Brealey Publications.

Chapter 8

Ethical Issues in Recruitment and Selection

LEARNING OBJECTIVES

After reading this chapter, you will be able to understand:

1. Definitions and concepts of ethical recruitment and selection
2. Dimensions of ethics in recruitment and selection
3. Importance of ethics in recruitment and selection
4. Ethical due diligence
5. Gender mainstreaming and recruitment ethics
6. Ethics-compliant recruitment policy
7. Ethical framework of recruitment and selection
8. Social media and recruitment ethics
9. Recruitment and selection ethics in public sector enterprises
10. Ethical breaches

Recruitment Ethics for HR Managers

Talent sourcing is always a challenge for Summer Salt, a company that provides creative HR solutions to clients. HR managers of the company being always on talent hunt, make employment commitment right in the interview board after salary negotiation, once they are convinced that the new hires are the right-fit for the jobs. Such selected new hires are told that they will get the job offer letters soon, and should be prepared to join within a week time. While communicating this information to a new hire, who is currently working with one of the top competitors of the company, the job candidate said in his company three months' notice period is mandatory, else he has to give three months' notice pay to the company. HR manager of Summer Salt then recommended the candidate to better resign from the job and start taking leaves, while continuing to work with them. The job candidate refused to do so, citing that this would be gross violation of employment ethics, which he had learnt from his present company. Even after this the HR manager of Summer Salt was insistent, and was urging the candidate to join. Subsequently, the HR manager agreed to give some joining bonus to cover three months' notice pay and additional incentive of ₹50,000. The candidate thereafter agreed to join and asked the HR manager to prepare the letter of appointment by the next day, so that he can come and collect it in person.

INTRODUCTION

Ethical business practices in organizations have now become extremely important. Like other business functions ethical issues also encompass recruitment and selection process. To attract talent, it is important for organizations to get identified as ethical organizations. Organizations can give such ethical signals to job aspirants, embracing ethical organizational and recruitment practices. Beu and Buckley (2004) could study the ill-effect of poor ethical decisions, which not only damages reputation of companies, even wipes out billions of dollars, ultimately causing organizational collapse. We have many such examples in the corporate world. For recruitment and selection, ethical issues are particularly important because job seekers prefer such ethics-compliant organizations, and feel the urge to apply for the job.

In organizations, ethical issues in recruitment and selection are primarily understood from certain common perspectives. These are like presenting job positions to prospective talent, process of identifying talent, and the manner of conducting the interview. In cases, where professional guidelines for the specific jobs are available, say chartered accountant, company secretary, doctor, lawyer, etc., ethical issues largely encompass the same. Some companies may have their own ethical guidelines in recruitment and selection, which even they make public through their web-sites. Such documented ethical guidelines for recruitment and selection process not only help in ethical decision-making process, but also provide valuable ethical signals to prospective talents.

In this chapter, ethical issues for recruitment and selection have been discussed in terms of both theories and corporate practices.

DEFINITIONS AND CONCEPTS

Before we define and conceptualize ethical issues in recruitment and selection, it is important for us to comprehend the differences between the ethics and values, particularly, in the context of recruitment and selection. Values are our possessed or deeply held beliefs, which get reflected in our actions, choices, and attitudes. Ethics are certain principles that we need to follow while we do our job. Hence ethics are more like moral rights and duties, which elicit our responses for doing things rightly. Often, we confuse ethics with religious mandates, and even as legal requirements. Complying with religious mandates or legal provisions by default cannot make our decisions ethical. For example, uniformity in diversity as a practice in recruitment and selection may comply with legal requirements, but certainly not guarantee ethical compliance, which additionally requires diversity inclusivity approach in recruitment and selection. We need to have better clarity on diversity uniformity and diversity inclusivity. A diversity neutral recruitment and selection process is compliant with legal requirements for an organization. Contrarily, diversity inclusivity in recruitment and selection would only be there when we recruit merit without factoring the diversity constructs.

In recruitment and selection, ethical compliance denotes adopting fair practices without any discrimination. Asking job applicants any question that may elicit personal information, which has no bearing with the job, can also be construed as ethical violation. Although we do not have adequate research information on ethical recruitment and selection, from the organizational practices, we can deduce certain decision-making processes, which can be adjudged as ethical. These are not just standalone ethical decisional model for recruitment and selection alone. It is applicable for any managerial decision-making process in organizations. Ethical recruitment and selection decision-making process ensures (Fig. 8.1):

FIGURE 8.1 Decision-making process for ethical recruitment and selection.

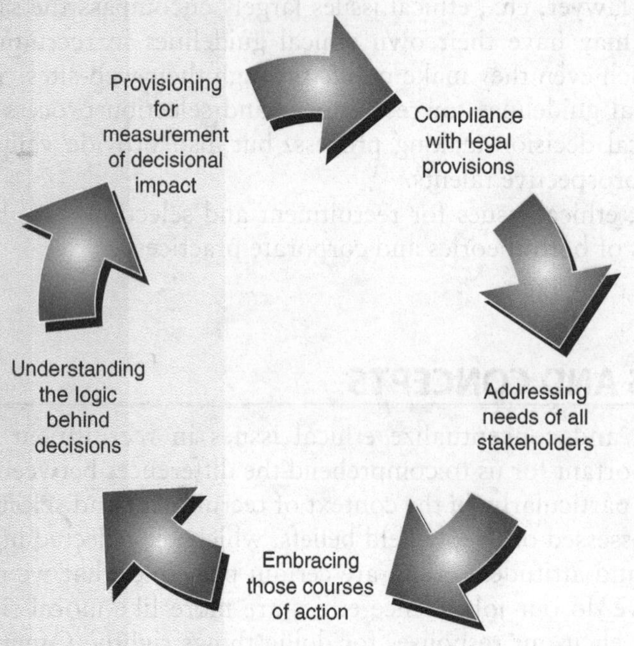

(1) Compliance with legal provisions
(2) Addressing needs of all stakeholders
(3) Embracing those courses of action, which can do more good than harm
(4) Understanding the logic behind decisions
(5) Provisioning for measurement of decisional impact

Compliance with the legal provisions to a great extent can alleviate the problems of our decision-making process in recruitment and selection. In fact, it reduces the chance of unethical decisions. Similarly by meeting expectations of different stakeholders (to the extent rational), we can ensure ethical compliance. HR managers confound with multiple options while taking recruitment and selection decisions. When they consider the best decision alternative, which can do more good than harm to organizations and its stakeholders, ethical compliance is best achieved. Interpreting the logic behind decisions, provisioning for measurement of decisional impact, HR managers can also achieve ethical compliance. Often HR managers confront with the problems of deciding between two decisions, as they appear as equally correct. Particularly in recruitment and selection-related decision making, such problems are common. In such cases, it is always recommended that HR managers must go for that decision alternative which in terms of ethics best-fit than the other alternative. The final test, however, is to take a call on ourselves, are we right, and are we meeting our core values and beliefs. Therefore, thinking and acting ethically in recruitment and selection for HR managers is difficult and not unachievable. Without ethical compliance in recruitment and selection, HR managers will not be able to build the brand value of the organization, and attract talent for selection against future job positions. Also for not considering the ethical issues, HR managers will also fail to achieve business goals and strategic intents of the organizations.

DIMENSIONS OF ETHICS IN RECRUITMENT AND SELECTION

For HR managers, it is important to understand various ethical dimensions of recruitment and selection functions. However, the problems here are the pattern of decisions on employee selection. Smart recruiter needs to be more practical, more capable to take instantaneous decisions, etc. Ethics not just influence during the selection of candidates, it even starts with the initial process of job design.

For better understanding of ethical dimensions in recruitment and selection, as HR managers and recruiters we have to first understand moral or ethics attached to the process. We select the candidates who in future emerge as winners contributing to business goals of organizations. This means they will emerge as valuable members of the organizational talent pool. Recruitment and selection involves wise decision making, based on the holistic assessment of the candidates, and sustained vigilance through the process of manpower planning, acquisition, selection interview, and reference-checking processes.

Ethical dimensions encompass the actual decisions on recruitment and selection, i.e., exactly at the time we take decisions on offering a job to the candidate, and at the same time, and also the relationships between the candidates and the recruiting member of the organizations. What are the job position requirements, and what candidates we are hiring, is a serious ethical issue, which many organizations, knowingly or unknowingly, violate. We have enough evidences from the corporate world, when selected talents have been assigned to some jobs, which are not within their areas of expertise; as a result, such talents fail to deliver the results, and gradually quit the organizations. Such talents, on whom organizations have shadowed unethical behavior, later share their experiences in social media like LinkedIn, Glass Doors, etc., which eventually destroy their reputation. Again, we have examples of organizations also that unnecessarily raise the bar, rendering many right-fit candidates unsuitable for the job positions. Doing so, they feel they can get better talent for the job positions. This is also another important unethical behavior in recruitment and selection process.

Ethical implications in recruitment and selection process are also evident from the way companies advertise or direct-source for the job positions. Knowingly or unknowingly, organizations often leave the scope of misinterpretation by the candidates. Both overdoing and underdoing with the information and facts about the organizations are not reflections of ethical behaviors.

During the interview process also we have to be careful about the ethical implications. Often organizations restrict their interview process, without assessing all relevant aspects, asking questions to the candidates. Such flawed selection process again is unethical, as such selected candidates may not succeed in doing future assigned jobs efficiently and effectively. Hence, ethical considerations during the interview process demand holistic assessment of knowledge, skills, and competencies, on-job experiences (when required), and the antecedents of the candidates. Objective is to achieve the right job-fit for mutual benefit of candidates and organizations. Often organizations fail to invest time during interview process. This is also not ethical. Job candidates must be given adequate opportunity to showcase their talents, capabilities, so that both organizations and candidates can take win-win decisions.

During the interview process ethical behaviors also demand correct sharing of information about the job, about the organization, compensation and benefits program, career development opportunities, learning and development programs, etc.

Similar ethical diligence organizations should show while verifying the antecedents of the prospective candidates.

Globally, it is now recognized that ethical compliance in recruitment and selection not only helps organizations to avoid future litigation, but even benefits in creating the talent pool, which is essential for long-term sustenance and growth.

Showcasing of Ethical Values on Recruitment and Selection

Hunter Water, a state-owned organization of Australia, with headcounts of 466 is engaged in water supply to about 6 lakh people, spreading across 6671 kilometers. This organization has showcased their ethical compliance in recruitment and selection process as under:

(1) Hunter Water attracts and retains high caliber employees.
(2) Hunter Water applies merit principle.
(3) Hunter Water follows ethical and transparent recruitment and selection process.
(4) Hunter Water adheres to legal provisions on Anti-Discrimination and Equal Employment Opportunity.
(5) Hunter Water applies the values of impartiality, openness, and integrity to ensure ethical recruitment and selection process.
(6) Hunter Water's ethical values on recruitment and selection are supported by their core values on customer services, team work, adaptability, reliability, and accountability.

Conforming to such ethical issues Hunter Water ensures the best employee selection.

IMPORTANCE OF ETHICS IN RECRUITMENT AND SELECTION

In Chapter 1, we have defined both the terms recruitment and selection. Recruitment is attraction of job applicants (Barber, 1998), more specially, attracting those who are talented. More specifically, recruitment involves attracting potential employees who have knowledge, skills, and abilities (Allen, Van Scotter, & Otondo, 2004). Hence, recruitment functions encompass a wide range of activities, ranging from recruitment planning to interview of the job applicants. In some organizations, recruitment functions also require preparing required materials to showcase the company before job applicants, and also prepare a detailed behavioral requirement of interviewers (Taylor & Bergmann, 1987). From job seekers' point of view, choosing a job involves successive decisions at each stage of the recruitment process (Gatewood, Gowan, & Lautenschlager, 1993). Hence, as recruitment and selection involves successive hurdles, it is important for HR managers to comply with ethical issues at different stages of the recruitment process.

Importance of ethics in recruitment and selection can be better understood, when we see it as a holistic decision-making process. Obviously, the first ethical compliance issue is how we attract potential candidates for a job in the organization. Prima facie every job applicant would like to assess the degree of fit between their personal characteristics and the attributes of the organization (Schneider, et al., 1995). This is what we call organizational attraction (Bretz, Ash, & Dreher, 1989). However, as has been stated in the previous paragraph, job attraction of job applicants may change during the recruitment process for moderating effect of ethical issues. Therefore, an ethical issue from a job applicant's point of view deserves our attention, at the time of job application, job selection process, and during the process of job choice (Barber, 1998). However, job applicants may not have complete information about the organization, before they decide to apply for the job position in an organization. They process the incomplete information or the signals, based on some observable factors (Hannon & Milkovich, 1996). The ethical or unethical behavior during recruitment and selection process can give signal to the talents, who are job applicants. When such signal is negative, such candidates may decide not to join, even when they are offered the job. Nicotera and Cushman (1992) rightly observed ethical actions (by managers) follow a continuum and it has both legal and moral implications. When managerial decisions are unethical either in legal or moral terms, people in general discard it (Jones, 1991). Trevino et al. (2006) observed ethical behavior of managers at the individual level judged in terms of generally accepted moral norms of behavior. Hence, decision-making process in compliance with ethical issues cannot be isolated from social norms, and so also from social environment or culture (Payne & Giacalone, 1990; Trevino, 1986), it combines both individual and situational variables.

ETHICAL DUE DILIGENCE

Ethical due diligence in recruitment and selection process ensures selection of best talent in organizations, who can further extend support to organizations to reinforce the ethics and values. Also, such talent will always endeavor to uphold the image of the organization, by not compromising with the ethical issues in their decision-making process. Many organizations embed their core values with the recruitment and selection process. Declaration of core values provides opportunity to new hires to understand the culture of the organization, and assess whether they are the appropriate fit with the organization.

To enforce ethical due diligence in recruitment and selection process, organizations need to follow certain distinct steps as under (Fig. 8.2):

(1) Document characteristics for profiling an ethical employee. Such characteristics may be the requirement of knowledge, experiences, and skills, understanding of ethical challenges for the job position, values that the organization is looking for, etc.

FIGURE 8.2 Steps for ethical due diligence in recruitment and selection process.

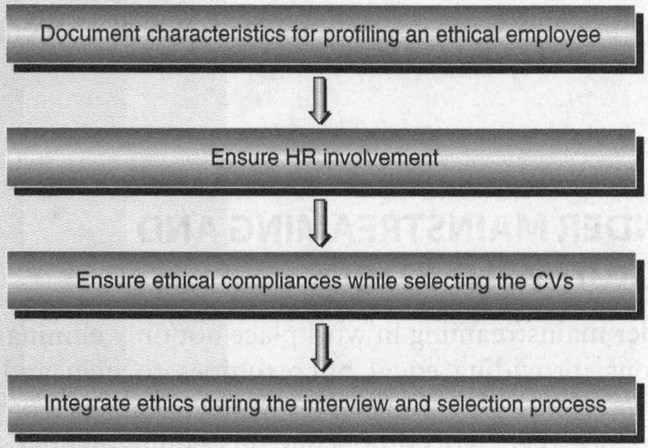

(2) Ensure HR involvement, so that HR can appropriately embed the ethical characteristics in the recruitment and selection process.
(3) Ensure ethical compliances while selecting the CVs of those who otherwise qualify for the job position.
(4) Integrate ethics during the interview and selection process. This can be done by asking candidates to discuss scenarios on some ethical issues, which might have been faced by them in their previous employment, asking direct questions to assess candidates' knowledge on ethical issues, and so also candidates' understanding of organizational core values, etc.

Following the above steps, HR managers can ensure compliance with ethical issues in recruitment and selection.

For Starbucks Ethical Compliance Is Embedded in All Spheres of Activities

For Starbucks, employees are partners; hence, each employee personally feels responsible to support core values. To support core values of Starbucks, employees need to comply with both regulatory and institutional norms. While regulatory norms are legal requirements, institutional norms are ethical conduct at Starbucks. The company has developed Standards of Business Conduct to ensure their core values are reflected in each of their stores, across the globe. The company believes in commitment to integrity, honesty, ethical, and legal compliance to achieve success. With an ethics and compliance helpline, the company helps employees, whenever they face ethical challenges in decision-making process.

GENDER MAINSTREAMING AND RECRUITMENT ETHICS

Gender mainstreaming in workplace not only eliminates gender discriminations, providing equal opportunities to men and women, but also creates a level playing field for women employees, giving them space to balance their work-life. Thus, by valuing gender diversity, not only organizations gain, with economic empowerment, the society also benefits. However, creating equal opportunities both for men and women is not so easy at the organization level. At the outset it requires agreement to the philosophy of gender diversity by the top management of the organizations, and then embracing gender diversity as a necessity, duly documenting it in organizations' ethical code of conduct, rather than a legal compulsion. Only after this can we create the required platform for gender mainstreaming culture. This is followed by a series of actions, including developing policies, its implementation, and time-to-time checking of conformance.

Having gender-sensitive human resource management (HRM) policies, conforming to regulatory requirements, ethical and social norms, and adherence to such policies in managing organizations is considered to be the most important step after agreement to the philosophy of gender diversity by the top management. For example, reflection of gender-sensitive HRM policies can be better understood from the recruitment and selection process of the organizations. Unless the job specifically requires male members, organizations should be neutral between male and female employees. Degree of such neutrality can be understood by calculating number of women employees recruited from the number of women applicants for the job, and by comparing the same with the recruitment of male employees. Many organizations have their policies for gender mainstreaming, but in practices, they still lack spontaneouity. Good examples are discrimination between male and female employees in giving annual increments, discrimination in promotion, overt and covert pressure on whistleblowing for sexual harassment, bias in performance reviews, etc.

Therefore, at organization level, gender mainstreaming requires not only embracing diversity-inclusive policies and programs, but also requires adequate monitoring mechanism for its strict adherence. Employees of organizations also will start cooperating, once they are convinced on its benefits to organizations. However, it requires systematic training and awareness programs.

ETHICS STRATEGY

It is desirable for organizations to have their ethics strategy, encompassing all business practices. Recruitment and selection functions can also be built around the ethics strategy. This way organizations can increase ethical compliance, and gradually can build their ethical image to attract future talents.

Ethics strategy helps in realizing ethical goals, and to frame it organizations need to follow certain steps as under (Fig. 8.3):

(1) Clarity on ethical standards
(2) Formation of ethics committee

FIGURE 8.3 Steps for ethics strategy.

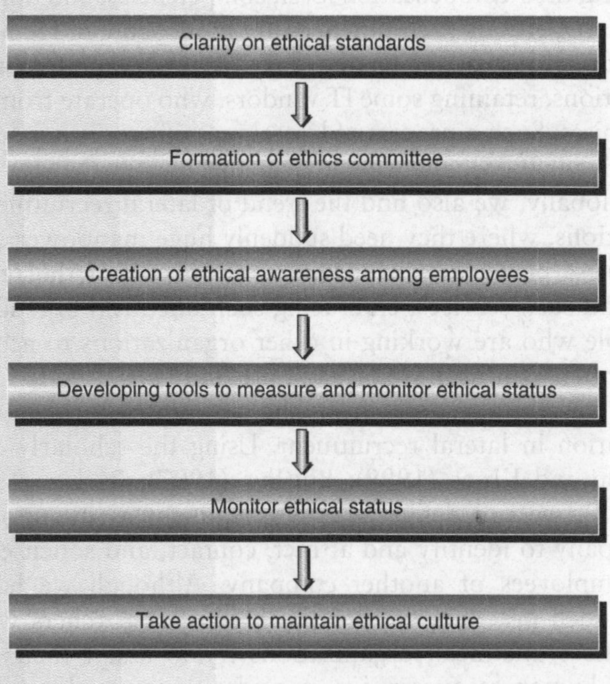

(3) Creation of ethical awareness among employees
(4) Developing tools to measure and monitor ethical status
(5) Monitoring ethical status
(6) Taking action to maintain ethical culture

Many organizations systematically conduct ethics audit. Such audits also help organizations to understand the ethics environment, and make necessary changes in the ethics strategy, standards, and business practices.

THE ETHICS OF LATERAL RECRUITMENT

For obvious talent crunch, many companies go for lateral hiring. In this process, companies often fail to comply with ethical practices. One good example, which we commonly see, is company's attempt to sensitize passive job seekers. Like forced or unsolicited job applications, companies also take chance to attract talent sending unsolicited letter of appointment to some identified people, who may be working in competiting organizations. The idea behind is not to get large response from these people, i.e., the passive job seekers, rather to take chance at least to persuade some of these people to accept the job offer. The process requires extensive data mining and information about these people, like their performance track record, their compensation level, competencies, and things they are capable of doing, etc. As such practices are more acute in IT industry, many organizations, instead of having their IT set-up, prefer outsourcing their IT functions, retaining some IT vendors, who operate from the organizational premises. Such a process of lateral recruitment is not at all a good practice (Sullivan, 2005), and even it is unethical.

Globally, we also find the trend of lateral recruitment in bulk in organizations, where they need suddenly huge manpower either for their new business plans, or new projects, etc. Most of the recruitment agencies extend such services, embracing such unethical practices, i.e., persuading people who are working in other organizations to accept the unsolicited job offer with promise of pay raise and better service conditions. We can have several anecdotes from the corporate world to explain the ethical violation in lateral recruitment. Using the scholarly contributions from Baron and Kreps (1999), Bui-Eve (1997), Barber (1998), and Cappelli (1999), we can define lateral recruitment as intentional actions of one company to identify and attract, contact, and solicit employees or group of employees of another company. Although we have more opinions that such practices are unethical, some researchers warned calling such practices unethical; organizations try to assert their property rights on their human resources, i.e., consider their people more as organization-specific human capital rather than social capital. Adler (2005) and other researchers said, providing misleading information to people to persuade them to join the company may be unethical, but the practice as such has competiting justification.

DEVELOPING ETHICS-COMPLIANT RECRUITMENT POLICY

To ensure ethics-compliant recruitment and selection decisions in organizations, HR managers at the outset need to develop recruitment policy, detailing the step-by-step actions and the procedural norms in taking such actions with ethical overtone. In addition, HR managers also require taking employees in general through compulsory training on ethics, including training on ethical recruitment and selection practices. For assessing the extent of compliance with the ethical values in recruitment and selection, or the effect of training transfer (as evident from the performance outcomes), periodic audit or monitoring is important.

In some organizations we also see well-documented ethical code of conduct. Such code of conduct being prepared with ethical overtone, also helps in sending ethical signals to the employees, which gradually embrace such code of conduct in their decision-making processes. A well-documented ethical code of conduct, among others, emphasizes on reflection of competence required for a job, legal requirements for the job, requirement for dignity in the workplace, need for balancing interests, confidentiality, conflict of interest, fairness and justice, etc.

> For ITC people-centric ethical practices are evident from their core values. ITC believes in respect for people upholding the humanness and human dignity. This is despite subscribing to a performance-driven work culture, which requires setting of high-performance standards for the organization, individuals, and teams. ITC acknowledges every individual brings different perspectives and capabilities to the team. The company is committed to achieving leadership through teamwork.

ETHICAL RECRUITMENT AND SELECTION FRAMEWORK

Value-based recruitment and selection decisions are considered ethics-compliant decisions. To ensure recruitment and selection decisions are ethics-compliant or ethical, many organizations develop their own framework of recruitment of selection. Such a framework is carefully developed so that at every stage ethical issues are taken care of. Organizational values, principles, individual values, social norms, etc., are integrated with this framework. Normally, organizations profess their own values, expecting their employees also to espouse those values. Organizational values gradually develop organizational culture and also gradually get embedded with business practices. Some of the values, which are commonly embraced by organizations, are commitment to profession, ethical decision making, respectfulness, accountability, and impartiality. Other examples of such values for ethical recruitment and selection practices are collaboration, integrity, meeting stakeholders' interest, professionalism, objectivity, accuracy, and confidentiality.

The 1957 US-based company Enterprise Rent-A-Car with current business turnover of US$14.10 billion and headcounts exceeding 70,000 over the years developed their ethics-compliant recruitment and selection framework, which they are successfully following. The company hires approximately 1000 people every year for their business expansion programs throughout the world.

The framework of the company first defines the purpose of recruitment. In the new recruits, the company looks for availability of those sets of competencies which not only meet the present job requirements, but also for the future job roles of such new hires, pacing with the changing business needs of the company. With clarity on the purpose of recruitment and selection, the company then prepares job description, and employee specification. While job description process defines the job role listing the tasks involved, employee specification characterizes the attributes and qualities which are essentially required in doing the job. The company studies the person job-fit by integrating person specification with the job description.

The framework then can be explained as under:

(1) Attracting applicants for vacant job position in companies
(2) Screening candidates with standardized person-job-fit analysis
(3) Selecting eligible candidates for interview
(4) Two-tiered interview, i.e., both with the recruitment manager, and the branch manager
(5) Shortlisting of candidates based on the interview results
(6) Taking shortlisted candidates through assessment centers
(7) Appointing the best candidate(s) for the job

At every stage, the company ensures rigorous ethical compliance, based on their internal recruitment and selection policy.

SOCIAL MEDIA AND RECRUITMENT ETHICS

Social media is an important game changer for the recruitment and selection functions in organizations. While it benefits organizations to mine through the profiles and information about prospective candidates for the jobs, identify the talent at more precision level, it also calls for extra precaution from organization side, particularly to guard against the ethical-compliant issues. For social media, organizations today are open to the world. Their managerial practices, customer services, products or services quality, employee management issues, and so also their general commitment to ethics are transparent. Many organizations maintain their Facebook and LinkedIn account and obviously there are innumerable followers. With increased number of followers, companies enjoy the sense of pride, but at the same time run the risk of negative publicity, once they violate the ethics. Followers report their experiences with the company, the type of questions they were asked during interview, their general feelings about the company, etc. It is the responsibility of the companies to manage the social media, strategically responding to different queries of the followers, and answering to the experience-sharing stories, when they find those conflicting with the company's interest.

RECRUITMENT AND SELECTION ETHICS IN PSES

Public sector enterprises (PSEs) in India and abroad are bound by ethical and regulatory norms for recruitment and selection functions. Code of conduct, ethical guidelines, statements of values, and ethical principles are commonly seen almost in all PSEs both at the center and at the state level. What constitutes ethical guidelines widely vary across the countries from organizations to organizations. However, for PSEs we find ethical guidelines universally constitute:

(1) General values
(2) Democratic values
(3) Professional values

In the context of recruitment and selection, general values broadly encompass honesty and integrity, fairness, sense of responsibility and accountability, sense of mutual respect and sense of decency. Democratic values are moderated by law, practice of neutrality, openness, and responsiveness. Finally, professional values encompass effectiveness, efficiency, service, innovation, and quality, in addition to people-oriented values like caring, tolerance, compassion, and humanity (Kernaghan, 2003).

In PSEs ethical overtones become evident from the thoughts and actions of the public servants. Such thoughts and actions of the public servants largely get influenced by the respective structure and culture of such organizations. In some PSEs ethical compliance is considered synonymous to bureaucratic behavior, in conformity with the thought of Max Weber (Cooper, 2006). It means in such organizations, ethics are complying with formal structure, rules, and job roles. Also in such organizations public servants consider ethics as ethos, commitment, integrity, and trust (March & Olsen, 1989). Finally, ethics are also seen as impression management and image building for building trust of the organizations (Brunsson, 1989).

For recruitment and selection in PSEs, we find emanation of ethical considerations from all the above three values. As these organizations develop their recruitment and selection policies, aligning with ethical and legal norms, we hardly find ethical violation.

Wipro the World's Most Ethical Company

Wipro, one of the flagship conglomerates in India in information technology and consulting, fast moving consumer goods, electrical and computer peripherals, has been adjudged as the most ethical company of the world. Such honor was conferred by Ethicsphere Institute in 2015. Such recognition is given to those companies that are able to create material impact at every level of business, on the way of their doing business, fostering transparency, and ethical culture. Wipro believes in ethics, integrity and responsible citizenship, and successfully correlates ethical business practices with their performance.

ETHICAL BREACHES FOR SENIOR-LEVEL RECRUITMENT AND SELECTION

Senior-level recruitment and selection processes in organizations often encounter ethical breaches. For such recruitment, organizations usually constitute search committee, represented by external experts. Although it is desirable to ethically act while conducting search for prospective candidates, often in the name of attracting talent, search committee members may recommend prospective names, without appreciating the degree of fit of such candidates with job positions and so also with organizations. In our country, such propensities are more visible in senior-level recruitment process of public sectors, educational institutions, departmental undertakings, etc. Such unethical practices question the integrity of the organization, and put their reputation at stake (Fig. 8.4).

Some of the recommended actions to avoid ethical breaches are as under:

(1) Keep search open for all
(2) Extensive training of search committee members on dos and don'ts in recruitment and selection process
(3) Help search committee members to understand and recognize required credentials for the job position
(4) Make honest and candid job offer
(5) Ensure confidentiality in the recruitment and selection process

FIGURE 8.4 Recommended actions to avoid ethical breaches.

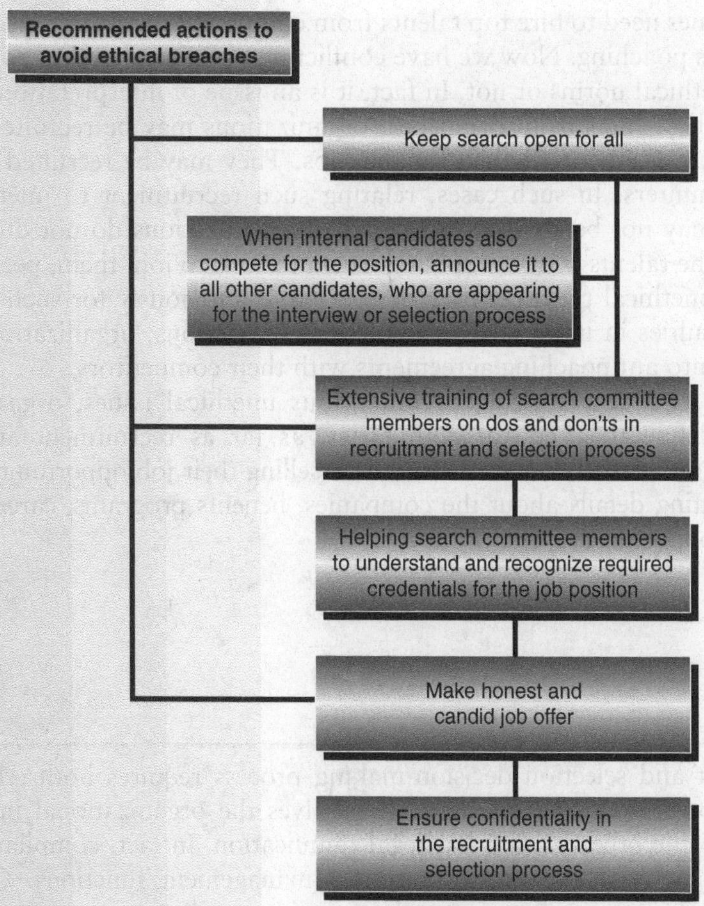

(6) When internal candidates also compete for the position, announce it to all other candidates, who are appearing for the interview or selection process

Although the above-recommended actions can help in controlling ethical breaches in recruitment and selection, it is always desirable to have periodic ethical audit, even for recruitment and selection functions. Moreover, better results can be obtained by gradual embracing of ethical culture and ethical business practices.

UNETHICAL RECRUITMENT AND SELECTION PROCESS

When recruitment and selection process violates ethical norms, we call it unethical recruitment. At times apparently for business reasons, companies need to hire top talents from competing organizations. Technically, it is poaching. Now we have conflicting opinions whether poaching violates ethical norms or not. In fact, it is an issue of interpretation. For example, these hires from competing organizations may be recruited because they have directly applied for the jobs. They may be recruited through headhunters. In such cases, relating such recruitment to unethical practices may not be correct. Hence when organizations do not directly persuade the talents from competing organizations to join them, perhaps the tag of unethical practices may be too harsh. Obviously for such technical difficulties in interpreting the recruitment actions, organizations today enter into antipoaching agreements with their competitors.

To deal with such contentious unethical issues, organizations often define their ethical boundaries, as far as recruitment and selection is concerned. They resist from overselling their job opportunities by exaggerating details about the companies, benefits programs, career development opportunities, etc.

SUMMARY

- Recruitment and selection decision-making process requires both ethical and legal considerations, as on the one hand it involves the organizational image and prestige, and on the other hand it has legal ramification. In fact, compliance with ethics literally encompasses all human resource management functions. Obviously, this requires organizations to promote ethical culture, so that in recruitment and selection, employee onboarding, performance management, compensation design, training and development, succession planning and career development, and even in employee relations, we demonstrate ethical values. Demonstrating ethics or ethical values in human resource management decisions need not require compromising with strategies and business goals. Also ethics or ethical values, being derived from the social and cultural norms, do not confront with legal and institutional requirements. With an inclusive approach to ethics, organizations can embed the culture of ethical compliance in every managerial decision, including recruitment and selection.

- Organizations come out with ethics-based human resource plans and strategies, so that employees engage in ethical actions for creating uniformity, which is a precondition for a sustainable ethical culture and climate. For ethical recruitment and selection process, it is important to incorporate ethical constructs right from the stage of human resource planning so that subsequent employee selection decisions and strategies become more and more ethics-compliant. Many organizations feel creating a clean and ethical image would be enough to attract the talent pool. But this is not enough, as ethics need to get cascaded into organizational practices. For recruitment and selection it indicates ethicality in realistic job design, appropriate selection test and interviewing, reference checking, etc. At every stage ethical considerations must not get compromised.

Key Words

Values: Values are our possessed or deeply held beliefs, which get reflected in our actions, choices, and attitudes.

Ethics: Ethics are certain principles that we need to follow while we do our job.

Ethical signals: Signals on ethical practices in the organizations.

Uniformity in diversity: Uniformity in diversity is a process of complying with legal requirements, but it cannot guarantee ethical compliance, which additionally requires diversity inclusivity approach in recruitment and selection.

Ethical dimensions: Ethical dimensions help us to study the scope of ethics in managerial decision-making process.

Ethical due diligence: Ethical due diligence is the process of ensuring that ethical issues are not compromised in decision making.

Gender mainstreaming: It is a process of eliminating gender discriminations by providing equal opportunities to men and women in organizations.

Ethics strategy: Strategy to help organizations in realizing ethical goals.

Review Questions

1. Explain the concepts of recruitment and selection ethics. What are its different dimensions?
2. In recruitment and selection process, why is ethical compliance so important? Answer with examples.
3. What is ethical due diligence? Why is ethical due diligence necessary in recruitment and selection?
4. Design an ethics-compliant recruitment and selection policy for a car manufacturing company.
5. Design a recruitment and selection framework with ethical overtone.
6. Explain how recruitment and selection ethics of an organization may get influenced by social media. Discuss this with examples.
7. What are ethical breaches? Explain with examples.
8. Write short notes on:
   (a) Gender mainstreaming
   (b) Ethical due diligence
   (c) Lateral recruitment
   (d) Ethics strategy
   (e) Code of conduct
   (f) Democratic values
   (g) Talent poaching

Critical Review Questions

1. Develop two different situations, in one case you justify recruiting top talent of your competitor is not unethical. In another case you take the role of your competitor, and build your arguments, such talent poaching is unethical.
2. Critically evaluate an ethics-compliant recruitment and selection policy of a company.

Multiple Choice Questions

1. Ethical issues in recruitment and selection can be understood from the following perspectives, except:
   (a) Presenting the job positions to prospective talent
   (b) Process of identifying talent
   (c) Manner of conducting the interview
   (d) All of the above
   (e) None of the above

2. Identify the incorrect statement in the context of recruitment and selection:
   (a) Values are our possessed or deeply held beliefs
   (b) Values get reflected in our actions, choices, and attitudes
   (c) Ethics are certain principles that we need to follow while we do our job
   (d) Ethics are more like moral rights and duties, which elicit our responses for doing things rightly
   (e) Ethical compliance by default taken care of by religious mandates and legal requirements

3. Uniformity in diversity as a practice in recruitment and selection indicates:
   (a) Legal requirements
   (b) Ethical compliance
   (c) Diversity inclusivity
   (d) Diversity neutrality
   (e) Only (a) and (d)

4. Ethical recruitment and selection decision-making process ensures the following, except:
   (a) Compliance with legal provisions
   (b) Addressing needs of all stakeholders
   (c) Embracing those courses of action, which can do more good than harm
   (d) Understanding the logic behind decisions
   (e) None of the above

5. Identify the incorrect statement in the context of recruitment and selection:
   (a) Ethical dimensions of recruitment and selection functions can be understood from the pattern of decisions on employee selection
   (b) Ethics not just influence during the selection of candidates, it even starts with the initial process of job design
   (c) For better understanding of ethical dimensions in recruitment and selection, we have to first understand moral or ethics attached to the process
   (d) Ethical dimensions encompass the relationships between the candidates and the recruiting member of the organizations
   (e) None of the above

6. Ethical implications in recruitment and selection process are evident from the following, except:
   (a) The way companies advertise or direct-source for the job positions
   (b) When companies overdo or underdo information and facts about the organization and also about the job position
   (c) When organizations restrict their interview process, without assessing all relevant aspects, asking questions to the candidates
   (d) When the scope of ethical diligence does not encompass verification of the antecedents of the prospective candidates
   (e) None of the above

7. Adherence to ethical due diligence in recruitment and selection process, requires organizations need to follow certain distinct steps, other than:
   (a) Document characteristics for profiling an ethical employee
   (b) Ensure HR involvement, so that HR can appropriately embed the ethical characteristics in the recruitment and selection process
   (c) Ensure ethical compliances while selecting the CVs of those who otherwise possess quality for the job position.
   (d) Integrate ethics during the interview and selection process
   (e) Take into account the ethical background of the family

8. Ethics strategy helps in realizing ethical goals, and to frame it, organizations follow certain steps, except:
   (a) Clarity on ethical standards
   (b) Formation of ethics committee
   (c) Creation of ethical awareness among employees
   (d) Ensuring ethical issues do not compromise with the business needs
   (e) Developing tools to measure and monitor ethical status

9. Value-based recruitment and selection decisions are considered as ethics-compliant, and this can be achieved when organizations:
   (a) Show commitment to profession (b) Emphasize on ethical decision making
   (c) Are respectful (d) Feel accountable
   (e) All of the above

10. Ethical guidelines do not consider:
   (a) General values (b) Democratic values
   (c) Professional values (d) Personality values
   (e) Moral values

11. Some of the recommended actions to avoid ethical breaches are as under, except:
   (a) Keeping search open to target-group
   (b) Extensive training of search committee members on dos and don'ts in recruitment and selection process
   (c) Helping search committee members to understand and recognize required credentials for the job position
   (d) Making honest and candid job offer
   (e) Ensuring confidentiality in the recruitment and selection process

Answers:

1. (d) 2. (e) 3. (e) 4. (e) 5. (e) 6. (d) 7. (e) 8. (d)
9. (e) 10. (d) 11. (a)

CASE STUDY

Uncovering Ethical Standards in Recruitment and Selection

Assessing ethical sense of job candidates requires Human Resource Management (HRM) team of any organization to design the interview questions to ensure meaningful discussions. The idea behind is to elicit honest and meaningful answers to the interview questions. Standardizing the ethical questions to assess the ethical sense of the job candidates is difficult. Therefore, companies go for behavioral questions. As such questions are related to some hypothetical situation, and answers help us to understand how the job candidates responded to such situations in the past, and how he or she would like to respond in future, we can measure the ethical sense more effectively.

Some of the behavioral questions for assessing ethical sense of job applicants are listed below:

(1) When you are required to comprise with the workplace ethics?
(2) How do you define accountability, confidentiality, and stability?
(3) As you are experienced, narrate some uses and abuses of code of conduct in workplaces?
(4) In your previous workplaces, did you have training on business ethics? If your answer is yes, can you narrate your experiences?
(5) Is there any difference between the ethical individual and ethical corporation?
(6) Share some of your experiences when you were ethically challenged?
(7) Interpreting the web-site of a company, can you identify the reflection of ethics? If so how and where?
(8) In your previous workplaces, did you have experience of working with people from different cultures?
(9) What did you do when you confronted with ethical issues in your work?
(10) How do you relate customers' dissatisfaction with workplace ethics?

Getting answers to such elaborate questionnaire items may not be necessary for recruitment and selection decisions in all the cases. However, for human resource management positions, it is always advisable to assess the ethical senses of the job applicants, so that the company recruits ethical persons with expectations of reflection of their ethical sense in future decision-making processes.

However, we face real challenge when we integrate ethics with strategy. While organizations across the globe have already matured in embedding ethics or ethical issues with their business models, pacing with strategic issues, it is said, often it becomes challenging, when it confronts with the strategy.

Marks & Spencer, one of the largest retailers in the UK, to ensure workplace ethics came out with enormous number of measurable commitment, centering around five pillars like climate change, waste, sustainable raw materials, fair wages to workers in supply chain, and health. Even this company faced the ethical challenges particularly when their supply chain partners at Rana Plaza of Bangladesh collapsed, causing death of large number of workers. With such a catastrophe, the company faced the ethical challenge of sourcing and to corporate social responsibilities. The company, after such incident, enforced compliance with strict ethical standards, even for suppliers, as a pre-condition to work with them. Such compliance not only encompasses workers' security and safety issues at workplaces, but also the compliance with payment of living wages, ensuring payment of the cost price benefits to workers. Also the company enforces that workers with their supply chain partners do enjoy the privilege of unionization, right to collective bargaining, freedom of association, good working conditions, respect, etc. The company today has more than 500,000 workers in their supply chain (2015). Ensuring ethical compliance in the workplaces of their suppliers, the company engaged compliance managers, who with the help of independent third-party auditors are to check the ethical-compliant issues.

Question: Why are ethical issues important in recruitment and selection?

REFERENCES

Adler, L. (2005), Ethics, poaching and competitive intelligence, http://www.eremedia.com/ere/ethics-poaching-and-competitive-intelligence accessed on 19th June, 2015.

Aiman-Smith, L., Bauer, T.N. and Cable, D.M. (2001), "Are you attracted? Do you intend to pursue? A recruiting policy-capturing study", *Journal of Business and Psychology*, 16, 219–237.

Allen, D.G., Van Scotter, J.R. and Otondo, R.F. (2004), "Recruitment communication media: Impact on pre-hire outcomes", *Personnel Psychology*, 57, 143–171.

Barber, A.E. (1998), *Recruiting Employees: Individual and Organizational Perspectives*. Thousand Oaks: Sage.

Baron, J.N. and Kreps, D.M. (1999), *Strategic Human Resources: Frameworks for General Managers*. New York: John Wiley & Sons, Inc.

Bauer, T.N. and Aiman-Smith, L. (1996), "Green career choices: The influence of ecological stance on recruiting", *Journal of Business and Psychology*, 10, 445–458.

Beu, D.S. and Buckley, M.R. (2004), "Using accountability to create a more ethical climate", *Human Resource Management Review*, 14, 67–83.

Bhattacharyya, D.K. (2014), *Organizational Behaviour*, 2nd edition. New Delhi: Oxford University Press.

Boswell, W.R., Roehling, M.V., LePine, M.A. and Moynihan, L.M. (2003), "Individual job-choice decisions and the impact of job attributes and recruitment practices: A longitudinal field study", *Human Resource Management*, 42, 23–37.

Bretz, R.D., Jr., Ash, R.A. and Dreher, G.F. (1989), "Do people make the place? An examination of the attraction-selection-attrition hypothesis", *Personnel Psychology*, 42, 561–581.

Brunsson, N. (1989), *The Organization of Hypocrisy: Talk, Decisions and Actions in Organizations*. Chichester: Wiley.

Bui-Eve, H. (1997), "To hire or not to hire: What Silicon Valley companies should know about hiring competitors' employees", *Hastings Law Journal*, 48, 981–1027.

Cable, D.M. and Turban, D.B. (2003), "The value of organizational reputation in the recruitment context: a brand-equity perspective", *Journal of Applied Social Psychology*, 33, 2244–2266.

Carless, S.A. and Wintle, J. (2007), "Applicant attraction: The role of recruiter function, work-life balance policies and career salience", *International Journal of Selection and Assessment*, 15, 394–404.

Cappelli, P. (1999), "Career jobs are dead", *California Management Review*, 42(1), 146–167.

Cooper, T.L. (2006), *The Responsible Administrator: An Approach to Ethics for the Administrative Role*, 5th edn. San Francisco, CA: Jossey-Bass.

Cullen, J.B., Victor, B. and Stephens, C. (1989), "An ethical weather report: Assessing the organization's ethical climate", *Organizational Dynamics*, 18, 50–62.

Frederick, W.C. (1991), "The moral authority of transnational corporate codes", *Journal of Business Ethics*, 10, 165–177.

Gatewood, R.D., Gowan, M.A., Lautenschlager, G.J. (1993), "Corporate image, recruitment image", and initial job choice decisions, *Academy of Management Journal*, 36, 414–427.

Gilmore, D.C., Stevens, C.K., Harrell-Cook, G. and Ferris, G.R. (1999), Impression Management Tactics. In R. W. Eder and M. A. Harris (Eds.), *The Employment Interview: Theory, Research, and Practice*, 2nd Ed. 226–321. Newbury Park, CA: Sage.

Hannon, J.M. and Milkovich, G.T. (1996), "The effect of human resource reputation signals on share prices: An event study", *Human Resource Management*, 35, 405–424.

Highhouse, S., Hoffman, J.R., Greve, E.M. and Collins, A.E. (2002), "Persuasive impact of organizational value statements in a recruitment context", *Journal of Applied Social Psychology*, 32, 1737–1755.

Jones, T.M. (1991), "Ethical decision making by individuals in organizations: An issue contingent model", *The Academy of Management Review*, 16: 366–395.

Joo, B.K. and McLean, G.N. (2006), "Best employer studies", *Human Resource Development Review*, 5, 228–257.

Judge, T.A. and Bretz, R.D., Jr. (1992), "Effects of work values on job choice decisions", *Journal of Applied Psychology*, 77, 261–271.

Kernaghan, K. (2003), "Integrating Values into Public Service: The Values Statement as Centerpiece", *Public Administration Review*, 63(6): 711–19.

March, J.G. and Olsen, J.P. (1989), *Rediscovering Institutions: The Organizational Basis of Politics*. New York: The Free Press.

Nicotera, A.M. and Cushman, D.P. (1992), "Organizational ethics: A within-organization view", *Journal of Applied Communication Research*, 20, 437–462.

Payne, S.L. and Giacalone, R.A. (1990), "Social psychological approaches to the perception of ethical dilemmas", *Human Relations*, 43, 649–665.

Pirsch, J., Gupta, S. and Grau, S.L. (2007), "A framework for understanding corporate social responsibility programs as a continuum: An exploratory study", *Journal of Business Ethics*, 70, 125–140.

Powell, G.N. (1984), "Effects of job attributes and recruiting practices on applicant decisions: A comparison", *Personnel Psychology*, 37, 721–732.

Ryan, A.M. and Ployhart, R.E. (2000), "Applicants' perceptions of selection procedures and decisions: A critical review and agenda for the future", *Journal of Management*, 26, 565–606.

Rynes, S.L., Bretz, Jr., R.D. and Gerhart, B. (1991), "The importance of recruitment in job choice: A different way of looking", *Personnel Psychology*, 44, 487–521.

Schneider, B., Goldstein, H.W. and Smith, D.B. (1995), "The ASA framework: An update", *Personnel Psychology*, 48, 747–773.

Spence, M. (1974), *Market Signaling: Informational Transfer in Hiring and Related Screening Processes*. Cambridge: Harvard University press.

Spence, M. (1973), "Job market signaling", *The Quarterly Journal of Economics*, 87, 355–374.

Sullivan, J. (2005), The best practices of the most aggressive recruiting department, http://www.eremedia.com/ere/the-best-practices-of-the-most-aggressive-recruiting-department-part-2, accessed on 19th June, 2015.

Taylor, M.S. and Bergmann, T.J. (1987), "Organizational recruitment activities and applicants' reactions at different stages of the recruitment process", *Personnel Psychology*, 40, 261–285.

Trevino, L.K. (1990). A cultural perspective on changing and developing organizational ethics. In Pasmore, W.A. and Woodman, R.W. (Eds), *Research in Organizational Change and Development*, Vol. 4, 195–230. Greenwich, CT: JAI Press, Inc.

Trevino, L.K. (1986), "Ethical decision making in organizations: A person-situation interactionist model", *The Academy of Management Review*, 11, 601–617.

Trevino, L.K., Weaver, G.R. and Reynolds, S.J. (2006), "Behavioral ethics in organizations: A review', *Journal of Management*, 32, 951–990.

Turban, D.B. and Cable, D.M. (2003), "Firm reputation and applicant pool characteristics", *Journal of Organizational Behavior*, 24, 733–751.

Turban, D.B. and Dougherty, T.W. (1992), "Influences of campus recruiting on applicant attraction to firms", *The Academy of Management Journal*, 35, 739–765.

Turban, D.B. and Greening, D.W. (1996), "Corporate social performance and organizational attractiveness to prospective employees", *Academy of Management Journal*, 40, 658–672.

Victor, B. and Cullen, J.B. (1988), "The organizational bases of ethical work climates", *Administrative Science Quarterly*, 33, 101–125.

Chapter 9

International Recruitment and Selection

LEARNING OBJECTIVES

After reading this chapter, you will be able to understand:

1. Concepts and issues in international recruitment and selection
2. Approaches and types of international recruitment and selection
3. Selection of employees in international companies
4. Diversity and cross-cultural issues in international recruitment and selection
5. Assignment-specific international recruitment
6. Training and development of international recruitees
7. Compensation and benefits design of international recruitees
8. Performance management of international recruitees

Select the culture-fit when you source your manpower from abroad

Lobo Life, a multispecialty hospital in Kabul, Afghanistan, is struggling to recruit specialist nurses for orthopedic department. The hospital immediately wants to recruit 25 nurses from different countries, as locally such qualified nurses are not available. Accordingly, the hospital initiated the recruitment process. Afghanistan is a war-torn country, and Kabul is often a center of attack from different secessionist groups, making it unattractive to many Indian nurses, who prefer to take up international assignment. Indian nurses are preferred over nurses from other countries, as they are known for their dedication and quality services internationally. Lobo has to take the challenge of recruiting from China, where a large pool of qualified nurses are available, who are prepared to relocate to Afghanistan. All the 25 nurses have been recruited from China and deployed in orthopedic unit of the hospital. Within a week after their deployment, Lobo could identify the problem engaging this batch of nurses, as they engaged them in arguments, quarrels, and even fighting with patients and their relatives. Such incidents one after another, ultimately caught the attention of management committee of the hospital, and the HR head who personally steered this recruitment process was called for explanation.

HR head explained under what circumstances they had to recruit these nurses from China, knowing well the difference in culture and values. As the hospital had no provision for induction training for nurses, excepting the technical induction from the nursing head, these nurses could not be taken through the culture awareness program. Suggestion was to conduct such program, withdrawing all of them from their wards, and then to redeploy them. However, this also did not work, as many of these nurses could not keep pace with the culture shock, and ultimately expressed their willingness to leave the job.

INTRODUCTION

With globalization, organizations are now expanding their international business operations. Such operations in different forms help organizations to integrate their businesses with global markets. For example, multinational corporations or MNCs are the most popular type of international operations. Another form of international operations is transnational corporations, i.e., TNCs. Structurally, MNCs and TNCs are different, but both the organizations primarily focus on expanding their market spread to global markets. Characteristically, MNCs and TNCs operate differently. For example, MNCs expand their international business units in different countries giving full autonomy to the local units of host countries, so that they can pace with the local issues like taste and preferences of customers; economic, political, social and cultural issues, etc. Such local units function with autonomy without much of integration with their parent companies. Some MNCs, however, maintain their control over local units. Such companies are more evident among Japanese corporations, as Japan believes in ethnocentric management approach, irrespective of their place of operations. These types of MNCs are better known as global corporation. Some examples of MNCs and global corporations are Phillips, Shell, Matsushita, etc. Transnational corporations also achieve their local responsiveness, but at the same time focus on achieving efficiencies balancing between global and local issues through a network structure. Companies like Unilever, Ford, etc., are examples of transnational corporations.

Both MNCs and TNCs, apart from addressing the global business issues, require adherence to human resource management issues, primarily issues related to international recruitment and selection. These companies need to understand local issues and integrate their understanding in managing human resources in different countries of their operations. The biggest challenge for these companies is managing the cross-cultural issues, which literally encompass all human resource management activities, managing of organizational behavior, strategies, structures, technologies, etc. Differences between domestic and international HRM practices are largely attributed to cross-cultural issues. These apart we have certain international HRM issues, like relocation, onboarding, training, legal and taxation, and so also complete expatriate management. All these are characteristically different from domestic HRM issues. For managing international HRM issues, MNCs and TNCs require local expertise, need to train them, and make them the right-fit with their headquarters. In some MNCs and TNCs a core team of HR coordinates with their local units more as internal consultants to achieve seamless integration with the HR strategies of the headquarters. McDonald is a good example. With global HR information systems such tasks have now become easier.

INTERNATIONAL RECRUITMENT AND SELECTION CONCEPTS

In MNCs and TNCs, we find three important types of employees. Such employees may be expatriates (home country nationals or PCNs, i.e., parent country nationals), host country nationals (HCNs), and third-country nationals (TCNs). Sending expatriates or home country nationals to overseas units have all along been practiced by the multinational or transnational companies to achieve efficiencies in operations and so also to enforce direct control. However, such practice is gradually becoming redundant, as engaging home-country or host-country nationals better efficiency and control can be achieved with appropriate structure. Good example is Solvay, the Belgium-based chemical major, which is now managing their global operations, particularly in south-east Asian countries forming global business units (GBUs). GBUs are primarily staffed by local people. Such recruitment of local people is not only cost effective; it can add value to the organization in terms of better integration with the dynamics of local culture, social and political systems, and so also the market dynamics. Cost effectiveness can be achieved primarily for additional costs of compensation and benefits for the expatriates in host countries for cost of living adjustments, and for maintaining parity with the headquarters' based pay (when such pay level is higher than the pay level in host countries). In both the cases, compensation and benefits costs go up. Even in cases where MNCs and TNCs use HCNs or TCNs for staffing their international operations, they continue to send their headquarters' based employees to overseas operating units time to time to control and guide the local units, and to align with the goals and objectives, mission, and vision. Such alignment adds better value in terms of achieving global efficiency.

International recruitment and selection practices are different primarily for country-specific regulatory norms. Such differences in regulations require companies to follow different procedures in their different operating units, spread across different countries. In many countries, specific regulations for engaging foreign nationals exist. So also we find wide variations in country-specific regulations on the employment of the physically disabled, war veterans, or displaced persons, regulations on adherence to the diversity issues, issues related to diversity, work permit or visa, etc. Propensity of MNCs and TNCs to enforce similar recruitment and selection practices, as they enforce in their home countries, often lands them in trouble. Many Japanese MNCs and TNCs faced problems in different countries, including India for valuing their ethnocentric approach to management of human resources, and more specifically in recruitment and selection.

However, we also have some MNCs and TNCs that are known for their world-class HRM practices, particularly in recruitment and selection. These companies emphasize on merits to ensure the best qualified candidates are selected for job positions. Some MNCs and TNCs follow their own recruitment and selection policies like hiring on the basis of family tie, social status, language, race, etc. Such differentiated recruitment policies of these companies often confront with the country-specific regulations and social norms.

Like recruitment and selection for domestic job positions, in international recruitment and selection also we do initially human resource planning (HRP) in alignment with the business goals and strategies of the MNCs and TNCs. In addition, for international level recruitment, we need to specifically address the following important questions:

(1) Whom we are recruiting—TCNs, PCNs, or HCNs?
(2) How we are recruiting—more detailing on the techniques to be followed in other countries?
(3) How we are aligning our recruitment practices with our company's philosophy, vision, and mission?
(4) How we are aligning our staffing plans with the business goals?
(5) What on-boarding program we have designed for international recruitees?
(6) What plans we have for managing our own employees who are sent to international operation units (expatriates)?
(7) How we are going to address the diversity issues?
(8) How we are going to design our compensation and benefits program for international recruitees?
(9) What would be our training and development plans for international recruitees?
(10) What would be our career development programs for international recruitees?

APPROACHES TO INTERNATIONAL RECRUITMENT AND SELECTION

Based on their specific practices, and also depending on their country of origin, organizations vary in their international recruitment and selection approaches. Such approaches in international recruitment and selection of MNCs and TNCs can be grouped as under (Fig. 9.1):

(1) Ethnocentric
(2) Polycentric

FIGURE 9.1 Approaches to international recruitment and selection.

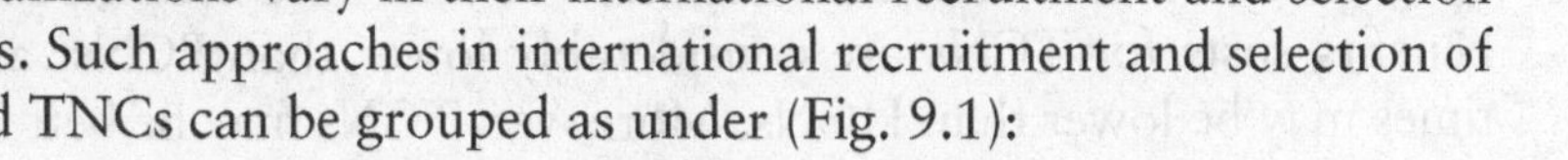

(3) Regiocentric
(4) Geocentric

Ethnocentric approach to international recruitment and selection indicates engagement of PCNs, i.e., people from home country. While engaging people from PCNs, organizations need to focus on issues like culture, language, personality, attitude, etc. Opposed to this is polycentric approach, as organizations following such approach recruit from HCNs. Such recruitment enables organizations to pace with the cultural, political, social, and local economic issues, and at the same time also enable organizations to manage international operations with a decentralized approach. International operating units of such companies enjoy functional autonomy and also in some case less of financial controls. Most of the GBUs, as mentioned above, follow this type or recruitment. Regiocentric approach denotes recruitment of people from other countries (TCNs), who have similar culture and follow similar managerial practices. Recruiting Indian workers for Kathmandu (Nepal) operations is a good example. Geocentric approach of recruitment emphasizes more on merit, and hence they recruit from different countries, both home and abroad, without considering the nationality and other diversity issues. With the recruitment of PCNs, organizations can enforce better control and coordinate with their operating units for achieving global efficiency. HCNs facilitate in better alignment of MNCs and TNCs with the local conditions, and with some control from the headquarters such organizations can also achieve global efficiency. Many organizations discriminate their HR practices between PCNs and HCNs. For example, career development opportunities for HCNs in subsidiaries of MNCs and TNCs are limited, compared to PCNs operating in headquarters. Also recruitment costs and overall HR costs for HCNs are considerably less than deputing PCNs from headquarters for managing international operations. Recruitment of TCNs for international operations is also cost effective for MNCs and TNCs. Compensation and benefits costs for TCNs are considerably lower than PCNs, and even at times may be lower than HCNs. Moreover, TCNs may be better informed about the culture and work environment of host countries.

Hybridization in International Recruitment and Selection

Till 1987 Korean MNCs used to follow the paternalistic HRM model, more like Japanese multinationals. After Asian financial crisis in 1997, Korean firms revolutionized their HRM practices aligning with the global standards. Introduction of individual performance-based incentives, performance-based pay systems, etc. are some of the examples. In managing their overseas subsidiaries, Korean MNCs now follow hybridization, balancing between global standardization and localization. Unlike the US and Japanese organizations, Korean firms have considerably reduced their ethnocentric approaches in managing their global subsidiaries, which resulted in recruitment of large HCNs in most work positions, with minimum control from headquarters. Few managerial talents, who are sent on assignment basis to overseas subsidiaries, work more as facilitators than regimenting the local business.

TYPES OF INTERNATIONAL RECRUITMENT AND SELECTION

Based on the nature and duration of the assignment, international recruitment and selection can be of the following types:

(1) Short-term assignment—for a maximum period of 3 months
(2) Extended assignment—between 3 months and 1 year time frame
(3) Long-term assignment—more than 1 year
(4) Commuter assignment—posting in difference countries with provisions for weekly or bi-weekly commuting between workplace and home. This is common in European countries.
(5) Rotational assignment—when posting is done on rotation basis. This is commonly practiced by petroleum and oil companies for staffing their oil rigs in different countries.
(6) Contractual assignment—more common for IT companies in the form of deputing their employees to clients' site.
(7) Virtual assignment—followed for managing operations in different countries from the country of origin. This is also followed in IT companies. A senior-level project manager may operate from the home country, but can be assigned to manage operations in client sites, located in several other countries. Technology-enabled network structure can help in such assignment.

SELECTION OF EMPLOYEES IN MNCS AND TNCS

MNCs and TNCs incur huge costs in recruitment and selection of international employees. Also cost of replacement of international employees is very high. Obviously, this requires exercise of stringent control and time investment in international selection decisions. Although selection process varies across MNCs, it is common to go for rigorous screening of employees' antecedents, to avoid any possible decisional error. Apart from the relevant skill and competencies, in international selection, companies also emphasize on assessing the coping abilities of the individual employees, their sensitivity to cross-cultural issues, their degree of awareness about the local culture, family situation, etc.

Depending on the country of origin of MNCs and TNCs, selection practices also vary. For example, technical competence is more valued in MNCs with North American origin, while MNCs of West European origin emphasize both on technical competence and coping abilities of individual employees. This is also common for MNCs of Japan. These apart MNCs assign weight on behavior, previous work experience, and natural interest of individual employees before selecting them for international assignments.

Like selection for domestic assignments, here also MNCs follow certain techniques as under:

(1) Interviewing—balancing between structured and unstructured interview techniques
(2) Compliance with norms, values, and ethics
(3) Psychological testing
(4) Use of assessment center and competency-based interview
(5) Assessment of cross-cultural skills
(6) Assessment of adaptability
(7) Assessment of adaptability of spouse and family members
(8) Assessment motivation for overseas assignments
(9) Assessment of interpersonal skills for building relationships with the employees of host countries
(10) Assessment of emotional stability

Adhering to above selection techniques to a great extent can reduce the selection errors, and can ensure better job-fit.

DIVERSITY AND CROSS-CULTURAL ISSUES IN INTERNATIONAL RECRUITMENT AND SELECTION

Workforce diversity in terms of culture, caste, gender, religion, language, etc., is now a global issue for MNCs and TNCs. Managing workforce diversity conforming to the principles of uniformity, and then achieving success leveraging the collective efforts of diverse workforce are now are important agenda of MNCs and TNCs. With inclusive workforce diversity management practices many global organizations become innovative and achieve excellence in business results. Primarily, this requires creation of a diversity-inclusive culture by creating level playing field for all cross-sections of employees, and embeds the culture with organizational human resource management practices.

Diversity and cross-cultural issues are more important for international and particularly for cross-border recruitment and selection because of country-specific variation in social and regulatory norms. Many global organizations comply with the diversity neutral recruitment and selection practices pacing with the country-specific regulatory norms. Such a practice, however, cannot guarantee business results. It requires careful integration of competing interests of diverse workforce.

GUIDELINES FOR RECRUITMENT AND SELECTION ACROSS CULTURES

International recruitment requires strong understanding of culture and diversity issues. While compliance with the regulatory norms is necessary, more effective results can be obtained when organizations come out with their guidelines on management of culturally diverse workforce, and adhere to their recruitment process. Based on the industry practices, we may consider the following guidelines:

- Making all employees aware on their cultural values
- Making all employees understand the culture of the organization
- Understanding the reality of cultural gap between their peers from different countries
- Understanding the culture of others
- Modulating behavior of employees aligning with the culture of host countries, where they may be deputed for work
- Documenting behavioral styles, values, beliefs, social norms, rituals of host countries, where the organizations are planning to expand their business
- Sensitivity to work systems of host countries, like pattern of communication, style of supervision, etc.
- Making employees aware about the need for diversity inclusivity
- Making employees aware about the importance of recruitment of people who are culturally diverse
- Conducting cross-cultural awareness training programs, and ensuring that employees earmarked for foreign deputation understand their foreign counterparts.

Based on the above guidelines, international organizations can draw their recruitment and selection plans, so that those who appropriately fit with the country-specific cross-cultural issues and diversity issues are only recruited. When cross-cultural and diversity issues are addressed, international organizations can get the benefit of innovation, productivity, and increased performance. Borderless business has now become important economic imperative, and it requires organizations to recruit people who are more and more mixed in their ethnic origin. Getting the best out of these people requires understanding of the diversity issues. Although culture is not only diversity issue, it is the most important one, among others. This is because culture develops the shared feelings, the most crucial glue to bind people to work together.

In addition to the cross-cultural and diversity issues, international organizations are also facing the challenge of dual career couple (DCC) issues, where both husband and wife are working. Deputing employees for international assignment often becomes impossible for spousal rejection. Some organizations have their structured programs on spousal training, so that they can get gainfully employed, while in abroad, and get appropriate children education support.

INTERNATIONAL SELECTION PROCESS

International selection process widely varies. Such variations are not only attributable to organizational practices, but also on country-specific cultural variation. Even different countries have different mandates and regulatory norms on interview guidelines. While understanding of culture is one part that can be weighed while selecting employees for international assignments, during selection it is also important to assess the awareness of the employees on the political, legal and socioeconomic systems of the host country, and more particularly the degree of differences between the home country and the host country. This is important for selecting expatriates among the existing employees who may be prepared to relocate abroad. For selecting employees from host countries who will be operating in their respective countries, selection process will emphasize on such employees' understanding of the organizational values, vision, mission, business goals, and also the work culture as a whole. For selecting third-country nationals for host country operations would consider issues explained above for expatriates (PCNs) and HCNs. TCNs or third-country nationals enjoy more cultural proximity with HCNs, which to a great extent make the selection process easier.

Thus, while technical skills, competencies, etc., are one important area that merits selection of employees for international assignments, on the other hand, equally important is cultural sensitivity, understanding of the values, norms, socio economic conditions, political systems, etc.

For selecting expatriates for international assignments, many companies have their own guidelines. The biggest challenge here is to ensure that employees with requisite technical skills are emotionally matured, empathetic, and diplomatic.

Many organizations for better selection of international assignees form a cross-functional selection plan, represented by experts from both the home and host countries. Such selection panel allocates differential weights to different selection criteria, based on the nature of assignment, type of jobs, profile of candidates, etc. For example, it is common to give more weights to previous international experiences. Similarly, weights are given for fluency in language of the host country, intercultural adaptability, etc.

Selections of employees for transnational teams, i.e., team members who represent different nationalities, also require specific focus on the above aspects. In all these cases, methods of selection are interviews, assessment centers, and tests. In some cases, companies also conduct interviews for the spouse to assess their coping strategy with the international environment. All these selection methods we have already been discussed in Chapter 6.

TRAINING AND DEVELOPMENT FOR INTERNATIONAL RECRUITEES

Success of international recruitment and selection process largely depends on appropriate training and development reinforcement immediately after selection and joining of the recruitees. To make employees fit in cross-cultural work environment, organizations need to train the recruitees on culture-mediated business practices, focusing on the countries where they require to work. For host country nationals, such training emphasize on understanding the organizational values, systems, processes, vision and mission, etc. Such recruitees (HCNs) are helped to adapt themselves with the organizational culture, so that gradually they can align themselves with the parent organization and achieve business excellence. Such HCNs recruitees are gradually empowered by the organizations and encouraged to form cross-functional work groups, so that innovation in a culturally-diverse work environment can be achieved, and organizations continue to sustain their competitive advantages.

Cross-cultural training emphasises on the understanding of people who represent different cultures. In terms of culture, people differ in their way of doing work, and their perception, understanding, rituals, and symbols widely differ. Cross-cultural training for the new recruitees helps them in building the required competence, and they feel more comfortable in integrating them with people from different cultures. Like any training delivery method, cross-cultural training can make use of structured lectures, showing videos, taking participants through role plays, field trips, simulation exercises, and sensitivity training. With such training reinforcement, new recruitees, as well as the identified expatriates, gradually become more adaptable and efficient in a culturally-diverse work environment. Some of the important areas of a cross-cultural training module are on:

- cultural constructs
- diversity
- culture of host country
- language, communication process, religions and rituals, symbols, etc., of the host country
- economic, social, and political systems of the host country
- business etiquette
- career development and mentoring
- work-life balancing

For international recruitees in most of the organizations, cross-cultural training emphasizes on marketing and selling in a cross-cultural environment, managing of sales employees, leading cross-cultural teams, understanding group dynamics of cross-cultural team, and customer services in a cross-cultural workplace. For expatriates a documented guideline on host countries information is provided, covering all the above areas, even after training reinforcement.

Some of important attributes of managerial employees recruited for international assignments are ability to seize strategic opportunities, capability to manage distributed operations, understanding of international issues, sensitivity to culture and diversity, capability to build interpersonal relations in a cross-cultural work environment, and ability to develop and manage cross-cultural teams.

COMPENSATION AND BENEFITS PROGRAMME FOR INTERNATIONAL RECRUITEES

Compensation and benefits design is one of the important areas of concern for international recruitees. This is for all categories of recruitees, i.e., PCNs, TCNs, and HCNs. Organizations spread their international operations to gain strategic advantage in terms of new market development, achieving cost efficiency, etc. But in the process, if compensation and benefits program is not suitably designed, it would be difficult to achieve efficiency. It is not just the benefits that international organizations derive relocating their manufacturing base in China. Closely related to the compensation issues are talent attraction and retention, country-specific legal issues, etc.

Most of the international organizations design compensation for the employees earmarked for global placement usual salaries plus cost of living expenses for meeting additional expenses while they are posted abroad. However, this is more a narrow approach. We have a number of issues on international compensation design. Some international companies design internationally equitable compensation across the nations. Depending on the tenure of recruitment, compensation designs largely vary. For example, we can classify international workforces as short-term transferees, permanent transferees, expatriates, third-country nationals, glopats, etc. A glopat is an international cadre employee who is sent from one international assignment to another. Also international compensation varies with respect to the cultural constructs of countries, where the employees need to work. This is more important for design of incentives with respect to the culture of individualism and collectivism, principles of equity, performance-related pay, ratio between fixed and variable pay, propensity of employees to put pay at risk, etc. Another area of concern in designing international compensation for the employees identified for global placement is wage-related and tax-related laws. Such laws vary with respect to countries. With respect to non-monetary benefits, pay equalization, etc. adherence to these laws are enforced.

Many organizations without changing the base pay provide allowances to their employees when they are sent on international assignments. For TCNs and HCNs, however, they match with the host country's legal norms to come out with structured compensation package. Some of the allowances for expats and glopats are:

(1) Foreign Service Allowance, which varies between 10 and 25% of base pay, depending on the organizations
(2) Special hardship allowance for distressed location abroad
(3) Cost of living allowances (COLA) for maintaining parity with the host country's standard of living
(4) Housing, utility, and furnishing allowances
(5) Education allowances for children
(6) Medical allowances, including payment of premiums for the medical insurance
(7) Relocation allowances
(8) Car and driver allowances
(9) Club membership allowances
(10) Allowances for additional tax liability

However, payment of such allowances is very much organization specific.

ASSIGNMENT-SPECIFIC INTERNATIONAL RECRUITMENT

Recruitment in MNCs and TNCs can be done in a number of ways. People are recruited from different countries which have different regulations related to labor matters, different tax laws, different culture and different social settings. Nature of international assignments varies depending on the specific needs of organizations. According to Mathis and Jackson (2005), international recruitment is done by organizations to meet their global manpower requirement, and such assignments could be a technical, functional, developmental, and strategic. Depending on such nature of assignment, skill and competency profile changes. For example, technical assignments are restricted to job-specific assignment, on completion of which employee returns to their original place of work. Most of the foreign technicians and experts come for installation of new machines (under technology transfer agreement) in India usually comes on technical assignments. Such employees may not have adequate cultural skills. Employees sent on functional assignments being for a longer duration for completion of assigned tasks, they need to have cross-cultural skills. Similarly, employees for developmental assignments are also expected to possess more cross-cultural skills. These groups of employees initiate development of overseas operations of MNCs and TNCs, aligning with the culture of the host countries. Strategic assignments denote deputing managerial employees for critical strategic job performance; hence this group of employees also requires critical cross-cultural skills. Therefore, while recruiting, when organizations consider the specific nature of deployment of new recruitees, can achieve better job-fit.

PERFORMANCE MANAGEMENT FOR INTERNATIONAL EMPLOYEES

Like compensation and benefits, performance management for international employees is also another important issue that deserves special attention. Most of the international organizations decide their performance management systems and processes for international employees, based on the place of their operations. For example, for TCNs and HCNs they tend to follow performance management systems that match with the local systems. For PCNs, however, they follow the home country systems of performance management. However, some international organizations which believe in performance-driven work culture maintain uniformity in performance systems, irrespective of the location of their employees. Whatever may be the systems adopted by the organizations, international performance management is essentially an important strategic function, as it emphasizes not only on evaluation of performance, but also focus on continuous improvement to achieve business excellence, across all the operating units, spread across the world.

Some of the objectives of international performance management systems for international employees can be listed as under (Fig. 9.2):

(1) Enables organization to ensure implementation of their strategies in subsidiaries for achieving global efficiency

FIGURE 9.2 Objectives of international performance management systems.

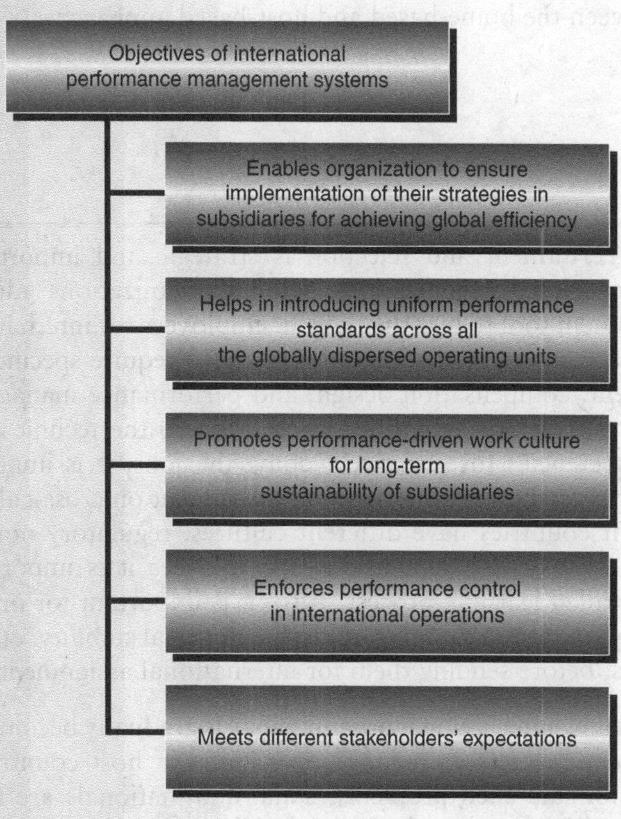

(2) Helps in introducing uniform performance standards across all the globally dispersed operating units
(3) Promotes performance-driven work culture for long-term sustainability of subsidiaries
(4) Enforces performance control in international operations
(5) Meets different stakeholders' expectations

Performance management systems at international level are a complex process, as it requires understanding of dynamics of work environment, which is mediated by country-specific culture and work systems. Moreover, aligning with the parent organization's systems may not be always possible for cultural incongruence. Also, there may be problems of information asymmetry, knowledge asymmetry, goal incongruence, difference in rating patterns, difference in dissemination of performance feedback and review reports, etc. International organizations, depending on the type of employees, i.e., PCNs, HCNs, and TCNs follow either home-based approach, i.e., compliance with the performance management systems followed in the headquarters, host-based approach, i.e., following the practices of host countries, or an integrative approach, i.e., balancing between the home-based and host-based approaches.

SUMMARY

- International recruitment and selection is strategic and important for long-term sustainability of global organizations. Global organizations adopt more effective selection assessment tool to hire the right-fit employees for international assignments. International recruitment and selection issues also require specific focus on training and development, compensation design, and performance management systems for both talent attraction and retention. In addition to the technical and professional skills and competencies for effectively doing the jobs, it is important to focus on sensitizing new recruitees for international placement on cross-cultural and diversity issues. Different countries have different cultures, regulatory norms, social norms, values, rituals; and before deputation of employees it is important to take them through the detailed learning process. Also, it is important for organizations to test the adaptability (in terms of coping ability), emotional stability, and natural interests of the assignees, before sending them for international assignments.

- Talent attraction by international organizations is gradually becoming tough. Sending expats from headquarters to manage operations in host countries often becomes difficult. To eliminate such problems, some multinationals are following "reverse expat" strategy. This strategy helps in developing managers from host countries, so that they can develop as glopats for managing operations of the companies in different countries.

Key Words

MNC: MNCs expand their international business units in different countries giving full autonomy to the local units of host countries, so that they can pace with the local issues like taste and preferences of customers; economic, political, social, and cultural issues, etc. Such local units function with autonomy without much of integration with their parent companies.

TNC: Transnational corporations achieve their local responsiveness balancing between global and local issues through a network structure.

Ethnocentric approach: In international recruitment and selection, this approach denotes engagement of parent country nationals, who are sent as expatriates to overseas operating units.

Commuter assignment: Posting in difference countries with provisions for weekly or bi-weekly commuting between workplace and home. This is very common in European countries.

Cross-cultural training: It is training on the understanding of people who represents different culture.

Glopat: A Glopat is an international cadre employee who is sent from one international assignment to another.

Review Questions

1. Explain the concept of international recruitment and selection. Why is it different from domestic recruitment and selection?
2. List the important issues in internal recruitment and selection. How such identified issues can help you in managing international recruitment and selection?
3. What are the different types of international recruitment and selection? Detail important techniques of international recruitment and selection.
4. Explain why diversity and cross-cultural issues are important in international recruitment and selection.
5. What guidelines do you recommend to follow for embedding diversity and cross-cultural issues in international recruitment and selection process?
6. For international recruitees, why do we need to consider compensation and benefits design issues?
7. Indicate performance management issues for international recruitees.

8. Write short notes on:
   (a) TCNs
   (b) Regio-centric approach
   (c) Hybridization
   (d) Virtual assignment
   (e) Diversity inclusivity
   (f) DCC
   (g) COLA

Critical Review Question

1. Prepare a cross-cultural training module for identified expatriates of your company. These expatriates are due for departure for one of your production units in China. You may refer to web-sites, but you must have some logic for including any particular training area in this training module.

Multiple Choice Questions

1. International recruitment and selection issues require understanding of the following issues, except:
   (a) Local issues and integrate their understanding in managing human resources in different countries of their operations
   (b) Managing the cross-cultural issues
   (c) Managing of organizational behavior, strategies, structure, and technologies
   (d) Understanding of differences between domestic and international HRM practices
   (e) None of the above

2. Parent country nationals denote:
   (a) Expatriates
   (b) HCNs
   (c) TCNs
   (d) DCNs
   (e) MCNs

3. GBUs are primarily staffed by:
   (a) TCNs
   (b) Expatriates
   (c) HCNs
   (d) Inpatriates
   (e) PCNs

4. International-level recruitment addresses the following important questions except:
   (a) How we are recruiting—more detailing on the techniques to be followed in other countries
   (b) How we are aligning our recruitment practices with our company's philosophy, vision, and mission
   (c) How we are aligning our staffing plans with the business goals

(d) How much weight we assign for recruiting people from local source
(e) What on-boarding program we have designed for international recruitees

5. International recruitment and selection of MNCs and TNCs can be grouped as under:
(a) Ethnocentric (b) Polycentric
(c) Regiocentric (d) Geocentric
(e) All of the above

6. Identify the incorrect statement:
(a) Ethnocentric approach to international recruitment and selection indicates engagement of PCNs
(b) Polycentric approach to international recruitment and selection indicates recruitment from HCNs
(c) GBUs do not follow polycentric approach to international recruitment and selection
(d) Regiocentric approach denotes recruitment of people from TCNs
(e) Geocentric approach of international recruitment emphasizes more on merit, and hence they recruit from different countries

7. Indicate which is not a type of assignment in international recruitment and selection:
(a) Short-term assignment (b) Extended short-term assignment
(c) Long-term assignment (d) Commuter assignment
(e) Rotational assignment

8. Selection errors in international recruitment and selection process can be reduced adopting the following approaches, except:
(a) Assessment of cross-cultural skills
(b) Assessment of adaptability
(c) Assessment of adaptability of spouse and family members
(d) Assessment motivation for overseas assignments
(e) Assessment of IQ rather that EQ

9. Workforce diversity in MNCs and TNCs requires:
(a) Conformance to the principles of uniformity
(b) Achieving success leveraging the collective efforts of diverse workforce
(c) Creation of a diversity inclusive culture
(d) Creating level playing field for all cross-sections of employees
(e) All of the above

10. Which is not a part of guideline in international recruitment and selection:
(a) Making all employees aware of their cultural values and the culture of the organization

(b) Modulating behavior of employees aligning with the culture of host countries, where they may be deputed for work
(c) Documenting behavioral styles, values, beliefs, social norms, rituals of host countries, where the organizations are planning to expand their business
(d) Sensitivity to work systems of host countries, like pattern of communication, style of supervision, etc.
(e) Restricting recruitment of culturally diverse workforce to reduce future complications

11. Important area(s) of a cross-cultural training module is/are on:
(a) cultural constructs
(b) diversity
(c) culture of host country
(d) language, communication process, religions and rituals, symbols, etc., of the host country
(e) All of the above

12. Common allowance(s) for expats and glopats is/are, except:
(a) Foreign Service Allowance, which varies between 10 and 25% of base pay, depending on the organizations
(b) Special hardship allowance for distressed location abroad
(c) Cost of living allowances (COLA) for maintaining parity with the host country's standard of living
(d) Housing, utility, and furnishing allowances
(e) Professional development allowances

13. International performance management systems for international employees designed by organizations focus on the following, except:
(a) Implementation of strategies in subsidiaries for achieving global efficiency
(b) Introduction of differentiated performance standards across all the globally dispersed operating units
(c) Promotion of performance-driven work culture for long-term sustainability of subsidiaries
(d) Enforcement of performance control in international operations
(e) Meeting different stakeholders' expectations

Answers:

1. (e) 2. (a) 3. (c) 4. (d) 5. (e) 6. (c) 7. (b) 8. (e)
9. (e) 10. (e) 11. (e) 12. (e) 13. (b)

CASE STUDY

International Staffing of Coca Cola

With its beginning in 1886 and operations in more than 200 countries with market capitalization of US$184.3 billion and headcounts of seven lakhs, Coca Cola is truly an international company with time-tested experience in international staffing. The company follows a mixed approach in international staffing, i.e., combination of ethnocentric, polycentric, and geocentric approaches. Ethnocentric approach is followed by the company for deputing senior-level managerial personnel from headquarters to establish control over subsidiaries, particularly in finance. However, for other managerial and nonmanagerial employees, the company focuses on polycentric, regiocentric, and geocentric approaches. The appropriate mix of employees facilitates in giving international business units the required autonomy to manage their operations responding to market needs, and country-specific human resource management practices. Geocentric approach to international recruitment facilitates the company to develop glopats who can take up different cross-border assignments. Such employees gradually develop their capabilities to adapt with multi-cultural work environment. With such mixed approach in international staffing, Coca Cola today is the most successful company in the world.

The embedded philosophy of "think globally, act locally" prepares every associate (employee) of the company to prepare their mind-set to see their company from a global perspective. Such mind-set of the employees further gets reinforced when they engage them in cross-border knowledge sharing, collaborative innovation, and cocreation. Spontaneous international mind-set of employees helps the company to identify willing and competent expatriates for international assignments. Such identified employees are then taken through training on cross-cultural issues, understanding of the social and business dynamics of the host countries, regulatory norms, values, languages, rituals, etc.

However, the company faces the problem of discrimination in compensation and benefits program, when they pay their expatriates as per US benchmarked rate, while they are posted in a host country like India, Brazil, etc. Often this dissuades the HCN managerial talents to join the company. However, the company tries to address this issue with their total rewards strategy, which in addition to the monetary part of compensation, emphasizes on accelerated career development opportunities, including international assignments.

Question: Indicate how Coca Cola's experience can help other multinationals operating in India?

REFERENCES

Au, K.Y. and Fukuda, J. (2002), "Boundary spanning behaviors of expatriates", *Journal of World Business*, 37(4), 285–297.

Bartlett, C.A. and Ghoshal, S. (1989), *Managing Across Borders. The Transnational Solution*. Boston, MA: Harvard Business School Press.

Black, J.S. and Gregersen, H.B. (1999), "The right way to manage expats", *Harvard Business Review*, 77(2), 52–62.

Collings, D.G., Scullion, H. and Morley, M.J. (2007), "Changing patterns of global staffing in the multinational enterprise: Challenges to the conventional expatriate assignment and emerging alternatives", *Journal of World Business*, 42(2), 198–213.

Dowling, P.J., Festing, M. and Engle, A.D. (2008), *International Human Resource Management: Managing People in a Multinational Context* (5th ed.). London: Cengage Learning.

Ghoshal, S. and Nohria, N. (1993), "Horses for courses: Organizational forms for multinational corporations", *Sloan Management Review*, 34(2), 23–35.

Harzing, A.W.K. (1995), "The persistent myth of high expatriate failure rates", *International Journal of Human Resource Management*, 6(2), 457–475.

Mathis, L.R. and Jackson, J.H. (2005), *Human Resource Management*. Ohio: Thompson, South Western.

Sparrow, P., Brewster, C. and Harris, H. (2004), *Globalizing Human Resource Management*. London: Routledge.

Tung, R.L. (1981), "Selection and training of personnel for overseas assignments", *Columbia Journal of World Business*, 16(2), 68–78.

Chapter 10

Employee Onboarding

LEARNING OBJECTIVES

After reading this chapter, you will be able to understand:

1 Concepts of onboarding
2 Difference between onboarding and orientation
3 Strategic onboarding
4 Designing onboarding program
5 Onboarding and employer branding
6 Cocreating individual-level onboarding program
7 Gamification of onboarding

Make Your Onboarding Program Meaningful

Employee onboarding program of a global software developer with presence in more than 20 countries starts with multiple level of induction programs, extending over three months. The company earlier used to provide a year-long induction for their new recruitees, which even had one-month-long international tour at least in four to six European countries, where the company has strong business presence. Truncating year-long induction program to three months is primarily attributable to high attrition rate, which enhanced the manpower replacement costs sky high. This three months' induction program is well researched in several countries, where the company has their presence, excepting in India. The program starts with general orientation, which they call new-hire orientation, followed by skill-family orientation, project orientation, general information sharing about the company's policies, culture, career development opportunities, etc. After this induction, employees are placed to each mentor, who helps employees in on-the-job learning. Mentors are made personally accountable to develop these new hires and also in retaining them with best possible guidance and also coaching. With personal interaction with their bosses, new hires in the company feel more satisfied and gradually develop their self-confidence in doing their jobs with high level of precision. They find meaning in their jobs, identify them with the organization, and decide to stay. The success in India, when studied further, lies in the fact that the collegiality in boss–subordinate relationships could make such a great difference.

INTRODUCTION

Onboarding is now a strategic learning and performance issue for the new hires. Companies develop their onboarding program for transforming new hires to achieve top performance level with series of briefing and debriefing sessions over a period of 1 year or so. Some companies, however, crafted their onboarding program for the new hires for 90 days and even could achieve results. Successful onboarding program also engages new hires and increases their retention. Globally, attrition rate of the new hires has reached to an alarming level. Cocreating individual-level onboarding program effectively, interacting with the newcomers, and using gamification as a tool for onboarding, organizations are now trying to make their onboarding program satisfying for the newcomers. Such satisfaction of the new hires also adds to organizational brand value, as satisfied newcomers share their positive onboarding experience in social media. This helps organizations also in talent attraction. Effective onboarding programs also lend support to succession planning in organizations, as during this process, organizations can identify potential employees for future leadership roles.

DEFINITIONS AND CONCEPTS

Onboarding is not *per se* dazzling new hires. It is a structured approach to transform new hires, so that they can quickly integrate them with organizations, understanding its values and culture. Also they get trained, develop internal network for collaboration, and become effective in their future performance.

The term onboarding is more encompassing than induction. While onboarding and orientation are often used interchangeably, unlike orientation—which is what a company provides to new hires during the initial days of employment—onboarding is an approximately 90-day process of orienting and integrating new hires so that they can deliver results as efficiently, effectively, and energetically as possible.

Induction is the process of sensitizing newcomers to the existing systems and processes of organizations. Induction programs are conducted for a short duration more for compliance, rather than achieving a successful transition of new hires to the organizations. It is a mechanical process of bringing newcomers to a pre-existing institutional order. It describes the history and mission of the organization, teaches new hires about company rules, summarizes compensation and benefits plan, and introduces the work systems.

It has now been acknowledged by many researchers that social relations have important role in facilitating learning and performance (Adler and Kwon, 2002; Bandiera et al., 2008; Lin, 2001; Nahapiet and Ghoshal, 1998). In organizations such social relations of new hires are built through onboarding program. Through onboarding process, the organization helps new employees to learn their work and to align with the workplace (Ashforth et al., 2007; Bauer et al., 1998). Based on organizational practices, onboarding program for the new hires provides detailed guidelines about job, organizational culture and mission, and the process of interaction with other members of organizations. For newcomers, such learning experience engages them with organizations. They derive job satisfaction, achieve improved performance, and also feel committed to organizations.

DIFFERENCE BETWEEN ONBOARDING AND ORIENTATION

The terms induction, organizational socialization, and orientation are interchangeably used. Based on our discussion above, we can articulate the difference between onboarding and orientation program as given in Table 10.1:

TABLE 10.1 Difference between onboarding and orientation program.

Onboarding	Orientation
A long-term structured process of integration of new hires with the organizations.	A short-term structured program essentially coordinated by HR department of organization.
More encompassing in scope, as it takes the new hires through the understanding of organizational policies and procedures, processes, structure, mutual expectations, and the scope of employee development.	Emphasizes more on understanding of employee benefits, policies, and procedures.
Emphasizes on more holistic understanding of the organization, including cross-departmental functions.	General orientation is followed up with specific orientation related to the job of new hires.
Facilitates in employee engagement, reduced employee turnover, and increased performance.	More focused on compliance training.

STRATEGIC ONBOARDING PROGRAM

Managing onboarding strategically requires organizations adjusting new recruits to social and performance aspects. Focus is more on smooth transition, so that new hires can quickly fit them with their job and organization. Globally, onboarding is a challenging function, as it helps organizations in avoiding the initial phase of attrition, technically known as attrition during "induction crisis." Even in Fortune 500 companies such attrition rate is so high, several estimates could observe that more than half of new recruits (including directly recruited managerial employees) tend to leave their job within 18 months. During the onboarding program new hires learn attitudes, knowledge, skills, behaviors, and all these are critical for their success in their jobs.

Strategic onboarding programs widely vary across organizations. It has gradually now become not only a talent retention tool, it is also used for talent attraction. Many organizations today showcase their onboarding program to attract talents. Good examples are Samsung and IBM. Samsung attract young talent retaining celebrities from different walks of life in their onboarding and mentoring program. IBM offers onboarding program, which is having high learning value. Many Indian companies like Aditya Birla, Tech Mahindra, NTPC, etc. put more thrust on their onboarding programs, and for new hires such program itself is adding tremendous self-transformation value.

Compositional shift in the nature and type of new hires have also emphasized on the need for managing onboarding function strategically. For example, companies are now sourcing their manpower globally. Geographically, dispersed people have their own culture and set of priorities. Hence, apart from business alignment, strategic onboarding program requires helping new recruits to align with the culture of the

L'Oreal's Strategic Onboarding Program

With 32 international brands, US$22.53 billion sales turnover, and head counts of 78,600 dedicated workforces drawn from 156 different countries, L'Oreal today operate from 130 countries. With 59% women managers, and 45% representation of women in executive committees, the century-old company truly represents a culture of diversity inclusivity. All new recruits of L'Oreal go through two-year-long formal onboarding program. The tailor-made induction program helps new recruits to develop their confidence in taking up new challenges. The six-step strategic onboarding program of the company starts with a successful welcome, followed by developing employees to experience field and products, training and round-table discussions, personalized meeting program, on-the-job learning, and even individual guidance through mentor and HR support.

organizations. Failing which, organizations will be more prone to the risk of attrition. Nevertheless it is also important to remember that competition or talent has now increased to an alarming level. Hence with organizational priority to achieve enhanced performance, improved retention, high employee engagement, improved employee satisfaction, and higher commitment and loyalty from new hires, onboarding programs are now becoming more strategic. Depending on the strategic priorities, organizations are revisiting their onboarding programs, and time to time bringing changes for achieving better results.

Realizing the strategic importance on onboarding program, Microsoft has now made their onboarding as "everyone's job" extending its responsibility beyond HR department. The suggested four-C model for strategic onboarding program of Bauer (2011) requires us to adhere to compliance, clarification, culture, and connection issues. Compliance issues focus on legal and policy-related, clarification processes help new hires to understand their jobs, including expectations from the jobs. Culture issues familiarize new hires on formal and informal norms of organizations. Finally, connection facilitates new hires to establish interpersonal relationships, and information networks. The extended model of strategic onboarding, based on organizational practices, is connecting, communicating, cocreating, collaborating, and checking.

Strategic onboarding function has been integrated with the talent management function by most of the organizations. With strategic onboarding, new hires can develop their relationships and networks within the organization, which later helps in achieving their performance goals and fulfilling their career aspirations. Through the process of acculturations, new hires can quickly get integrated with organizations. Some of the benefits of strategic onboarding are:

(1) Help new hires to get familiarity with company's processes and way of working.
(2) Help new hires to deliver performance results without much of time-lag.
(3) Help organizations to achieve higher retention of new hires.
(4) Enhance engagement of new hires with the organization.
(5) Enable organization to share all work-related relevant information, including career opportunities, compensation, benefits program, etc.
(6) Help organization to integrate new hires with its culture.
(7) Help organization to understand expectations of new hires.
(8) Benefit new hires to achieve their career goals.
(9) Develop sense of pride in new hires.
(10) Ensure identity in new hires.

DESIGNING ONBOARDING PROGRAM

Onboarding is a process of imparting knowledge and skills to new hires so as to make them an effective member of a company. We also call it employee orientation, "learning the ropes" and even "first day at work." Also some researchers use the term "organizational socialization." Despite such theoretical debates, operationally we find that orientation or socialization process lasts for a short duration, while onboarding can last up to 90 days, and in some organizations, even more. Many research studies could establish linkage between onboarding and employee retention, increased job satisfaction and reduced levels of stress.

Onboarding is an extended program, which starts with the recruitment and continues beyond orientation. More appropriately, it is defined as assimilation into the workplace so that new hires feel at ease and start performing better. Effective onboarding can help in enhancing employee retention. Organizations that follow effective onboarding program can also attract talent. In designing onboarding program, organizations try to focus on those issues, which can integrate the new hires with the culture, and make employees feel they are in the right place. This requires putting those issues in onboarding program, which can mutually fit and make the program successful. Failure in onboarding program leads to immediate attrition, we call induction-phase crisis. Some research reports of consulting organizations like Bersin, etc. indicated such attrition can go up to 26% in less than two months' period. Minimum ninety days' onboarding program has now become the industry practices. Although we do not have any one-size-fit-all solution to effective onboarding program designing, but organizations, based on their experiences, frame their onboarding program as per the outline below:

(1) **Making introduction personal:** It is important on the first day itself that the new recruitees are taken through office tour. Also organization chart is shared with them with pictures of the team members with whom they will be working. Introductions need not be formal only; use humor, even stories can make such interactions more meaningful. Purpose is to help new employee to feel at home, and in the process to reduce their attrition. Many organizations make such introduction program for new employees more formal like any one-time event. Organization chart with pictures to a great extent can address such situation; else new hires with information load may not remember their team members. Videographing the introduction and later on sharing the same with the new hires also can substantially benefit new

hires to connect his/her colleagues and make him/her feel more comfortable at work.

(2) **Sharing of training information:** Sharing on-the-job and cross-departmental training information with the new hires can help them to understand their job requirements, job responsibilities, etc., which in the process make organizational onboarding program successful. Many researchers agree cross-departmental training during onboarding better prepares new hires to collaborate across organizational boundaries, and in the process to get things done. Some organizations use video training particularly in explaining the job roles of the new hires. This is very effective.

(3) **Integrate the new hire with the organizational culture:** It is important for organizations to integrate new hires with their culture. Organizational culture speaks on the unique way of working of the organizations. Cultural orientation helps new hires to prioritize their own unique set of values. Here also video can be useful. Through video presentation and gamification, organizations can share the messages from management and team members, making new hires feel more engaged in terms of experiential learning of culture and values of the organizations.

(4) **Making everything ready:** Effective onboarding program design requires everything ready right from day one. Detailed scheduling of onboarding program with stage-wise action plans can benefit organizations in getting the business results.

Thus, appropriate design of onboarding program facilitates in listing the details of activities involved and the possible way to perform those activities, so that new hires can integrate them successfully, and they increasingly feel themselves aligned with their organizations.

In addition to the design of onboarding programs as per the details above, it is also important to share certain information with the new hires during onboarding. The degree and extent of such information sharing widely varies with respect to the job roles of the new hires, and so also with the culture of the organizations. Some of the general information shared with the new hires is (Fig. 10.1):

(1) Information about the key stakeholders
(2) Information on organizational strategy
(3) Information on organizational goals and objectives
(4) Information on how the new hires can get access to top leaders of the organization
(5) Information on new hires participation in different meetings
(6) Information on different training programs designed for the new hires during the period of onboarding

FIGURE 10.1 Information shared with the new hires.

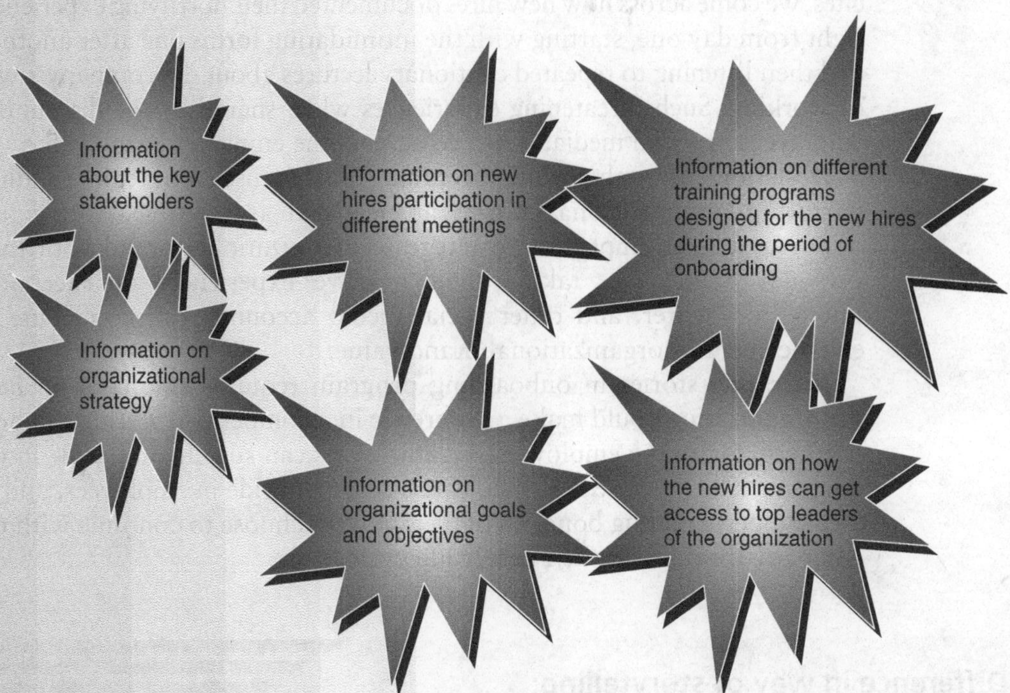

ONBOARDING AND EMPLOYER BRANDING

Effective onboarding program not only helps in employee engagement and retention, it can also reinforce employer branding, which benefits organizations in terms of talent attraction. When newcomers are satisfied with their onboarding program, they share this experience in social media. For example, Glassdoor carries many such stories shared by the employees. Similarly, organizations also briefly discuss about their onboarding program in career sites, without, however, compromising with the strategic issues. On a positive note, these help in employer branding. We have discussed the cases of L'Oreal and IBM. Both these companies could successfully make their onboarding program a strategic employer branding tool. Hence, showcasing organizational onboarding program with appropriate story highlighting culture, values, career opportunities, compensation and benefits program, and overall organizational expectations, including the time schedule and contents, with thrust on training and development and team building to a great extent benefit organizations to increase their brand value as employers.

Many organizations make their onboarding too mechanical, bothering too much for compliance, legal, and process issues. Referring to social media cites, we come across how new hires documented their horrifying experiences right from day one, starting with the intimidating forms one after another, and then listening to repeated cautionary lectures about the company's way of working. Such threatening experiences when shared by the disgruntled employees in social media, it can go against the employer brand value.

Designing an onboarding program that focuses on team-building, narrating organizational stories as personal as possible, and giving opportunities to employees to integrate organizational brand with their personal brand, i.e., taking their positive experiences in Facebook, LinkedIn, Twitter, and other social media accounts, can contribute to enhancement of organizational brand value.

Narrating stories in onboarding program requires emphasis on how the organization could make a difference in a competitive world, and how partnering with the employees, organizations can sustain and grow in the long run. The purpose is to inculcate a sense of pride in employees, and to create a perpetuating bond, so that employees choose to continue with the company throughout their career life-cycle.

Difference in way of storytelling: Lessons from Putney

Putney, a small-scale US-based low-cost quality vet generic drug manufacture for cats and dogs with less than 50 headcounts, have an excellent way of sharing story with the newcomers. Being a small-scale company, the Chairman of the company Jean Hoffman narrates her real-life story directly with the newcomers. The story is how the company from their experience of adopting cats and nurturing them till their old age, felt the compelling need to form the company, so that people can look after their pets till their old age. The company was formed in 2006 and is growing, achieving high engagement of employees promoting a team work culture. The spirit behind the story is that all the employees of the company work for a cause, that is, love for animal.

SUCCESSION PLANNING AND ONBOARDING

Many organizations in their onboarding program clarify to newcomers about their succession planning program, i.e., the process of identifying talent for future leadership role. With clarity on future leadership positions, and the criteria of selection, newcomers can feel the urge of continuing in their employment. Detailing on talent pipeline creation process in alignment with the changing business goals and strategies of the organization, and explaining to the newcomers how they can increase their value proposition to accelerate their career growth opportunities, to a great extent benefit organizational succession planning process. Some of the areas on information sharing on succession planning during onboarding process are how the company differentiates high potential from others, internal hiring, promotion from within policy, company's policy on diversity inclusivity, how employees can identify roadblocks in their career path, and how it can be avoided, etc.

Co-Creating Individual-Level Onboarding Program

Literally, co-creation denotes establishing strategic interactive relationships for value addition. In marketing involving customers companies can co-create value-adding experience, which can ultimately benefit organizations in product innovation and even in new product development. It also helps in understanding customers better and the way they take decisions while they purchase goods and services produced by organizations. In onboarding, co-creation with new hires helps in designing individual-level programs, which mutually benefits both the organizations and the new hires themselves. Such an approach of consultative cooperation emotionally engages new hires with the organization, helps them to experience satisfaction, and in the process makes the onboarding program successful.

Organization-wide approach to co-creation of personal level onboarding program varies. According to Bradt and Vonnegut (2009) to develop individual-level onboarding plan, it is important to co-create with new hires, so that they can accommodate, assimilate, and accelerate and align them appropriately with the organizations. Through co-creation both the new hires and the organizations establish their working relationships. New hires also get the message how they are valued in organizations.

Gamification in Onboarding

One of the primary objectives on onboarding program in any organizations is to engage new hires with the culture of the organizations. Learning, skill and knowledge enhancement, competency development are simultaneously reinforced through different phases of onboarding. But without engagement all these will be meaningless. To elicit response from the new hires, and to arouse their interest, organizations now use gamification as a tool. Gamification as an onboarding tool that makes onboarding program successful by aligning the process with the business goals of the organizations. Also, it drives performance, improved employee engagement, and higher retention of new hires.

For engaging employees, gamification is used in training programs. Gamification in onboarding is now gaining importance, as new hires through game-based learning can understand their job roles, acquire new skills and knowledge, develop competencies, and even quickly go through the process of acculturation. According to Kapp (2014), there are two types of games: structural and content-based. In structural games contents remain fixed, only elements are added depending on the learning needs. This is more a reinforced learning tool, as the learners can engage them in learning through rewards. Content gamification has the provision of altering content, depending on the learning goals. Goal of gamification in onboarding can elicit better responses from the new hires as they feel more engaged with the learning process, and can quickly develop their understanding to become job-ready. Such engagement of the new hires helps organizations in their retention, in achieving productivity and the business results. Realizing such importance, many organizations have started gamifying their onboarding programs. For example, Deloitte has gamified their onboarding program.

SUMMARY

- Onboarding is the process of alignment of the new hires with the organization through different stages of learning. It is different from orientation, as in orientation we emphasize more on compliance issues, and it is also conducted for a shorter duration. Effective design of onboarding requires certain stage-wise action. Organizations now manage their onboarding process with strategic approach, as it can better align new hires with their business and culture, and it can engage and motivate new hires. Strategic onboarding practices enhance retention of new hires. Successful onboarding program can promote brand value of organizations, as new hires share their positive experience in social media. This also helps in talent attraction. Designing individual-level onboarding program through co-creation to a great extent improves retention of new hires. Organizations for getting better success in their onboarding programs use various gamification tools.

Key Words

Onboarding: Onboarding is developing the desired behaviours, skills, knowledge and expertise that will be the foundation of new hires' long-term success.

Orientation: It is a program for new hires to familiarize with the history and mission of the organization, teaching about company rules, summarizing employee benefits, etc.

Strategic onboarding: Process of adjusting new recruits to social and performance aspects for their smooth transition to the job and organization.

Employer branding: Process of promoting an employee for talent attraction.

Succession planning: It is a process of identification of talent for future leadership role in organizations.

Co-creating onboarding program: It denotes establishing strategic interactive relationships with new hires and then develop individual level development programs for mutual benefits of new hires and the organizations.

Gamification in onboarding: Use of game-based learning in onboarding program for helping new hires in understanding their job roles, acquire new skills and knowledge, develop competencies, and even quickly go through the process of acculturation.

Review Questions

1. Define the concepts of onboarding. How onboarding is different from orientation?
2. What is strategic onboarding? How it benefits organizations?
3. What are the important areas of consideration while we design an onboarding program?
4. Explain how onboarding can help in organizational branding?
5. What is the importance of co-creating individual level onboarding program? How can this be done?
6. Discuss how onboarding program can be gamified.
7. Write short notes on:
   (a) Induction
   (b) Strategic onboarding
   (c) Four C Model
   (d) Employer branding
   (e) Story telling

Critical Review Question

1. Select an international level Indian organization. Study their onboarding program, collecting information from their websites, published reports, including previous research paper or articles, if any. Also refer to the shared experience of their employees

from social media sites. Document your observation and critically comment on their onboarding practices.

Multiple Choice Questions

1. Indentify incorrect statement on onboarding:
   (a) Onboarding is the other name employee socialization
   (b) Onboarding is strategic learning and performance issue for new hires
   (c) Successful onboarding program engages new hires and increases their retention
   (d) Gamification is an important tool used in onboarding program
   (e) Effective onboarding programs lend support to succession planning in organizations

2. Identify the correct statement(s) about onboarding
   (a) Onboarding transforms new hires
   (b) Onboarding helps new hires to quickly integrate them with the organizations
   (c) Onboarding promotes developing of internal network for collaboration
   (d) Onboarding dazzles new hires
   (e) All of the a, b, and c

3. Employee induction denotes as:
   (a) Process of sensitizing new recruits with organizational systems and processes
   (b) Induction is more encompassing than onboarding
   (c) Induction is more encompassing than orientation
   (d) Induction programs are usually conducted for a longer duration
   (e) Induction helps organizations to bring newcomers to future institutional order

4. Indicate which is not a feature of onboarding program:
   (a) A long-term structured process of integration of new hires with the organizations
   (b) Takes the new hires through the understanding of organizational policies and procedures, processes, structure, mutual expectations, and the scope of employee development
   (c) Emphasizes more on understanding of employee benefits, policies and procedures
   (d) Emphasizes on more holistic understanding of the organization, including cross-departmental functions
   (e) Facilitates in employee engagement, reduced employee turnover and increased performance

5. Indicate which is/are not benefit(s) of strategic onboarding:
   (a) Helps new hires to get familiarity with company's processes and way of working
   (b) Helps new hires to deliver performance results without much of time-lag
   (c) Helps organizations to achieve higher retention of new hires
   (d) Enhances engagement of new hires with the organization
   (e) Helps new hires educational support

6. Strategic onboarding helps new hires
   (a) Integrate with corporate culture
   (b) Share their expectations with the organizations
   (c) Develop sense of pride
   (d) Achieve career goals
   (e) All of the above

7. Effective onboarding program designing does not require:
   (a) Making induction personal
   (b) Sharing of training information
   (c) Integrating new hires with the culture of organizations
   (d) Making everything ready as the situation arises
   (e) All of the above

8. General information shared with the new hires during onboarding does not include:
   (a) Information about the key stakeholders
   (b) Information on organizational strategy
   (c) Information on organizational goals and objectives
   (d) Information on how the new hires can get access to top leaders of the organization
   (e) None of the above

9. Success of onboarding programs depends on its:
   (a) Focus on team-building
   (b) Narrating organizational stories as personal as possible
   (c) Giving opportunities to employees to integrate organizational brand with their personal brand
   (d) All of the above
   (e) None of the above

10. In onboarding, co-creation with new hires helps in all these, excepting:
   (a) Designing individual level programs
   (b) Ensuring mutually beneficial onboarding program for both the organizations and the new hires
   (c) Adopting approach of consultative cooperation to emotionally engage new hires with the organization
   (d) Helping new recruits to feel dazzled
   (e) Helping employees to experience satisfaction

Answers:

1. (a) 2. (e) 3. (a) 4. (c) 5. (e) 6. (e) 7. (d) 8. (e)
9. (d) 10. (d)

CASE STUDY

IBM's onboarding program

IBM's onboarding program is well crafted to ensure every new employee starts their job on the right foot. Right from day one, every newcomer starts getting their value-added onboarding sessions, which hone their knowledge and skills, and gradually make them right-fit for the company. Couple of onboarding information company shares with the new hires through e-mail before their joining. On the very first day, onboarding coordinators assist the new hires to complete mandatory documentation with sharing of complete information about the company, compensation and benefits, opening of salary account, and also answer any of queries from the new hires. This is followed by next-day orientation session to kick start IBM's own "Succeeding@IBM" two-year rigorous program with system and resource support, including series of learning activities. During this phase, new hires, after they grasp the basics, are encouraged to develop with support from their managers and colleagues. Side by side IBM intranet also provides information on career development and professional support to pursue employees' interest.

The first-day experience is not intimidating for the new hires, as new hires are helped by the onboarding coordinators. What new hires are required to bring while they report for the onboarding program on the first day are preinformed to them.

"Succeeding @IBM: Getting Oriented" after explaining to the new hires IBM's core values, rich heritage of technology leadership and innovation, and the role the new hires are required to play to drive growth and innovation for the company, provide detailed outline on phase-wise program during the period of onboarding. Designed in workshop format, new hires get opportunity to connect with other IBMers with different skill sets and expertise. This helps them to build internal networks. Entire onboarding program of IBM is more focused on experiential learning.

The initial phase is structured with the introduction of IBM and the "Succeeding@IBM" program, followed by explaining of IBM's history, strategy, business priorities, values, business conduct guidelines, diversity practices, global corporate culture, structure and organization, and the process of collaborating with other IBMers. Also new hires are explained about IBM's development path, introduction to the career development framework, and tools, and resources and programs for developing skills and expertise.

The next phase of onboarding is by the departmental managers to explain the tools and processes. The company calls it "Royal Blue Ambassador Program (RBA)," which connects new

IBMers with experienced employee (an advisor or buddy), who helps them to adapt quickly within IBM. This 30-day program is followed by a program to connect to "Grassroots Community," i.e., a group of proud and passionate IBMers. This group helps new IBMers to form a collaborative community for their smooth transition in the workplace.

Post the RBA program, you can also look forward to the "Grassroots Community" which is a group of proud and passionate IBMers who have come together to form a collaborative community to assist new IBMers transition into the workplace.

Subsequent phases over the two-year period provide tremendous learning value to new IBMers, which make them feel more attached, engaged, motivated, and productive.

Note: This case study has been developed based on website information of IBM:

Question: Critically evaluate IBM's onboarding program. How does such onboarding program benefit any organization to retain talent?

REFERENCES

Adler, P.S. and Kwon, S.W. (2002), "Social capital: Prospects for a new concept", *Academy of Management Review,* 27(1): 17–40.

Ashforth, B.E., Sluss, D.M. and Saks, A.M. (2007), "Socialization tactics, proactive behavior, and newcomer learning: Integrating socialization models". *Journal of Vocational Behavior,* 70(3): 447–462.

Bandiera, O., Barankay, I. and Rasul, I. (2008), "Social capital in the workplace: Evidence on its formation and consequence", *Labour Economics,* 15(4): 725–729.

Bauer, T.N. (2011), "Onboarding new employees: Maximizing success. SHRM Foundation's Effective Practice Guideline Series", SHRM Foundation, Alexandria, Virginia, USA.

Bauer, T.N., Morrison, E.W. and Callister, R.R. (1998), Organizational socialization: A review and directions for future research. In: Ferris GR (ed.) *Research in Personnel and Human Resources Management*, Vol. 16. Stamford, CT: JAI Press, 149–214.

Bradt, G. and Vonnegut, M. (2009), *On-Boarding: How to Get Your New Employees up to Speed in Half the Time*. Hoboken, NJ: John Wiley and Sons.

Kapp, K. (2014), *The Gamification of Learning and Instruction Field Book*. New York: Wiley.

Lin, N. (2001), *Social Capital: A Theory of Social Structure and Action*. Cambridge: Cambridge University Press.

Nahapiet, J. and Ghoshal, S. (1998), "Social capital, intellectual capital and the organizational advantage", *Academy of Management Review* 23(2): 242–266.

Sprogoe, J., and Elkjaer, B. (2010), "Induction – organizational renewal and the maintenance of status quo", *Society and Business Review*, 5(2): 130–143.

Chapter 11

Career Planning, Career Development, and Employees' Succession

LEARNING OBJECTIVES

After reading this chapter, you will be able to understand:

1. Definitions and concepts of career planning and career development
2. Interrelations between career planning, career development, and succession planning
3. Process of doing career planning
4. Process of career development
5. Importance and significance of career planning and career development
6. Succession planning
7. Management development and organizational development activities
8. Influence of career planning and career development on talent management practices

Career Development in IBM

IBM, the century-old global IT services major, with headcounts of 4.31 lakhs and sales revenue of US$ 99.7 billion believes in partnering with their employees. With the embedded culture of innovation through collaboration, the company always emphasizes on employee development. To meet such an objective, IBM has crafted their career development programs by focusing on individual career guidance to all cross-sections of employees and providing compulsory skill enhancement opportunities. The idea behind this is to prepare the talent pipeline. Career development program is blended with employees' self-development showcasing various career opportunities, so that employees themselves can make their informed career choices. Stretch assignments, job rotations, job shadowing, lunch and learn sessions, speed mentoring, etc., are used to help employees to make their career choices. IBM calls it "blue opportunities." Emphasis is also given on development of foundational competencies so that employees can develop desired behavior essential for critical job roles. For leaders they have advanced foundational competency programs. Through "Team Pac" programs the company develops essential skills for achieving team productivity, and also problem-solving ability. With reinforcement of outbound programs, IBM helps employees to achieve team cohesion and bonding.

INTRODUCTION

After successful transition of new hires into the organizations through onboarding, career planning and career development issues, including issues pertaining to succession planning, assume importance. Organization has to invest in career planning and career development of employees, else organization will face the risk of retention of employees. Employees with talent will also expect career development opportunities, so that they can continue with their job over an extended period of their career life cycle. Succession planning is an inseparable function from employees' career planning and development, as through this process, organizations can identify potential talent and design suitable career development programs to groom them for future leadership jobs. Cross-functional job mobility, global job market, and competitors' relentless pursuit for talent hiring, especially, made career planning and development function more challenging. Theoretically, the term career planning and career development is different. Career planning process for an employee communicates where they are at present, and where they can reach in the future within the organizations. With suitable career planning process, employees can make their informed choice about future career progression opportunity within the organization, and accordingly can develop their self-development plan within the organization. We can say it is a document career plan in alignment with the organizational goals and objectives, business priorities, strategies over a reasonable span of time. Contrarily, career development denotes process of assisting employees so that they can reach their career goals. Rather, it creates opportunities for employee development for future job roles. Despite such theoretical differences, in organizations we use these two terms interchangeably. Some organizations prefer using the term career development plan rather than using two separate terms, i.e., career planning and career development.

Challenge of talent retention accentuated the pace of career planning and career development functions in organizations. Many organizations use it as part of their total rewards program, while they attract and recruit talent. Through career planning, career development, and succession planning, organizations can also strengthen their talent pipeline, for internal hiring, particularly at the senior level. Another inseparable issue from career planning, and career development is management development and organizational development. This chapter also briefly highlights this aspect.

DEFINITIONS AND CONCEPTS

The term career indicates occupation, including the job roles, related to paid employment in organizations. In employment cycle, employees move from one job to another, play different job roles, and even experience cross-functional job movement. All these are different stages of career and at every stage, competency requirements vary. Organizations reinforce employees' career through training and development support. Employees make their career choices within their organizations, once they fail they move to other jobs, which we call career shift. A number of factors influence employees' career choices, more important among these being the opportunity to innovate, learn, and grow. Research studies indicate on average employment cycle of 25 years or so, we make five to eight career changes. Some of the reasons are opportunity to work in a new work environment which is more innovative, dynamic, and resilient, sustainable and growth-oriented, and finally which facilitates in work–life balancing.

Literally, therefore, career is succession of different jobs in the work–life cycle of an employee.

Career planning is a process of lending support to employees helping them to understand their career opportunities, and accordingly set their career goals. Career planning process is rationalized through the process of identification of employees' strengths. Organizations create career development opportunities on the basis of their career plans to retain talent. Availability of a structured career plan helps employees to make an informed choice about their career movement within and between occupations, and within and between organizations. Hence, it is also used as a self-development tool by employees. For organizations career planning is done by mapping sequence of jobs for employees. Career plans in organizations are done for both the short-term and long-term career goals for employees.

Effective career planning involves preparing career paths, developing employees' skill inventories, documenting career information systems, and providing career counseling services to employees. This is supported by job designs, developing of performance standards and systems of performance assessment, developing career goals, effective human resource planning, etc.

In alignment with the career plans, organizations undertake career development activities by creating both career opportunities and developing employees so that they can rise through career ladder. From this perspective, we cannot separate a career plan from career development, as in both the cases, our prime objective is to create opportunities for employees to progress through their career path. Career development was defined by Leibowitz, Farren and Kaye (1986) as an organized and formalized process of balancing between individual employees' and organizational goals. It is an ongoing process for individuals' development through different career stages over their work-life cycle (Greenhaus et al., 2000). Similarly, Hansen (1976) defined career development as an ongoing developmental experience of employees throughout their career life cycle.

The best way to define career development is as an ongoing process of managing learning and work so that employees of organizations gradually develop and rise through organizational hierarchy. Good organizations extend career development opportunities to all cross-sections of employees, and such practices not only help in employees' retention, but also attract talent. Process of career development largely varies across organizations; however, we find all organizations for effective career development emphasize on employees' development, transparency on career information, and wherever required providing coaching and mentoring support.

Career planning and career development process in organizations also relate to succession planning. Through succession plan, organizations identify potential employees for future leadership positions. It helps organizations to build the talent pipeline for making available competent human resources internally, thus reducing organizational dependence on external hire. In this world organizations compete for talent. Succession planning helps in building talent. With the recruitment of quality manpower, and with career planning and career development support, succession planning process becomes more effective. Like career planning and career development, succession planning also helps in employees' retention and increased level of motivation and performance.

Likewise, career planning and career development needs reinforcement from management development and organizational development initiatives, as these help in building employees' capabilities that are essential for future career growth. Talent management functions in organizations also get reinforced by career planning and career development activities.

Thus, career development increases employees' opportunities for career change through different hierarchical positions, whereas career planning establishes career progression path and career objectives. Career management, on the other hand, indicates all HR activities that facilitate career development. Such activities are recruitment, selection, onboarding, placement, succession planning, and performance evaluation.

ESSENTIAL ELEMENTS OF CAREER

In line with our above discussions, we can list essential elements of career as under:

- It indicates logical arrangement of job-related activities.
- It can be both individual-centered and organization-centered.
- It is an integrated pace of hierarchical movement in a job-family or occupation.
- It is a proactive process and involves concerted action.
- It is a transparent process of information collection and dissemination to help employees to take informed decisions about their career.
- It culls knowledge and skill gap for the future job positions.
- It succeeds in designing of career planning and career development programs.

IMPORTANCE OF CAREER DEVELOPMENT

We have already understood career development as a holistic approach to reinforce employees' career aspiration through training and development. Rather, it is a process of developing employees so as to help them rise through career ladder (Bhattacharyya, 2015). Also, career development issue is now embedded with the organizational rewards and recognition programs. Along with the competitive compensation and benefits, organizations need to provide career development opportunities to their employees. Barbeite and Maurer (2002) could observe good career development opportunities attract talent in organization. Also, it can contribute to enhancing job satisfaction and organizational commitment (Birdi, Allan, & Warr 1997), higher level of performance (Aguinis & Kraiger, 2009), etc.

From the above perspective we can enumerate significance and importance of career development as under:

(1) It helps in employee development through training and development balancing the individual and organizational needs.
(2) It enhances employees' performance and productivity.
(3) It supports the organizational process of building talent pipeline.
(4) It attracts and retains talent in organization.
(5) It facilitates in creating suitable organizational structure.
(6) It aligns with organizational vision, mission, goals, and strategies.
(7) It motivates employees, raising their level of satisfaction.
(8) It can support organizational restructuring and change management initiatives.
(9) It can enhance organizational competitive strength through employees' capability development.
(10) It can drive innovation in organizations.

Among all, most significant contribution of career development is attracting and retaining talent.

Again for Indian organizations, career development is a critical task, as many Indian organizations are now restructuring to respond to global competition, which render many jobs and skill-sets redundant. Redeploying employees, who are affected in this process, obviously requires organizations to develop career development program for skill renewal. Complexity of jobs with the changing environment requires organizations to focus on career development. For this perspective, career development program in any organizations can lend support for successful organizational change-building capabilities of employees. Similarly, structured career development programs can eliminate discretionary employee promotion, promote diversity inclusivity and culture of equity, and enhance the scope of job mobility.

Sun Microsystems, the 1982 company, despite facing intense competition from Microsoft, is able to attract talent creating a culture of having fun while innovating in organizations. Career development opportunities at Sun Microsystems align employees' fulfillment with the organizational needs. "Figure it out for yourself" is the Sun's approach to employees' career development. Employees are informed about career services through a variety of channels, which help them to make informed choices about their career.

The importance and significance of career development mentioned above are in reality core advantages. Such advantages may not be uniform across organizations. Similarly, we can chuck out purposes and objectives of career development from the above lists.

TYPES OF CAREER DEVELOPMENT PROGRAMS

Selection of appropriate types or methods of career development will vary depending on the target employees for whom organizations are initiating career development. Apart from training and development, career development process can be facilitated by job rotation, job shadowing, assignment of employees in committees, deputing employees to different conferences and forums, assignment of employees in some special projects, etc. All these we classify under experiential or on-the-job learning. These processes are further reinforced by coaching, mentoring, networking, workshops and seminars, class-room learning, and off-the-job learning. Traditionally in organizations class-room learning is considered synonymous of training and development. But to ensure better benefits through training transfer (viz., incremental change in performance results), organizations now embrace blended approach to training and development, like class-room training with e-learning, class-room learning with on-the-job training, class-room training with off-the-job learning (like deputing employees to attend conferences, seminars, workshops, or enrolment in some part-time educational programs), etc. For example, HUL follows blended approach to develop career of their employees. The company gives more thrust on on-the-job learning (70%), followed by coaching and mentoring (20%), and then class-room training (10%).

Apart from use of training and development as primary career development tool, organizations also make use of tools like management development and organizational development. Organizational development focuses on more holistic development of the organizations, primarily achieved through employee development; management development focuses on developing managers upgrading their skills and knowledge, so that they can pace with the changing processes, and also develop their competence for future promotional vacancies.

Therefore, we find career development programs of any organization encompass with the entire gamut of employee development functions. Whatever may be the differences, career development is inter-related with other human resource development functions of organizations.

IMPORTANCE OF CAREER PLANNING

Career planning matches individual employees' potential with their career aspiration, matching with organizational needs. Career planning helps organizations making available appropriate manpower with requisite knowledge and skill-sets at times of need. It helps in deciding the need for suitable training and development so that capable human resources can be made available without any time lag. It helps employees to understand their career progression path and also helps organizations to understand possible career stagnation, if any. When career stagnates in organizations, talent leaves, and organizations face the crisis of talent attrition. With identification of career stagnation at various levels, it is possible for organizations to initiate appropriate action, creating opportunities within the same job family, or even outside the job family (through cross-skilling). From these perspectives, career planning helps in opening new career opportunities in organizations. Career planning process also reinforces organizational succession planning.

Based on the above discussions, like career development, for career planning also we can list the significance as under:

(1) It provides opportunities to employees to understand their career growth prospects.
(2) It enhances employees' voluntary participation in training and development programs.
(3) It increases employees' loyalty to the organization, as they feel their organizations value their career aspiration.
(4) It helps employees to integrate individual career goals with the organizational goals.
(5) It improves organizational brand value, which as a result helps in talent attraction.
(6) It can address the problem of talent attrition.
(7) It provides support to organizational manpower planning process.
(8) It can align with the business goals.

(9) It helps employees to make their long-term career choice in organizations.
(10) It helps in succession planning.

DIFFERENCE BETWEEN CAREER DEVELOPMENT AND CAREER PLANNING

Both career planning and career development are operationally used in organizations as one and the same. Hence, it is difficult to draw a line between these two employee development tools, essential for attraction and retention of talent. However, from theoretical percepts, we can document the differences as under.

With career development programs, organizations can guide employees to achieve high performance level and reach through their career goals. With a career plan, organizations can chart the possible career progression path for employees. A good career plan raises employees' career aspiration, while a good career development program fulfils employees' career aspiration. With career development programs, organizations can attract and retain talented employees, while with career planning organizations can attract new talent. A career plan explains the career path up the organizational ladder (Fink, 1992), whereas career development programs help employees to rise through organizational ladder. By creating career development opportunities organizations can make their employees loyal and committed to raise their job satisfaction, and reduce their rate of attrition (Werther & Davis, 1992). With career plan organizations can develop employees' trust. Career development programs are developed by organizations based on career plans, whereas career plans are developed aligning with organizational goals and strategies. Career planning activities encompass career pathing, skill inventories, career information systems, career counseling, etc. Career development aligns such career plans with employees' capabilities. Organizations cannot go through career development process without a career plan, whereas career plan can be independent of a career development process.

DIFFERENCE BETWEEN CAREER PLANNING AND HUMAN RESOURCE PLANNING

Career planning is often considered synonymous with human resource planning (HRP). In fact, it is difficult to draw a line between these two concepts. However, career planning and HRP are different. HRP is facilitated by career planning process of any organization. Again, career planning process in organizations cannot be effective without inputs from HRP. The reason is that organizations integrate their HRP with corporate plans; hence such inputs can be used in career planning process, while charting career progressing path in sync with organizational goals and strategies. Thus, both these processes are interdependent. Some of the differences between HRP and career planning process can be as follows.

HRP documents availability of talent in terms of skills, knowledge, and competencies duly developing skills inventory. Using such skills inventory organizations can take stock of their talent pipeline and frame their long-term strategies accordingly. Career planning, on the other hand, facilitates in individual employees' career movement and thus grooms them and makes them available whenever required by organizations. HRP can provide information on human resource availability, based on which organizations can draw their business plans. Career planning helps in replacement of human resources internally in case any form of manpower wastages, like voluntary attrition, retirement, death, dismissal, etc. Career planning process in any organization cannot be done without HRP but HRP can be done, although to achieve results from HRP, it is important to have an effective career planning process.

DIFFERENCE WITH SUCCESSION PLANNING

Succession planning is a process of identification of potential talent in organizations for future leadership roles. Usually, scope of succession planning gets limited to key managerial positions, as these employees require grooming over a long period of time through management development programs. Scope of career planning, on the other hand, encompasses all employees, including managers and executives, who are not covered under the succession plans. Thus while succession plans require management development programs, career plans require training support so that career development of employees can be achieved. Succession planning is one element of career management process in any organization, while career planning is the process of career management. Through a career plan organizations help employees to identify their career goals and accordingly strive to achieve the same with career development support. Through succession plan, organizations identify potential employees and then take them through planned development. A career plan is for the entire career cycles of an employee, i.e., till he/she retires from the organization. A succession plan is time bound, i.e., from 2 to 10 years or so. Nevertheless succession plan is continuous.

CAREER DEVELOPMENT CYCLE

Career goals and aspirations of employees widely vary with respect to their age-group. Hence, organizations need to factor employees' age-group while designing career plan and developing opportunities for career development. Difference in employees' perceived internal career with respect to their age group can be grouped as exploratory, establishment, maintenance, and the stage of decline. Exploratory age employees are in the beginning of their career life cycle. Such employees take longer time to integrate them with the organization even after effective onboarding process, and often quit their jobs when they feel incompatibility in their education, knowledge, and skills are not in sync with their job roles and even with the organization. Crafting career development programs for this age-group of employees requires appropriate job sculpting, so that they can identify that their jobs are interesting. Also organizations need to provide these employees with autonomy, take them through compulsory job rotation, etc.

The second phase of career development cycle is known as establishment stage. It is at this stage employees start looking at their job as career and gradually decide to be with the organizations over a long time frame. At this stage, organizations provide systematic performance feedback to the employees, help them to understand their performance setbacks, if any, and also help them to understand their performance strengths, their important contributions to the organizations, etc. Also wherever required organizations provide support to employees to overcome their functional deficiencies. All these processes emotionally engage employees, enhance their loyalty and commitment to the organizations, and at the same time, ensure their retention.

Maintenance stage is the third phase of career development cycle of employees. We also call it mid-career stage of employees' career life cycle. At this stage, employees put their best efforts to retain their name and fame; hence, they put their relentless efforts for their development. Organizations also extend support to employees' skill renewal, knowledge updating, and competency development with structured career development support, so that these mid-career stage employees can become more productive and decide to stay permanently. Else organizations will face the crisis of mid-career job switch. Indian organizations are facing crisis of middle level managers for their high attrition, primarily because of lack of career development support.

Decline stage is the final stage of career development cycle. At this stage, employees actually mentally prepare them for retirement. Employees gradually feel that their role in the organizations will get reduced, and they will be shredded off from their responsibilities. Some of the behavioral complexities of old age, like sense of insecurity, loss of confidence, poor self-esteem, etc., gradually reduce their performance. Career development process of organizations for this stage of employees focuses on mentally preparing employees for retirement, and through counseling helps them to develop their coping strategies, so that they can adjust with their families and also with the society.

In line with Schein (1990), we can document the issues in career development process of employees at different career stages as represented in Table 11.1:

TABLE 11.1 Issues in career development process of employees.

Exploratory	Establishment	Maintenance	Decline
Sharing of career information with newcomers	Identify best possible talent	Provide performance feedback, career counseling, long-term career plans and ensure proper deployment of employees so that they can feel challenged, motivated, and committed to the organization	Ensure that employees do not destroy their self-worth
Integrate newcomers with organizations through onboarding	Create correct and positive image about organization	Ensure productive utilization of career-plateaued (those who are unsuitable for promotion) employees	Prepare retirement plan
Acquaint new comers on organizational careers through job rotation and internship	Develop employees' positive attitude about organization	Help employees for their transition from specialist to generalist cadre so as to provide them opportunity to rise through career ladder	Identify possible engagement of retired employees in part-time job (mostly in advisory nature) matching with their knowledge and experience

(*Continued*)

TABLE 11.1 Continued

Exploratory	Establishment	Maintenance	Decline
Take newcomers through training and learning programs	Allocate challenging jobs to employees to enable them to put their abilities and skills on test	Create adequate career paths to enable employees to avail career growth opportunities with work–life balancing	Send birthday wishes to retired employees
	Provide performance feedback and help employees to understand their strengths and weaknesses	Help employees to develop coping strategies while they experience career transition from operational jobs to advisory jobs	Arrange annual meet of retired employees for effective social networking
	Design suitable career development plans in line with employees' strengths and weaknesses	Help employees to prepare for retirement	

However, all these issues may not be relevant for organizations. Employees at different stages of their career life cycle assess career-related information and make their informed choice about their career either within or outside the organization. As career development issues are critical for employees' retention, organizations need to design appropriate career development plan for their employees at different career stages, and make such information transparent for employees.

CAREER ANCHORS

According to Schein (1990), all of us have some specific orientation toward our work and we all prioritize and attach values to work. This we do combining our competence and motives, which in the process helps us in making our professional work choices. Schein has used the term "career anchors" to indicate this concept. Career anchors' concept helps employees to make their appropriate career choices in alignment with their talent, attitude, motives, and values. It drives a person to make his/her career choices. Career anchors can be defined as employees' self-perceived talent and abilities, values, and motives with respect to their career. As it is employees' self-understanding, organizations, when understand career anchors of employees, can make them more productive, allocating employees job of their choices.

Employees also knowing their career anchors, based on their self-perceived talents, attitudes, motives, and values, select appropriate career options. When employees are able to identify their career anchors they show their unwillingness to relinquish, as a result of which absence of desired career choices in their present organizations, may persuade them to go for job switch, creating crisis of attrition in organizations. In a sense, employees are pulled back to right-fit career, which we use metaphorically as an anchor (Evans, 1996). Thus, important components of career anchors are self-perceived talents and abilities, self-perceived motives and needs, and self-perceived attitudes and values of employees.

Schein (1990) based on the research carried out at MIT identified eight career anchors for employees. Depending on the motives, needs, attitudes,

TABLE 11.2 Categories of career anchors and their traits.

Categories of career anchor	Traits
Technical/ functional	Strives to achieve excellence. Propensity to become expert in their domain. Like challenge in job to put their expertise to test, and have capability to do their job better than others.
Managerial	Bestowed with problem-solving abilities and show interest to take responsibility.
Autonomy/ Independence	Propensity to work under their own rules and enjoy working in silos.
Security/Stability	Primarily driven by stability and job security.
Entrepreneurial	Creative and have propensity to invent things. Have strong sense of ownership with their jobs.
Service/dedication	Prefer doing jobs that can help others.
Pure challenge	Prefer challenging and difficult jobs.
Life style	Prefer integrating work and life.

and values, individual employees assign priorities to their preferences. Employees in general remain anchored in one area. In Table 11.2, we have documented categories of career anchors and traits for the same.

Using the above template, employees can analyze their traits and match with the relevant career anchors. While making such an analysis, one can weigh the relevant career anchor in terms of its importance to career. Also for better rationalization, it is recommended to match the career anchor with the current post. In both the cases, 5-point scale is used, where 1 indicates not important, while 5 indicates very important. Depending on the degree of match, one case assesses whether he or she is in the right career anchor or not.

SUCCESSION PLANNING

Succession plan identifies and develops potential employees for future leadership positions in organizations. Organizations based on their short-term and long-term plans envisage future requirements of human resources for managerial job positions. Potential employees who are identified through the process of succession plans are taken through tailor-made training and development programs, and also exposed to relevant jobs through on-the-job training under coach or mentor. Through this process, such potential employees develop their capabilities, and make them perfect fit for the future leadership roles. From these perspectives we can call succession planning a process of leadership continuity so that performance of the organizations does not get affected for absence of key managerial level people. Again, it is a process of manpower replacement planning, particularly at senior level. Importance of succession planning has increased in organizations particularly for developing in-house talent pipeline for future leaders. While selecting potential employees for succession plan, in addition to performance data, organizations factor issues like personality, education and training, family background, interpersonal skills, age-group, emotional maturity, etc. However, all these depend on specific priorities of organizations.

After identification of potential leaders for future job roles through the process of succession planning, organizations need to develop them so that they acquire requisite skills and knowledge and competencies, matching with the envisaged job requirements. Such development initiative is taken based on the gap analysis, i.e., taking into account the available competencies and required competencies in the future. Accordingly, organizations develop training and mentoring programs. Usually in succession planning, identified potential leaders are put under a mentor (fairly at senior level). Some organizations emphasize on selection of mentors who need to be replaced by the identified potential employees. Problem-solving and decision-making abilities are given priorities. Potential employees shadow the mentors and gradually develop such skills through experiential learning. Gradually, these potential employees start attending top management meetings, get them involved in decision-making process, engage in budgeting, goal-setting, resource allocation, and strategy framing.

With all the above time-bound programs, spreading over few years, top management of the organization assesses the potential employees and then deploys them in the leadership jobs. In between organization needs evaluation of their succession plan programs to bring the required changes, if any.

Steps of Succession Planning

Effective succession planning can be possible once we follow a structured approach with successive steps. These are as under:

Preparing and developing managerial employees' anticipated staffing plan in different time frames, say 5 years, 10 years, 15 years, etc. Some organizations may have staffing plan for short time-frame like one to two years also. While developing such staffing plan possible manpower wastages need to be factored. Manpower wastages could occur even for premature death, disability, premature retirement, etc., in addition to voluntary attrition like employees' preference for a job switch, or unwillingness to continue with job and taking sabbatical for long vacation, studies, etc. In addition, organizations also require factoring exogenous issues like economic factors, labor market situation, etc.

The second step of a succession plan is to recruit and develop identified potential employees. Recruitment and selection can be done either from within or outside the organizations. For internal recruitment, promotion and transfer is used as tool. After recruitment, organizations identify potential employees and plan for their systematic development using several employee development tools like training, job rotation, creating "assistant-to" job positions, temporary assignment to job that requires higher responsibilities, project assignment, board assignment, performance counseling, coaching and mentoring, etc.

The next step for effective succession planning results requires organizations to develop a performance-driven work culture along with a congenial work environment. This will facilitate in developing potential employees, and they will feel increased attachment with the organizations.

In the fourth step, organizations streamline their performance management systems giving constant feedback to employees, helping them to understand shortcomings and ways to improve their performance.

Feedback on their strengths also can help employees to focus on those jobs which match with their skills and competence.

The final step of a succession plan is to prepare inventory of potential managers with information like biographical details, performance records, skills, knowledge, career goals and career paths, career anchors, etc. These potential managers will then be deployed in suitable jobs time to time, pacing with organizations' business goals and strategies.

Drawing Lessons from Apple

Steve Jobs, erstwhile CEO from Apple, before two years of his resignation introduced his successor Tim Cook, the then chief operating officer of the company. His announcement two years before had some initial effect on the stock prices of Apple, which went down by around 5%. However, the shock was for a very short period, as the market could realize that the company had a plan. With shareholders' voting, Tim Cook could become the CEO of the company and take the company forward, as we see it today. CEO succession planning is a strategic move, which company has to decide well in advance. This at least enables the company (as it happened in the case of Apple) to follow a process of transition.

MANAGEMENT DEVELOPMENT

Effective career planning and development along with a succession plan makes use of management development for grooming of potential managers. Management development is a training process for managerial level employees to build and enrich their knowledge and skills so that they can gradually be groomed to take up future senior managerial or leadership roles in organizations. Management development programs are more holistic and focus on developing conceptual and human relations skill of managers. Usually, such programs are conducted for a longer duration. Many organizations do not have their in-house facilities for conducting management development programs. Such organizations can make use of the services of professional institutions and agencies.

Characteristically, management development programs are conducted as a continuous process to update knowledge and for building capabilities of managers, bring their attitudinal change, stimulate their higher competence, and build their self-confidence. Scope of management development activity also encompasses job rotation, short-term assignments for jobs requiring higher responsibility, creating "assistant-to" job positions, projects and boards assignment, etc.

SUMMARY

- Recruitment and selection without employees' career planning and development would render the process meaningless, as new hires may gradually leave their jobs for better career prospects in other organizations. We already know the cost implications of employee attrition. Also negative vibes will not attract new talents for the organization. Career planning and development is a holistic process of identifying the career progression path for employees and creating opportunities for their upward movement through their career ladder. Even though these two terms are different, we use it interchangeably in organizations.
- Career planning and development process not only retains potential employees, it also attracts new talents, and helps in organizational strategic planning, making available future ready human resources. Also it helps in designing need-based training and development programs.
- Career planning and development process are facilitated by a series of employee development activities, like training and development, management development, job rotation, creating "assistance-to" job positions, assigning employees to projects and boards, temporarily assigning employees to jobs with higher responsibility, etc.

Key Words

Career planning: A charted career progression path for various categories of employees in an organization.

Career development: Process of creating opportunities for employees to rise through the career progression path.

Succession planning: Process of identifying potential successors among employees for future leadership positions.

Career cycle: Career development stages of an employee, more related to age group and promotional levels.

Career anchors: Syndrome of talents, motives, and values, which gives stability and direction to a person's career.

Career paths: Career paths are logical mapping jobs indicating potential progression tract that an employee may follow over time.

Review Questions

1. Define career development. Explain how it helps in talent retention. Does it differ from career planning?
2. What is the difference between individual centered and organization centered career planning? Briefly discuss the career planning program of a hypothetical organization.
3. Discuss how an organization can make their career planning process successful.

4. Discuss the important steps in career planning process.
5. Define Succession Planning. Enumerate the steps involved in succession planning.
6. Write short notes on:
   (a) Career plateauing
   (b) Career ladders
   (c) Job families
   (d) Skill inventories
   (e) Career anchors

Critical Review Question

1. Design a career development plan for a manufacturing organization.

Multiple Choice Questions

1. Career planning and career development issues encompass the following, except:
   (a) Issues pertaining to succession planning
   (b) Issues pertaining to career development opportunities for employees
   (c) Helping employees in understanding their career life cycle
   (d) Issues pertaining to cross-functional job mobility both within and outside the organizations
   (e) Helping employees in career anchoring

2. The term career indicates:
   (a) Occupation
   (b) Job roles
   (c) Cross-functional job movement
   (d) All of the above
   (e) None of the above

3. Identify the incorrect statement:
   (a) Career is succession of different jobs in work-life cycle of an employee
   (b) Career planning is a process of lending support to employees helping them to understand their career opportunities, and accordingly set their career goals
   (c) Career planning process is rationalized through the process of identification employees' strengths
   (d) Organizations create career development opportunities based on their career plans to retain talent
   (e) Sharing a structured career plan with the employees make them feel less aspirational

4. Effective career planning involves:
   (a) Preparing career paths
   (b) Developing employees' skill inventories
   (c) Documenting career information systems
   (d) Providing career counseling services to employees
   (e) All of the above

5. Identify the incorrect statement:
   (a) Career development is organized and formalized process of balancing between individual employees' and organizational goals
   (b) It is an ongoing process for individuals' development through different career stages over their work-life cycle
   (c) It is an ongoing developmental experience of employees throughout their career life cycle
   (d) All of the above
   (e) None of the above

6. Indicate which is not an element of career:
   (a) Logical arrangement of job-related activities
   (b) It is an individual-centered approach
   (c) It is an integrated pace of hierarchical movement in a job-family or occupation
   (d) It is a proactive process and involves concerted action
   (e) It is a transparent process of information collection and dissemination to help employees to take informed decisions about their career

7. Career development is significant for organizations because of the following, except:
   (a) It helps in employee development through training and development pacing with the individual needs
   (b) It enhances employees' performance and productivity
   (c) It supports the organizational process of building talent pipeline
   (d) It attracts and retains talent in organizations
   (e) It facilitates in creating suitable organizational structure

8. Career development process can be facilitated by:
   (a) Job rotation
   (b) Job shadowing
   (c) Assignment of employees in committees
   (d) Deputing employees' to different conferences and forums
   (e) All of the above

9. Career planning is significant because:
   (a) It provides opportunities to employees to understand their career growth prospects
   (b) It enhances employees' voluntary participation in training and development programs
   (c) It increases employees' loyalty to the organization, as they feel their organizations value their career aspiration
   (d) It helps employees to integrate individual career goals with the organizational goals
   (e) All of the above

10. Which is not a valid statement about career planning:
    (a) It improves organizational brand value, which as a result helps in talent attraction
    (b) It succeeds career development
    (c) It can address the problem of talent attrition
    (d) It provides support to organizational manpower planning process
    (e) It can align with the business goals

Answers:

1. (d) 2. (d) 3. (e) 4. (e) 5. (e) 6. (b) 7. (a) 8. (e)
9. (e) 10. (b)

CASE STUDY

For Godrej career planning and development is a serious business

For Godrej industries, the 115-year-old conglomerate with headcounts of 15,000 and sales revenue of US$1.4 billion, attracting and retaining talent is a major challenge. With a tag of one of the best companies in India to work, the company today envisages to grow adding additional headcounts of 3000 by 2017. The company believes customer centricity approach in business, and contemporary business practices are making them a magnetic force to attract new talent. The feel-good experience of employees is created by the company institutionalizing a healthy environment of learning, empowerment, and rewards. Exchange of ideas between employees is encouraged to foster innovation.

Career development opportunities of employees are reinforced by best-in-class technology-enabled training and development support with more emphasis on "on-the-job" learning. As a practice, the company believes in accentuating commitment from employees, creating career development opportunities. Career development programs are designed with inputs from the employees and these are reinforced by reward and recognition program.

Management trainees from different business schools are taken through year-long onboarding program, known as GALLOP (The Godrej Accelerated Learning, Leadership and Orientation Program). GALLOP focuses on holistic development of management trainees so that they can look forward to a galloping career. All pervasive approach to empowerment with a flat organizational structure ensures information transparency and satisfaction for the employees. Identified potential employees for future leadership roles are additionally taken through total talent management program. "High Values–High Performance" the dominant work culture makes Godrej a rewarding career for employees.

The identified leadership competencies of the company are professional competence, ability to make things happen, ability to uphold Godrej values, vision and infective passion, decisive and entrepreneurial, drive for achieving excellence and organizational change, customer-centric nose, etc.

Today, Godrej industries with quality manpower are able to produce internationally competitive quality products and export their produced items to 40 countries. With a positive employee development approach through career development, the company aspires to grow, adding approximately 1000 head counts every year.

Question: List the important lessons on career planning and career development from Godrej's case.

REFERENCES

Aguinis, H. and Kraiger, K. (2009), "Benefits of training and development for individuals and teams, organizations, and society", *Annual Review of Psychology*, 60: 451–474.

Barbeite, F. and Maurer, T. (2002, April), "Importance of learning and development opportunity to job choice decisions", Presented at the annual conference of the Society for Industrial and Organizational Psychology, Toronto, Ontario, Canada.

Bhattacharyya, D.K. (2015), *Training & Development*. New Delhi: Sage.

Birdi, K., Allan, C. and Warr, P. (1997), "Correlates and outcomes of four types of employee development activity", *Journal of Applied Psychology*, 82(6): 845–857.

Evans, C. (1996), "A Review of career anchors in use", *European Journal of Work and Organizational Psychology*, 5(4): 609–615.

Fink, S. (1992), *High Commitment Workplaces*. New York: Quorum.

Schein, E.H. (1990), *Career Anchors: Discovering Your Real Values*. San Diego, CA: Pfeiffer & Co.

Werther, W. and Davis, K. (1992), *Personnel Management and Human Resources*. New York: McGraw-Hill.

Chapter **12**

Research on Recruitment and Selection

LEARNING OBJECTIVES

After reading this chapter, you will be able to understand:

1. Introduction and concepts of recruitment and selection research
2. Types of recruitment research
3. Concept of recruitment research
4. Importance of recruitment and selection research
5. Literature review for recruitment research
6. Model building for recruitment research
7. Process of recruitment and selection research
8. Learning curve as tool for recruitment research
9. Recruitment research at organization level
10. Cost–benefit analysis for recruitment research
11. Predictive analytics for recruitment research

For Sears Recruitment Is Core to Their Business

For Sears, the retail giant, recruitment is aligned with the business. The company hires 1,40,000 to 1,60,000 sales people. This apart they have regular lateral hiring at managerial and executive levels. The company manages such massive recruitment volume using predictive analytics, which the company could design through sustained research. Recruitment activity for Sears is continuous. On a given day, they announce vacancies for 10,000 to 12,000 people of different categories. From a pool of 60 lakhs applicants every year, the company has to identify talents and their predictive analytics to a great extent help in achieving such intents. Considering the volume of applications and recruitment, the company starts their recruitment activity through the online filling of job applications by the candidates, including a simulation test on retail. This 35-minute simulation test has been designed by the company more like a video game. Applicants here are exposed to a real and interactive sales scenario, and are expected to sell to a heterogeneous group of customers. Such types of customers obviously include those who are angry, impatient, and indecisive in nature. With such initial screening of potential candidates for the job, Sears start predictive analytics to select the appropriate fit for various job positions. For managerial and executive-level recruitments, Sears measure the potential candidates with their leadership model that distinctly specifies a certain set of competencies. Sears feel with predictive analytics they could not only reduce their recruitment and selection cycle time, but also significantly reduce their recruitment cost. Moreover, with quality recruitment and selection, the company is able to drive their performance, and consolidate their business position, which in the recent past had the experience of significant drop in revenue.

INTRODUCTION

Recruitment research is a scientific process of analyzing and managing recruitment functions duly exploring various unknown facts, mostly the facts on the prospective talents. The primary purpose of recruitment is to identify, attract, and retain talents. With research bent, recruitment functions can be better structured, and recruitment decisions can be made more scientific. Effective recruitment research can help in framing recruitment strategies establishing causal connections between various variables, which help us to control "effect" or "cause" variable, so that we can achieve our desired goals and objectives. Also recruitment research helps us to track vital recruitment metrics, interpret big data using recruitment analytics, and take vital cost-effective recruitment decisions. Using recruitment research we can carry out descriptive research, which can help in managing recruitment operations more efficiently. This can be possible collecting and interpreting data, and then drawing suitable action plans for intervention to reduce the cost burden, bringing desirable changes, etc.

Recruitment activity is essentially a process of attracting and recruiting suitable candidates for the job of organization. It aligns such new recruits with the organization through effective onboarding program, and then deploy them in suitable jobs of the organizations. Extended recruitment activity also focuses on employees' development and retention. Obviously, it is one of the important strategic activities of the organization. For any organization, recruitment activities are managed with some structured processes, ethical guidelines, and legal restrictions. From the strategic management point of view, recruitment activities also require inputs through constant research. Such recruitment research may be both at the organization level or research at broader level, which can facilitate in developing new theories, concepts, models, metrics, or analytics on recruitment and selection. Recruitment and selection with research inputs can benefit organizations in meeting both their planned and unplanned manpower needs, and so also the unforeseen needs of manpower which may arise in the organizations due to sudden spurt of resignations.

Most of the recruitment researches so far carried out indicate that such researches circled around essentially on topics such as recruitment sources, recruiters, and realistic job previews. Obviously, such research pursuits did not help in new theory development, grounding on empirical data. Another group of recruitment research stimulated our pursuits for analysis of recruitment and selection process in organizations with the use of metrics and analytics. Barber (1998) did show us how recruitment research could establish recruitment objectives and strategy development duly delineating issues such as generating applicants, maintaining applicant status, and influencing job choice decisions. Certain recruitment activities influence the number of types of individuals who apply for a job position. Similarly, certain activities such as professional treatment during a site visit, etc., and certain recruitment actions may have positive or negative influence on the job applicants. All these research outcomes when considered in framing recruitment strategy, can substantially benefit organizations.

TYPES OF RECRUITMENT RESEARCH

Process of recruitment research may vary from organizations to organizations. It can be academic, theoretical, or action-oriented. Pure basic recruitment research resolves, illuminates, and exemplifies some theoretical issues. Hence, this type of research contributes to enhancement of our knowledge and understanding. This benefits HR managers who can gradually mature themselves in understanding the recruitment functions.

Objective recruitment research focuses on overcoming general application problem of our established knowledge, rather than focusing on solution of any specific problems pertaining to recruitment decisions. It helps in testing the validity of established knowledge in a given situation.

Evaluative recruitment research helps us in assessing various aspects of organizational function, analyzing effectiveness of a given research problem. For example, the effect of organizational compensation structure with attraction of new talents in organizations can be studied through an evaluative research method. Evaluation recruitment research therefore helps HR managers to develop "scientific neutrality" for objective interpretation of various recruitment issues.

Applied recruitment research is carried out by application of appropriate knowledge to identify which specific steps can facilitate in effective management of recruitment functions. Also, it is more specific to solve a given problem in recruitment and selection function. For example, why the organization is unable to attract more talents can be better understood through this type of research.

Action research in recruitment and selection function helps in building our stock of knowledge, while we manage any recruitment issue. Such a research outcome being more situation-specific, cannot be replicated; hence, it suffers from the crisis of validity (Fig. 12.1).

FIGURE 12.1 Types of recruitment research.

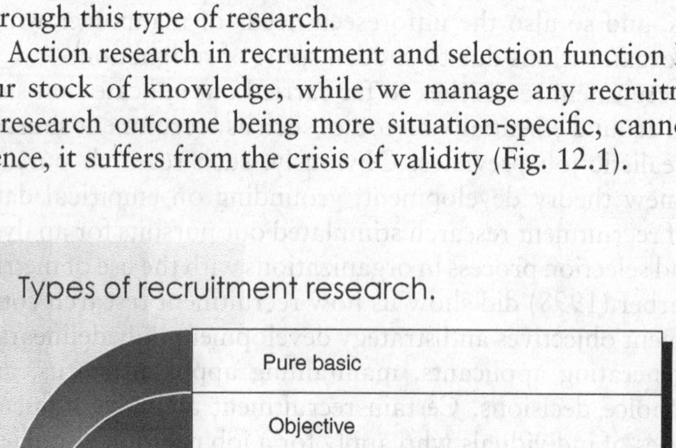

Which type of research will be used in which situation, for achieving what purposes, highly depends on HR managers' understanding and general data availability.

CONCEPT MAPPING FOR RECRUITMENT AND SELECTION RESEARCH

Effective recruitment and selection research requires exploring of knowledge and gathering of information through a concept map. A concept map is a formative assessment and a research tool. It helps us in visualizing the relations between concepts with a cognitive approach. It also helps in idea generation. Therefore, in recruitment and selection research, concept mapping helps in:

- Understanding body of knowledge
- Exploring relationships between information
- Assessing our previous knowledge-base
- Gathering new knowledge and information
- Sharing knowledge and information gathered
- Designing structures and processes
- Facilitating problem-solving

Thus, concept mapping is visual organization of the ideas bringing together different stakeholders with a shared vision for any future actions. For recruitment research concept mapping addresses the needs of different stakeholders, integrates various HR inputs, and binds our decision-making process with a common strategic vision. A well-designed concept map is a readable graphic or a pictorial form which can integrate all possible information, which can facilitate effective recruitment decision-making process. It is also known as mental mapping or concept-webbing.

LITERATURE REVIEW FOR RECRUITMENT RESEARCH

Literature review for recruitment research requires summarization of previous research on recruitment and selection, including human resource planning and talent management functions. It can be review of various research projects on recruitment and selection, review of thesis, review of scholarly papers published in scholarly journals, etc. Through literature reviews, we try to assess our specific research issue or issues for better understanding of the research problem, try to understand knowledge gap, if any, assess the degree of agreement or disagreement on the research topic, etc. Effective literature review helps us to ground our research topic on the scholarly premises, and accordingly we can make our scientific enquiry and come to a more objective conclusion. For HR professionals recruitment research is anchored toward corporate practices, and learning from best practice organizations, etc. For example, Samsung recruits young talents with a long-term focus, retaining the world-class celebrities in their mentor group.

Literature review *per se* conveys what knowledge and ideas exist on the research topic, strengths, and weaknesses of the research ideas, familiarizes us with different contrasting perspectives and viewpoints on the research topic. Therefore, the reasons for literature review for recruitment research are:

- Understanding what needs to be investigated
- Understanding the available explanation for any variations in behavior and phenomenon
- Identifying potential relationships between concepts and researchable hypotheses
- Understanding how other researchers define and measure the key concepts
- Identifying the data sources used in previous researches
- Developing alternative research approach
- Establishing link with the previous research, etc.

MODEL BUILDING IN RECRUITMENT RESEARCH

In recruitment research model building represents designing of a framework which can establish cause and effect relationships between different phenomena. A model is a dynamic framework or a scheme to portray the key concepts and propositions of a theory. It represents a process or a system that shows relative importance of various variables in the recruitment process or system. With analysis of such variables, HR managers can get better insights into the recruitment process. A model being not an explanation, rather model being a structure that discusses functions of a system or a process (say, recruitment system or process), in recruitment research we need to test a model (after we develop) gathering data, analyzing data, and then developing our reasoning.

Also a recruitment model can be the end result of a recruitment research. This is however more in those cases, where we find prevailing conceptual framework is not strong enough to explain the scientific logic. Therefore, building a recruitment and selection model based on research inputs is a sophisticated process. Like any other model, model in recruitment and selection also follows three important functions like description, explication, and simulation. With support of computers and advanced statistical tools, we can develop models.

Various types of models can be developed through research on recruitment and selection. These are presented below:

(1) **Verbal/written/descriptive/physical models:** Such models can explain the situation scaling it down to a manageable limit. It can explain a situation in words, or by a physical replica. Such models are also known as iconic models.
(2) **Explicative models:** Such models can extend application of existing theoretical connotations, and that can improve our understanding of key concepts.
(3) **Schematic models:** Such models help us to explain the relationships between different variables using charts, graphics, maps of routings, network diagrams, etc.
(4) **Mathematical models:** Such models establish functional relationships among different variables using mathematical symbols and equations. In recruitment research commonly used mathematical models are optimization models and heuristics models. Optimization models analyze problems and also suggest solutions. Heuristics models establish decision-making procedures to solve a problem.

SIGNIFICANCE OF RECRUITMENT AND SELECTION RESEARCH

Systematic recruitment and selection research has now become important for its strategic relevance. Organizations globally compete for talents, and need to attract, recruit, and retain talent. Through recruitment research, organizations can understand why their previous decisions did not yield better results in terms of recruiting and retaining talents, and accordingly organizations can adopt appropriate strategies to make their future decisions more foolproof. Using the research results, at corporate level, it is now possible to take effective recruitment and selection decisions. With models, theories, and research findings, recruitment research can meaningfully contribute to better decision-making process. We can understand the need for systematic recruitment research from logic explained below:

- People are now strategic resource for any organization. Attracting, recruiting, and retaining people now require more scientific decisions, which can substantially be made possible with recruitment research.
- Systematic recruitment research can help in aligning recruitment process with the organizational goals and strategies.
- Recruitment research output can help in designing and implementing scientific recruitment and selection process, pacing with the needs of the organization.
- Recruitment research also helps in assessing human resource requirements, and then in identifying the people with the right set of competencies, who can significantly contribute to achievement of organizational objectives.

These apart, recruitment research helps us to develop, implement, evaluate human resource management functions, computing various ratios and developing metrics. Such value addition benefits organizations in terms of assessment of the performance and productivity.

TYPES OF RECRUITMENT RESEARCH

Like any other research, recruitment research can also be classified into three important types as under:

- **Applied vs. basic research:** Applied research solves a particular problem in a particular circumstance. Good example is solving current recruitment crisis for high rate of attrition. Basic research, on the other hand, helps in understanding underlying principles behind human behavior. For a recruitment research, basic research helps us to identify important reasons for feeling attracted with various job positions of organizations.
- **Exploratory vs. confirmatory research:** Exploratory research is research into the unknown, like investigating certain recruitment issues (say diversity inclusivity), without actually knowing what to look for in particular. Confirmatory research, on the other hand, helps in understanding how an existing theory or concept can be supported by the facts. For example, we know with high organizational brand value, more people feel attracted to apply for a job position. Using a confirmatory research tool, we can collect data and assess our established assumption.

- **Quantitative vs. qualitative:** Quantitative recruitment research measures variables using some numeric scales. However, qualitative recruitment research interprets behavior to understand a phenomenon. Confirmatory recruitment researches are more quantitative in nature, while qualitative recruitment researches are qualitative in nature.

Some of the important areas of recruitment research are research on talent attraction, talent retention, career and succession planning, pre-employment and employee testing, job boards, online media, print media, background investigations, workforce analytics, etc.

HUMAN RESOURCE PLANNING FOR RECRUITMENT RESEARCH

Human resource planning facilitates in recruitment research immensely. In fact, more than 50% of recruitment research activities encompass human resource planning issues. For example, human resource planning initially requires forecasting of future manpower requirements, preparing inventory of present manpower, anticipating problems of manpower, meeting manpower requirements, etc. For these activities, we make use of both quantitative and qualitative tools, and these are commonly applicable for recruitment research too. For example, forecasting of future manpower requirements can be done either in terms of mathematical projections or in terms of judgemental estimates. Mathematical projections are done extrapolating factors like economic environment, development trends in industry, etc. Judgemental estimates, on the other hand, are done depending on the specific future plans of a company by managerial discretion, which is based on past experience.

Similarly, for preparing inventory of present manpower, we have to build quantitative index attributing values on employees' skills, abilities, performance, qualification, experience, etc. For internal recruitment or sourcing of manpower, such inventory immensely helps.

We can also project present set of competencies of our manpower into the future and compare the same with the new set of competencies required, and accordingly we can anticipate likely problems of future manpower, and accordingly can initiate actions to reduce such problems, closing the gap in competencies. Many organizations take appropriate initiative like building capabilities of existing employees through future leadership programs.

Finally, another important initiative taken for meeting manpower requirements could be planning for recruitment and selection, training and development, induction and placement, promotion and transfer, motivation and compensation to ensure that future manpower requirements are correctly met.

Doing all these activities require selection of appropriate research tools. For obvious strategic significance of human resources, recruitment research has now assumed significance as any recruitment decisions without back-up may transpire to be wrong, which organizations just cannot afford to survive in competition.

For doing recruitment research, HR managers require to follow certain steps like doing job analysis to collect requisite information about a job. These require collection of job information from various sources and then relate the same with the specific nature of job of the organization. Even this also requires adequate research. Quite often, organizations feel compelled to hire professional job analysts to chart the job content, without knowing even the person himself/herself or his/her supervisor. For technical jobs, technology vendors' product literatures also contain lot of information about the job. Scope of job analysis is just not limited to HR to take recruitment decisions; it also helps in other important HR decisions like compensation design, job re-engineering, training and development, performance management, and health and safety issues.

The succeeding step of job analysis is job description and job specification. Job description is recording of duties, responsibilities, and conditions needed for satisfactory performance of a particular job. Analyzing the job content (through job analysis), we need to create job family, grouping homogeneous nature of jobs. This helps to name a job (job description), which is the major role of HR manager. Even though operationally we use the terms job description and job specification interchangeably, theoretically, they are different. Job description denotes job content (conditions, tasks, and responsibilities) and job specification defines the job requirements (i.e., qualities necessary) for satisfactory performance of the job. Thus, job specifications translate job descriptions into human qualifications, experience, skill-sets, etc., required for successful performance of a job.

Recruitment research also requires development of work rules, which are some predetermined decisions about certain courses of action that may be taken when certain contingencies arise. Organizations develop such work rules in documented form and use the same as a control device to ensure predictability of behavior. Starting and stopping of work, rest periods, time-keeping, insubordination, fighting or drinking on the job, smoking, report of injuries, etc., are normally incorporated in such work rules.

In recruitment research, it is also necessary to understand various applications of industrial engineering techniques (work study, method study, and work measurement techniques). These techniques provide opportunity for effective use of plant and equipment, effective use of human efforts, measurement of human work, better ways of doing things, developing predetermined standard time, etc.

Miscellaneous other factors in recruitment research is layout plan, compliance with statutory requirements, shifts planning (including flexi-work issues), leave reserve, etc.

LEARNING CURVE AS A TOOL FOR RECRUITMENT RESEARCH

In the long run, both employees and organizations become efficient. Primary reason is for doing the same tasks repeatedly. While time requirement for doing the first task would be considerably higher, when people do the same task repeatedly, time requirement will considerably get reduced. We call it learning curve effect. In recruitment research, we also use learning curve as a tool, as it significantly influences our hiring decisions. We have three important assumptions in learning curve effect. These are:

(1) The time requirement for a given task decreases when the same task is performed again and again.
(2) The rate of decrease will be in a decreasing rate.
(3) The rate of decrease will follow a predictable pattern.

Learning curve effect on a job can be calculated using exponential decay function. It means time requirement for doing a task repeatedly will decrease exponentially. The standard equation is as follows:

$$T_n = T_1 n^b$$

where

n = the unit number (1 for the first unit, 2 for the second unit, etc.)
T_1 = the amount of time to produce the first unit
T_n = the amount of time to produce unit n
b = the learning curve factor, calculated as $\ln(p)/\ln(2)$, where $\ln(x)$ is the natural logarithm of x
p = the learning percentage

Production time for successive units will decrease by the percentage p. This is shown in the following calculation:

Imagine that we have T_1 = 10 hours and $p = 90\% = 0.90$. We can calculate the production time for the first 10 units as follows:

$$b = \ln(0.90)/\ln(2) = -0.152 \text{ (learning curve factor)}$$

$$T_1 = 10\ (1^{-0.152}) = 10$$

$$T_2 = 10\ (2^{-0.152}) = 9$$

$$T_3 = 10\ (3^{-0.152}) = 8.46 \text{ (rounded to two decimal places)}$$

$$T_4 = 10\ (4^{-0.152}) = 8.10$$

$$T_5 = 10\ (5^{-0.152}) = 7.83$$

$$T_6 = 10\ (6^{-0.152}) = 7.62$$

$$T_7 = 10\ (7^{-0.152}) = 7.44$$

$$T_8 = 10\ (8^{-0.152}) = 7.29$$

$$T_9 = 10\ (9^{-0.152}) = 7.16$$

$$T_{10} = 10\ (10^{-0.152}) = 7.05$$

Therefore, although time requirement for doing the first unit of job was 10 hours with the learning rate of 90%, time requirement for the 10th unit will be 7.05 hours. Based on this, HR managers can calculate the average time required and convert it to man hour requirement, and then calculate headcounts to be recruited for accomplishing the organizational business goals.

CAUSE AND EFFECT MODEL IN RECRUITMENT RESEARCH

Using a compact equation, HR managers can assess the surplus and shortage of manpower in future year *t*, and accordingly can frame their recruitment strategy. The equation goes as under:

$$X_t = {}_{at\ ct}\, S_t - (D_t/Q_t)N_t$$

Here product ${}_{at\ ct}\, S_t$ indicates projected manpower supply in year *t*. Component S_t is the number of manpower projected to be alive in a year *t*. Component ${}_{at}$ is the fraction of those manpower who will be professionally active in year t, and component $_{ct}$ is the fraction of those manpower who will be professionally active and also available for service. The product $(D_t/Q_t)N_t$ represents the projected demand or requirements of manpower in a year t. Variable D_t denotes the projected average number of manpower services needed or demanded in year t. Q_t is the projected average number of manpower services produced in year t. N_t is the volume of jobs to be attended.

Although Reinhardt (1987) used this model for occupation-specific macro level demand prediction of manpower, at organization level recruitment research, we can also replicate this model.

RECRUITMENT RESEARCH AT ORGANIZATION LEVEL

Recruitment research at organization level is carried out in four different stages: investigation, forecasting, planning and control, and utilization. At every stage, researcher performs specific task carefully to decide on optimum level of recruitment in organizations. For example, at investigation stage, researcher develops his/her understanding of the organizational human resources. The researcher here performs SWOT analysis taking into cognizance labor market situation, understanding performance and productivity trends in organizations, work culture and working practices in organizations, and so also organizational, operational and strategic plans. With effective SWOT analysis researcher can develop his/her research plan, factoring present and future skill gaps in the organization. Some of the tools used at this stage by a researcher are cause–effect diagram (fish-bone diagram), labor market review through Annual Economic Survey, Year Book on Indian Labour, Survey of Indian Industries, ILO International Year Book on Labour, Reports of Planning Commission on manpower, etc. At organization level, researcher considers various operational data, performance data, current employment practices and methods, strategic plans and objectives, etc.

In forecasting phase, the researcher assesses the demand and supply of manpower, using different demand forecasting models and supply analysis, factoring both internal availability and availability in labor market for external hire. Internal manpower supply analysis is done factoring organizational career planning and development systems, training and development and succession plan aspects, along with their policies and procedures.

At the third stage of recruitment research at the organization level, i.e., the stage of planning and control of manpower, researcher translates his/her forecasts into HR policies, encompassing HR issues like recruitment, training and development, etc.

At the final stage, i.e., the stage of utilization, researcher measures success in terms of achievement trend, both quantitatively and qualitatively. Quantitative achievement can be measured in terms of productivity trend, manpower cost, etc. Qualitative achievement is assessed in terms of organizational achievement of objectives, impact on industrial relations, motivation and morale, grievance patterns, etc.

COST BENEFIT ANALYSIS AND RECRUITMENT RESEARCH

Appropriate recruitment and selection through adequate recruitment research can substantially reduce not only the manpower acquisition cost, but even reduces the cost of training. Organizations also get the benefit of high employee retention, increased productivity, and can institutionalize the culture of performance. All these are applicable for recruiting talents both from external and internal sources, although for recruitment from internal sources, partially such expenses are less. Therefore, irrespective of recruitment from external or internal sources, recruitment process involves expenses. Hence with cost–benefit analysis, we can adjudge the efficiency of any organizational recruitment systems. Recruitment costs cover the period from the initial decision to recruit till it retains the new employees, to obtain the optimal level of performance (Compton, 2009). For example, if an organization used advertisement and college recruiting to fill a position, yield ratios would be calculated for each method:

- advertisement generates 200 applications and 10 qualified for an interview
- college recruiting generates 50 applications and 10 qualified for an interview

The yield ratios would be 5% (10/200) for advertisement, and 20% (10/50) for college recruiting. Therefore, the college recruiting provided the best yield ratio (Buhler P., 2002).

Cost is an important factor in the recruitment process. Effective recruitment indicates organizational ability to attract qualified applicants (Buhler, 2002). Through effective recruitment organizations can gain sustainable competitive advantage. Costs of effective recruitment are very high (Sims, 2002). This is why optimizing costs of effective recruitment is one of the priority areas in recruitment research.

The overall costs of recruitment and selection can be broadly classified into acquisition costs and learning costs (Flamholtz, 1999). Acquisition costs again could be direct or indirect. Direct acquisition costs are costs associated with hiring of individual employees through external sources, and indirect costs are internal recruitment through promotion from within. Likewise, learning and development costs associated with recruitment and selection can be direct costs or indirect costs. Direct costs are formal training, training on-the-job and indirect costs are the time of in-house trainers, loss of productivity, etc.

Some of the direct heads for recruitment costs are:

- Cost of recruitment advertisement
- Cost of consultants' fees
- Cost of incentives for employee referrals
- Cost of employee selection process
- Cost of onboarding, etc.

Therefore, recruitment costs can broadly be categorized into preselection costs, selection costs, formation costs, and then time costs of recruitment team of the organizations.

Through cost–benefit analysis all these costs can be measured and optimized aligning with the strategic needs of the organizations. This naturally positions cost-benefit analysis as one of the important areas of recruitment research.

PREDICTIVE ANALYTICS FOR RECRUITMENT RESEARCH

Using big data for recruitment research, we can develop predictive analytics. Such predictive analytics can help us in understanding the future trends and help us in taking strategic decisions on recruitment management. Predictive analytics are developed based on the existing data, and then using algorithms so that we can look deeper into meanings and connotations. It combines data sets, looks for underlying patterns, and allows accurate predictions about future needs and future performance. One of the biggest areas where predictive analytics can be applied is recruitment-related decisions. Many organizations still make use of metrics. But metrics cannot tell us what will happen in the future. It can only tell us what happened in previous years. Use of metrics in recruitment research approximates past trend to understand the future. Obviously, such metrics-driven approximation limits our research results. Contrarily, predictive analytics helps us in understanding what is going to happen. Obviously, this benefits organizations in reducing the decisional errors.

In recruitment, predictive analytics is used to look for patterns in performance, employee turnover, training needs, and career progression. It can determine the likelihood of particular types of employee leaving, or the set of competencies and skills that will create the best fit for a position. It can foresee future training and recruitment needs. It can even help in identifying where dissatisfaction is likely to arise, and so help in staff retention. Using this organizations can assess the challenges ahead, and type of manpower that would be required to meet such a crisis. Also, it can help in assessing the required manpower availability within and outside the organization. For example, in external hiring, predictive analytics can help organizations to take a forward-looking approach. Based on the algorithms drawn on factors like gross domestic product (GDP), economic trend, employment rates, trend in regional market, attrition data, etc., companies can estimate category-wise availability of manpower in labor market, and can draw suitable strategies to attract talent from the labor market. Also predictive analytics in recruitment research unveils trends, which were not known to the organizations earlier. As it can align with the human resource management practices of the organizations, it helps in scientific factoring of other HR-related and business-related information for recruitment research.

USING PREDICTIVE ANALYTICS FOR RECRUITMENT RESEARCH

In recruitment research, predictive analytics helps in optimization of recruitment levels in organizations. For example, it can help in assessing who are the likely talents, how these talents can be attracted to company's job positions, how a talent pipeline can be planned and developed factoring both endogenous and exogenous factors, how company can optimize responses for their job postings, what would be the probability that the new recruits will perform and stay with the organizations, etc. Thus, in recruitment research, predictive analytics can effectively be used in processing, managing, and optimizing recruitment decisions. Rather than taking reactive decisions in recruitment, predictive analytics facilitate in establishing the link between goals and the strategic intents of the organizations. Standard predictive analytics modules of different software vendors can help in profiling and segmenting of present employees and assessing the nature of future profiles of employees, developing learning algorithms for building talent pipeline, analyzing the employee attrition and loyalty, developing skill inventory, forecasting organizational manpower capabilities and recruitment needs for both the present and the future, profile matching, etc.

Some of the areas of analysis done by recruitment researchers with the use of predictive analytics are descriptive analysis, correlation and simple regression, and multiple regressions. Descriptive analysis helps in data visualization. It can track and compare the data to assess whether the past recruitment decisions were effective and how such decisions could give ROI. At this level, however, it is not predictive. Correlation and simple regression help a recruitment researcher to assess relationships between two variables, but it cannot assess the causes. This analysis also cannot be predictive. Multiple regressions establish relationships between several factors, and obviously can be used as a tool for predicting the future outcome. For recruitment research this is very important. But we need to understand that descriptive and correlation analyses are not redundant. Recruitment managers can make use of these two primary-level analyses for better visualization of the data trend, and then fit their results for multiple regressions. In fact, predictive analytics helps not only in trend visualizations, in assessment of relationships, in understanding of multiple predictors; but also in predicting multiple outcomes, calculating ROI and in determining causation. More relevant example is developing of structural equations modeling for better decision making with predictive analytics.

PREDICTIVE ANALYTICS FOR RECRUITMENT RESEARCH—LESSONS FROM ORGANIZATIONS

In recruitment and selection, predictive analytics helps us to improve our quality of hire. At least this is evident from the experiences of several world-class organizations, which have embedded predictive analytics for their HR decisions. The company, however, could implement this with a research bent. For example, by linking the hiring process to performance, engagement survey information, pre-employment assessment results, interview results, recruiting sources, turnover data, and other data pertaining to employee lifecycle, companies can design models. Based on these models, companies can measure implications of future recruitment decisions, and calibrate decision to avoid any eventual risk. Thus, predictive analytics can indirectly help companies achieve their business goals.

Also in recruitment research, we can use predictive analytics to source manpower more efficiently and effectively. For example, HR managers can trace the hire back to the original hiring source and then link that to the quality of hire. This enables HR managers to optimize their recruitment decisions. We can use a similar approach to evaluate in-house recruitment process, third-party recruiting firms, and other recruiting sources. Thus, when recruitment decisions are backed by research with use of analytics, it can significantly improve the return on investment.

Likewise using predictive analytics in recruitment research, we can improve the speed of hire. Once we understand potential talents, we can immediately establish contact with them to take our recruitment process further.

From all the above perspectives, use of predictive analytics in recruitment research can give us the opportunity to take more effective and rationalized recruitment decisions. However, predictive analytics require investment in technology, build organizational capabilities for business intelligence, training of HR people entrusted with the responsibility of recruitment, and teamwork. In organizations, predictive analytics for recruitment is also known as hiring algorithms.

SUMMARY

- This chapter introduces the concept of recruitment and selection research and discusses how such research can benefit organizations in terms of quality hire and reducing the cycle time for recruitment. Organizations can make their recruitment process smart enough to avoid decisional errors in recruitment, restricting hiring decisions for only those who could be the best-fit and who could be developed and retained. After explaining various types of recruitment research, the chapter discusses concept mapping, literature review model building, and importance of human resource planning for recruitment and selection research.
- Finally, the chapter discusses how recruitment and selection research results are used in organizations, and how cost–benefit analysis and predictive analytics to a great extent influence recruitment and selection decisions, and make such decisions more effective.

Key Words

Recruitment research: Recruitment research is a scientific process of analyzing and managing recruitment functions duly exploring various unknown facts, mostly the facts on the prospective talents.

Concept mapping: Concept mapping is a formative assessment and a research tool. It helps us in visualizing the relations between concepts with a cognitive approach. It also helps in idea generation.

Job description: Job description is recording of duties, responsibilities, and conditions needed for satisfactory performance of a particular job.

Cause and effect model in recruitment research: A compact equation model that can assess the surplus and shortage of manpower in future year *t*, and accordingly can frame the recruitment strategy.

Predictive analytics for recruitment research: Using big data for recruitment research, we can develop predictive analytics. Such predictive analytics can help us in understanding the future trends and help us in taking strategic decisions on recruitment management.

Review Questions

1. Discuss the concepts of recruitment and selection research. What are the different types of recruitment and selection research?
2. Why does organization need recruitment and selection research? How does it influence decision-making process in recruitment?
3. What is the significance of literature review in research? Explain how recruitment and selection is carried out in organizations.
4. How learning curve as a tool is used in recruitment research?
5. What is the cost–benefit analysis in recruitment research?
6. Explain the concepts of predictive analytics in recruitment research.
7. Write short notes on:
   (a) Recruitment activity
   (b) Recruitment research
   (c) Evaluative recruitment and selection
   (d) Applied recruitment and selection
   (e) Recruitment research models
   (f) Learning curve effect

Critical Review Question

1. Visit website of any major technology company. Understand their recruitment process and explain how they make us of results of recruitment research? Also document benefits organization can derive from recruitment research.

Multiple Choice Questions

1. Recruitment research denotes:
   (a) Scientific process of analyzing and managing recruitment functions
   (b) Exploring various unknown facts

(c) Identify, attract, and retain talents
(d) Structuring of recruitment decisions
(e) All of the above

2. Effective recruitment research can help us in doing the following, except:
(a) Framing recruitment strategies
(b) Establishing causal connections between various variables
(c) Control "effect" or "cause" variable
(d) Track vital recruitment metrics
(e) None of the above

3. Recruitment activities require inputs through constant research because of the following reasons:
(a) Facilitate in developing new theories, concepts, models, metrics, or analytics on recruitment and selection
(b) Benefit organizations in meeting both their planned and unplanned manpower needs
(c) Understand unforeseen needs of manpower
(d) All of the above
(e) None of the above

4. Recruitment research can be:
(a) Academic
(b) Theoretical
(c) Action-oriented
(d) All of the above
(e) None of the above

5. In recruitment and selection research, concept mapping helps in the following, except:
(a) Understanding body of knowledge
(b) Exploring relationships between information
(c) Assessing our previous knowledge-base
(d) Gathering new knowledge and information
(e) Designing compensation structure

6. Indicate which is not a valid statement for literature review for recruitment research:
(a) Review of various research projects on recruitment and selection
(b) Review of thesis, review of scholarly papers published in scholarly journals
(c) Review of published data in company reports
(d) Review of primary data
(e) None of the above

7. Following are the reasons for literature review, excepting:
(a) Understanding what needs to be investigated
(b) Understanding the available explanation for any variations in behavior and phenomenon

(c) Identifying potential relationships between concepts and researchable hypotheses
(d) Understanding how other researchers define and measure the key concepts
(e) Establish link with the future research

8. In recruitment research model building represents:
(a) Designing of a framework which can establish cause and effect relationships between different phenomena
(b) Portraying the key concepts and propositions of a theory
(c) Representing process or a system that shows relative importance of various variables in the recruitment process or system
(d) Only (a) and (b)
(e) Both (a), (b), and (c)

9. Systematic recruitment and selection research is important for:
(a) Scientific decisions
(b) Aligning recruitment process with the organizational goals and strategies
(c) Designing and implementing scientific recruitment and selection process, pacing with the needs of the organization
(d) Only a and b
(e) Both a, b, and c

10. Indicate which is not a type of recruitment research:
(a) Applied research
(b) Unobtrusive research
(c) Basic research
(d) Exploratory research
(e) Confirmatory research

Answers:

1. (e) 2. (e) 3. (d) 4. (d) 5. (e) 6. (d) 7. (e) 8. (e)
9. (e) 10. (b)

CASE STUDY

Google—the company that believes in making their recruitment process research driven

Google, the 1998 company with 40,000 headcounts, does exemplary recruitment research using their in-house people analytics. Any recruitment decision in Google is taken based on analytics. For a company like Google to sustain their position in the top bracket of market capitalization cannot be possible unless they attract, recruit, and retain talent. Instead of giving weights to academic records of prospective hires, Google using their people analytics measure leadership skills, cognitive ability, humility, and ownership. This enables Google to recruit more and more talented people, build robust talent pipeline, improve recruitment-related decision-making process, and transform recruitment process faster and efficient. Chucking out the best-fit from two million resumes every year is no joke for Google. People analytics even analyze rejected candidates with a systematic approach and ensures no candidate otherwise good is wrongly rejected. It was Google's experience with return visits of rejected candidates; the company could identify great potential candidates.

Even Google's interview practices rest on research. Interview results show a pattern of predictability. Interestingly through people analytics, Google could find success of potential job candidates no way relates to their abilities to solve quizzes and puzzles. Better understanding of potentialities can be possible when responses of candidates are measured using consistent rating scales against some common set of questions. With reduced cycle time for recruitment, and possibility of better understanding of candidates, Google's research-based people analytics could take the company to a new height.

Question: Why Google's interview practices is different from other organizations? Do such recruitment practices really help?

REFERENCES

Barber, A.E. (1998), *Recruiting Employees*. Thousand Oaks, CA: Sage Publications.

Buhler, P. (2002), *HRM: All the Information You Need to Manage Your Staff and Meet Your Business Objectives*. MA: F+W Pub., Inc.

Compton, R.L., Morissey, W. and Nankervis, A.R. (2009), *Effective Recruitment and Selection Practices*. Australia: McPherson's Printing Group.

Flamholtz, E.G. (1999), *HR Accounting*. Massachusetts: Kluwer Academic Pub.

Reinhardt, U.E. (1987), "Projecting Long-Term Trends in Health Manpower: Methodological Problems, Indicators and Trends", in Detlef Schweel edited Health and Health Care, Springer, Berlin Heidelberg, pp. 87–107.

Sims, R.R. (2002), *Organizational Success Through Effective Human Resources Management*. USA: Greenwood Pub. Inc. Group.

Index

A

Ability requirements scales, 103
AM. *See* Assistant Manager (AM)
Ambiguous policy statements, 133
Apple (mobile company), drawing lessons from, 313
Applicant tracking systems, 179
Applied recruitment research, 326
Aptitude assessments, 175
Assignment-specific international recruitment, 270
Assistant Manager (AM), 71–74
Automatic internet sourcing tool, 180

B

Basic recruitment research, 326
Behavioral interview, 183
Big Five Model, 110–111, 190
Business plans
- aligning recruitment and selection policies, 139–141
- business process, 174
- connecting recruitment and selection, 164–165

C

Cambridge model, 74–75
Career, 299
- anchors. *See* Employess(s)
- development cycle, 307–309
- paths, 300
- transition process, 174

Career development process, 299–303
- career development cycle, 307–309
- career planning *vs.*, 305
- essential elements of career, 301
- Godrej career planning and development, 317–318
- in IBM, 298
- management development process, 313
- types of, 303–304

Career planning process, 298–301, 304–305
- career anchors, 309–311
- career development, 298, 305
- essential elements of career, 301
- Godrej career planning and development, 317–318
- HRP *vs.*, 305–306
- management development process, 313

Cattel's theory, 188
Cause and effect model in recruitment research, 330–331
CMQ. *See* Common metric questionnaire (CMQ)
CNC. *See* Computerized machining center (CNC)
Co-creating individual-level onboarding program, 289
"Coercive" pressures, 138
COLA. *See* Cost of living allowances (COLA)
Collaborative tools, 180
Common metric questionnaire (CMQ), 100, 103
Commuter assignment, 263
Compa-ratios, 218
Compensation design, equality in, 217–219
Competency, 57
- competency-based assessments, 175
- gaps, 51, 59

Computerized machining center (CNC), 65
Concept-webbing. *See* Concept mapping
Concept mapping for recruitment and selection, 323
Confirmatory recruitment research, 326
Constitutional mandates, 212
Constitution of India, 213
Cost benefit analysis, 332–333
Cost–benefit analysis of human capital. *See* Rate of Return Approach (RRA)
Cost of living allowances (COLA), 269
Country-specific legal compliance, 206
CRM. *See* Customer relationship management (CRM)
Cross-cultural issues, 259, 264–265
Cross-cultural training, 267
Culture job-fit, 107–108
Customer relationship management (CRM), 88

D

DCC issues. *See* Dual career couple issues (DCC issues)
Decision-making process, 132, 231, 236, 241
Deficiency approach, 210
Delphi technique, 89–90
Democratic values, 243
Department of Public Enterprises (DPE), 217
Depth interviews, 185
Descriptive models, 325
Designing onboarding program, 285–287
Developing ethics-compliant recruitment policy, 241
Digital recruitment, 176–177
Dimensions
  of ethics in recruitment and selection, 233–235
  of strategic recruitment and selection, 158–159
Direct planned interview, 19
Discrimination approach, 210
Diversity
  approaches to, 209–211
  diverse organization, 209
  inclusivity, 206, 208–209
  in international recruitment and selection, 264–265
  management, 208–210
  neutrality, 209
Dot.com generation. *See* Recruiting generation Y
DPE. *See* Department of Public Enterprises (DPE)
Dual career couple issues (DCC issues), 266

E

E-recruitment, 22, 176
  benefits and risks of, 178–179
  digital recruitment, 176–177
  using of social media, 179
  policy, 134
  SNS based recruitment, 177–178
  tools, 179–181
Ego states, 119, 120
Emotional intelligence (EI), 113, 194–195
  ability tests for recruitment, 197–198
  aspects and domains, 195
  ethical guidelines for psychological testing, 195–196
  NLP, 195
  recruitment analytics, 197
  recruitment metrics as recruitment tools, 196–197
Emotional Quotient (EQ), 113
  domains, 114–115
Employee(s), 156, 309–311
  induction, 25
  orientation, 25
  socialization, 25
Employee onboarding, 280–281
  designing onboarding program, 285–287

difference between onboarding and orientation, 282
onboarding and employer branding, 287–288
strategic onboarding program, 282–284
succession planning and onboarding, 288–290
Employer branding, 287–288
Employment testing, 190–191
EPQ. *See* Eysenck Personality Questionnaire (EPQ)
EQ. *See* Emotional Quotient (EQ)
Equality
in compensation design, 217–219
in recruitment and selection, 213–217
Ethical issues in recruitment and selection, 230–233
breaches for senior-level recruitment and selection, 244–246
developing ethics-compliant recruitment policy, 241
dimensions of ethics in, 233–235
ethical due diligence, 236–238
ethics, 235–236, 239–241, 243–244
gender mainstreaming and recruitment ethics, 238–239
framework, 241–242
recruitment ethics for HR managers, 230
social media and recruitment ethics, 243
uncovering ethical standards in, 251–252
unethical recruitment and selection process, 246
Ethical signals, 230, 241
Ethics, 231, 239–240
ethics-compliant organizations, 230
of lateral recruitment, 240–241
strategy, 239–240
Ethnocentric approach, 260, 262
Explicative models, 325
Exploratory recruitment research, 326
Exponential smoothing, 68–69
Exxon Mobil, 224–225
Eysenck Personality Questionnaire (EPQ), 109–110, 188–189
Eysenck's theory, 189

F

F-JAS. *See* Fleishman Job Analysis Survey (F-JAS)
FJA. *See* Functional job analysis (FJA)
Fleishman Job Analysis Survey (F-JAS), 103
Follow-up orientation, 25
Forecasting HR, 64–71
Framing policies, 132–133
Functional job analysis (FJA), 100, 103

G

GALLOP. *See* Godrej Accelerated Learning, Leadership and Orientation Program (GALLOP)
Gamification, 34, 180, 289–290
GBUs. *See* Global business units (GBUs)
Gender
diversity, 211–215
mainstreaming, 238–239
General orientation, 25
General values, 234
Generation Y recruiting, 30–33
Generation Z people, 34
Generation Z recruiting, 33–34
Global business units (GBUs), 260
Global corporation, 259
Globe competitive for talent, 170–171
Glopat, 269
Goal-setting theory approach, 31–32
Godrej Accelerated Learning, Leadership and Orientation Program (GALLOP), 317
Godrej career planning and development, 317–318
Group interview, 19

H

HCNs. *See* Host country nationals (HCNs)
HDS. *See* Hogan Development Survey (HDS)
Health and medical care, 60
Heuristics models, 325
Historical metrices, 28
Hogan Development Survey (HDS), 190
Hogan Personality Inventory (HPI), 188, 190
Host country nationals (HCNs), 158, 259, 267
Housing and Urban Development Corporation (HUDCO), 61
HPI. *See* Hogan Personality Inventory (HPI)
HR. *See* Human resource (HR)
HRD. *See* Human Resources Development (HRD)
HRIS. *See* Human resource information systems (HRIS)
HRM. *See* Human resource management (HRM)
HRP. *See* Human resource planning (HRP)
HUDCO. *See* Housing and Urban Development Corporation (HUDCO)
Human resource (HR), 152–153
 activities integration, 50
 aligning recruitment and selection policies with, 139–141
 department, 19
 planners, 53
 recruitment ethics for managers, 230
 requirements, 140
 utilization functions, 5
Human resource information systems (HRIS), 88
Human resource management (HRM), 3, 251
 international HRM issues, 259
 policies, 238
Human resource planning (HRP), 3, 50, 51, 54–56, 261, 305
 activities, 53–54
 analyzing environmental trends, 50–51
 career planning *vs.*, 305–306
 challenge of manpower planning and recruitment, 97–98
 challenging role of HR planners, 53
 importance for recruitment and selection, 51–53
 objectives, 57–82
 predictive statistics for organization level, 83–90
 and recruitment, 50
 for recruitment research, 327–329
 strategic alignment, 50–51
Human Resources Development (HRD), 5
Hybridization in international recruitment and selection, 262–263

I

IAMR. *See* Institute of Applied Manpower Research (IAMR)
Iconic models, 325
India
 gender diversity in, 212–215
 Indian Constitution, 212
 Indian Labor laws, 206
 legal briefing on recruitment and selection in, 219–221
Indian Society of Labor Economics (ISLE), 64
Indirect interview, 20
Induction, 23–28, 282
 crisis, 283
Industrial engineering techniques, 56
Informal interviewing, 184
Information Technology (IT), 23, 35
Institute of Applied Manpower Research (IAMR), 61, 63
Institutional theory, 138
Intelligence quotient tests (IQ tests), 112–113, 192–194

Intelligence test as employability test, 112, 192–194
Internal recruitment, 10–11
International recruitees
  compensation and benefits programme for, 268–270
  training and development for, 267–268
International recruitment and selection, 259–261, 263
  approaches, 261–263
  assignment-specific international recruitment, 270
  diversity and cross-cultural issues in, 264–265
  guidelines for recruitment and selection across cultures, 265–266
  international staffing of Coca Cola, 277
  performance management for international employees, 270–272
  selection of employees in MNCs and TNCs, 263–264
  selection process, 266–267
  training and development, 267–268
International selection process, 266–267
Internet-related sources, 175
Internet generation. *See* Recruiting generation Y
Interview(s), 19–21, 175, 182–184, 234
  depth interviews, 185
  direct planned interview, 19
  indirect interview, 20
  stress interviews, 19, 183
  structured standardized interview, 184–185
  telephone interviews, 185
IQ tests. *See* Intelligence quotient tests (IQ tests)
ISLE. *See* Indian Society of Labor Economics (ISLE)
IT-enabled services (ITeS), 23, 35
IT. *See* Information Technology (IT)
ITeS. *See* IT-enabled services (ITeS)

J

Job
  advertising, 174
  applications, 174
  descriptions, 55
  job-fit analysis, 105
  job-profile matching, 7
  questionnaire, 104
  sculpting, 104–107
Job analysis, 55, 100
  methods, 102
  social networking sites, 126
Jobs, Steve, 313
Johari Window model and personality and training on personality, 116–117

K

Key performance areas (KPAs), 217
Key performance indicator (KPI), 217

L

Labor
  economics, 63–64
  laws at State level, 207
  markets, 64
Labor laws governing recruitment and selection, snapshots on
  different approaches to diversity, 209–211
  diversity inclusivity, 208–209
  equality, 213–219
  gender diversity, 211–215
  legal briefing on recruitment and selection, 219–221
Lateral recruitment, ethics of, 240–241
Layout, 56
Learning curve effect, 329–330
Least-Squares Model, 84
Least squares line, 86–87
Leave reserve, 56, 66
Legal-compliant recruitment and selection process benefits, 207–208

Legal briefing on recruitment and selection in India, 219–221
Legal issues in recruitment and selection, 206
  benefits of legal-compliant, 207–208
  compliance issue, 132
  Exxon Mobil, 224–225
  snapshots on labor laws governing, 208–221
Linear regression, 83–84
Line of Best Fit, 84–86
Literacy and education, 60
Location tracking technology, 180

M

Macro level HRP, 59–61
  models, 61–62
Macro-level manpower planning, 61
Management Trainee (MT), 71
Manpower
  demand forecasting, 57–59
  difficulties in manpower forecasting, 87–89
  distribution, 70
  planning and recruitment challenge, 97–98
  planning models, 69
  requirements forecasting, 64–71
Manpower Requirement Approach (MRA), 61
Market Reference Points (MRPs), 218
Markov Chain Model, 71–75
Markov models—hierarchical systems, 69–71
Mathematical models, 325
Matrix structure, 140
Mayers–Briggs Type Indicator (MBTI), 110, 189
MBTI. *See* Mayers–Briggs Type Indicator (MBTI)
Memorandum of understanding (MOU), 170, 217
Mental mapping. *See* Concept mapping
Metamorphosis stage, 26
Micro level HRP, 59, 64
"Mimetic" pressures, 138
MNCs. *See* Multinational corporations (MNCs)
Mobile recruiting tools, 179–180
Model building in recruitment research, 324–325
Modern recruitment tools, 176
Monte Carlo simulation, 75–77
MOSAIC. *See* Multipurpose Occupational Systems Analysis Inventory-Closed Ended (MOSAIC)
MOU. *See* Memorandum of understanding (MOU)
MRA. *See* Manpower Requirement Approach (MRA)
MRPs. *See* Market Reference Points (MRPs)
MT. *See* Management Trainee (MT)
Multinational corporations (MNCs), 34, 258, 260
  selection of employees in, 263–264
Multipurpose Occupational Systems Analysis Inventory-Closed Ended (MOSAIC), 100–101, 103
Murray's theory, 188

N

NEO. *See* Neuroticism, Extraversion, and Openness (NEO)
Neuro-linguistic programming (NLP), 114, 195
Neuroticism, Extraversion, and Openness (NEO), 109, 111, 188, 190
Nike's policy changes on recruitment and selection, 134
NLP. *See* Neuro-linguistic programming (NLP)
Nominal group method, 90
Nondirective interview, 20

Nonperforming assets (NPA), 171
"Normative" pressures, 138
NPA. *See* Nonperforming assets (NPA)
NTPC attracting talent, 152

O

OAI. *See* Occupational analysis inventory (OAI)
Occupational analysis inventory (OAI), 103
Office of Personnel Management (OPM), 103
Onboarding, 282–283, 285, 287–290
Online recruitment. *See* E-recruitment
OPM. *See* Office of Personnel Management (OPM)
Optimization models, 71, 325
Orientation, 282

P

Panel or board interview, 19
PAQ. *See* Position analysis questionnaire (PAQ)
Parent country nationals (PCNs), 259, 262, 266
Patterned interview, 19
PBJA. *See* Personality-based job analysis (PBJA)
PCNs. *See* Parent country nationals (PCNs)
Performance
- intelligence test, 112–115
- management for international employees, 270–272

Performance-related pay (PRP), 217
Personality-based job analysis (PBJA), 108
Personality, 119–120
- assessments, 118–119, 175
- and career choice, 115–116
- emotional intelligence, 194–195
- and employment testing, 111
- profile, 183
- and recruitment, 108–109
- traits measurement, 109–111

Personality test for recruitment, 186–188
- Big Five model, 190
- intelligence test as employability test, 192–194
- measurement of personality traits, 188–189
- personality and employment testing, 190–191
- personality of potential hires, 186–187
- reliability, 192
- validity, 191–192
- work-related behavior, 186

Physical models, 325
Placement, 26, 57
- importance, 27

Police verification process, 176
Policy impediment for clogged talent pipeline, 148
Population planning and control, 60
Position analysis questionnaire (PAQ), 100, 102
- culture job-fit, 107–108
- job questionnaire, 104
- job sculpting, 104–107
- measurement of personality traits, 109–111
- PBJA, 108
- personality and employment testing, 111
- personality and recruitment, 108–109
- test of intelligence as employability test, 112
- validity and reliability of selection tests, 111–112

Predictive analytics for recruitment research, 333–336
Predictive matrices, 28–29
Predictive statistics for organization level, 83–90
Probabilistic simulation method. *See* Monte Carlo Simulation
Procedures for recruitment and selection, 132
Professional values, 243

Profile matching, 101–102
social networking sites, 126
Profile tracking systems, 179
PRP. *See* Performance-related pay (PRP)
PSEs. *See* Public sector enterprises (PSEs)
Psychological testing, 18–19
ethical guidelines for, 115–120, 195–196
for recruitment, 185–186
Psychometric assessments, 175
Psychometric tools, 174
Public sector enterprises (PSEs), 243
recruitment and selection ethics in, 243–244
Pull models. *See* Renewal models
Push models, 70
PWC's selection process, 8

Q

Qualitative models for better managerial judgment, 89–90
Qualitative recruitment research, 327
Quality management practices, 137
Quality of workforce, 154
Quantitative recruitment research, 327

R

Rate of Return Approach (RRA), 61–63
Real-time matrices, 28
Recruiting generation Y, 30–32
Recruitment and selection, 42–43, 174
ability tests for, 197–198
aligning with HR strategies and business goals, 139–141
analytics, 197
committee, 136
decision-making process, 30
development, 136–139
difference from selection, 6, 8–9
difference with recruitment, 8–9
e-recruitment, 22, 176–181
effective, 4–5
emotional intelligence, 195–198
ethics, 230, 238–239, 243
framing policies, 132–133
functions, 5, 10, 51
generation Y recruiting, 30–33
HR managers, 3
HRP importance, 51–53
importance and significance, 135–136
importance of human resources, 5
in India, 34–35
induction, 23
internal, 10–11
internet-related sources, 175
manpower procurement or acquisition, 4
matrices, 28–30
metrics as recruitment tools, 196–197
modern recruitment tools, 176
organizational practices and decisions, 4
outsourcing, 23
personal data, 45–47
personality test for recruitment, 186–195
policy, 132–133, 139
policy impediment for clogged talent pipeline, 148
primary intents, 134–135
process, 6–7, 14–16
psychological test for, 185–186
PWC's selection process, 8
recruitment, 174, 181–185
rules, 208
Skype or phone screening process, 7
through social media, 132
talent attraction, 2
techniques, 175
tools, 175
traditional recruitment tools, 175–176
Recruitment models, 181
depth interviews, 185
effective interviewing, 183–184
interview process, 182–183
staffing quality, 182
structured standardized interview, 184–185

telephone interviews, 185
types of interview, 184
Recruitment policy, 11, 13, 134
attitude measurement, 19
interview, 19–21
preliminary screening of applicants, 16–17
procedures, 13–14
psychological testing, 18–19
purpose, 12–13
reference checking, 18
and selection process, 14–16
template, 12
XYZ company, 12
Recruitment process outsourcing (RPO), 23, 135, 162
Recruitment research, 320
cause and effect model in, 330–331
concept mapping for, 323
cost benefit analysis, 332–333
human resource planning for, 327–329
learning curve as tool for, 329–330
literature review for, 323–324
model building in, 324–325
at organization level, 331–332
predictive analytics for, 333–336
significance of, 325–326
types, 321–323, 326–327
Reference checking process, 176
Regression analyses, 83
Reinforcement, 210
Renewal models, 71
Replacement theory, 80
Right to Equality in public employment, 213
RPO. *See* Recruitment process outsourcing (RPO)
RRA. *See* Rate of Return Approach (RRA)

S

SBU. *See* Strategic business unit (SBU)
Scatter diagram, 83–84
Schematic models, 325
Screening of applicants, 137
Securities and Exchange Board of India (SEBI), 34, 212
Selection research, 325–326
concept mapping, 323
literature review, 323–324
Semistructured interview process, 183
Senior-level recruitment and selection, ethical breaches for, 244–246
Senior Manager (SM), 71
SHRP. *See* Strategic human resource planning (SHRP)
Simulation process, 75
advantages, 79–80
disadvantages, 79–80
Situational interview, 183
16 personality factors (16 PF), 109, 188–189
Skills testing, 175
SM. *See* Senior Manager (SM)
SNS. *See* Social networking sites (SNS)
Social media, 243, 281
Social networking sites (SNS), 176
based tool, 179–181
Specific orientation, 25
SSE. *See* Sum of squared errors (SSE)
Staffing
process, 8
quality model, 182
strategic, 156
Staff replacement, 80–82
Strategic business unit (SBU), 140
Strategic human resource planning (SHRP), 52–53
Strategic onboarding program, 282–284
Strategic recruitment and selection, 161–162
benefits, 157–158
components of, 156
connecting with business plans, 164–165
connecting with strategies, 165–167

dimensions, 158–159
features, 159–161
globe competitive for talent, 170–171
HR functions, 155–156
human resources, 153
issues driving for, 156
perspectives, 154–155
process of developing plan, 152–153
purpose, 157
steps for developing, 162–164
strategic issues, 153
sustainability, 153–154
Strategic staffing, 156
Stress interviews, 19, 183
Structured interview approach, 183
Structured standardized interview, 184–185
Structure–strategy nexus, 141
Succession planning, 288–290, 298, 299–301, 311
career development in IBM, 298
difference with, 306
essential elements of career, 301
Godrej career planning and development, 317–318
identification of potential leaders, 311–312
management development process, 313
steps of, 312–313
Sum of squared errors (SSE), 85–86
Sun Microsystems career development process, 303
SWOT analysis, 331

T

TA. *See* Transactional analysis (TA)
TCNs. *See* Third country nationals (TCNs)
Telephone interviews, 185
Third country nationals (TCNs), 259
Time series analysis, 66
TNCs. *See* Transnational corporations (TNCs)
TR. *See* Transactional response (TR)
Trade unions, 16
Traditional recruitment tools, 175–176
Transactional analysis (TA), 119–120
Transactional response (TR), 119
Transactional stimulus (TS), 119
Transnational corporations (TNCs), 258, 260
selection of employees in, 263–264
TS. *See* Transactional stimulus (TS)
Two-Factor Theory of Intelligence, 193

U

Unethical recruitment and selection process, 246
Uniformity in diversity, 231
Unstructured informal interview, 184

V

Validity and reliability of selection tests, 111–112
Values, 231
Verbal intelligence test, 193
Verbal models, 325
Video interviewing tool, 180

W

Workload analysis, 66
Work profiling systems (WPS), 100, 103
Written models, 325